SCIENCE THROUGH THE MICROSCOPE

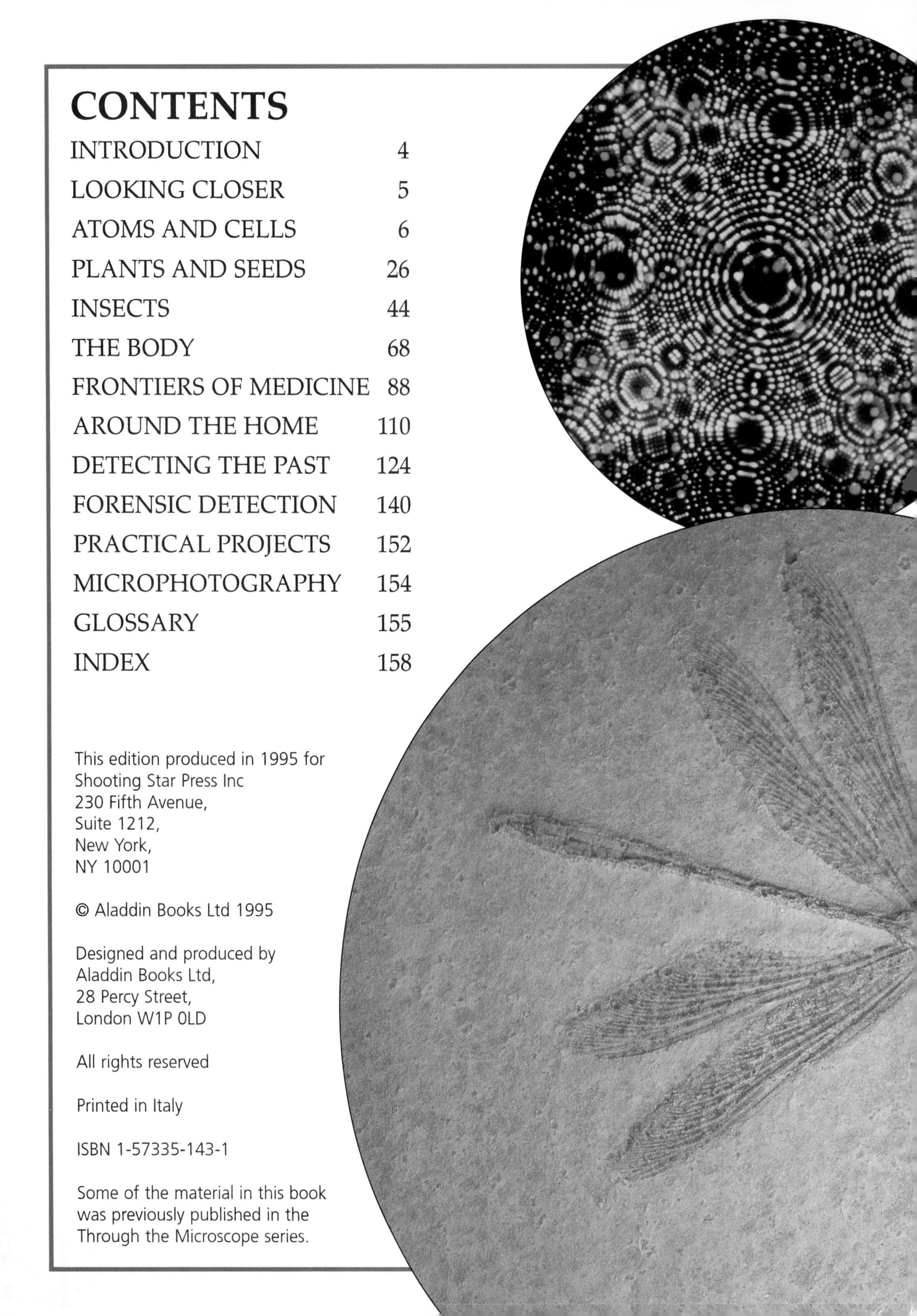

CONTENTS

This edition produced in 1995 for
Shooting Star Press Inc
230 Fifth Avenue,
Suite 1212,
New York,
NY 10001

Designed and produced by
Aladdin Books Ltd,
28 Percy Street,
London W1P 0LD

Printed in Italy

ISBN 1-57335-143-1

Some of the material in this book
was previously published in the
Through the Microscope series.

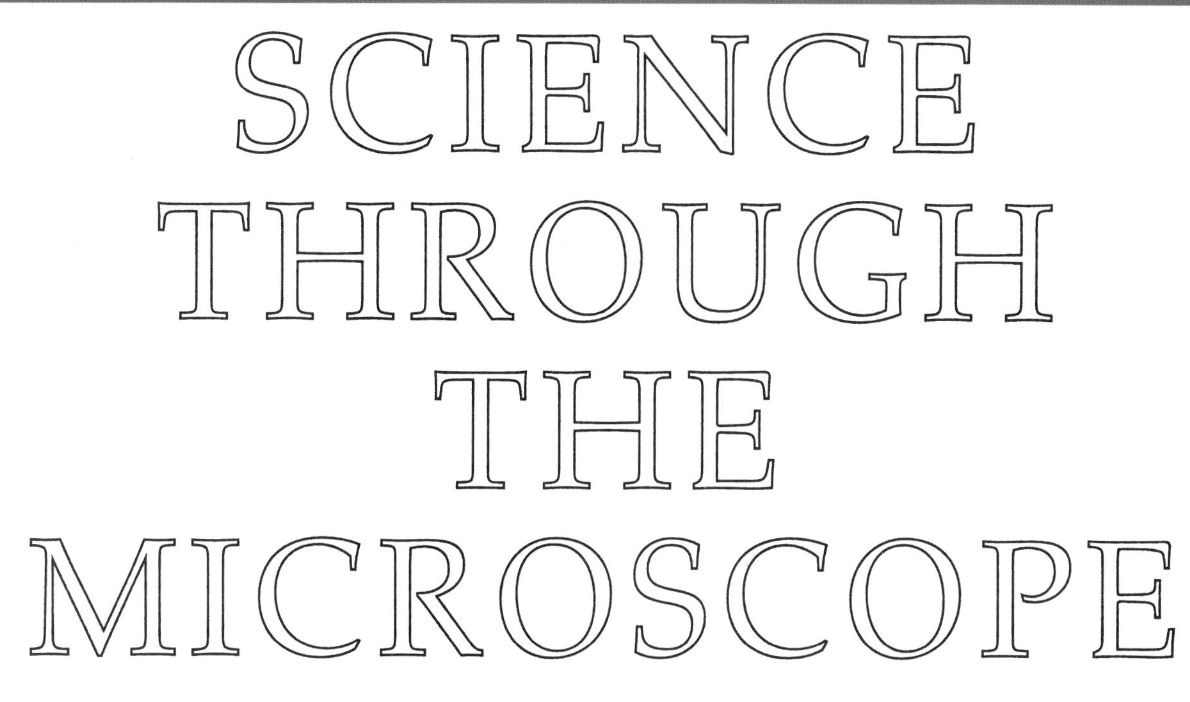

SCIENCE THROUGH THE MICROSCOPE

INTRODUCTION

The microscope has played a very important part in our understanding of the everyday world, as well as a key role in the inventions of modern technology and medicine. It examines those things on, in and around us which cannot be seen by the naked eye, revealing the complexity and beauty of nature.

Science Through the Microscope **contains pictures taken through different types of microscope, or with magnifiying lenses attached to cameras. Next to each picture is a symbol showing how each was made. This will give you an idea of the number of times (written x) the objects are magnified.**

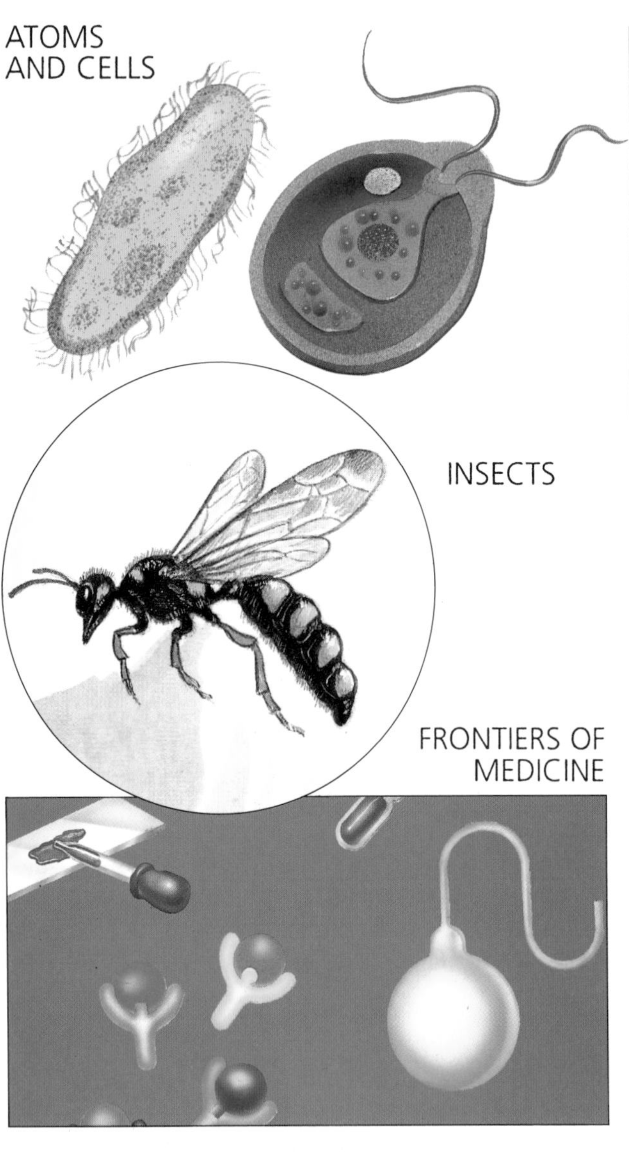

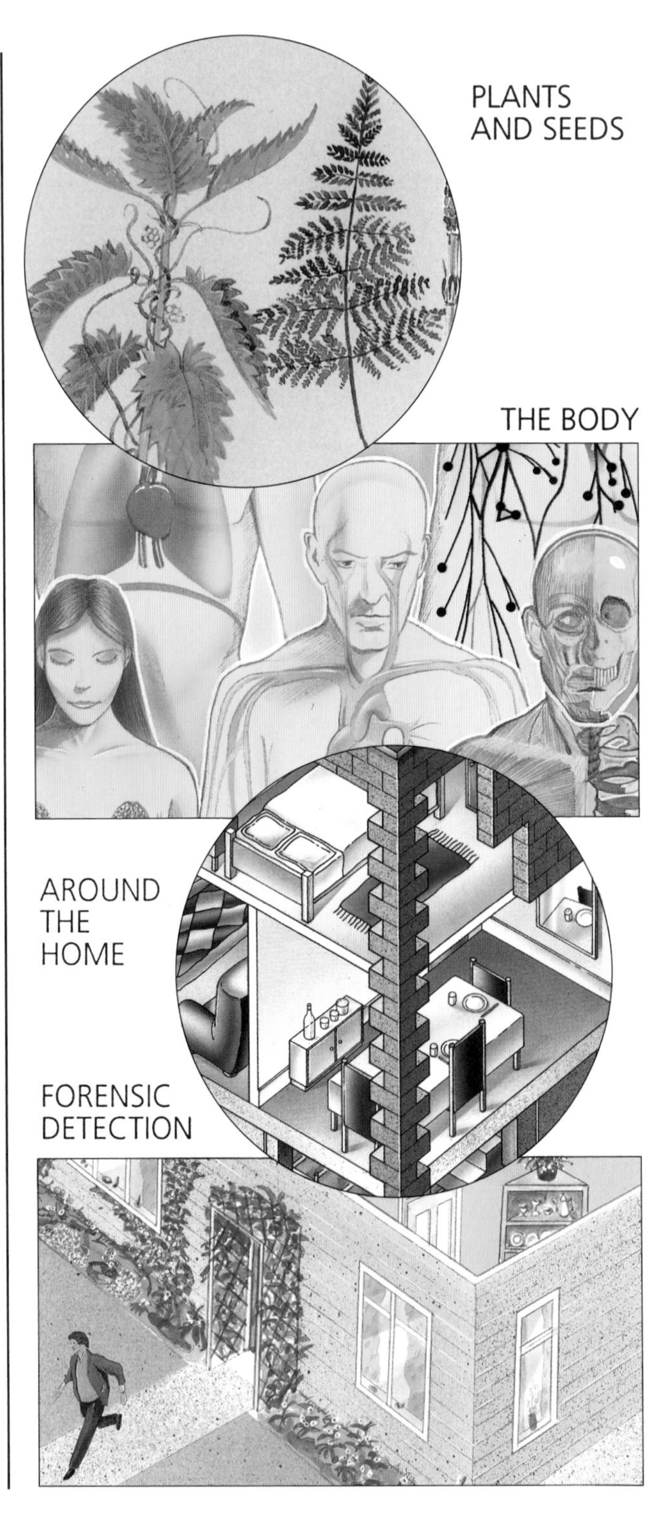

LOOKING CLOSER

Microscopes and magnifying glasses work by using lenses and light. A lens is usually a thin, circular glass, thicker in the middle, which bends rays of light so that when you look through it an object appears enlarged. A microscope uses several lenses. It will also have a set of adjustments to give you a choice over how much you want to magnify.

When we want to view something under a microscope, it must be small enough to fit on a glass slide. This is put on the stage over the mirror and light is reflected through so that the lenses inside can magnify the view for us. But not all microscopes work this way. The greatest detail can be seen with an electron microscope which uses electron beams and electromagnets.

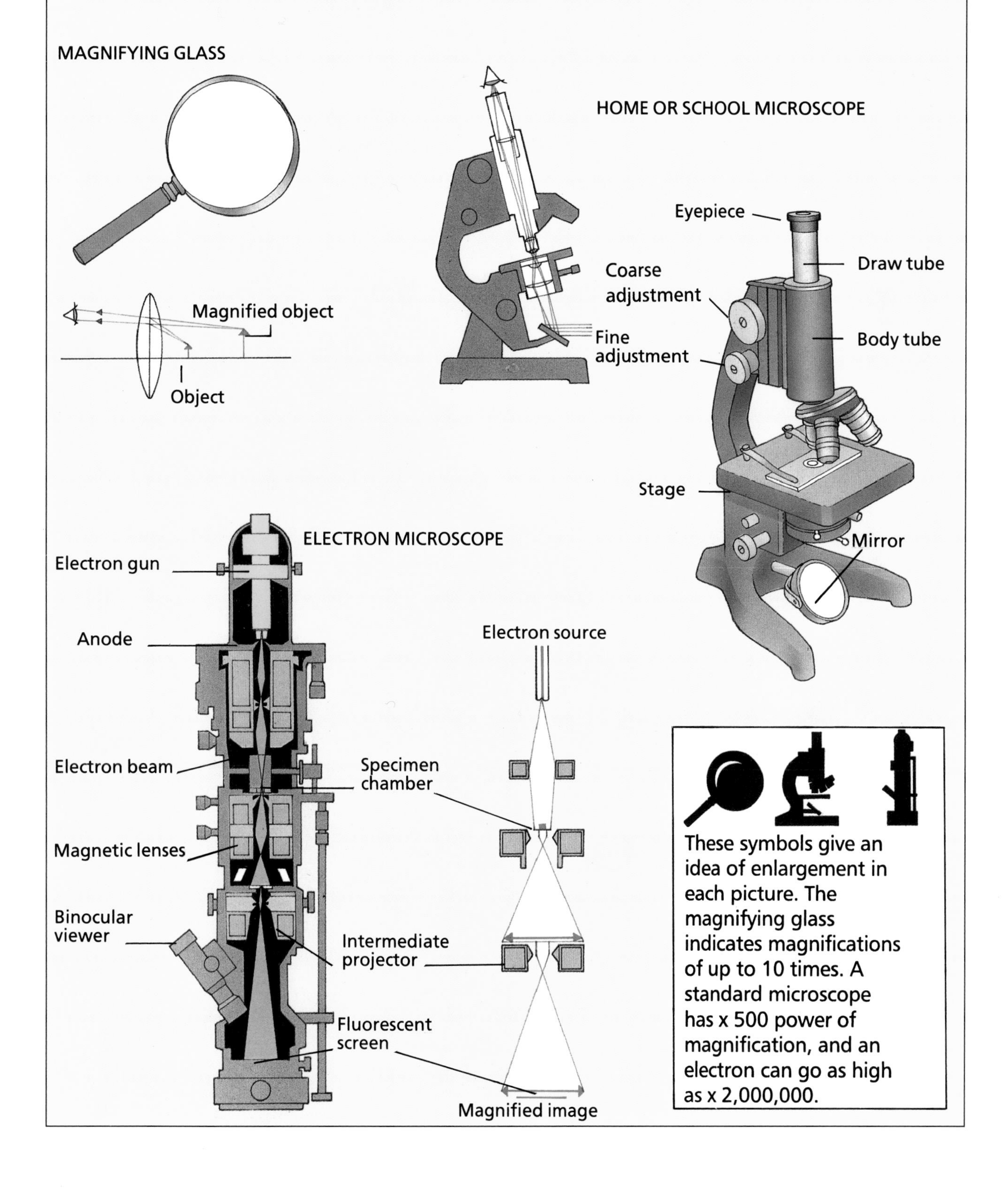

These symbols give an idea of enlargement in each picture. The magnifying glass indicates magnifications of up to 10 times. A standard microscope has x 500 power of magnification, and an electron can go as high as x 2,000,000.

CONTENTS

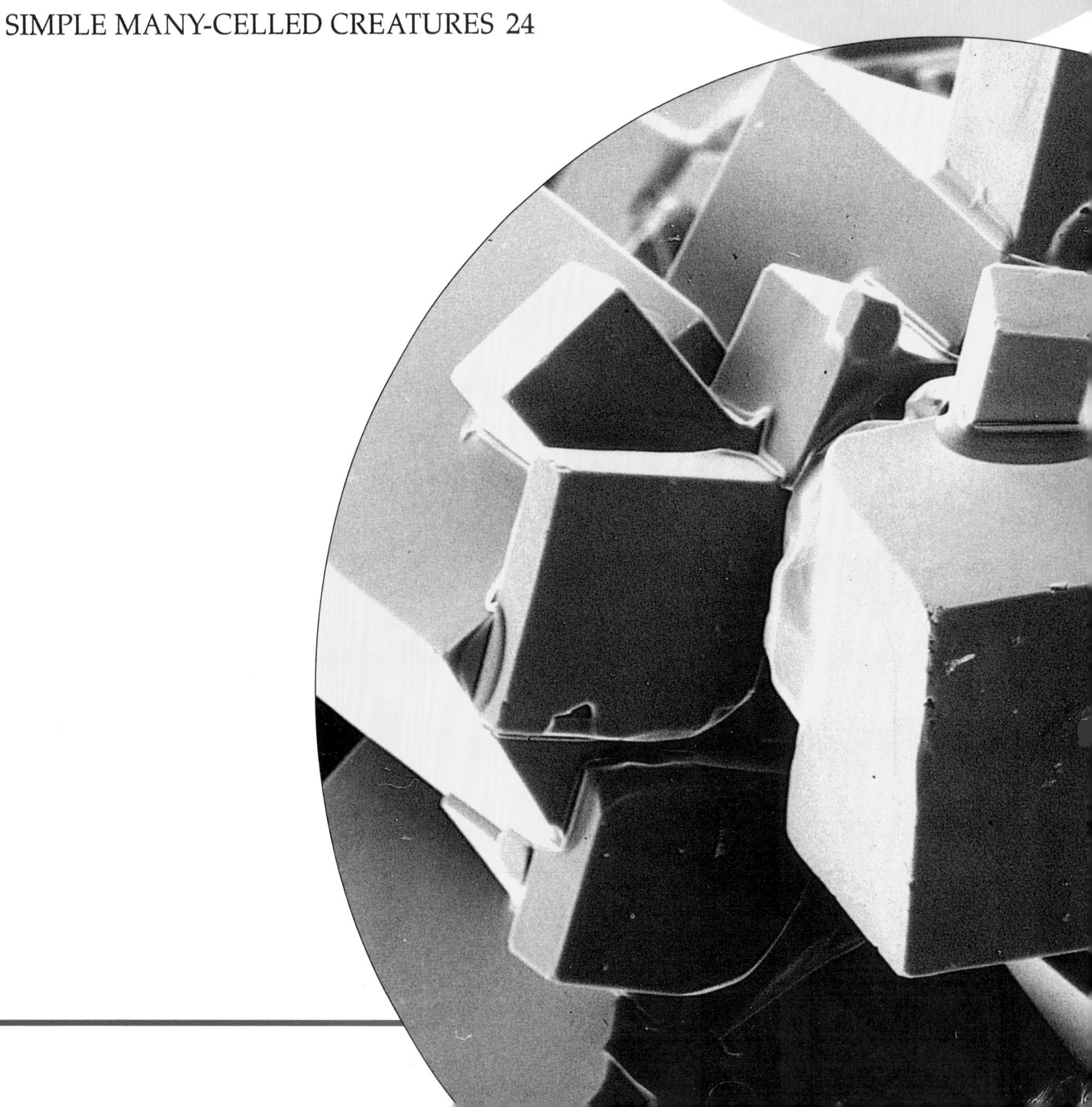

Atoms and Cells

Lionel Bender

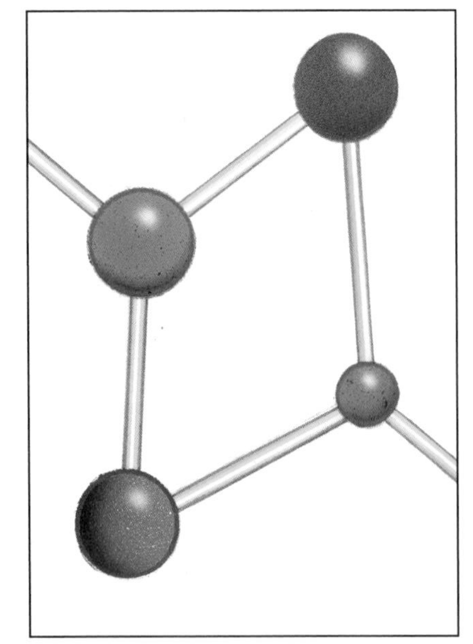

ELEMENTS AND MOLECULES

If you cut this page into smaller and smaller pieces, you would eventually get thousands of tiny fragments of paper. Under a microscope, and carefully using a very fine blade, it would be possible to cut up each of these fragments into thousands of yet smaller pieces. Finally, though, you would not be able to divide up the fragments any more. You would then have a mass of atoms. The word atom comes from the Greek, *atomos*, meaning uncuttable or indivisible. An atom is the smallest particle that can exist naturally. The pages of this book are each about 2 million atoms thick. In nature there are less than 100 different types of atom, yet these combine in endless ways to make bigger units known as molecules.

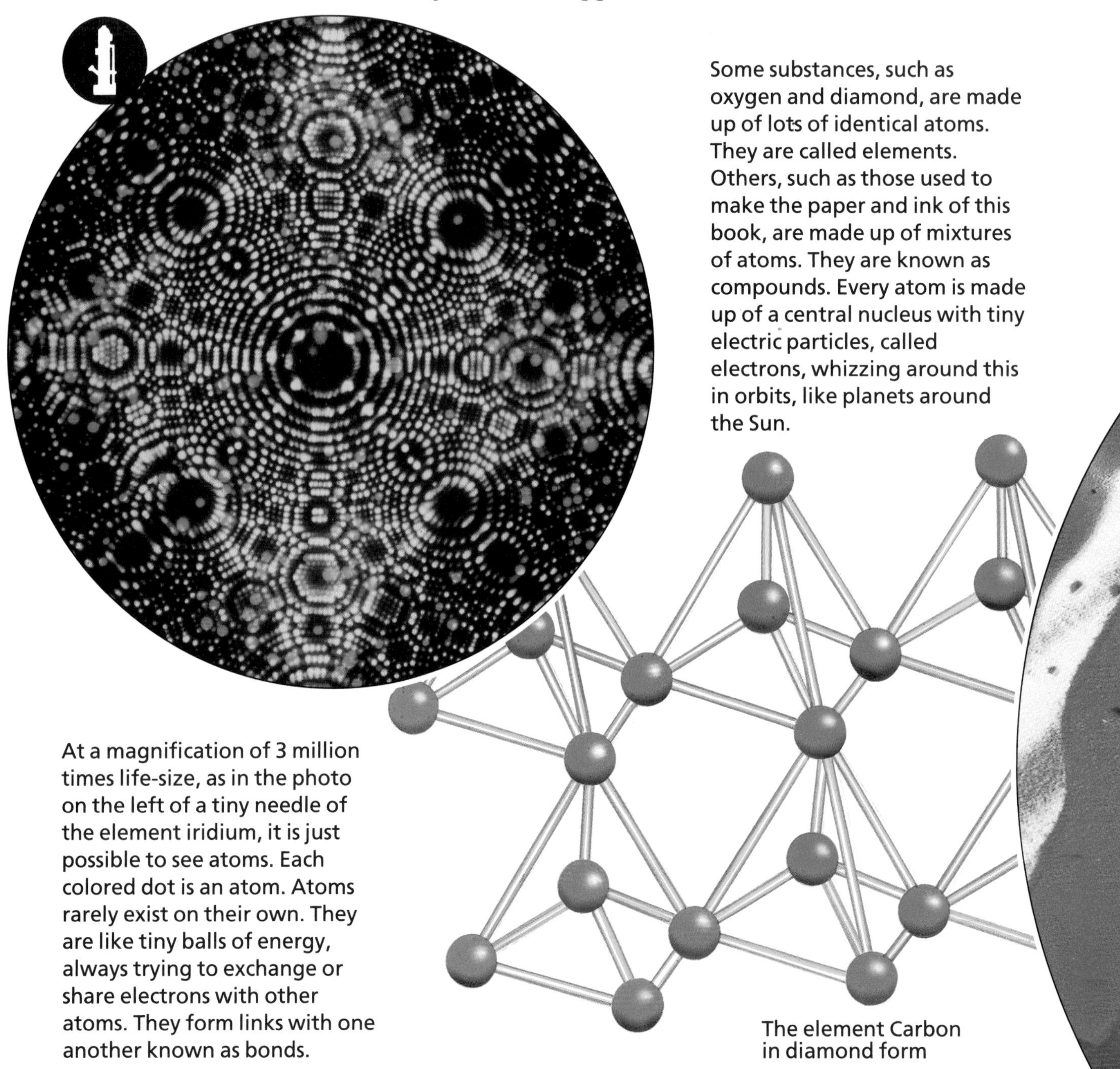

Some substances, such as oxygen and diamond, are made up of lots of identical atoms. They are called elements. Others, such as those used to make the paper and ink of this book, are made up of mixtures of atoms. They are known as compounds. Every atom is made up of a central nucleus with tiny electric particles, called electrons, whizzing around this in orbits, like planets around the Sun.

At a magnification of 3 million times life-size, as in the photo on the left of a tiny needle of the element iridium, it is just possible to see atoms. Each colored dot is an atom. Atoms rarely exist on their own. They are like tiny balls of energy, always trying to exchange or share electrons with other atoms. They form links with one another known as bonds.

The element Carbon in diamond form

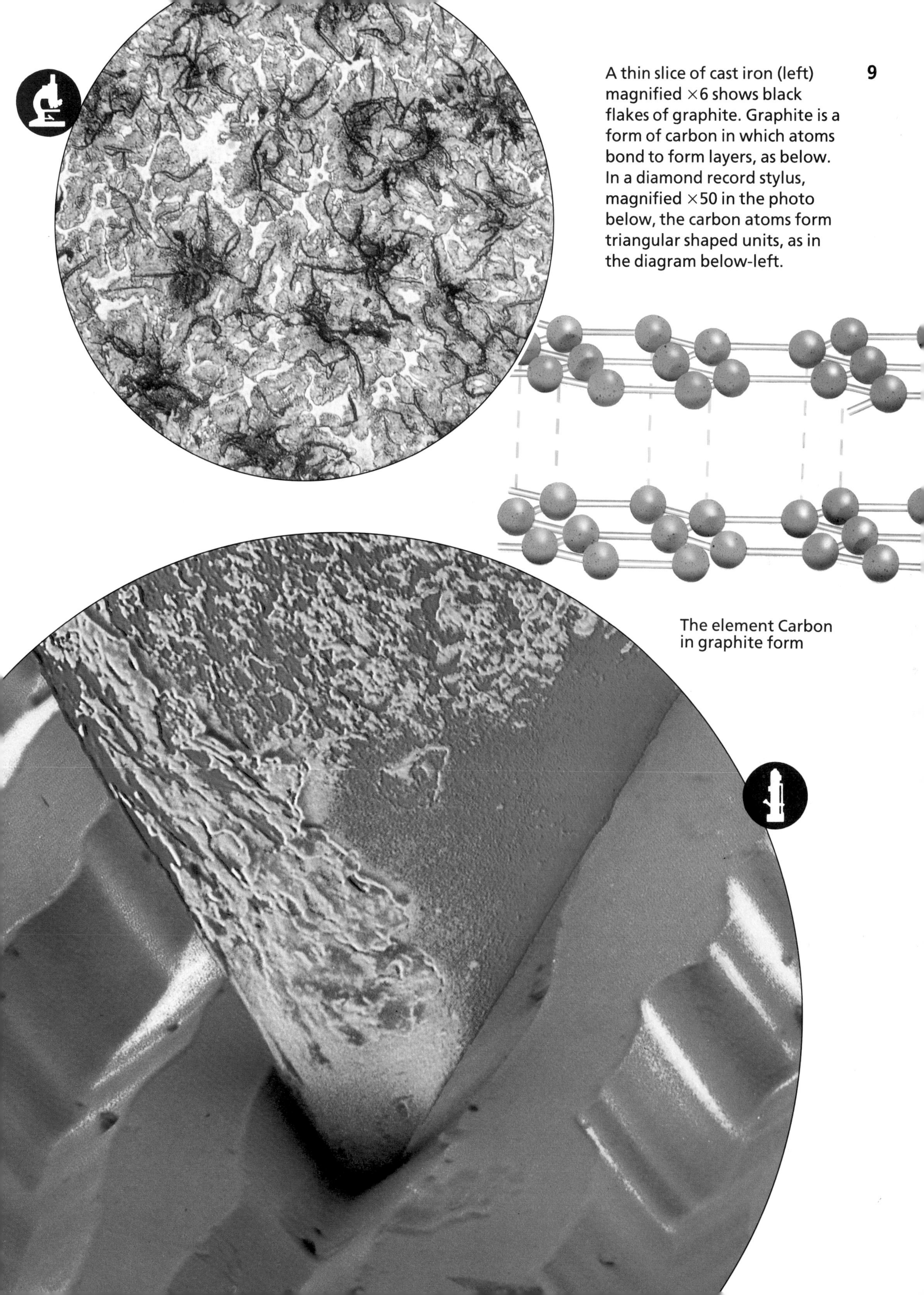

A thin slice of cast iron (left) magnified ×6 shows black flakes of graphite. Graphite is a form of carbon in which atoms bond to form layers, as below. In a diamond record stylus, magnified ×50 in the photo below, the carbon atoms form triangular shaped units, as in the diagram below-left.

The element Carbon in graphite form

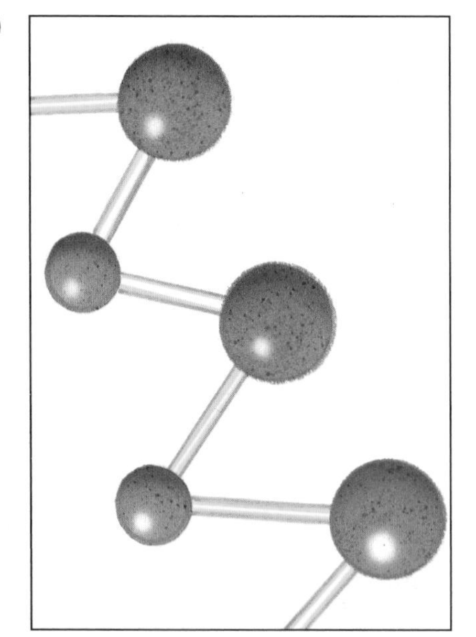

CRYSTALS AND CHAINS

Have you noticed how beautifully shaped the tiny grains of salt you have in your kitchen are? At a magnification of only ×15, as below, the grains look like minute cubes. Salt is made up of atoms of two elements, sodium and chlorine. These bond in a very regular way to form the structures we call crystals. Crystals are fascinating because they can grow even though they are not alive. Suspend a tiny crystal of copper sulphate, like one of those in the photo below-left, in a solution of the compound, and it will slowly increase in size to several inches across. Chemists – scientists who study the way that atoms bond – can make some atoms link together to form long chains of molecules.

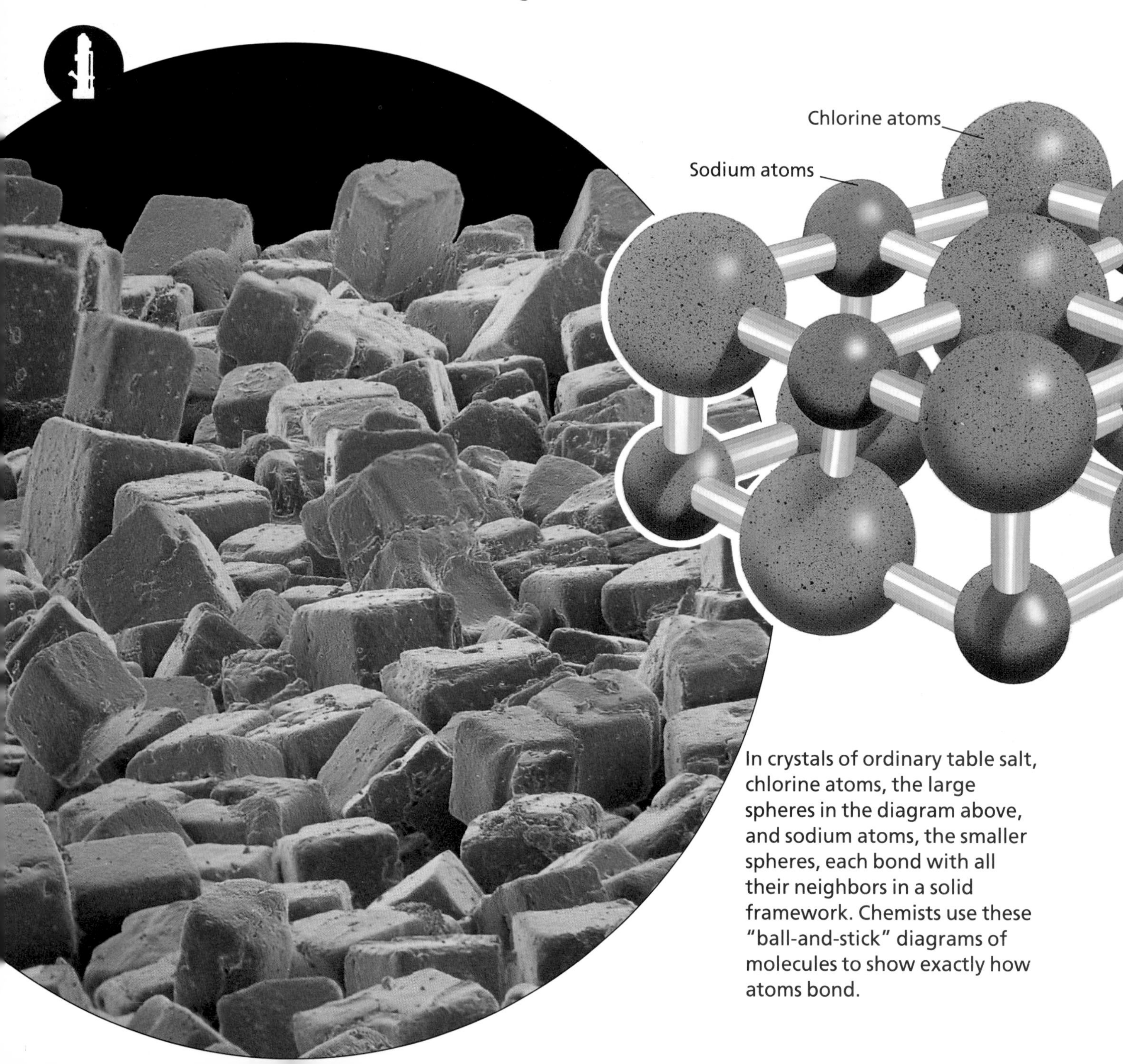

In crystals of ordinary table salt, chlorine atoms, the large spheres in the diagram above, and sodium atoms, the smaller spheres, each bond with all their neighbors in a solid framework. Chemists use these "ball-and-stick" diagrams of molecules to show exactly how atoms bond.

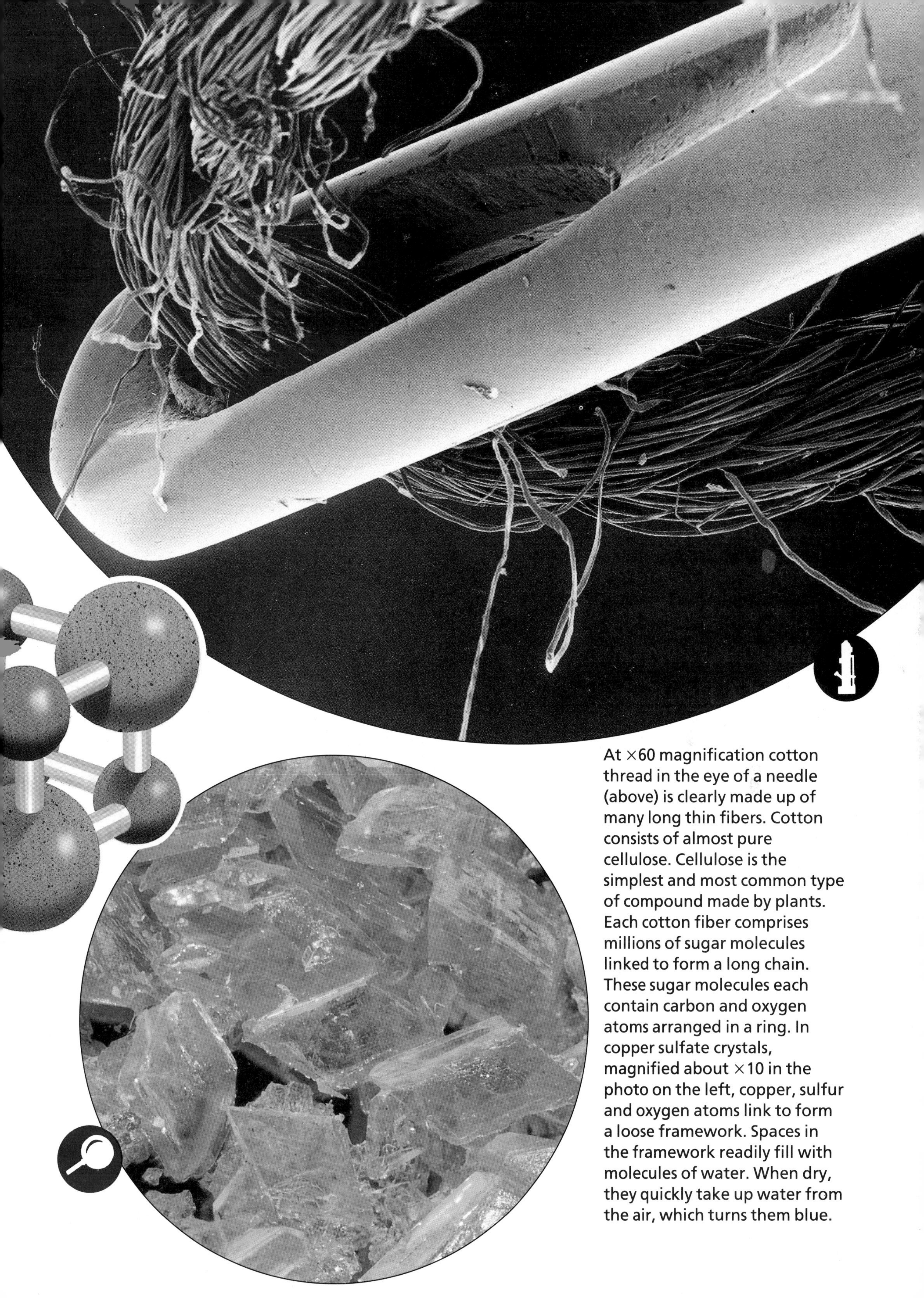

At ×60 magnification cotton thread in the eye of a needle (above) is clearly made up of many long thin fibers. Cotton consists of almost pure cellulose. Cellulose is the simplest and most common type of compound made by plants. Each cotton fiber comprises millions of sugar molecules linked to form a long chain. These sugar molecules each contain carbon and oxygen atoms arranged in a ring. In copper sulfate crystals, magnified about ×10 in the photo on the left, copper, sulfur and oxygen atoms link to form a loose framework. Spaces in the framework readily fill with molecules of water. When dry, they quickly take up water from the air, which turns them blue.

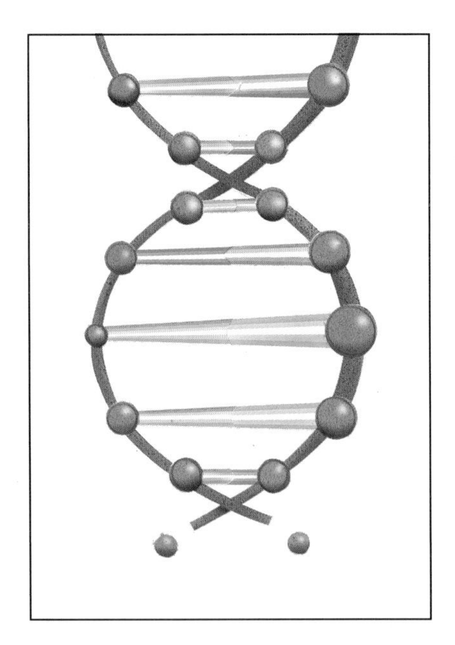

BIOMOLECULES

Carbon is one of the most important elements on Earth. All living things, including ourselves, depend on carbon compounds for growth, reproduction and repair. Those carbon compounds found in living things are called biomolecules – in Greek, *bios* means life. They include huge, but still microscopic, molecules that make up our food – fats, proteins and carbohydrates (sugars). One type of biomolecule, deoxyribonucleic acid (DNA), carries coded information that determines all the features of every animal, plant, and bacteria. Molecules of DNA are normally arranged in tiny ribbon-like structures known as chromosomes. The photos below are of human chromosomes.

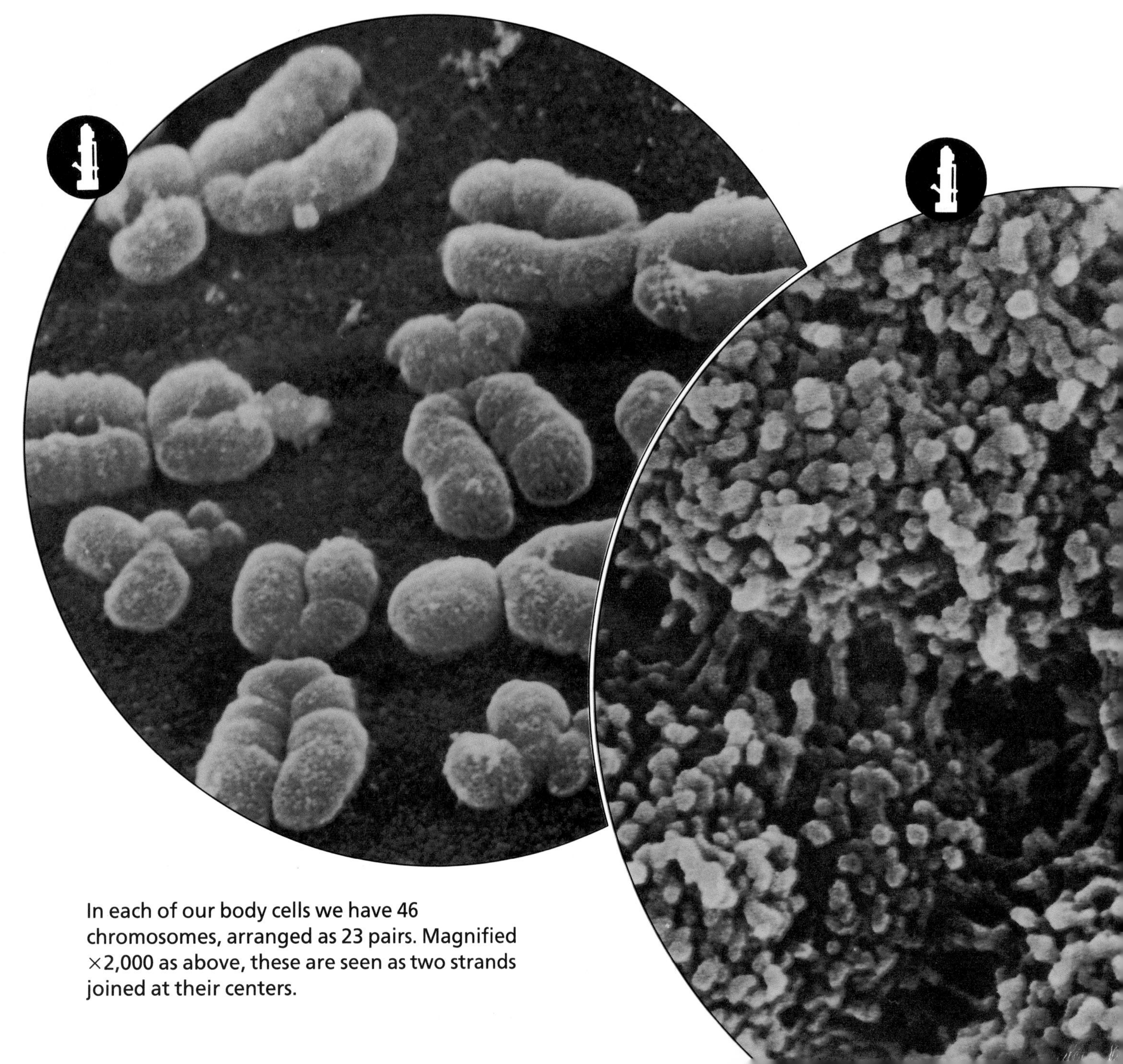

In each of our body cells we have 46 chromosomes, arranged as 23 pairs. Magnified ×2,000 as above, these are seen as two strands joined at their centers.

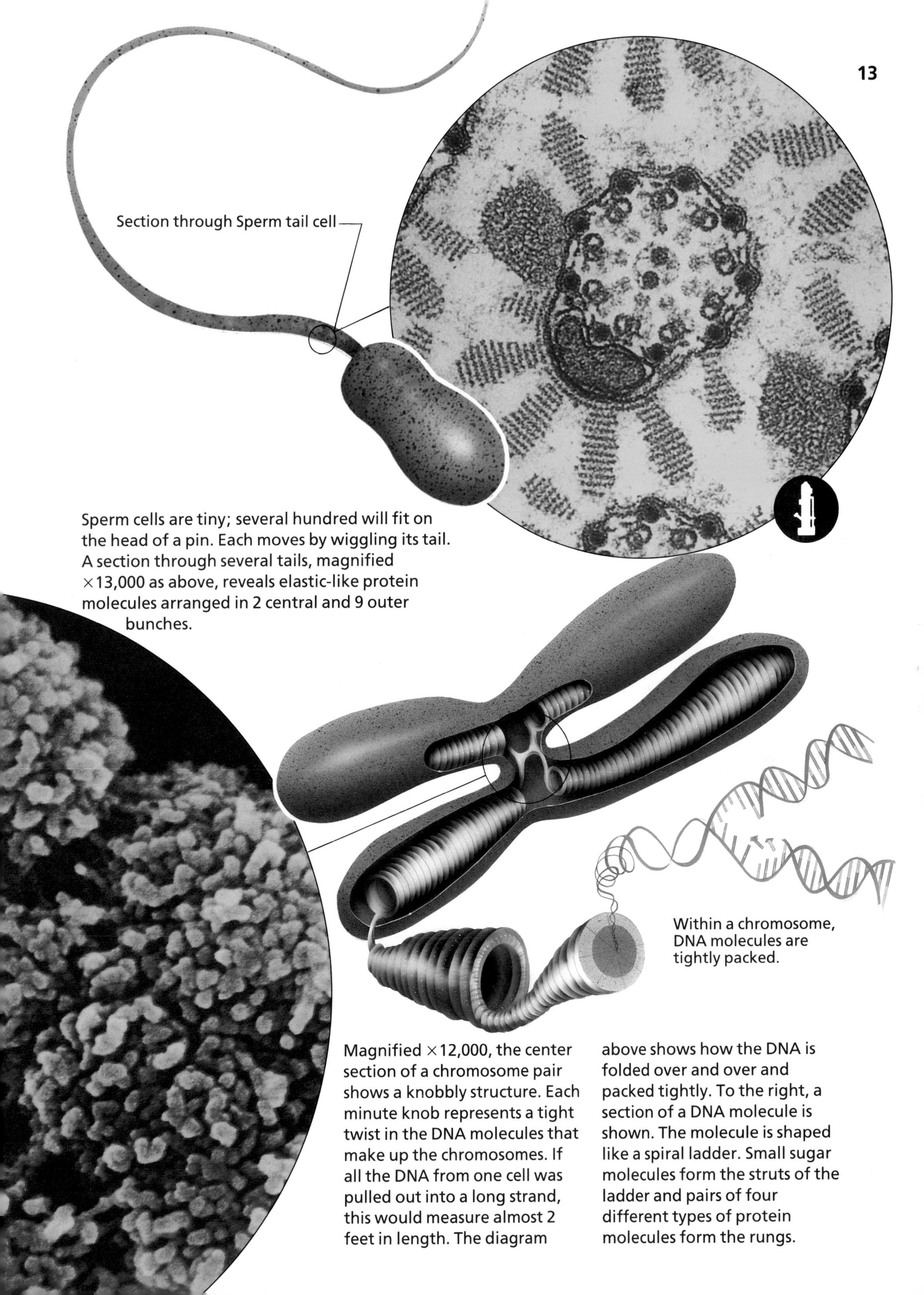

Sperm cells are tiny; several hundred will fit on the head of a pin. Each moves by wiggling its tail. A section through several tails, magnified ×13,000 as above, reveals elastic-like protein molecules arranged in 2 central and 9 outer bunches.

Within a chromosome, DNA molecules are tightly packed.

Magnified ×12,000, the center section of a chromosome pair shows a knobbly structure. Each minute knob represents a tight twist in the DNA molecules that make up the chromosomes. If all the DNA from one cell was pulled out into a long strand, this would measure almost 2 feet in length. The diagram above shows how the DNA is folded over and over and packed tightly. To the right, a section of a DNA molecule is shown. The molecule is shaped like a spiral ladder. Small sugar molecules form the struts of the ladder and pairs of four different types of protein molecules form the rungs.

VIRUSES

We say something is "living" if it can grow, reproduce and react to changes in its surroundings. A virus, by itself, can do none of these things. But once inside a live cell, a virus takes over that cell and turns it into thousands of new viruses. These escape from the dead cell and invade other cells. If the cells try to fight back, the virus can often change its shape and form to overcome their defenses. So viruses are on the borderline between living and non-living. They are in fact incredibly small packages of just two main types of biomolecules, proteins and nucleic acids (see pages 12-13). All viruses are too small to be seen with a home microscope, but electron microscope photos, as shown here, reveal them.

The photo above is of a human white blood cell infected with the AIDS virus, magnified several thousand times. The image has been colored using a computer.

The cell has a lumpy appearance due to the mass of viruses growing inside it. The tiny green blobs on the surface of the cell are AIDS viruses about to burst free.

Bacteriophages are viruses that infect bacterial cells. Each consists of a protein shell, a core of nucleic acid, a protein sheath and "legs." Shown at magnification ×5,000 in the photo left, are five bacteriophages about to invade a cell. The legs stick to the surface, the sheath contracts, and the nucleic acid is injected into the cell, as in the diagram below.

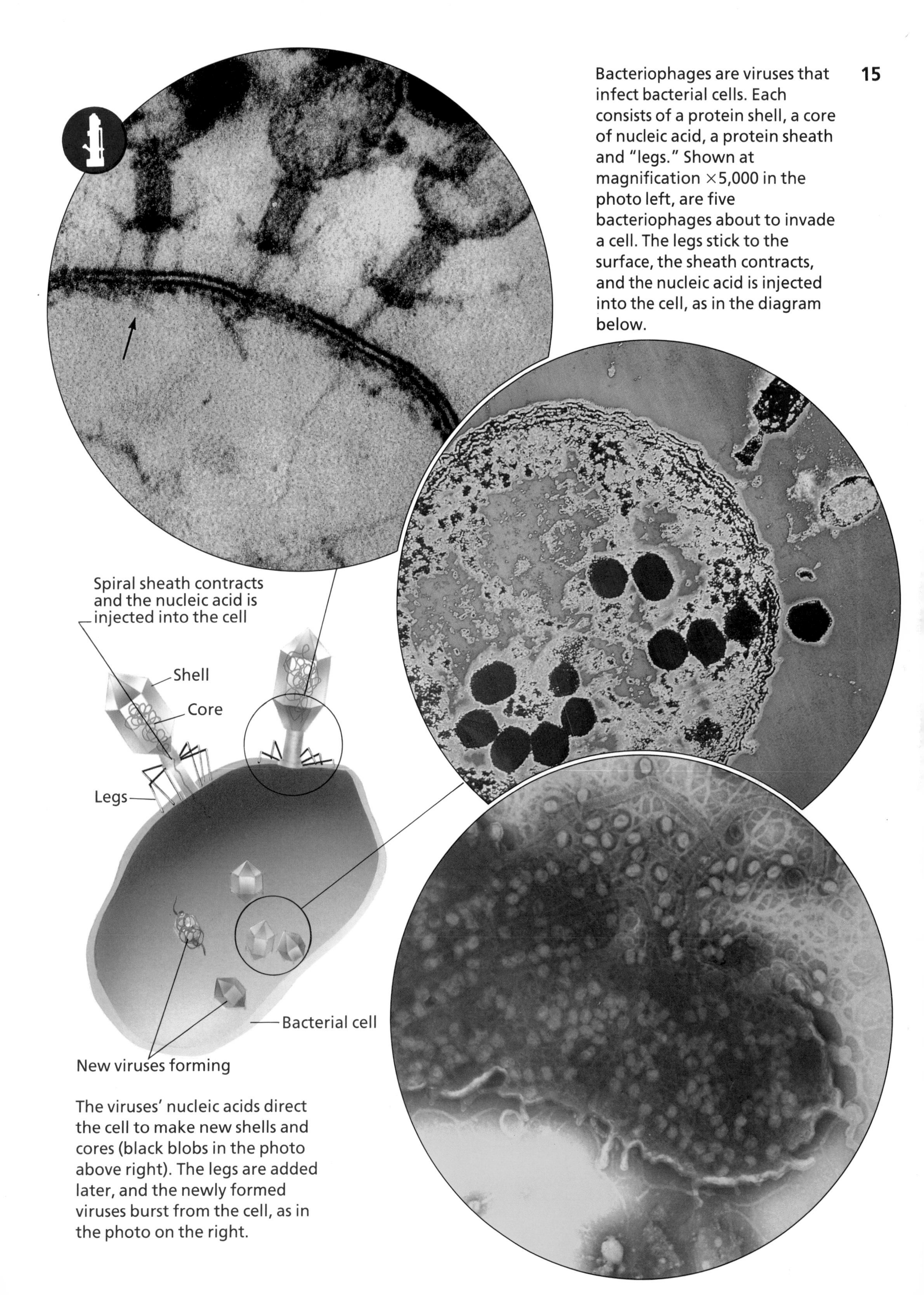

The viruses' nucleic acids direct the cell to make new shells and cores (black blobs in the photo above right). The legs are added later, and the newly formed viruses burst from the cell, as in the photo on the right.

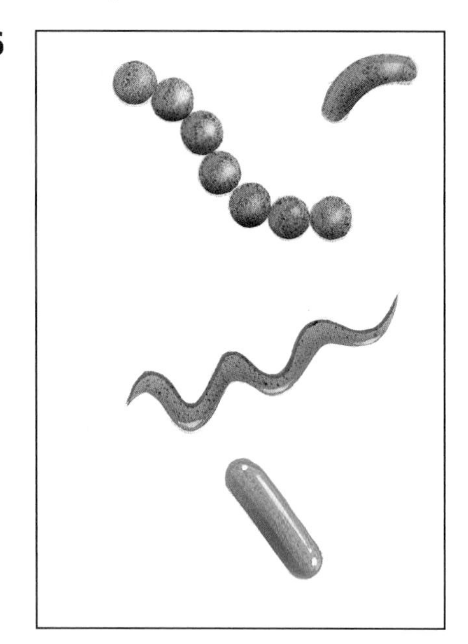

BACTERIA

Bacteria are tiny creatures that we often call germs. Indeed, most of us think of them as living things that cause nasty diseases. Bacteria are responsible for such human diseases as food poisoning and pneumonia. But many bacteria are extremely helpful to us. In the soil, some break down dead animals and plants and make their chemicals available to other organisms. Bacteria are also responsible for turning milk into yoghurt, cheese and butter. All bacteria are about 10,000 times larger than viruses but even the biggest of them can only just be seen with a home microscope. The photo below, at a magnification of more than ×1,000, shows that many thousands of bacteria can fit on the head of a pin.

Bacteria come in all shapes and forms. Some are simply round or oval, as in the photos below and on the right. Others are rod, comma, club or even spiral-shaped, as seen below left. The bacteria shown below live in water and cause Legionnaire's disease.

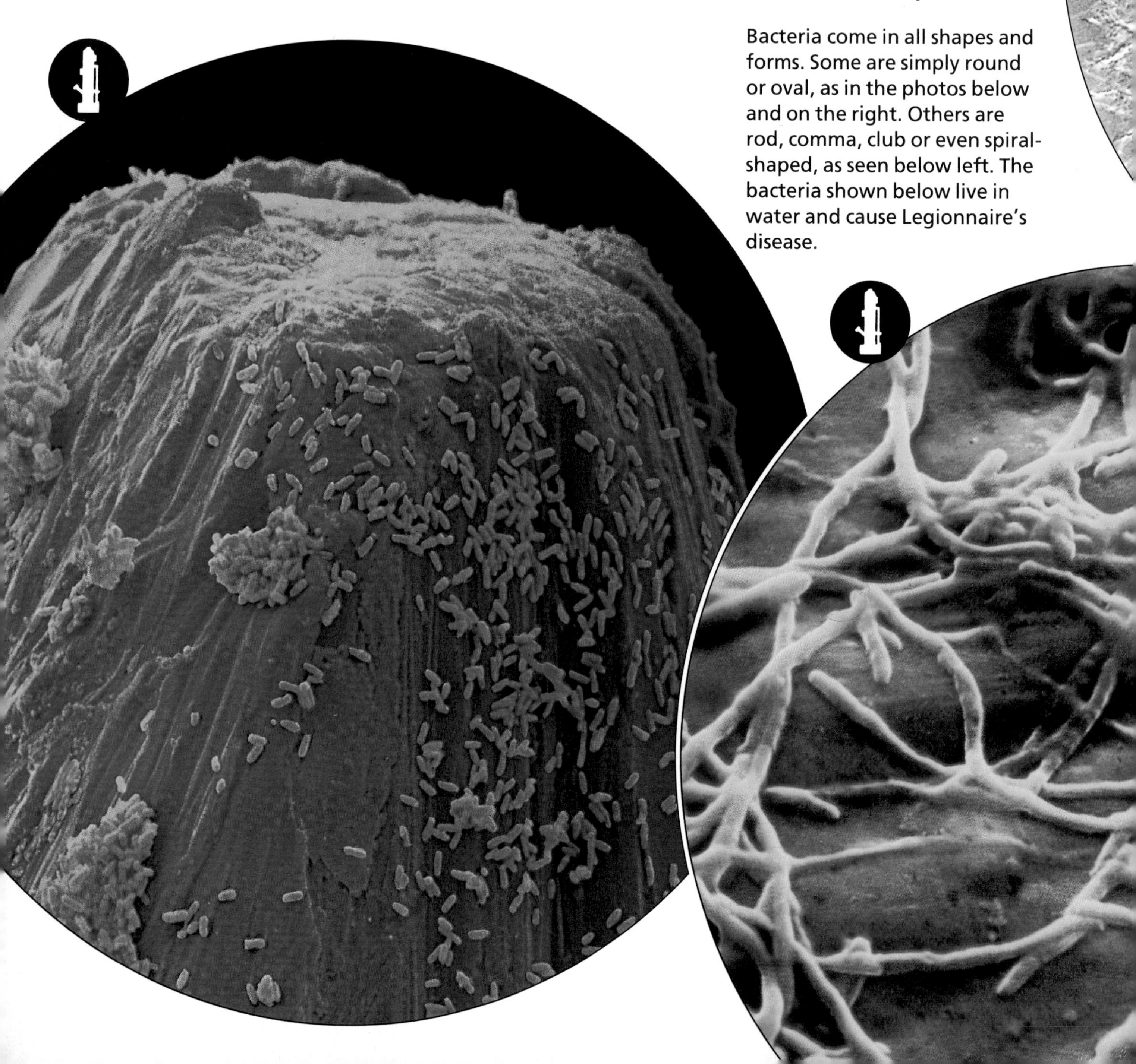

Each bacterium (plural bacteria) consists of just one cell, as in the diagram below. This cell is similar, but not identical, to animal and plant cells (see pages 18-19). On the outside is a thick wall. This is sometimes covered in tiny hairs and coated with a layer of slimy material. Inside is a jelly-like liquid, the cytoplasm, in which is embedded a mass of nucleic acid and other minute structures. Bacteria, such as those in the photo below, move through their watery surroundings by beating the hairs on their surface.

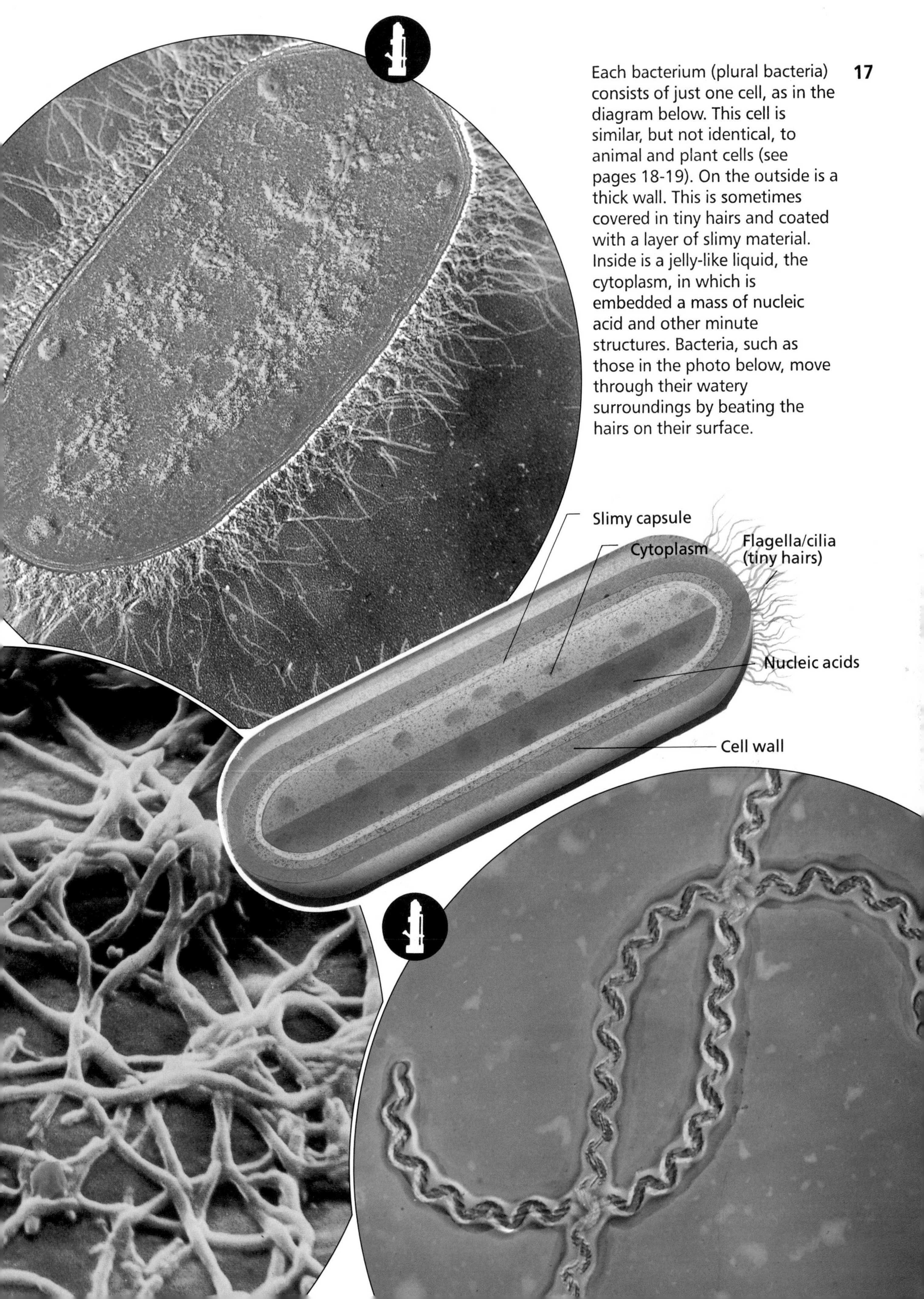

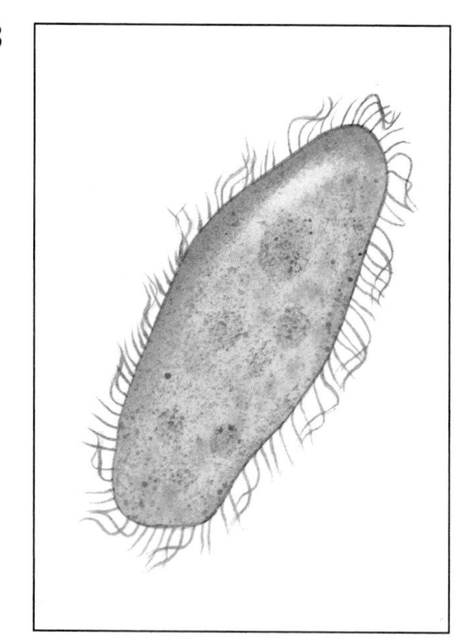

SINGLE-CELL ANIMALS

If you look at a drop of pond or sea water under a home microscope or even just a hand-lens, you are likely to see a number of tiny animals moving about. Some of these, like *Amoeba* and *Paramecium* photographed below, are single-cell creatures. A typical animal cell comprises a jelly-like outer membrane, the ectoplasm, and an inner liquid material, the endoplasm (or cytoplasm). Floating around in the cell are various structures such as the nucleus, the cell's control center. A contractile vacuole is responsible for collecting unwanted water in the cell and then, when full, bursting to get rid of its contents to the surroundings. Each single-cell animal is capable of feeding, growing and reproducing on its own.

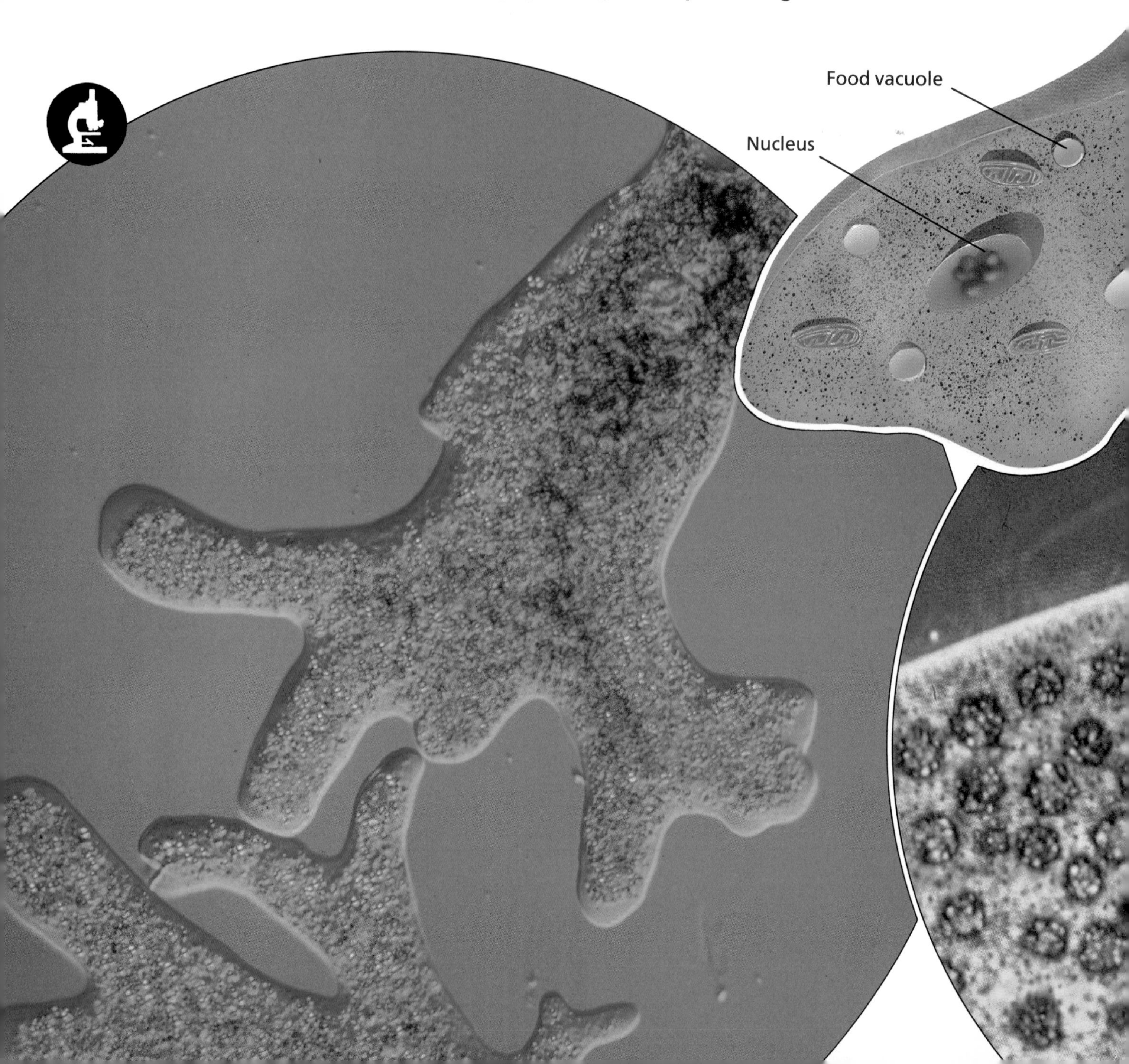

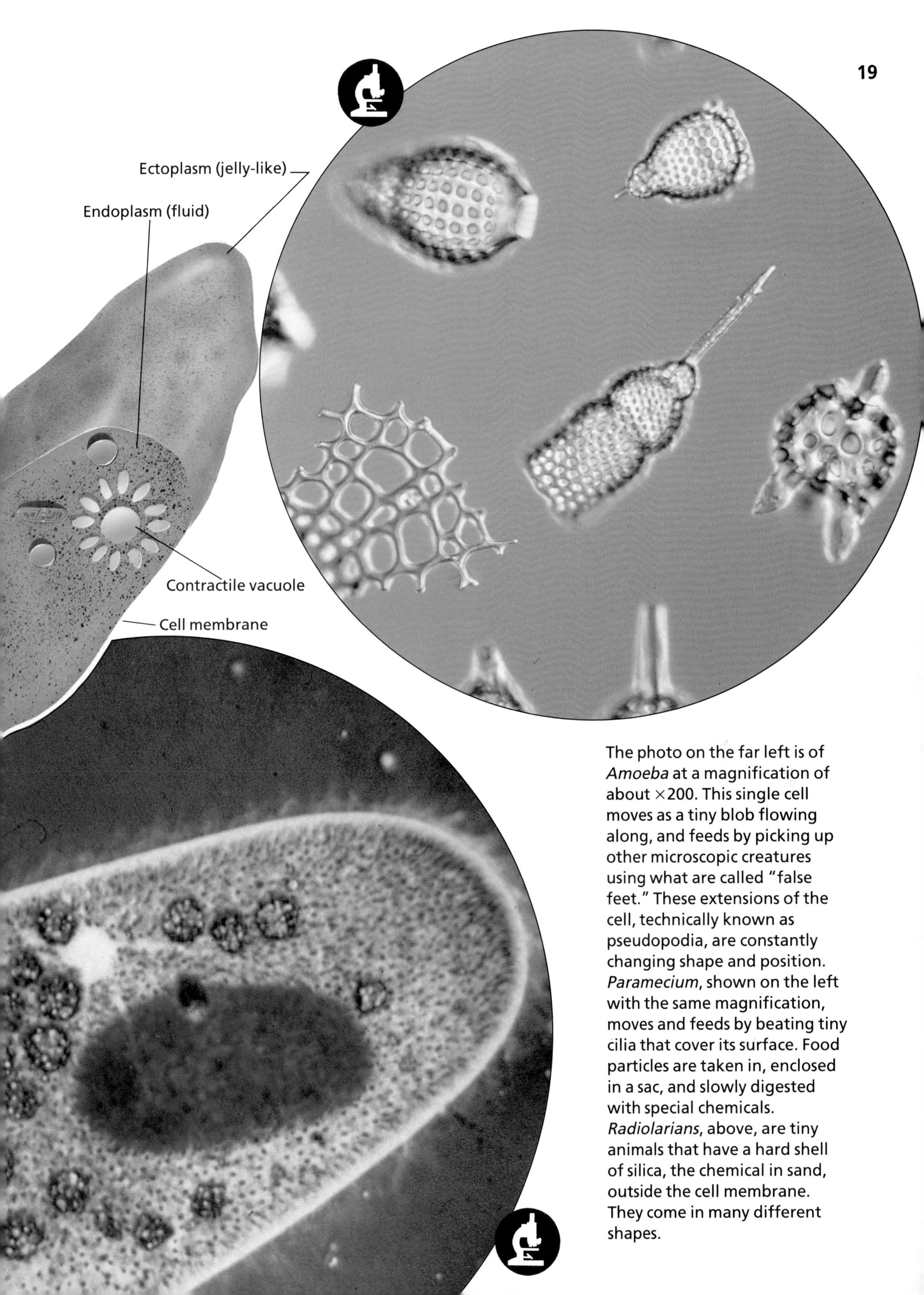

The photo on the far left is of *Amoeba* at a magnification of about ×200. This single cell moves as a tiny blob flowing along, and feeds by picking up other microscopic creatures using what are called "false feet." These extensions of the cell, technically known as pseudopodia, are constantly changing shape and position. *Paramecium*, shown on the left with the same magnification, moves and feeds by beating tiny cilia that cover its surface. Food particles are taken in, enclosed in a sac, and slowly digested with special chemicals. *Radiolarians*, above, are tiny animals that have a hard shell of silica, the chemical in sand, outside the cell membrane. They come in many different shapes.

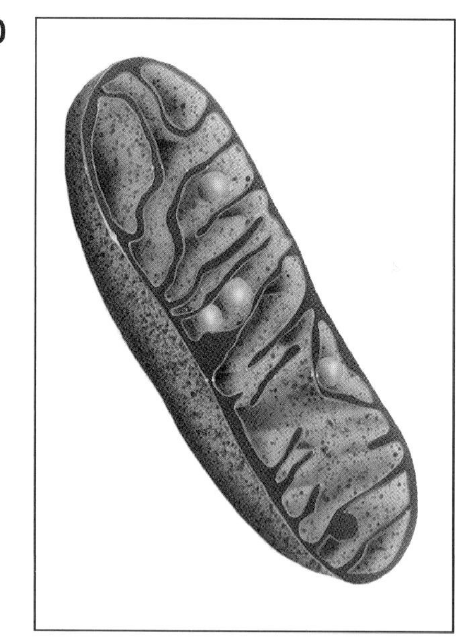

ORGANELLES

Cells are the building blocks of living things and the smallest units of life that can exist on their own. Within cells there are several minute structures called organelles, each of which has a specific job to do. Large cells, such as the human egg cell, or ovum, measure about 0.004 inches (0.1mm) across and can be seen with the naked eye. But only under a high power microscope can the organelles within them be seen. The largest of these is the nucleus. This directs all the cell's activities. Sausage-shaped organelles known as *mitochondria* are the main sites of energy production. Within many-celled creatures, each cell is adapted for a certain job. Some of these cells have organelles not shared by other cells.

The sausage-shaped organelles illustrated on the top left and right of these pages, are known as *mitochondria*. Only visible through a high-powered microscope, we can see them end-on in the picture below-left and also below-right.

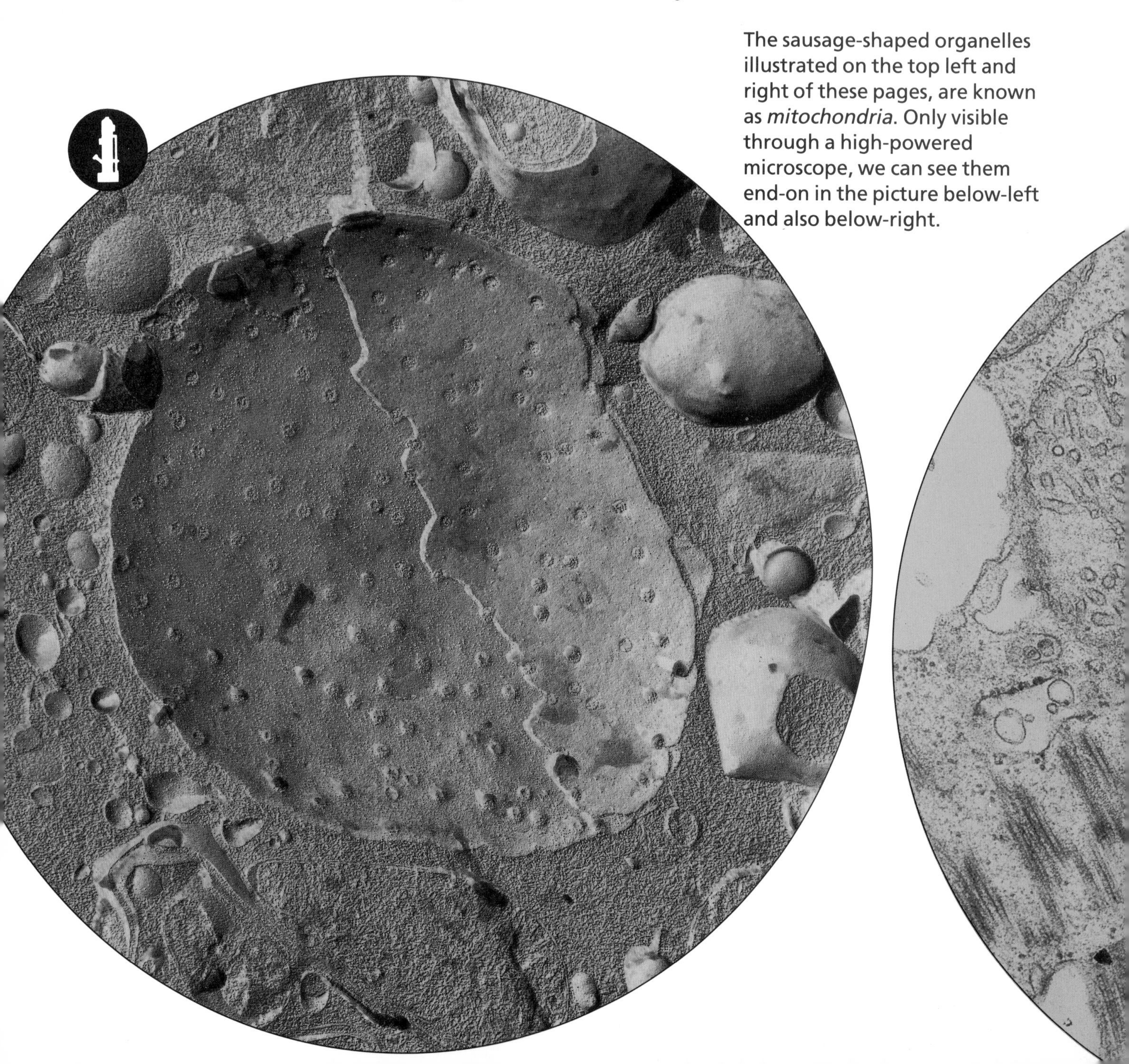

The cell nucleus, seen magnified more than 15,000 times in the photo below left, is surrounded by a thin membrane or covering which has many tiny holes in it. This envelope acts as a sieve, controlling the constant flow of chemicals to and from the nucleus. Surrounding each cell is another envelope, or membrane, which acts as a control gate for the entry of nutrients and the exit of wastes from the cell. In a cell from the human nose magnified ×7,000 (photo below), many minute hairs stick out from the outer membrane. These special organelles can beat from side to side to remove dust particles from the air a person breathes.

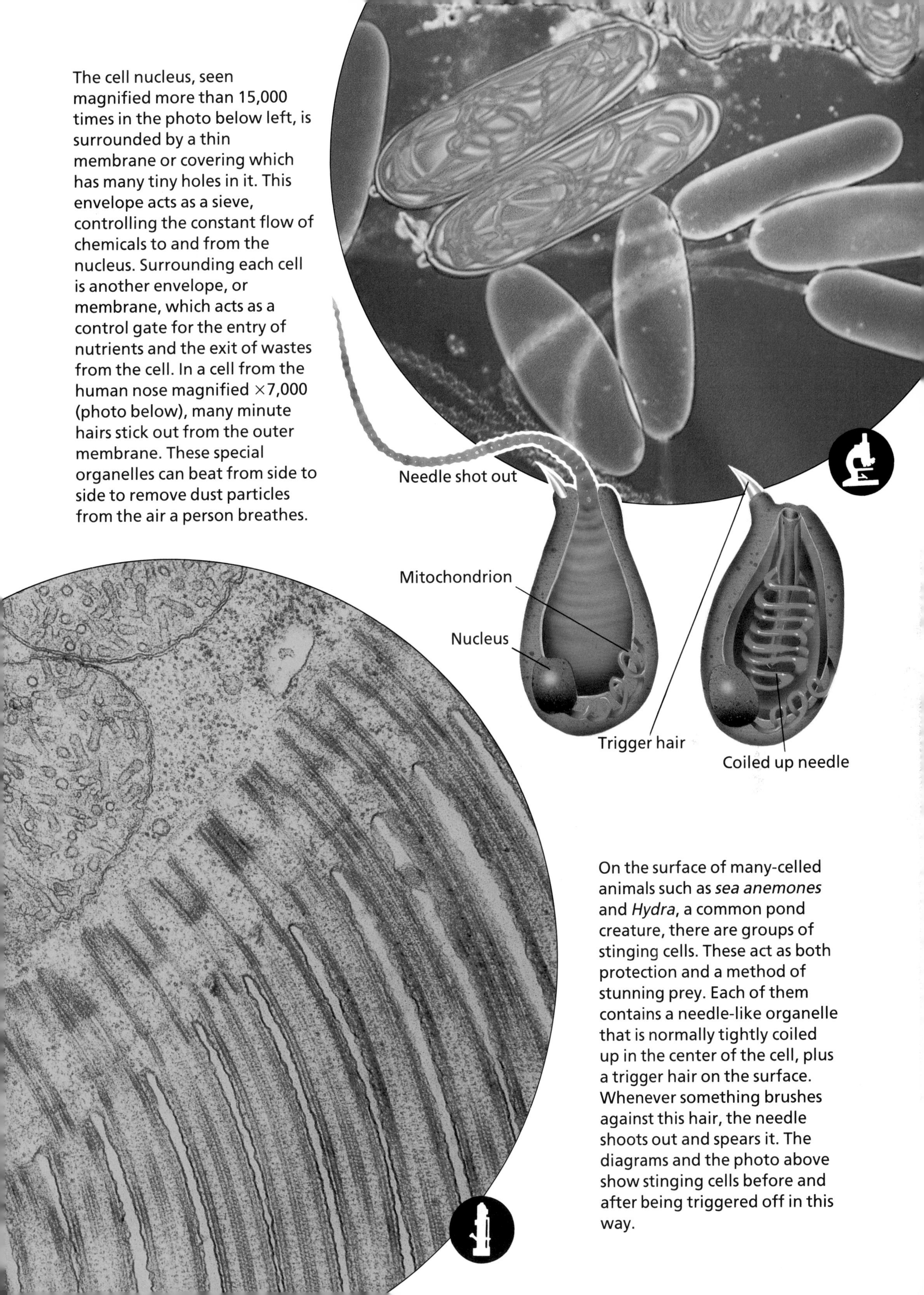

On the surface of many-celled animals such as *sea anemones* and *Hydra*, a common pond creature, there are groups of stinging cells. These act as both protection and a method of stunning prey. Each of them contains a needle-like organelle that is normally tightly coiled up in the center of the cell, plus a trigger hair on the surface. Whenever something brushes against this hair, the needle shoots out and spears it. The diagrams and the photo above show stinging cells before and after being triggered off in this way.

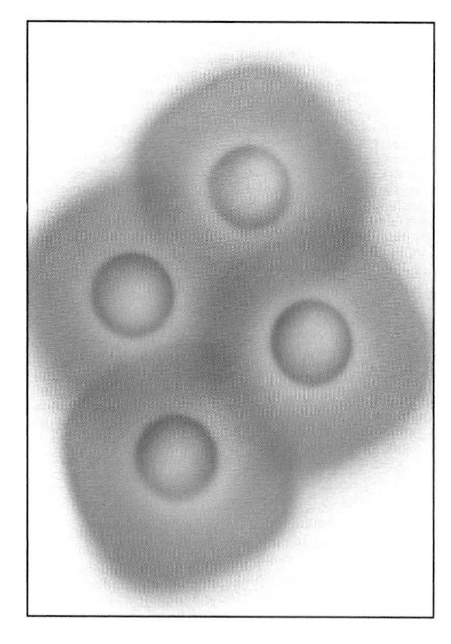

CELL DIVISION

All living things start life as a single cell. The cell grows and eventually it may split into two equal halves. In turn, each of these daughter cells divides into two. The root of a plant such as an onion gets longer and longer as cells within it – seen below at about 100 times life-size – divide repeatedly every few days. As babies, we all grow in size as many thousands of individual cells in our body each divide, until there are some hundreds of millions of cells. So that one cell can become two, all the organelles inside must be copied and shared out evenly. This happens in four distinct stages, as shown in the diagrams below. Here, the two new cells have exactly the same number and type of chromosomes (see pages 12-13).

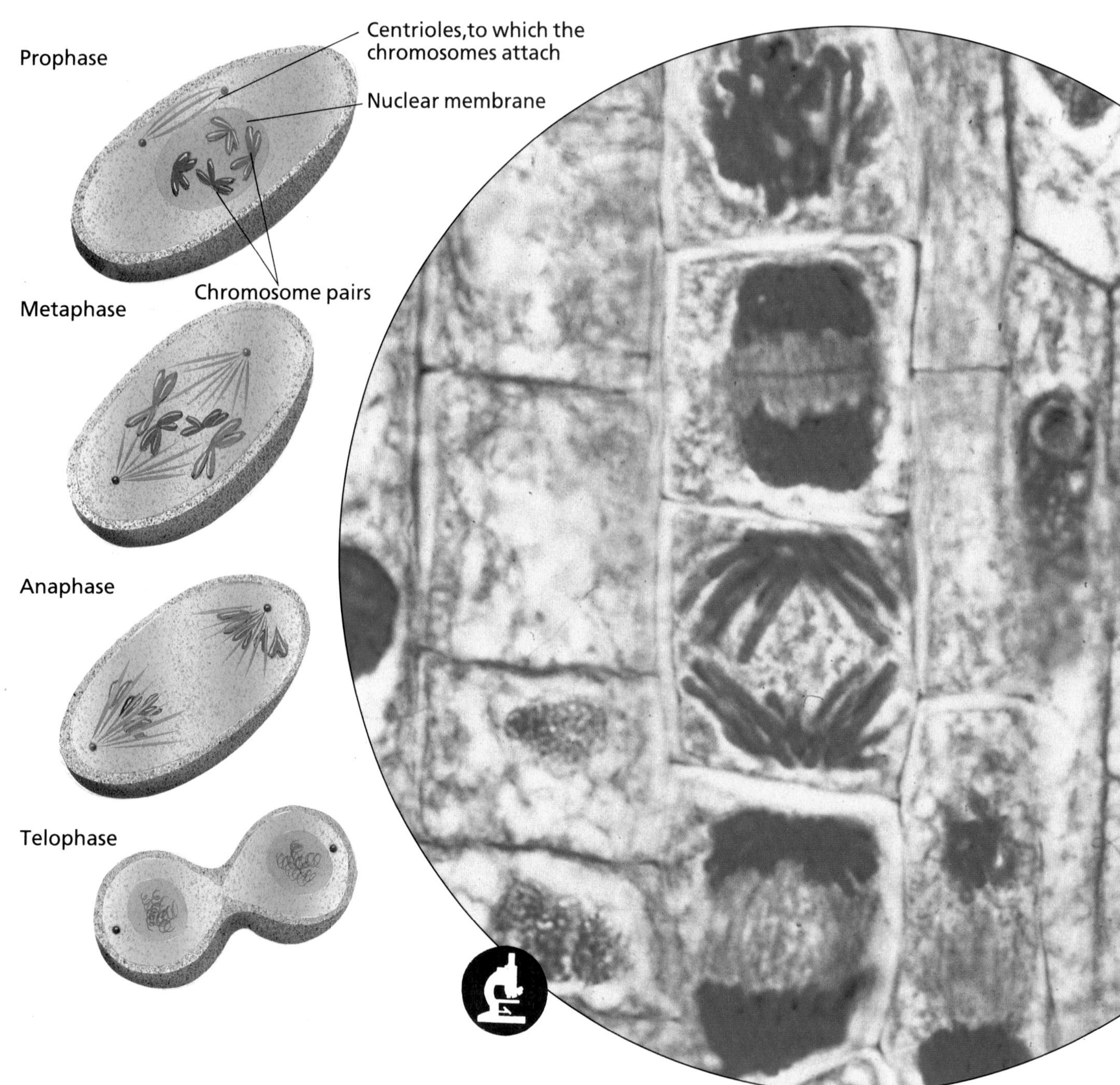

In an onion plant, food is made in the leaves and then sent to the stem and roots. Cells near the surface of the leaves are packed with chloroplasts. A groups of such cells, produced by simple division of just one or two cells, is shown in the photo on the right. Under the microscope, the chloroplasts appear as small green spheres. Note how each cell looks like its neighbors. In the photo below, a bacterial cell is in the last stage of cell division. Two nuclei have formed and each cell has its own outer membrane and wall, but the cells are still joined at the middle.

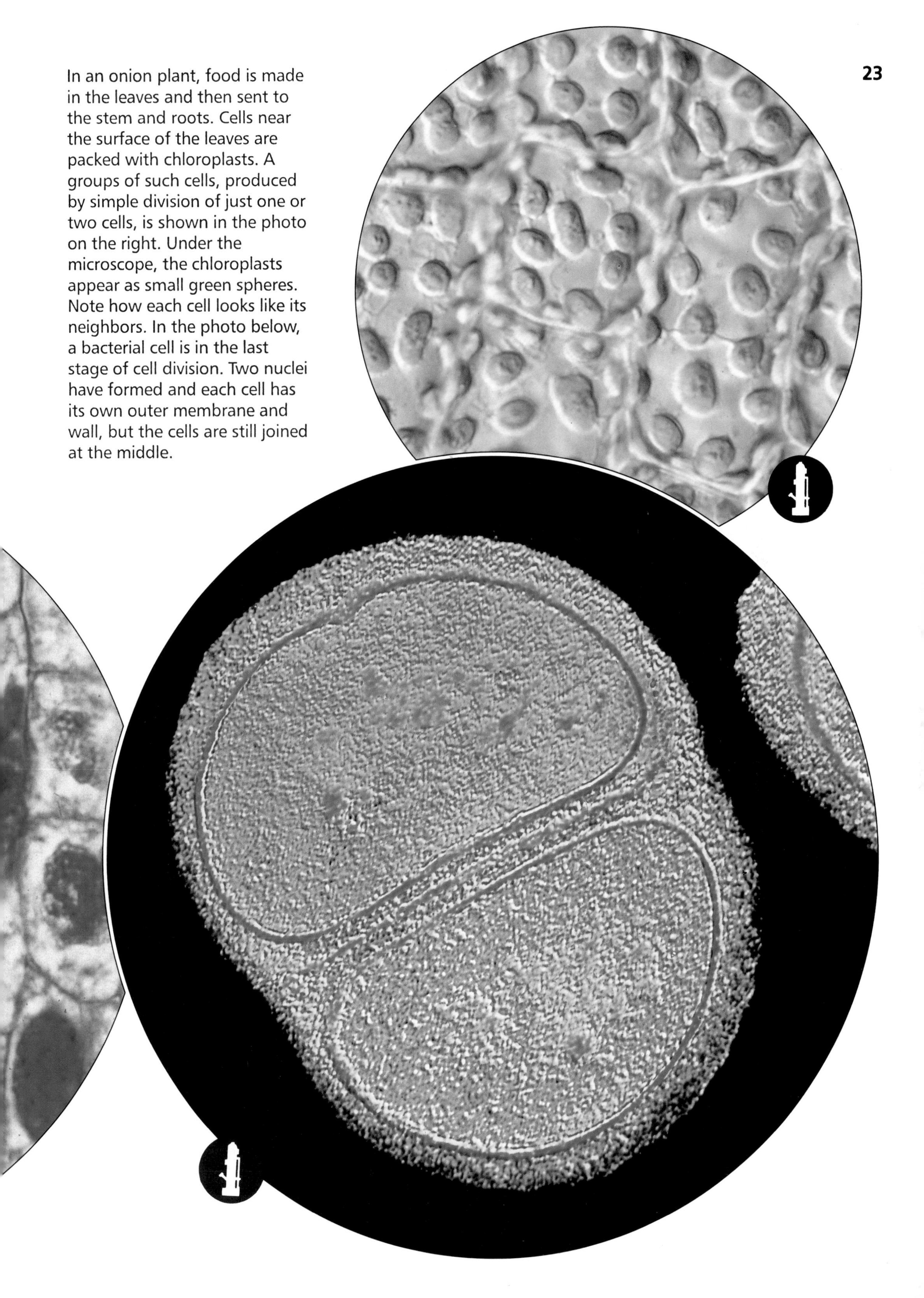

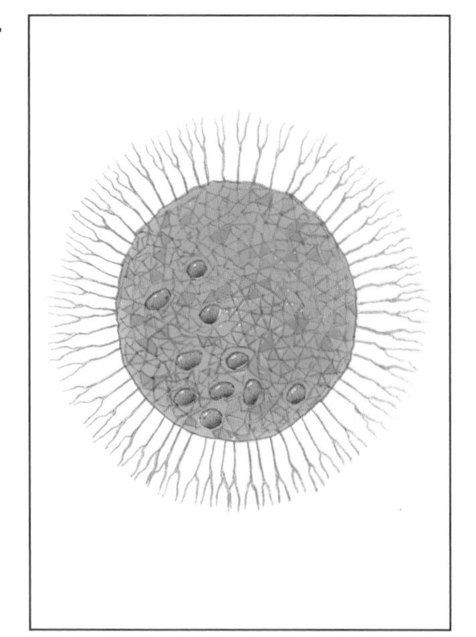

SIMPLE MANY-CELLED CREATURES

The alga *Spirogyra* is made up of many cells, each independent of its neighbor. In another simple creature, *Volvox,* shown below at a magnification of about x200, thousands of almost identical cells are joined together to form a hollow ball of cells. In this so-called "colony," the cells do interact with, and depend on, one another. The jellyfish and the water flea, *Daphnia*, shown opposite, also have a many-celled structure, although in these, different types of cells are present. These are arranged in groups called tissues, and groups of tissues form organs.

Volvox often reproduces by certain cells with the colony each dividing several times to form small daughter colonies. A few of these are visible near the center of the photo below. They break free from the parent colony by splitting it open.

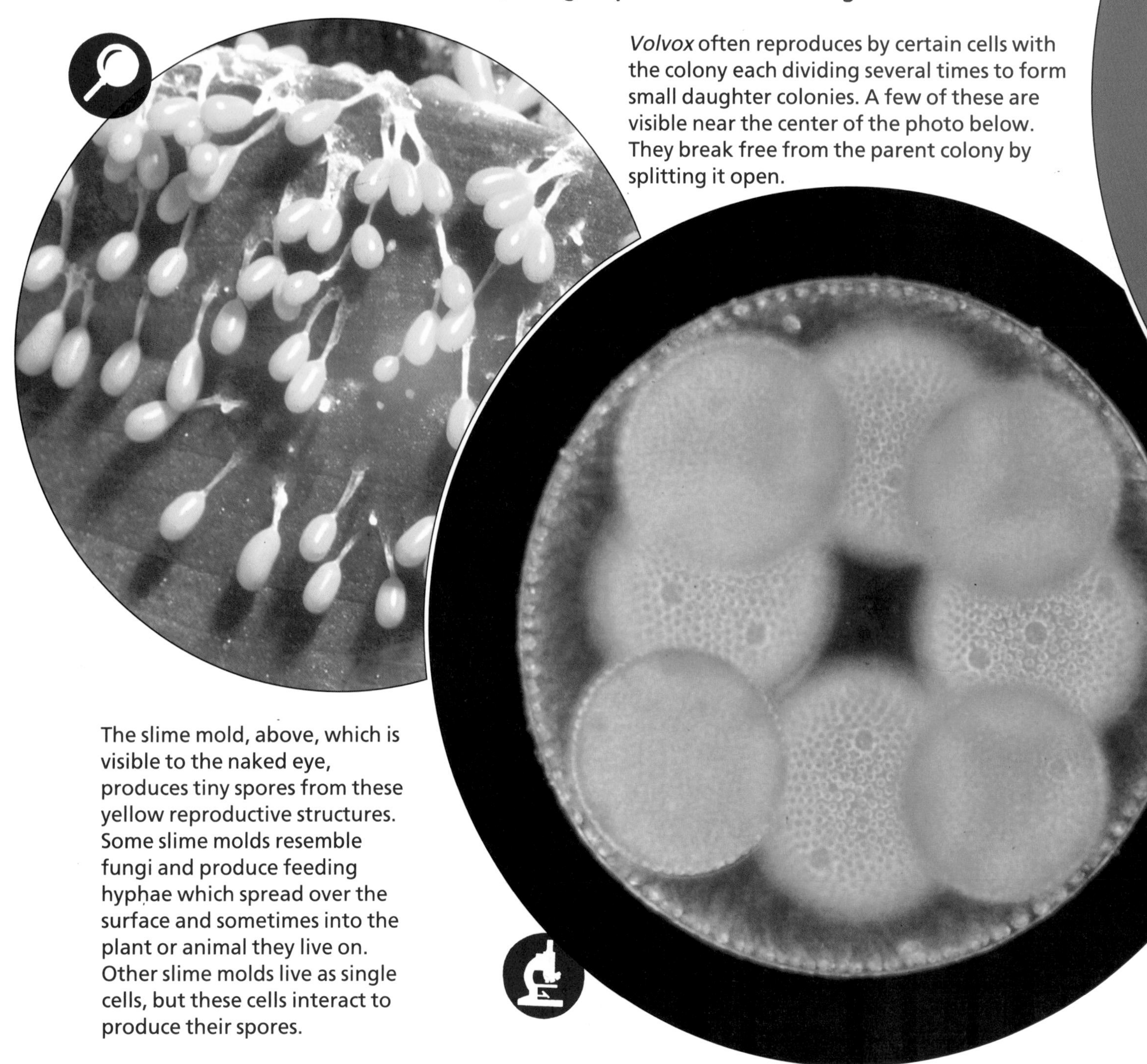

The slime mold, above, which is visible to the naked eye, produces tiny spores from these yellow reproductive structures. Some slime molds resemble fungi and produce feeding hyphae which spread over the surface and sometimes into the plant or animal they live on. Other slime molds live as single cells, but these cells interact to produce their spores.

Jellyfish, corals and sea anemones are made up of just two layers of cells. The outer layer contains stinging cells used to capture food (see page 20). The photo below-left shows a compass jellyfish with its strands of stinging cells trailing behind it.

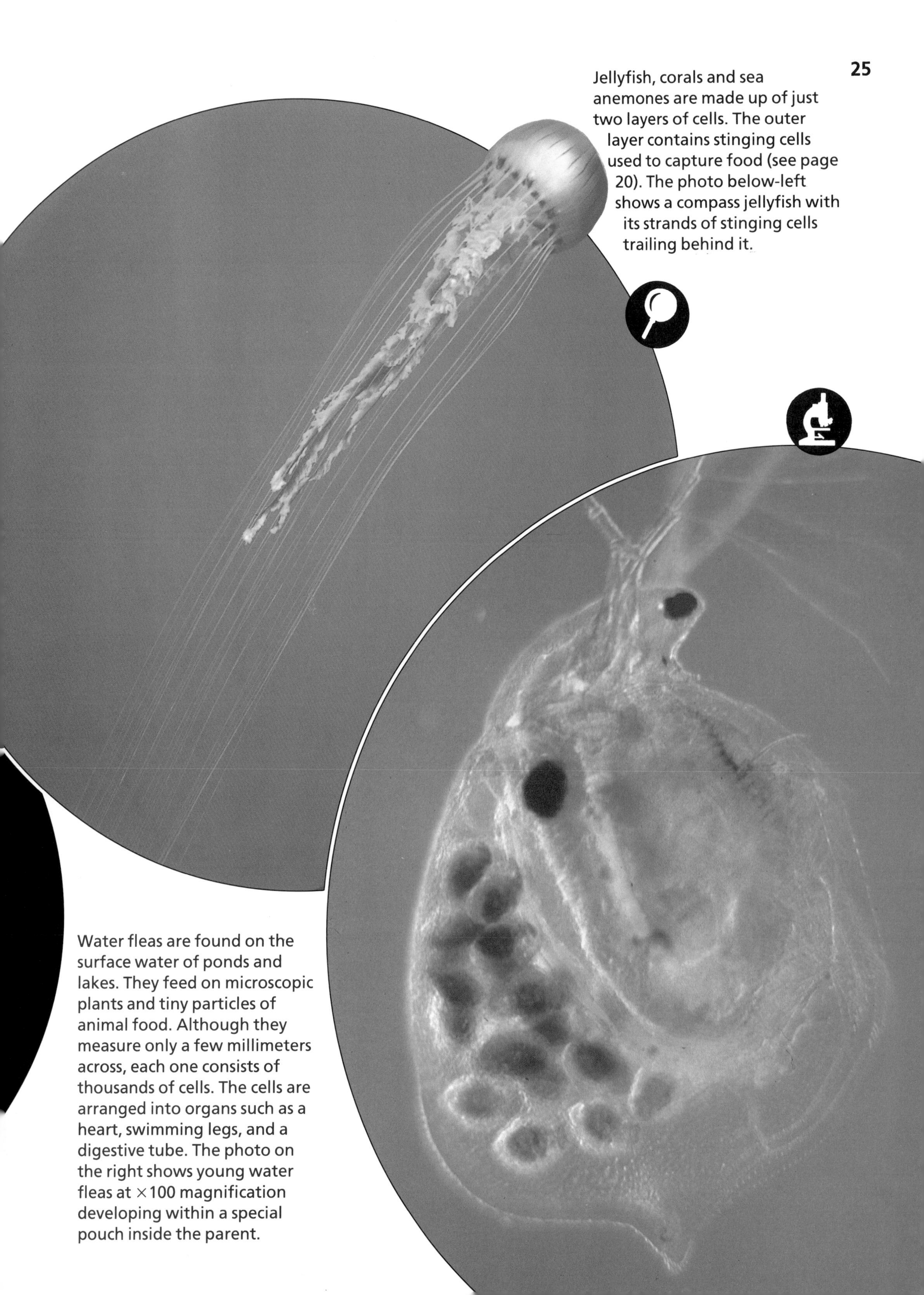

Water fleas are found on the surface water of ponds and lakes. They feed on microscopic plants and tiny particles of animal food. Although they measure only a few millimeters across, each one consists of thousands of cells. The cells are arranged into organs such as a heart, swimming legs, and a digestive tube. The photo on the right shows young water fleas at ×100 magnification developing within a special pouch inside the parent.

CONTENTS

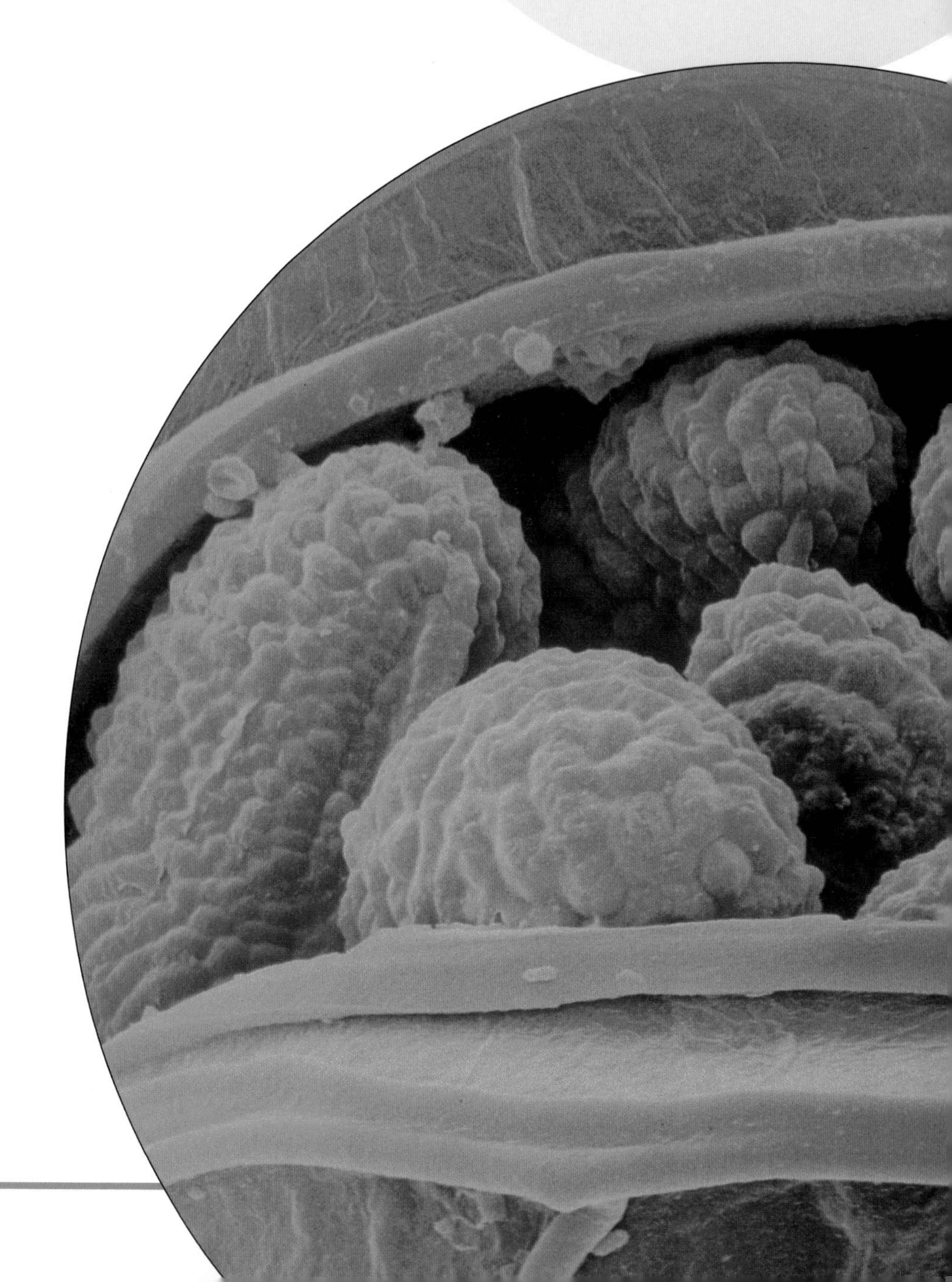

Plants and Seeds

John Stidworthy

FUNGI

Unlike true plants, fungi have no green chlorophyll, and cannot trap sunlight to help make food. Instead, many live as parasites on green plants or on animals. Others feed on dead or decaying plant and animal bodies. Yeasts are fungi that consist of just one cell. Most fungi, though, are made up of a mass of branching threads spreading over, or through, their food. These threads have a wall made of chitin, a tough material like that of insect skins. Every so often the fungus sends up a "fruiting body" which contains spores. Spores are released into the air and settle to grow into new fungi. Fruiting bodies may be simple, like the 'pin-heads' on bread mold, or they may be large like the toadstools and mushrooms.

In the photo (right) you can see a mold growing on a lemon. It has spread over the surface of the overripe fruit taking nourishment from it. This is at x14 magnification. The scanning electron microscope photo (far right) of bread mold was taken at x55 magnification. You can clearly see the network of threads, called *hyphae*, of this fungus as it spreads over and into a piece of bread. The deeper hyphae are very thin. Coming up from the mass of hyphae are stout vertical ones. Each is topped by a round fruiting body called a *sporangium*. It bursts when ripe to release the spores within.

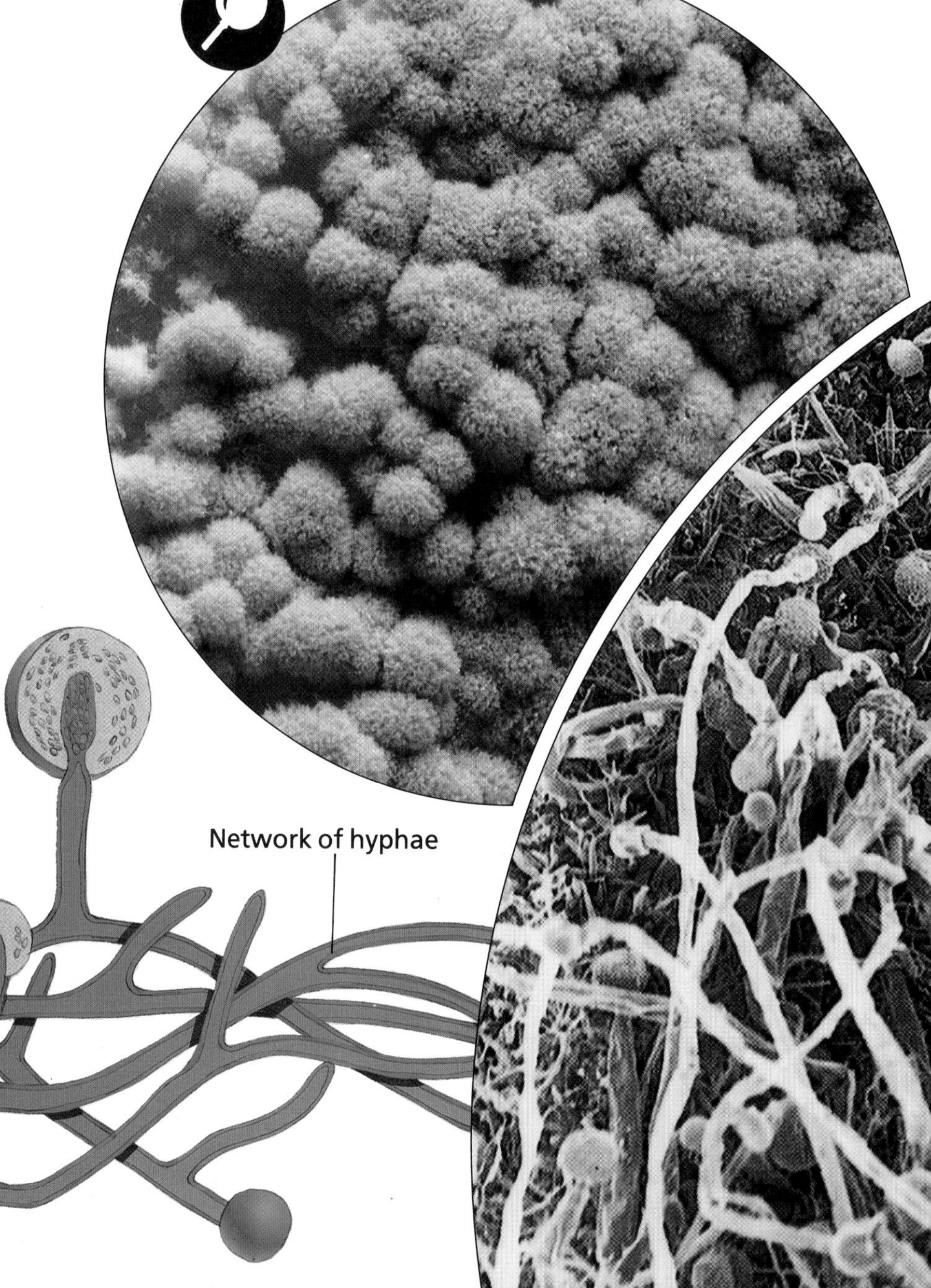

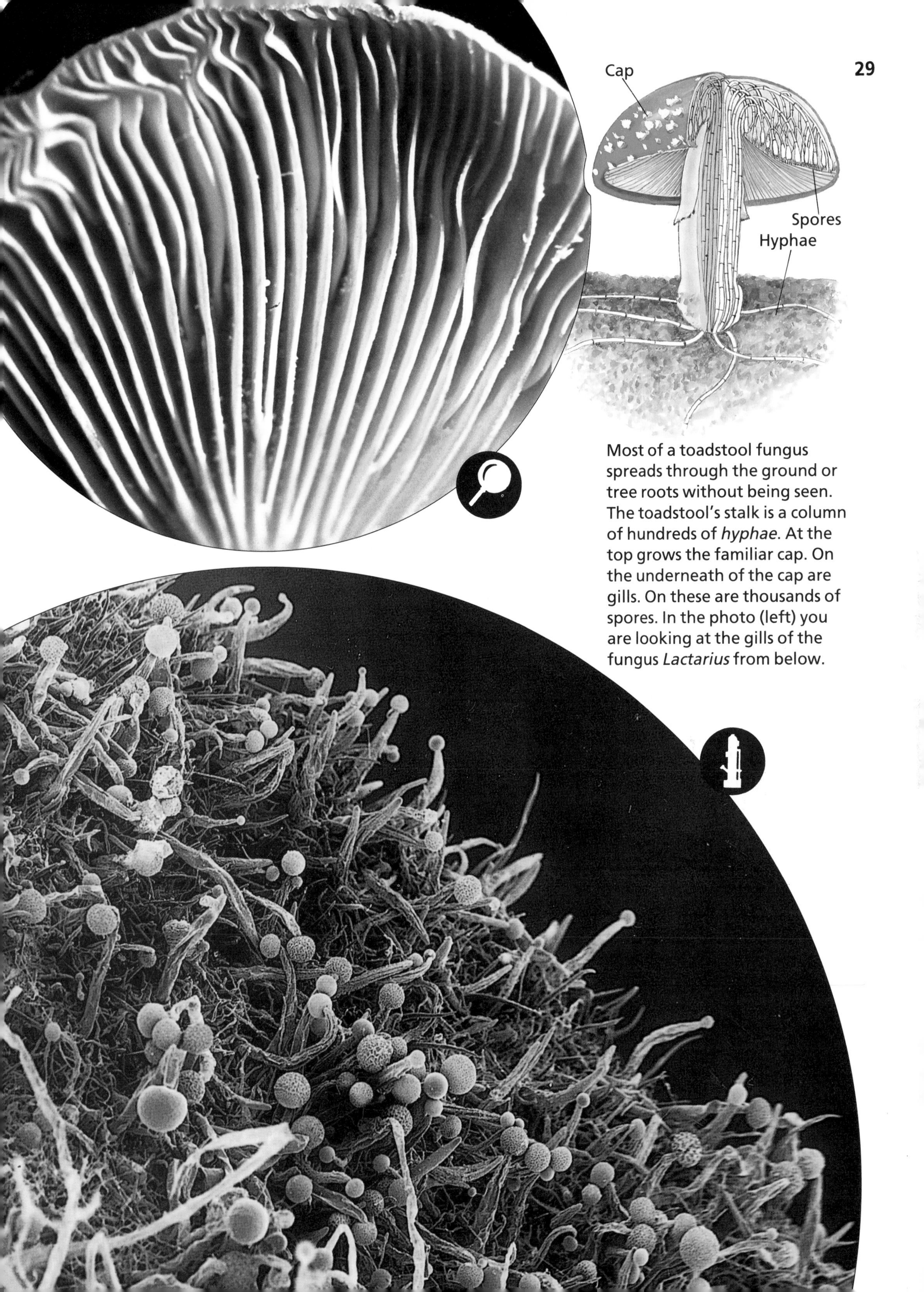

Most of a toadstool fungus spreads through the ground or tree roots without being seen. The toadstool's stalk is a column of hundreds of *hyphae*. At the top grows the familiar cap. On the underneath of the cap are gills. On these are thousands of spores. In the photo (left) you are looking at the gills of the fungus *Lactarius* from below.

ALGAE

Algae are simple plants which have chlorophyll and make their own food, but have no true roots, stems or leaves. The largest of the algae are the big seaweeds, but many kinds of algae are tiny. They live in sea water, freshwater, and in damp places. Some are single-celled, and can only be seen under the microscope, although there may be so many of them that they color the water or make a tree trunk's surface green. Others, such as *Spirogyra*, consist of a long chain of similar cells. Such chains may form a green scum on fresh water. Some algae live with fungi, the two combining to form the type of plant known as a lichen. The fungus provides shelter for the algae. Algae make food that the fungus can use.

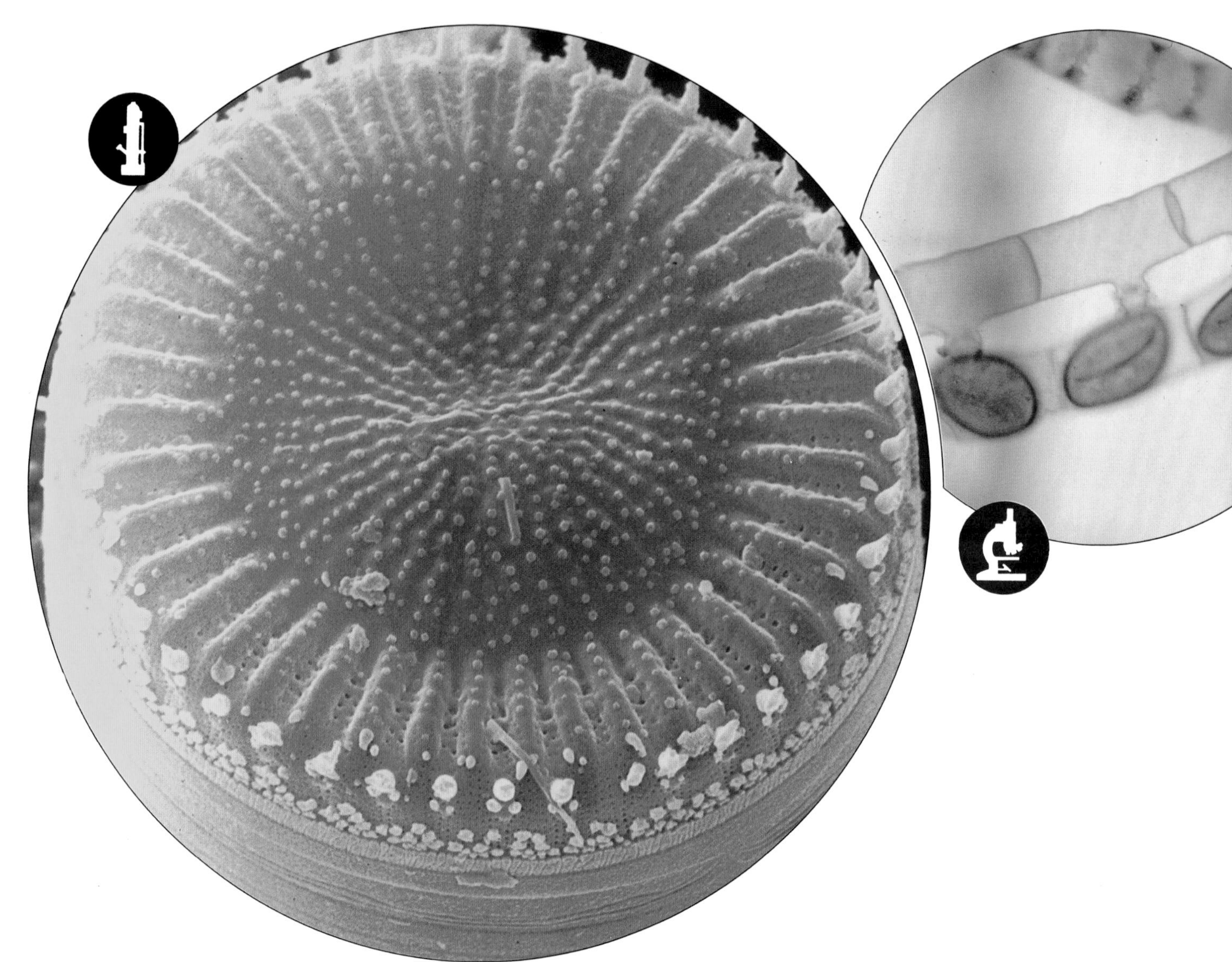

Cyclotella (photo above) is a diatom. Diatoms are single-celled algae that have a glassy shell in two parts. You can see here an electron microscope image of the "sculptured" upper shell of this lake-living alga, 0.002 inches across in life-size.

Spirogyra is an alga with cells joined end to end in a long thread as thick as a human hair. Above you can see two threads whose cells are taking part in a type of "mating." The cell contents of one thread have moved to join cells in the other.

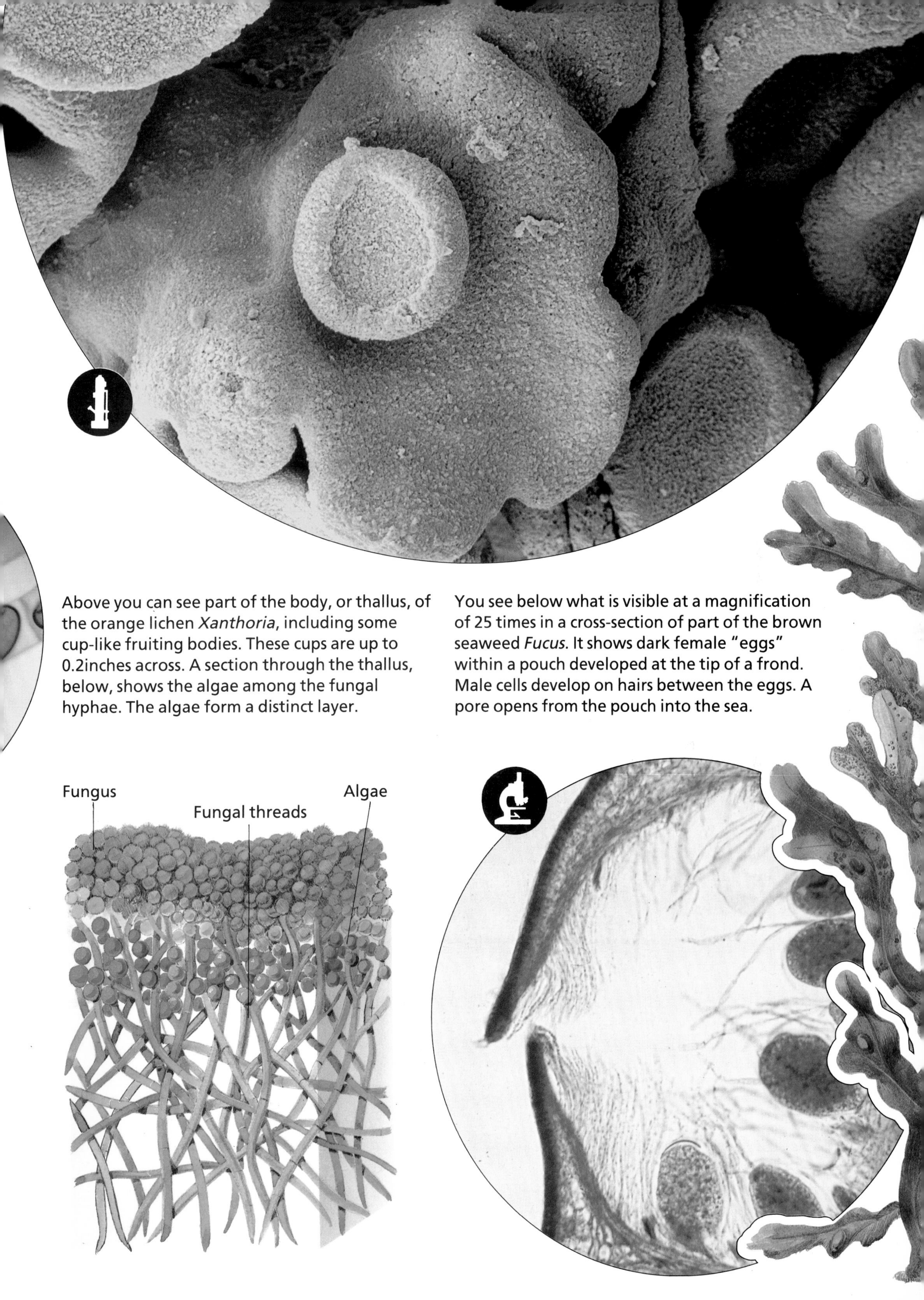

Above you can see part of the body, or thallus, of the orange lichen *Xanthoria*, including some cup-like fruiting bodies. These cups are up to 0.2inches across. A section through the thallus, below, shows the algae among the fungal hyphae. The algae form a distinct layer.

You see below what is visible at a magnification of 25 times in a cross-section of part of the brown seaweed *Fucus*. It shows dark female "eggs" within a pouch developed at the tip of a frond. Male cells develop on hairs between the eggs. A pore opens from the pouch into the sea.

CONIFERS

Some of the largest trees on earth are conifers. Conifers have needle-leaves, and are tough enough to live in many cold places. They have roots and stems with complicated systems of tubes for getting water and food through the plant. They have true seeds, and these develop in the cones on the tree. Conifers have both male and female cones. The small male cones produce large numbers of pollen grains which are carried by the wind to the larger female cones, where some come to rest over the ovules containing the female "eggs." In the pine it can take nearly a year for the pollen to grow down to fertilize the egg. After this, it takes two years for the seed to ripen, and for the woody female cone to open to release it.

Below-right you can see a photograph of a thin slice from the middle of a pine cone. The scales stretch from the core of the cone to the outside. Nestling at the base of some you can see the ovules with eggs inside. After fertilization, food reserves are added around the embryo, then a tough winged coat. The seed is then complete.

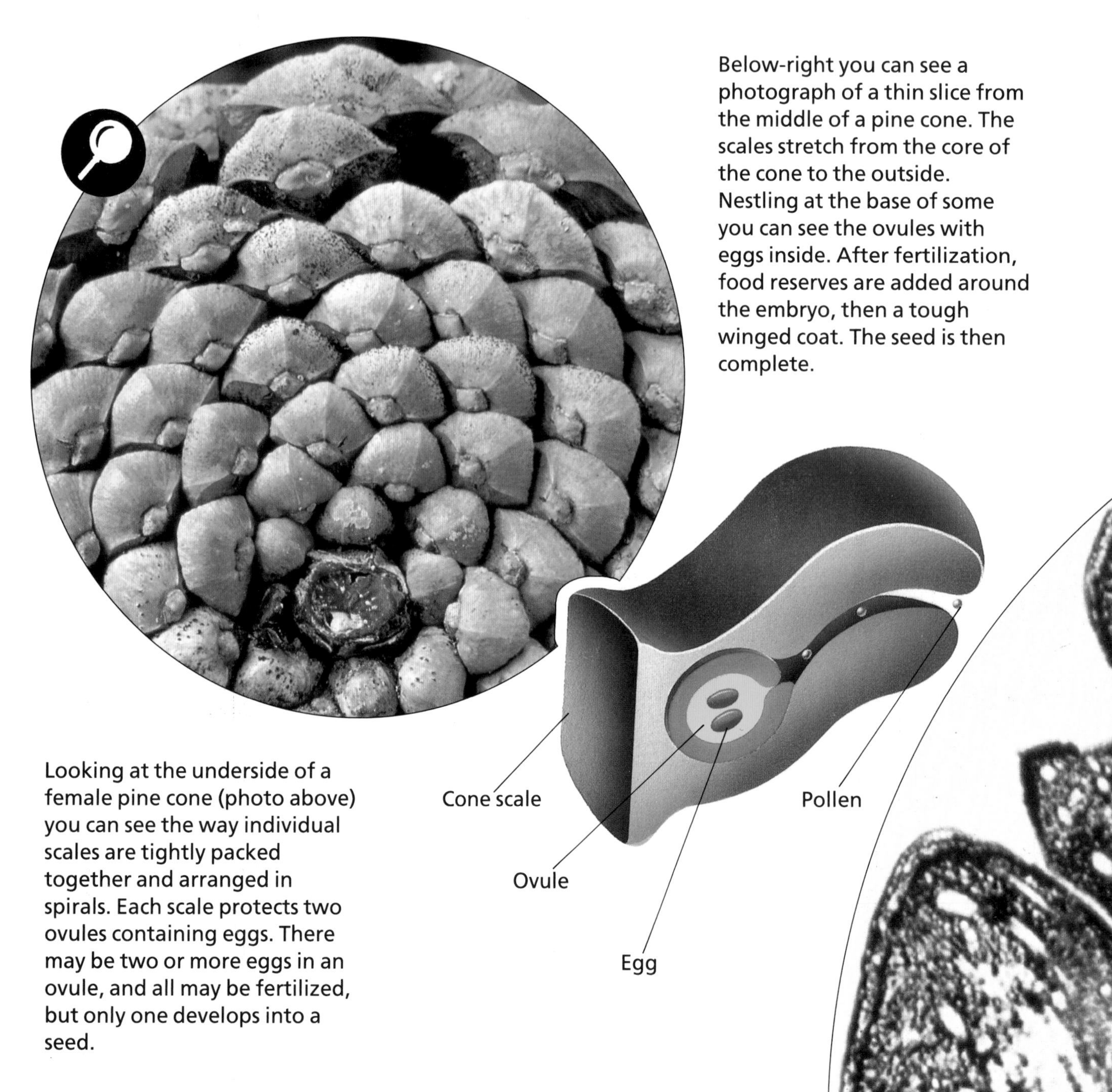

Looking at the underside of a female pine cone (photo above) you can see the way individual scales are tightly packed together and arranged in spirals. Each scale protects two ovules containing eggs. There may be two or more eggs in an ovule, and all may be fertilized, but only one develops into a seed.

A section of a pine tree magnified x100 (photo-right) shows many squarish cells called tracheids. These act as water pipes up the trunk. Large ones form in spring, smaller ones in late summer, creating the rings you see on a cut trunk.

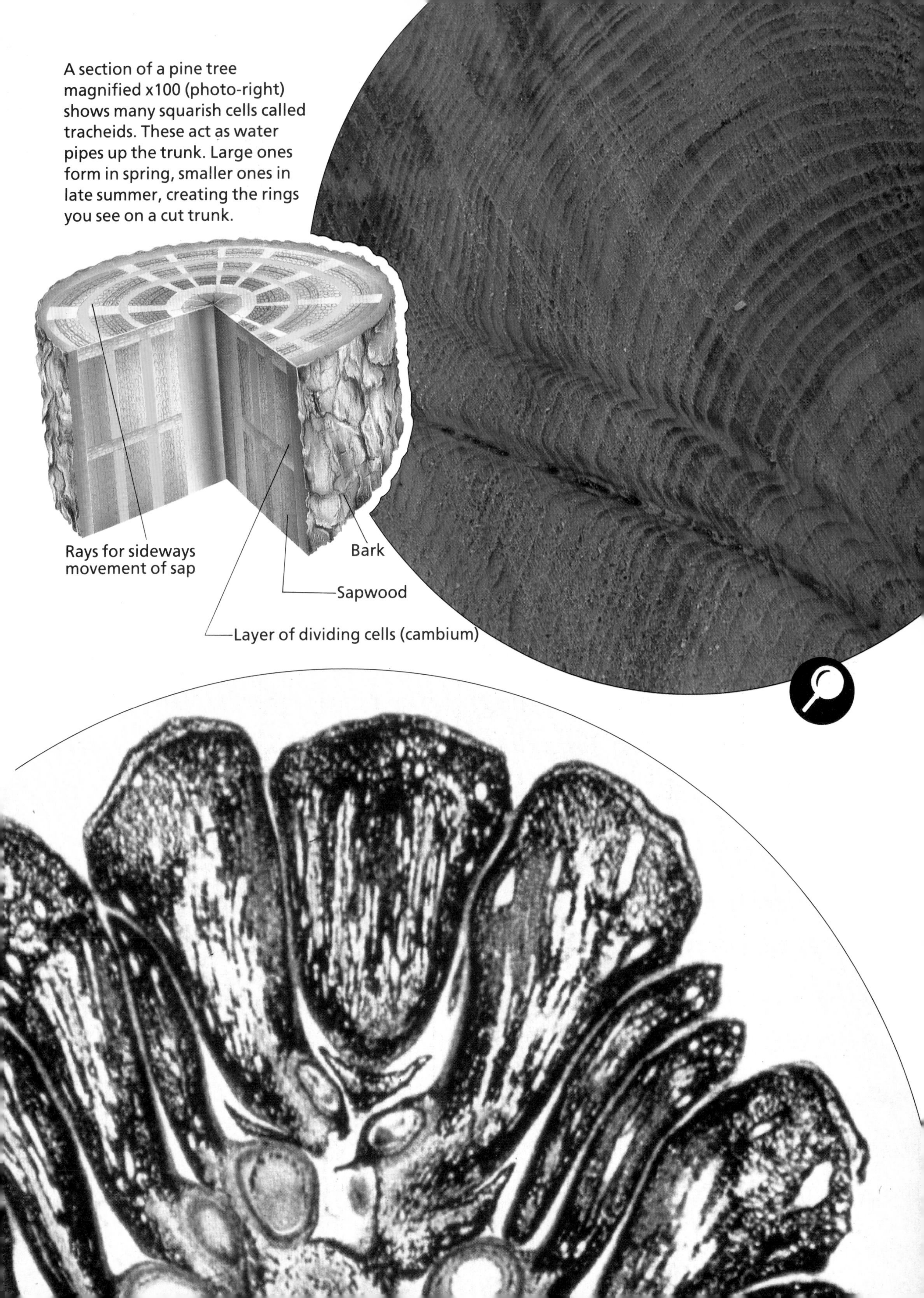

FLOWERING PLANT LEAVES

The leaf of a flowering plant is busy producing food for the plant. It is green because it contains chlorophyll that traps light for the plant to use. Some leaves, such as those of copper beech, have other colors but the all-important chlorophyll is still there. Most leaves are flat, and have a wide surface exposed to sunlight. Into the leaf run pipes made of cells that bring water carried up from the roots of the plant. Others may carry foods and salts in solution. As well as light and water, plants need carbon dioxide gas to make food. Under the leaf are many pores, called stomata, through which the plant can take in or let out gases. The leaf surface may have other structures, including "hairs" of various kinds.

On the left you can see the surface of a magnolia leaf. The veins show the course of the main water carrying vessels. One main vein starts at the leaf base. Branches come off from this all the way up the leaf, taking water to each and every one of the cells. These veins contain some of the strongest tissue in the leaf and help to strengthen and support it.

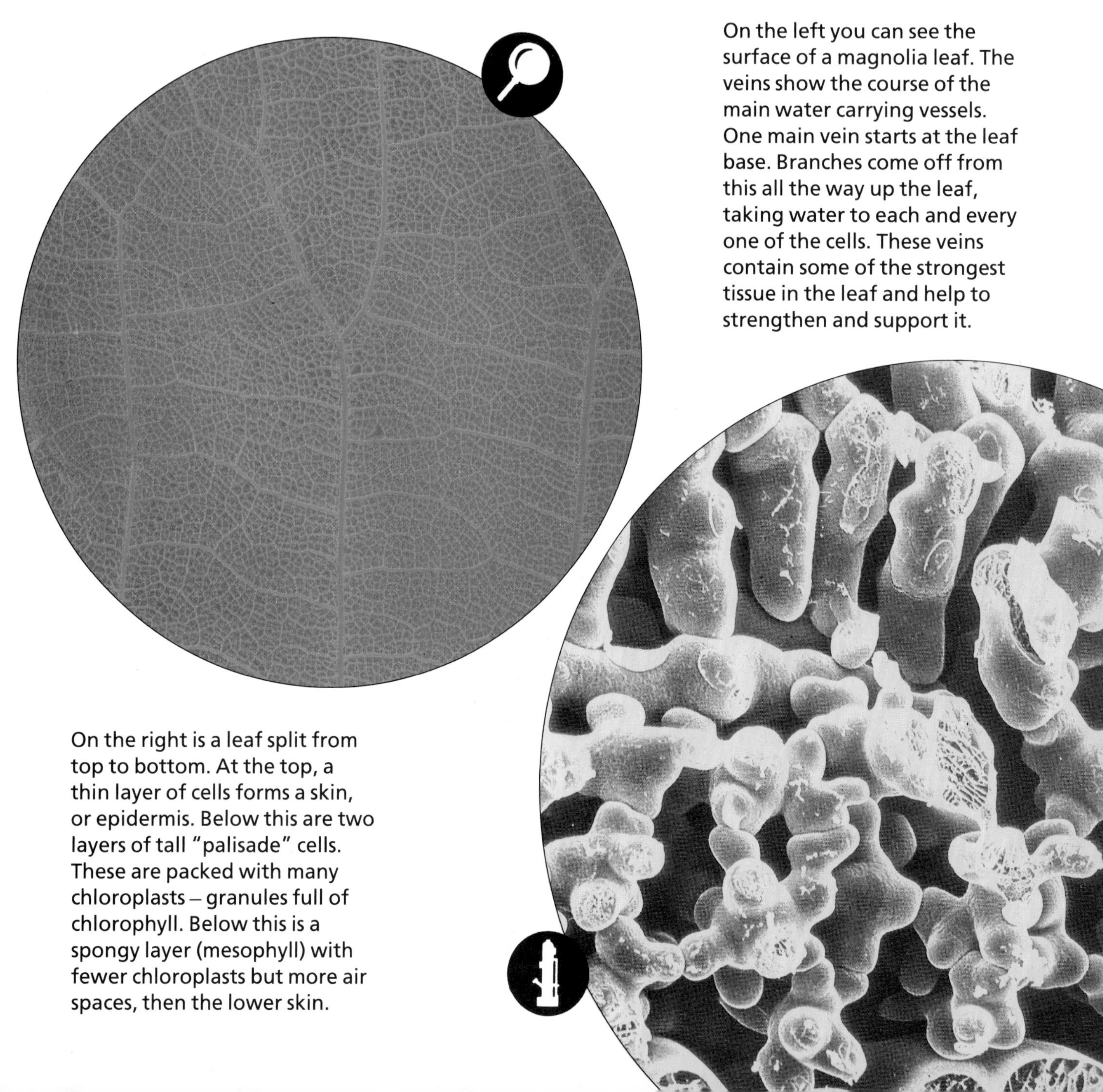

On the right is a leaf split from top to bottom. At the top, a thin layer of cells forms a skin, or epidermis. Below this are two layers of tall "palisade" cells. These are packed with many chloroplasts – granules full of chlorophyll. Below this is a spongy layer (mesophyll) with fewer chloroplasts but more air spaces, then the lower skin.

Plant leaves often have hairs on the surface to help protect leaves from heat or cold. Some hairs secrete poisons, as on nettle leaves. Others, like the short round hairs you can see on the *Coleus* leaf (right), secrete resins. On the surface of the tobacco leaf below you can see a long hair, and many stomata. Each has a pair of cells forming lips around the pore.

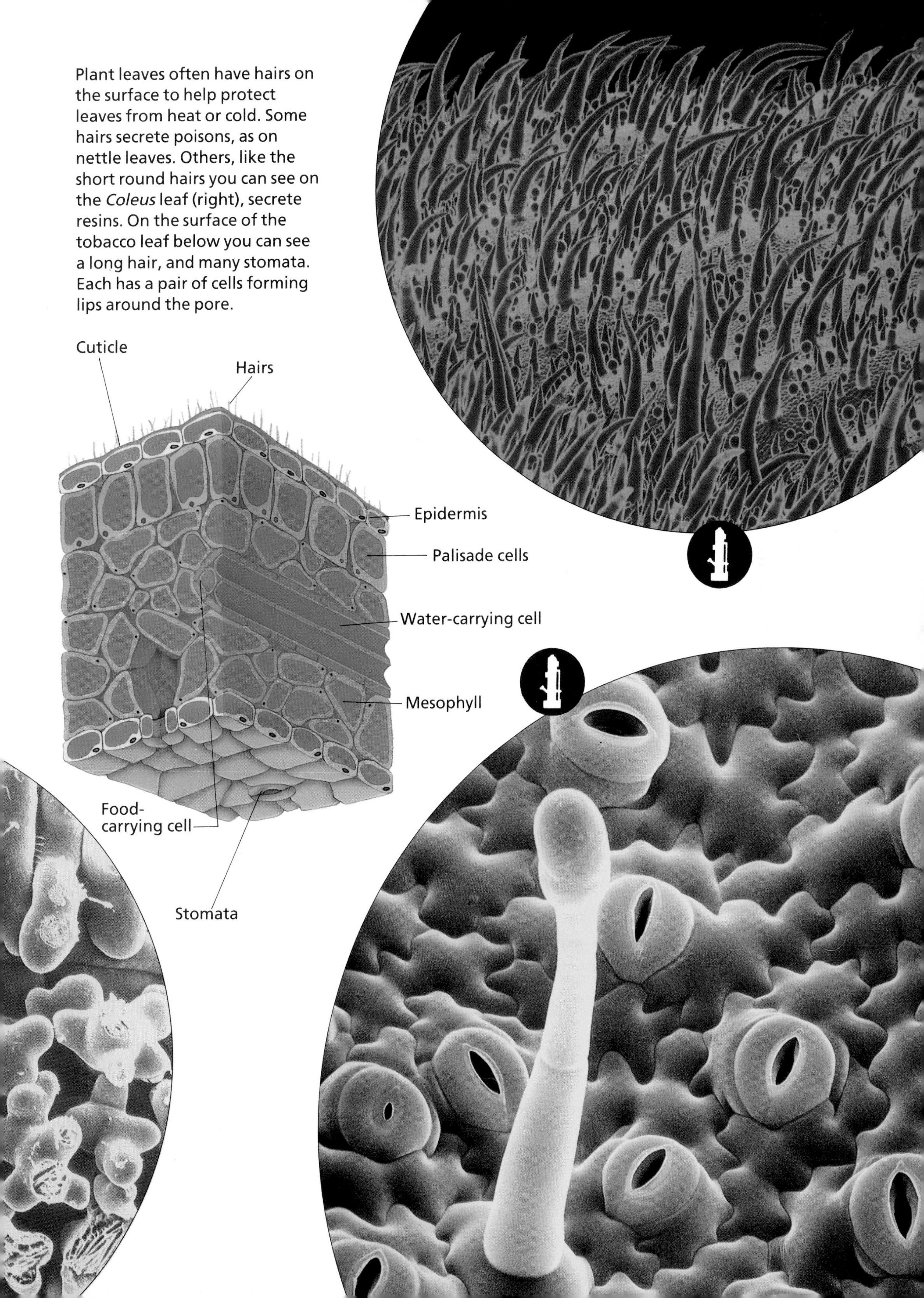

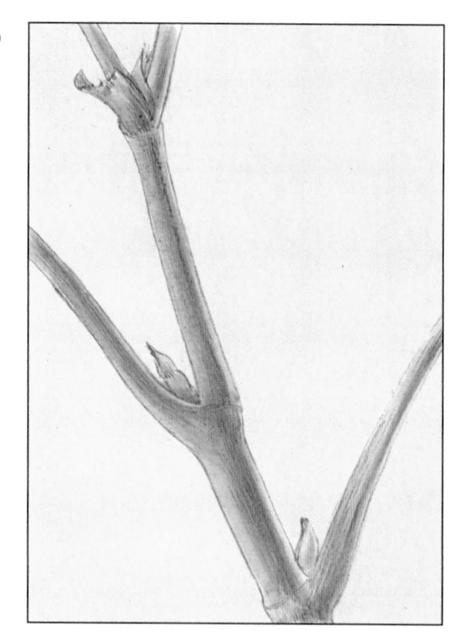

STEMS

Stems of most plants grow upwards toward the light. They carry leaves, and may branch, or they may have buds where new shoots will develop. There may be stomata on their surfaces, and some grow hairs or even spines. It is the job of a stem to hold leaves up toward the light so they can make the best use of it, and to keep the leaves supplied with water and minerals so they can do their job. "Pipes" carrying water and food run up the stem, and branch into the leaves. The pipes are made of specialized cells produced as the plant grows. Some of these cells are toughened with thick cell walls. They form bundles of pipes near the outside of the stem. Here they can also stop the stem from being bent by wind and weather.

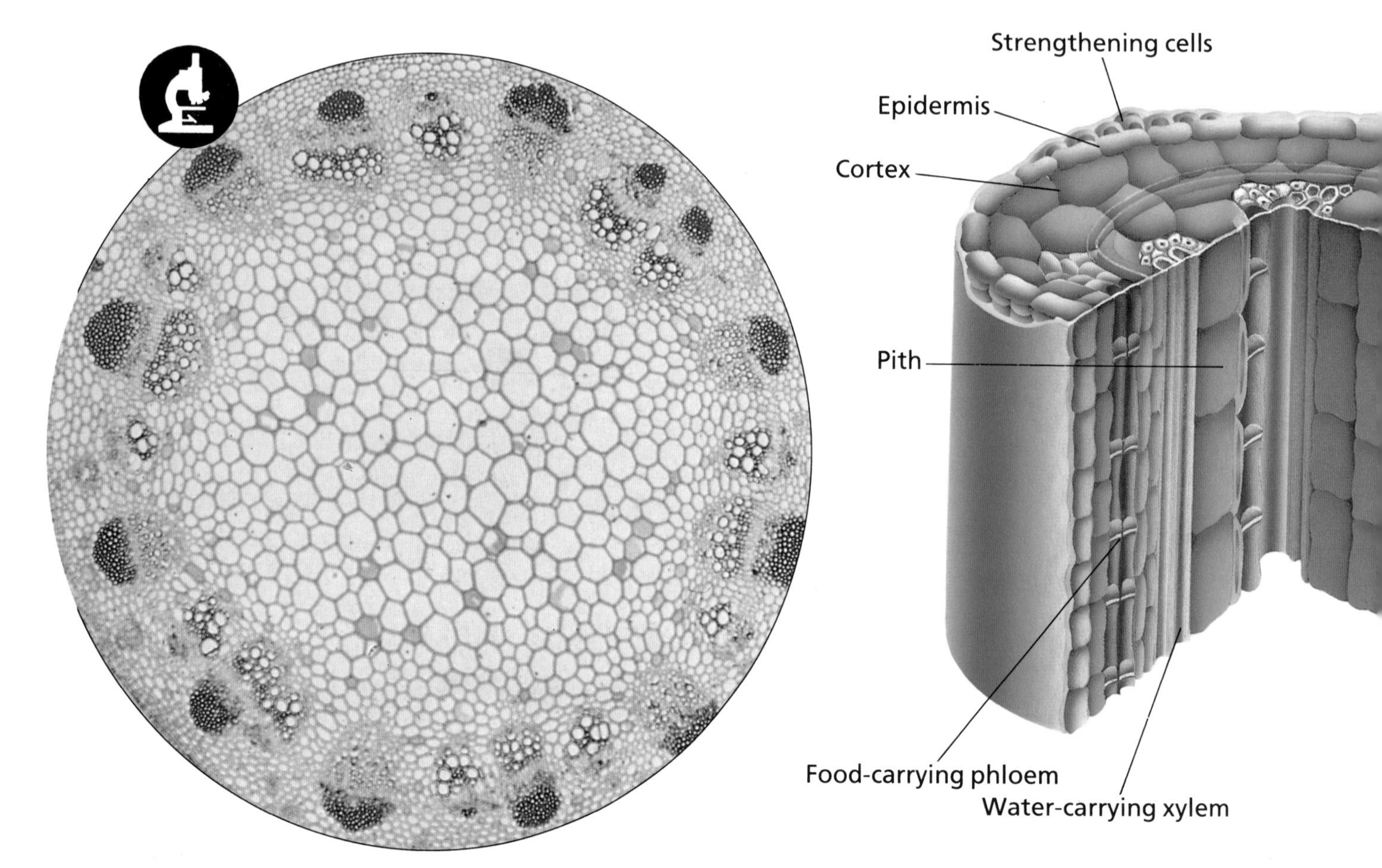

Above you can see a cut through the young stem of a sunflower plant. In the middle the pith cells are fairly large and open, but around the outside of the stem you can see the bundles of more tightly-packed cells that form the plant's pipework. Each bundle has cells called xylem in a bunch towards the pith. These are the water-conducting cells. Nearer the surface are phloem cells that carry foods. Outside these there are some tight-packed strengthening fibers, cells with thick cell walls and small centers. There are more strengthening cells just below the skin.

Between the phloem and the xylem is a thin band of cells called the cambium. These are dividing cells that produce new xylem and phloem. A thin band of cambium goes around the stem between the pipe and bundles. In older stems it produces xylem and phloem all around the stem, so you cannot see bundles of pipes, but get a stem with a woody cross-section.

The illustration below shows axillary buds growing in the angle between a leaf and the stem leaves. On the right, you can see a photo of a slice down such a bud. A number of leaves have started to form in the bud. They are folded around the top of the new shoot. Below is a greatly magnified view of some of the cells in a pine tree stem. You can see what is visible when a magnification of nearly 1000 times is used (as opposed to a 50 times magnification in the sunflower, far left). The long tubes are single water-carrying cells running up the wood. The rounded structures connect one cell to another.

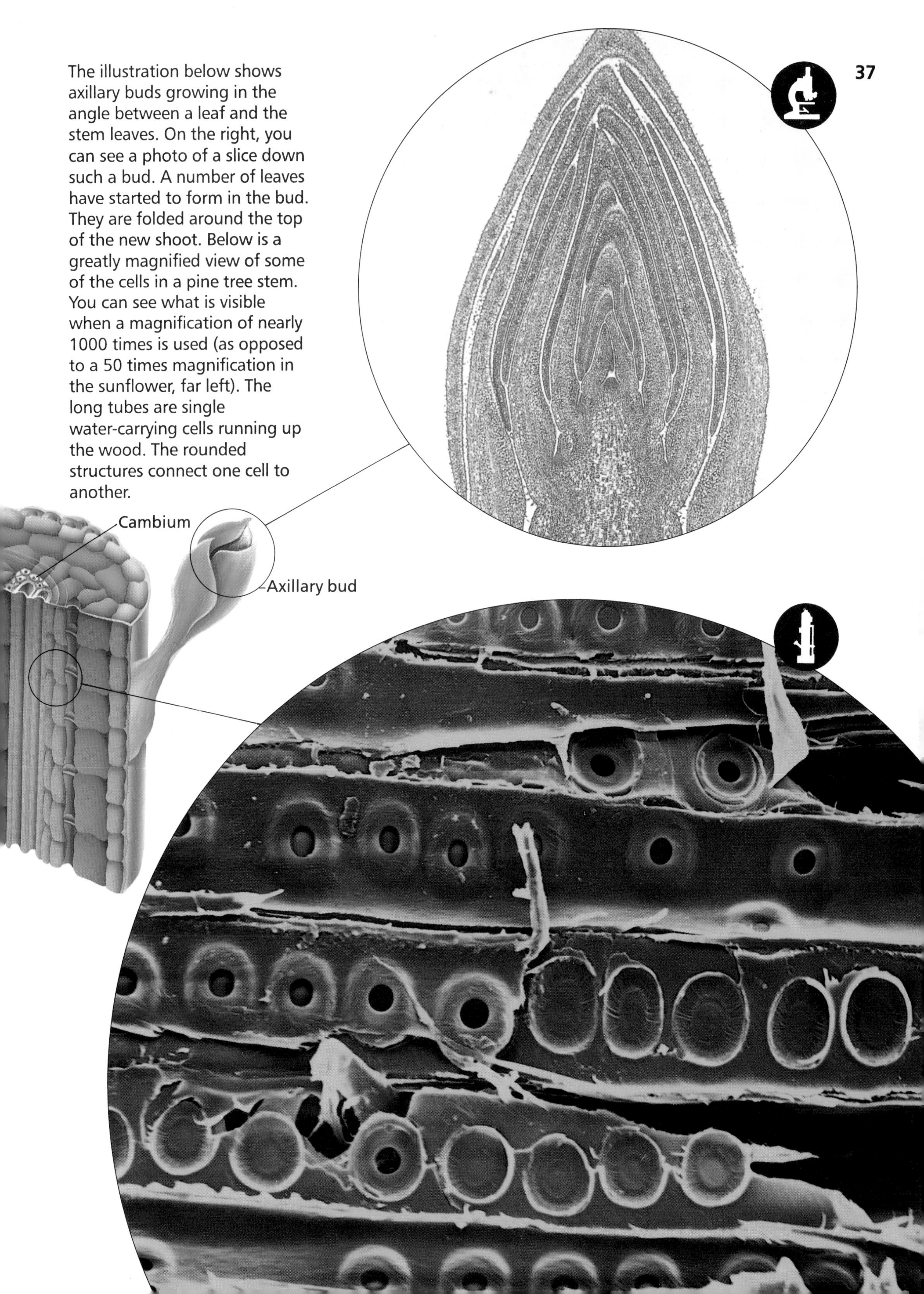

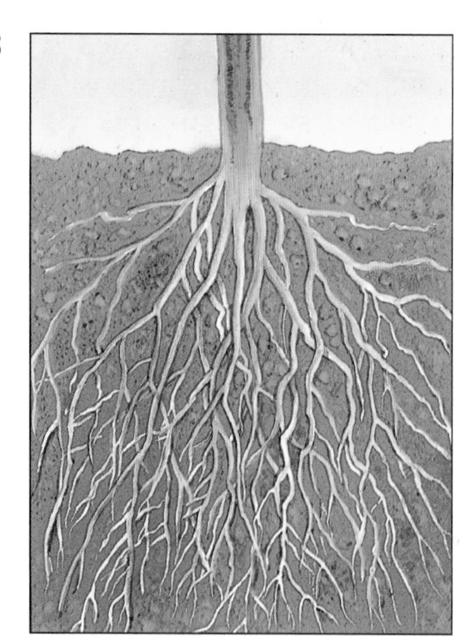

ROOTS

Roots anchor the plant in the soil and take up water from the soil so that the plant can live and grow. Water is taken in through fine root hairs that stick out into the surrounding earth. These hairs are extensions of the cells of the epidermis. Water moves through the root tissue into the xylem, and flows up to the stem. The pipework of a root runs up through the middle. In the roots of some plants, especially those of the pea family, certain bacteria live. These can take nitrogen from the air and turn it into a form the plant can use for growth. The bacteria multiply, surrounded by root tissue, forming little nodules like this one, one hundredth of an inch across which you can see (photo right) on the surface of a pea root.

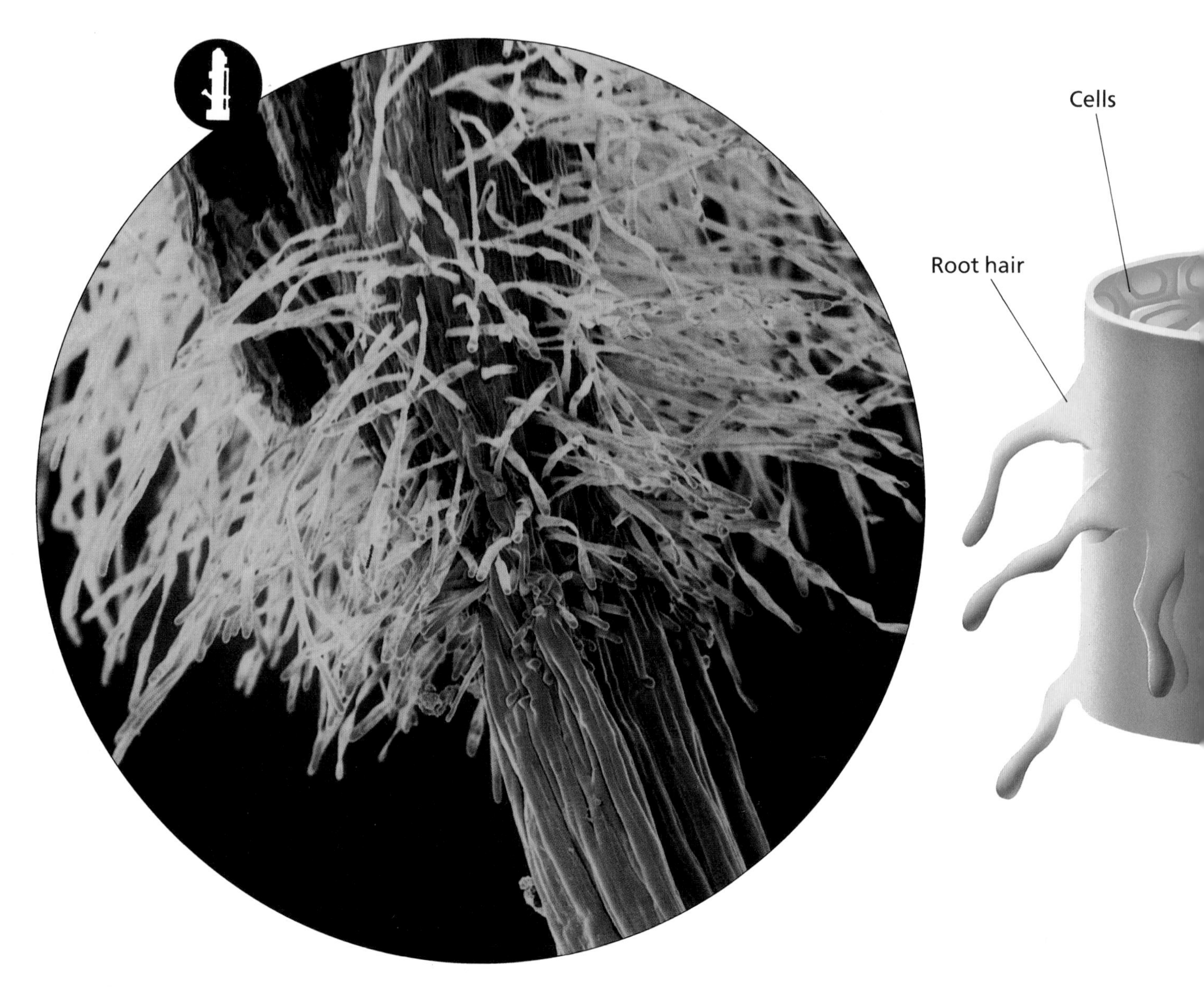

When a root is magnified 100 times, you can easily see the tangle of root hairs covering the surface almost down to its tip. Most plants can take up all the water they need using just a small proportion of these hairs, but as water may not be evenly distributed in the soil, it pays to have a good network. Root hairs are short-lived, but new ones keep being produced near the tip.

A root has to push its way through the soil as it grows. Some roots exert a surprising force for their size, but for them to slide between the soil particles it helps to be slippery. The cells at the tip produce a slime (photo below) that helps the root push through the soil.

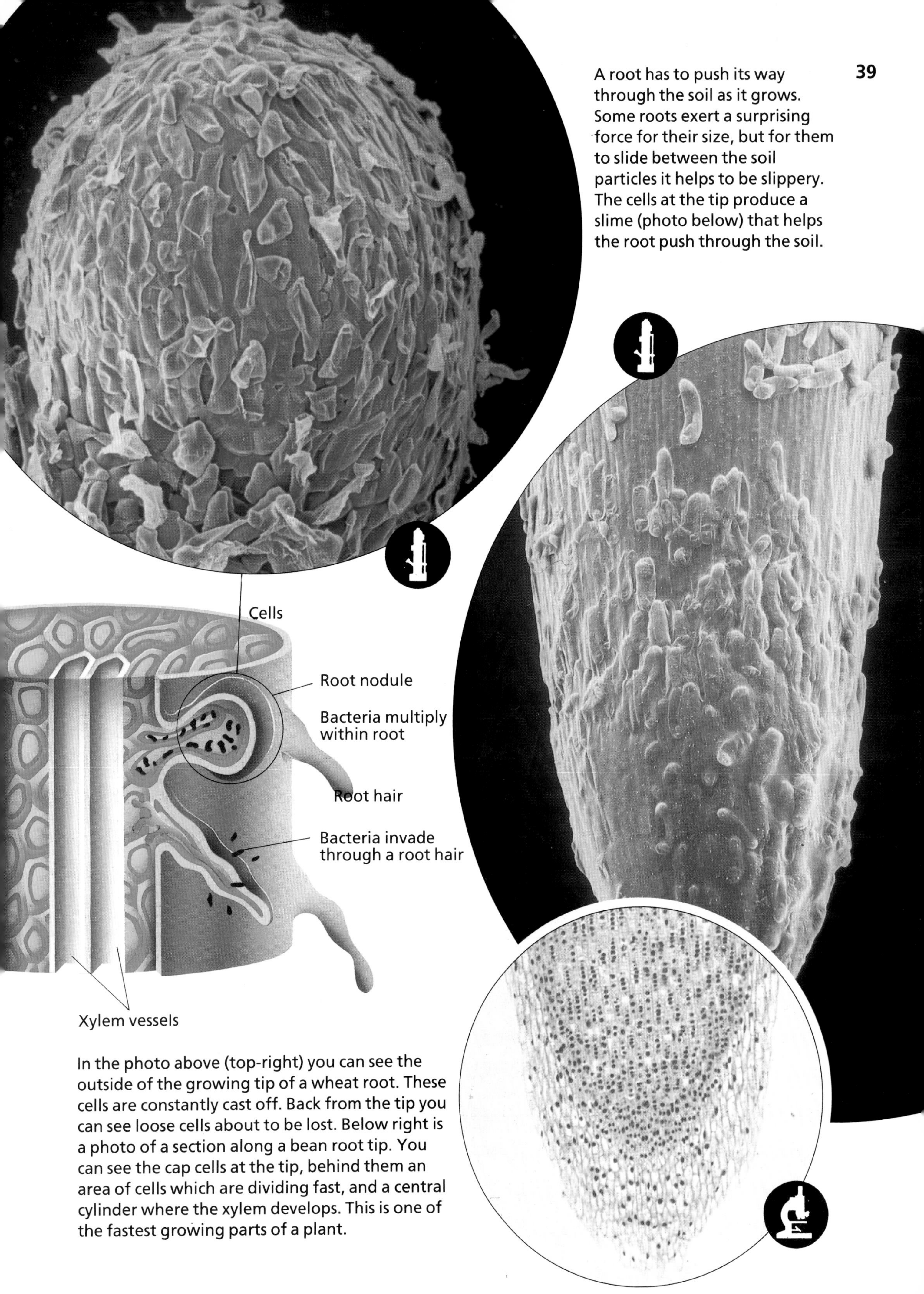

In the photo above (top-right) you can see the outside of the growing tip of a wheat root. These cells are constantly cast off. Back from the tip you can see loose cells about to be lost. Below right is a photo of a section along a bean root tip. You can see the cap cells at the tip, behind them an area of cells which are dividing fast, and a central cylinder where the xylem develops. This is one of the fastest growing parts of a plant.

FLOWERS

Flowers are devices to make sure that the plant reproduces successfully. Many of them are pretty, with bright petals or other colored parts. They often smell fragrant. However, their attractiveness is not really directed at humans, but at insects that can help carry pollen between flowers. Others may have their pollen carried by the wind. The pollen of a flower grows on the stamen, the male part of the plant. The egg, or ovule, is tucked away inside the ovary within the female part of the flower. Above the ovary is the stigma, the surface on which the pollen must land to reach the ovary. In some flowers the stigma is on a stalk, called the style. The stigma may have glands or hairs to help hold the pollen.

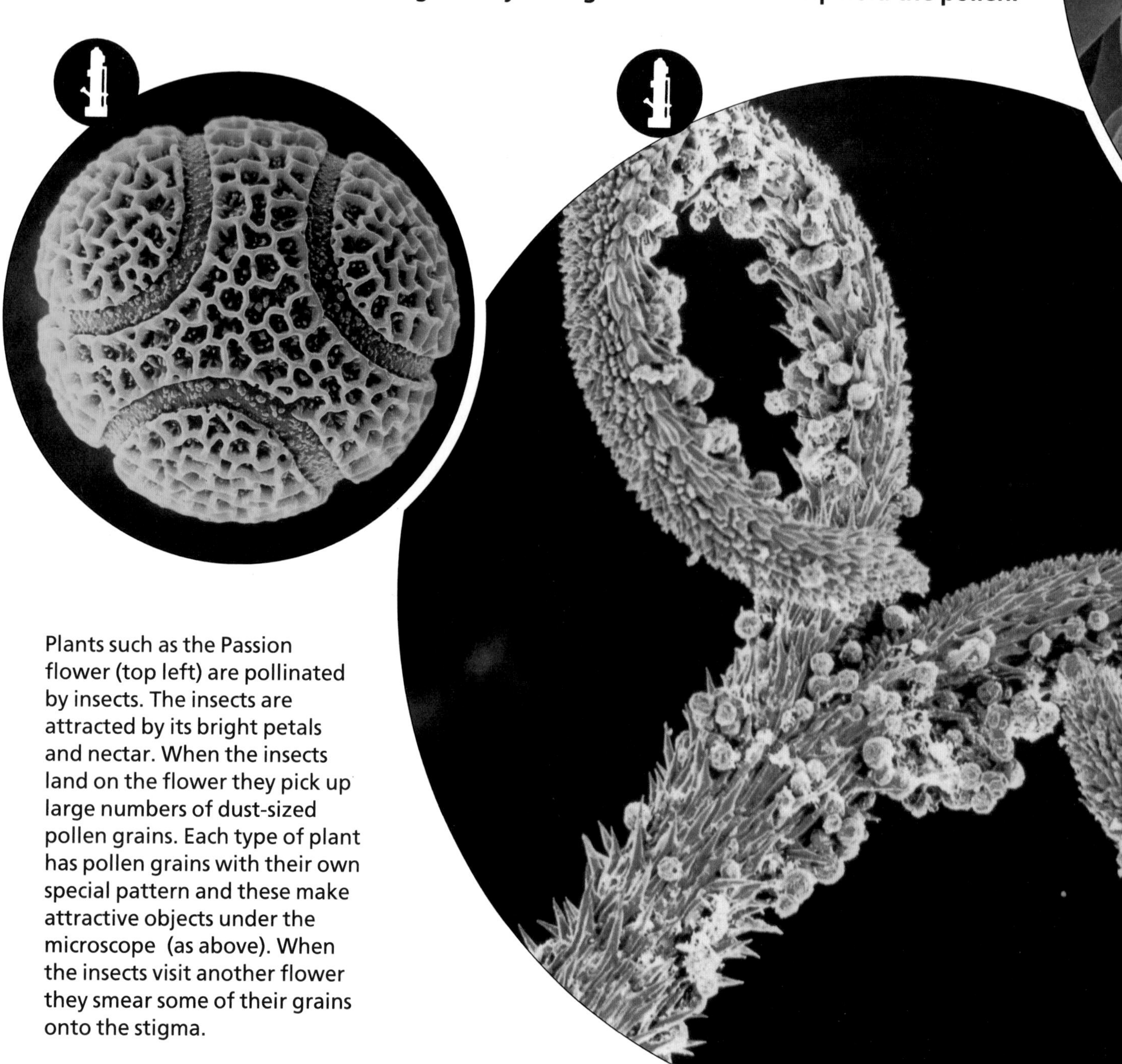

Plants such as the Passion flower (top left) are pollinated by insects. The insects are attracted by its bright petals and nectar. When the insects land on the flower they pick up large numbers of dust-sized pollen grains. Each type of plant has pollen grains with their own special pattern and these make attractive objects under the microscope (as above). When the insects visit another flower they smear some of their grains onto the stigma.

The photo below-left shows the stigma of a dandelion. The dandelion flower head is made up of a whole cluster of tiny flowers. A style grows up through the center of one of the tiny flowers, and on top the two arms of the stigma open out and curl back, as you can see in the photo. The sticky surface of the stigma collects pollen grains, as you can see here. The stigma in this flower is quite tiny, magnified 130 times. In the photo below-right, you are looking at the top of the capsule in the middle of a poppy flower. The rays radiating from the middle are the stigmas. They have hairs and glands to help them catch any pollen that arrives. The photo on the left (top) shows what happens after the pollen grains arrive on the stigma. Magnified 250 times, you can see the pollen grains swelling and splitting. Then a pollen grain is sent down a tube into the stigma and down into the ovary. The contents of the pollen grain go down this tube and fuse with, or fertilize, the egg.

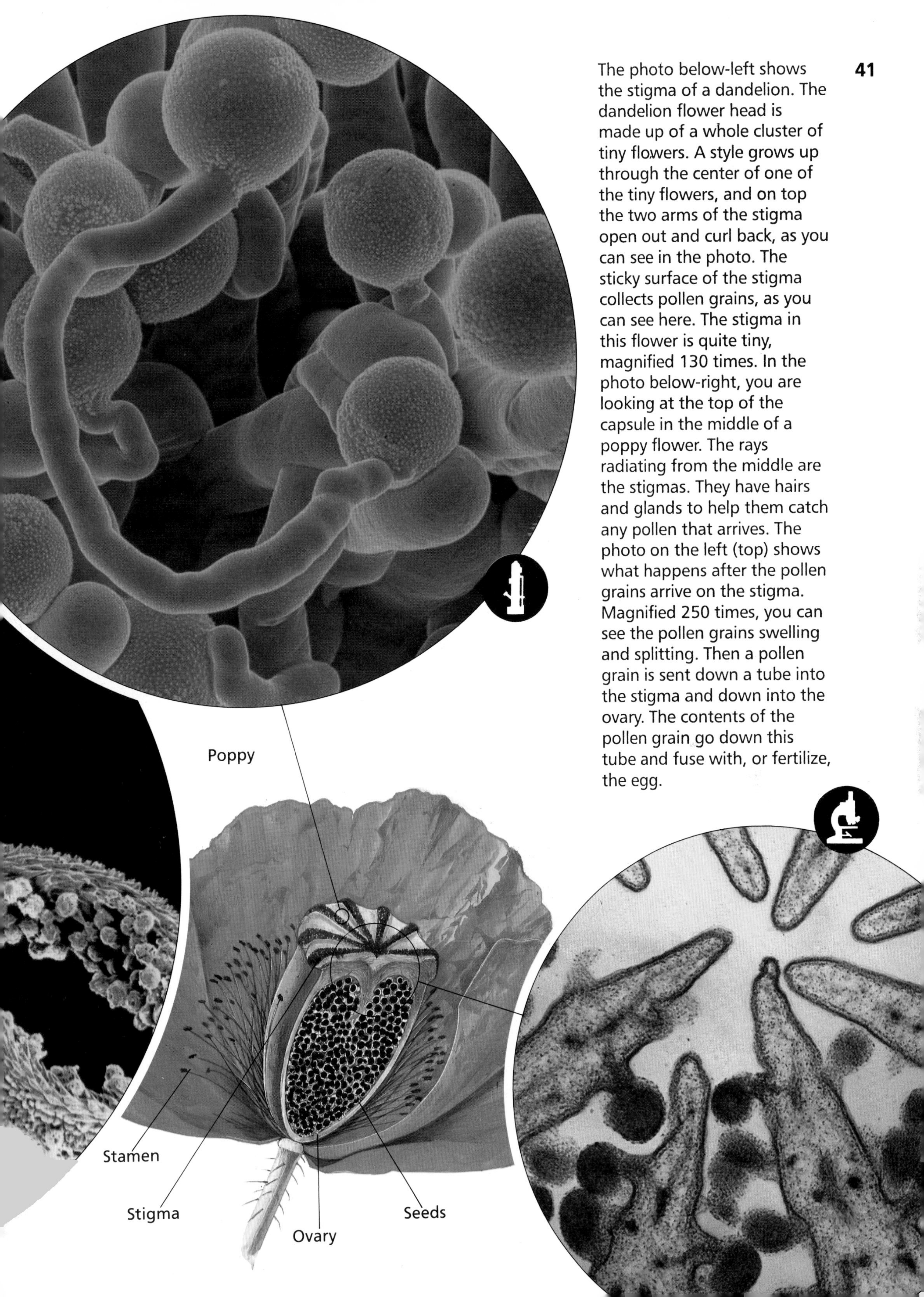

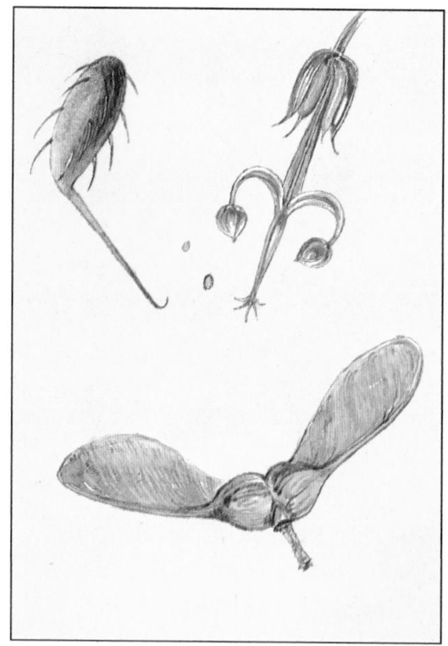

SEEDS

A seed contains the embryo of a new plant, and also food for the first stages of its growth. In a tiny seed the food supply is small, but in a bean or nut the food reserves are very large. Within a seed it is usually possible to recognize the beginnings of the root (the radicle) and the stem (the plumule). There are also seed-leaves, called cotyledons. There are two in most kinds of flowering plant, but just one in grasses and related narrow-leaved plants. The cotyledons are special storage leaves, and their fleshy bulk contains food that may take up most of the seed. Often seeds form part of a fruit, the structure that develops from a ripe ovary. Some fruits, such as an acorn, have a single seed. Others, like tomatoes, have dozens.

The okra, or lady's finger, has a narrow edible fruit about 4 inches long. In the cross section (photo left) you can see seeds arranged around a central core, with a fleshy wall outside. The stored food in the seeds contains a high proportion of oil.

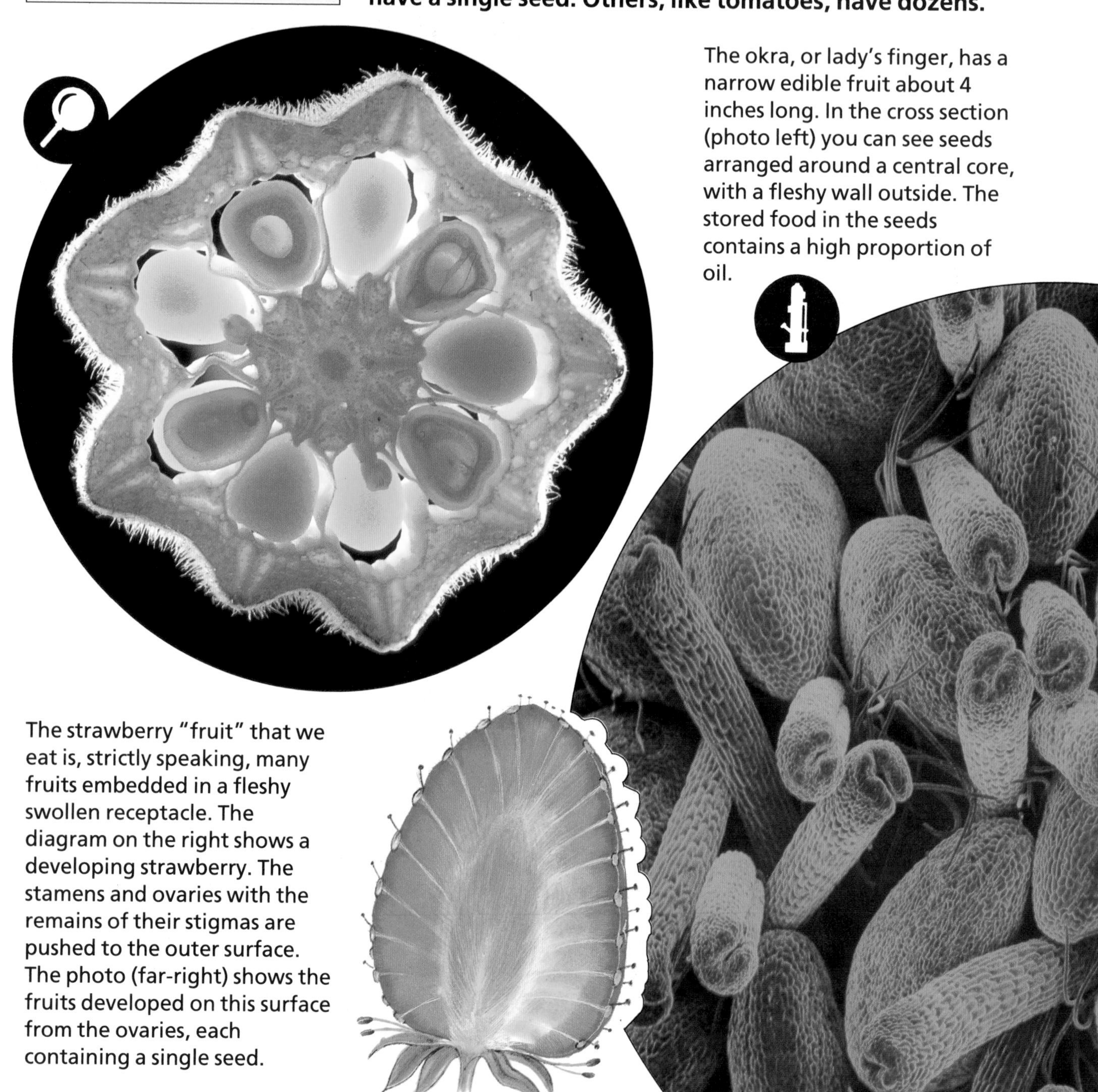

The strawberry "fruit" that we eat is, strictly speaking, many fruits embedded in a fleshy swollen receptacle. The diagram on the right shows a developing strawberry. The stamens and ovaries with the remains of their stigmas are pushed to the outer surface. The photo (far-right) shows the fruits developed on this surface from the ovaries, each containing a single seed.

The fruit of the dandelion is very characteristic. It consists of a single seed enclosed in the remains of the ovary. This has a stalk above which ends in a pappus – a whorl of feathery hairs. A fruiting head contains many of these fruits, making up the familiar dandelion "clock." The photo (right) shows ripe dandelion fruits. The pappus is a useful parachute, allowing the seed to travel with the wind and fall to earth slowly. With this help, the seeds can disperse far away from the parent.

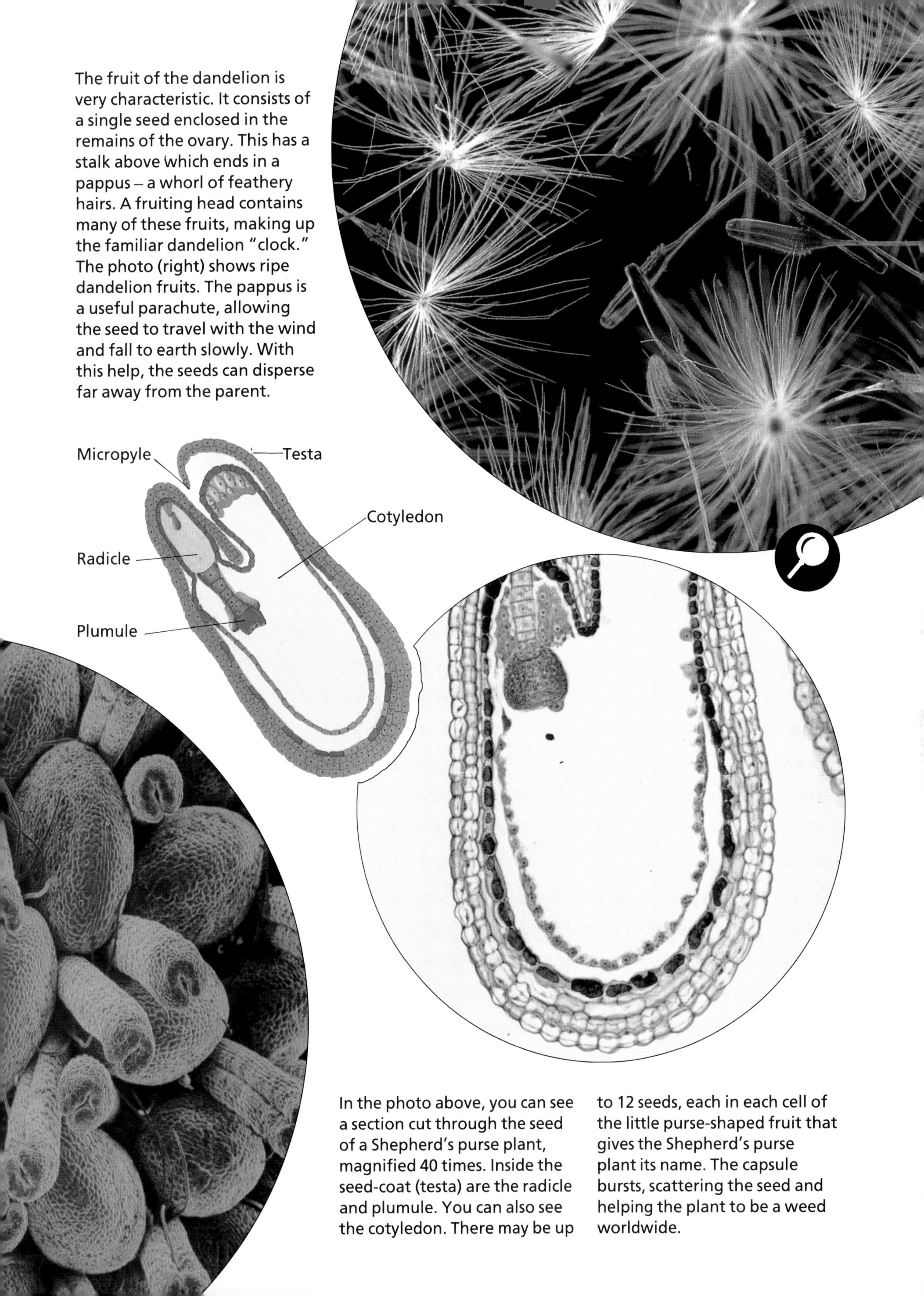

In the photo above, you can see a section cut through the seed of a Shepherd's purse plant, magnified 40 times. Inside the seed-coat (testa) are the radicle and plumule. You can also see the cotyledon. There may be up to 12 seeds, each in each cell of the little purse-shaped fruit that gives the Shepherd's purse plant its name. The capsule bursts, scattering the seed and helping the plant to be a weed worldwide.

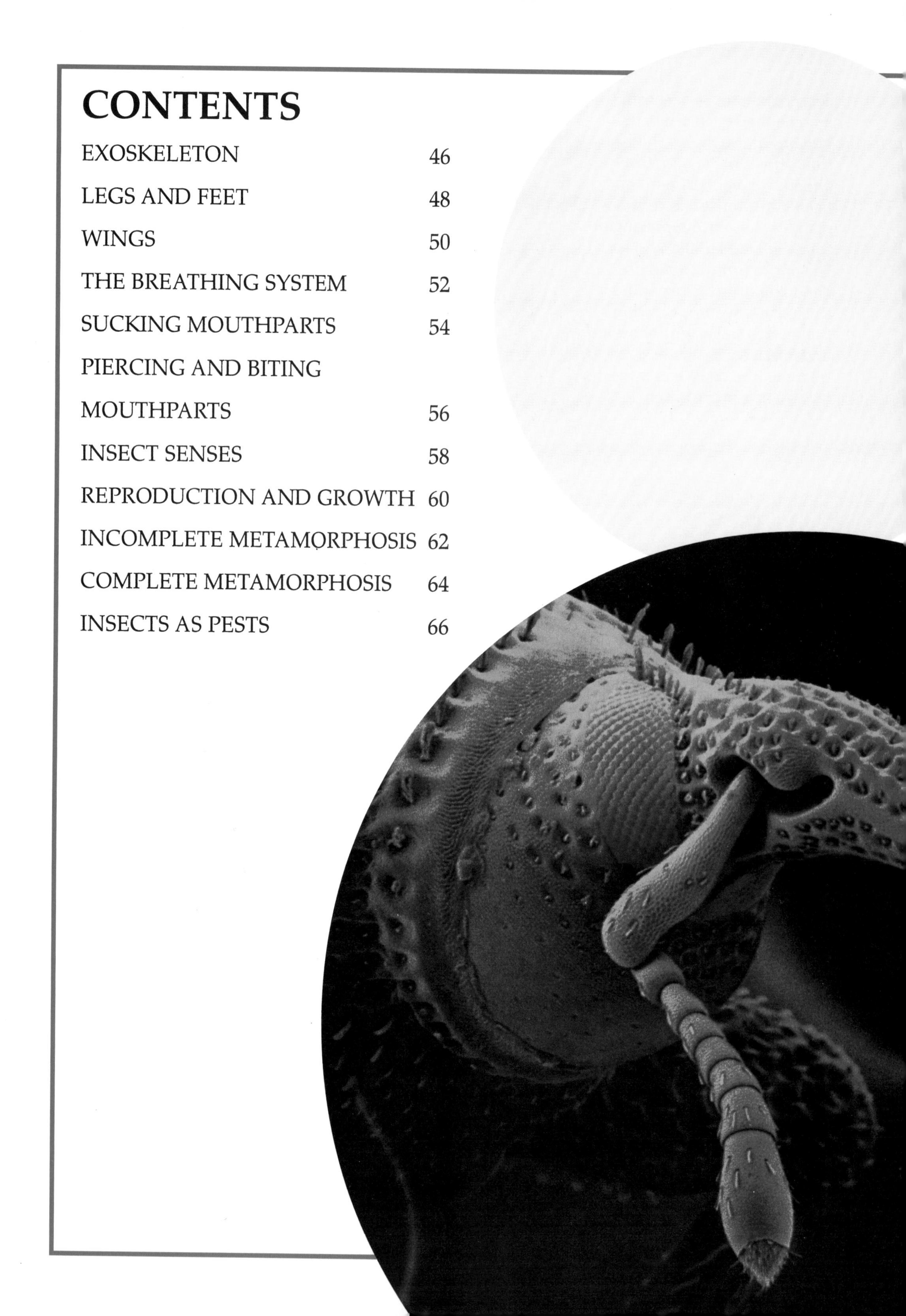

CONTENTS

Insects

John Stidworthy

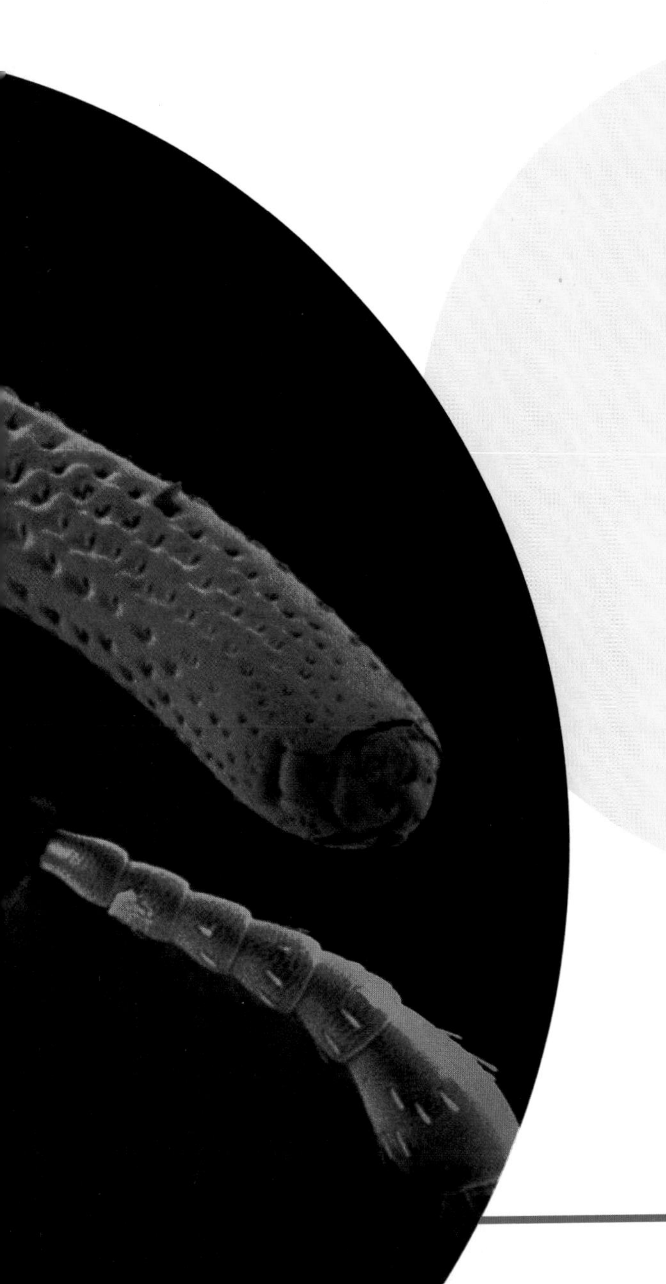

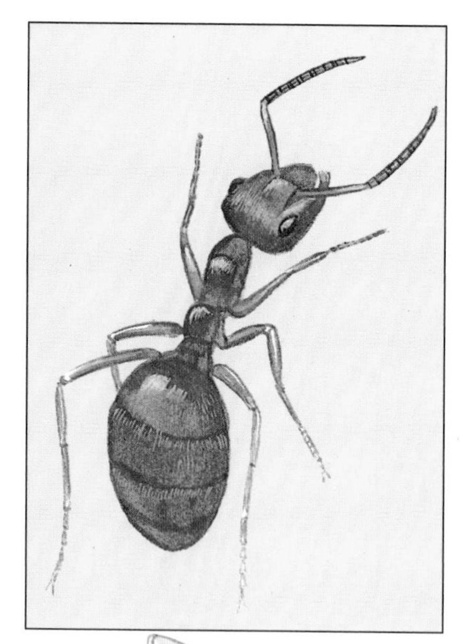

EXOSKELETON

There are no bones in the body of an insect. Instead it has an exoskeleton, or outside skeleton, which shapes, supports and protects it. This skin is made of a tough, light material called chitin, a substance related to sugar. Sometimes this is very thin, but it can be thickened to form a kind of "armor" if needed. A covering of waxy layers makes the exoskeleton watertight, so that it seldom lets moisture leak either in or out. Some insects have smooth exoskeletons. Others are covered with bumps, grooves, or ornaments. If we take a closer look at the body of an insect with a magnifiying glass we will see a large number of tiny hairs which are called setae. Some of them work as sense organs.

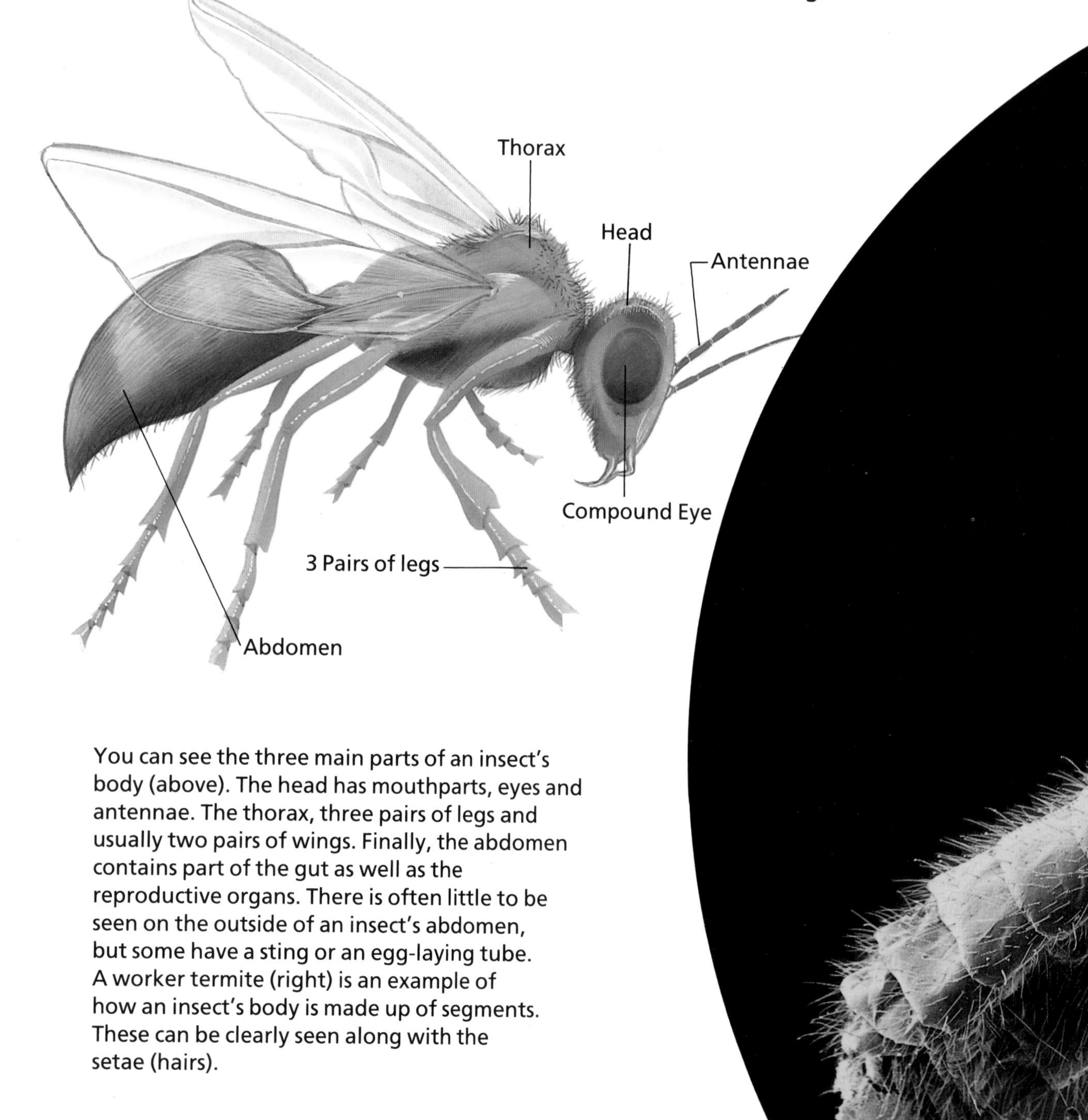

You can see the three main parts of an insect's body (above). The head has mouthparts, eyes and antennae. The thorax, three pairs of legs and usually two pairs of wings. Finally, the abdomen contains part of the gut as well as the reproductive organs. There is often little to be seen on the outside of an insect's abdomen, but some have a sting or an egg-laying tube. A worker termite (right) is an example of how an insect's body is made up of segments. These can be clearly seen along with the setae (hairs).

An electron microscope shows us that the head of a garden ant (right) has plates of exoskeleton joined tightly together. This "armor" forms a helmet to protect the brain and other organs within. The ant's antennae are sunk into sockets that allow them to turn. Its mouth is hard, so that it can bite and chew through tough materials easily.

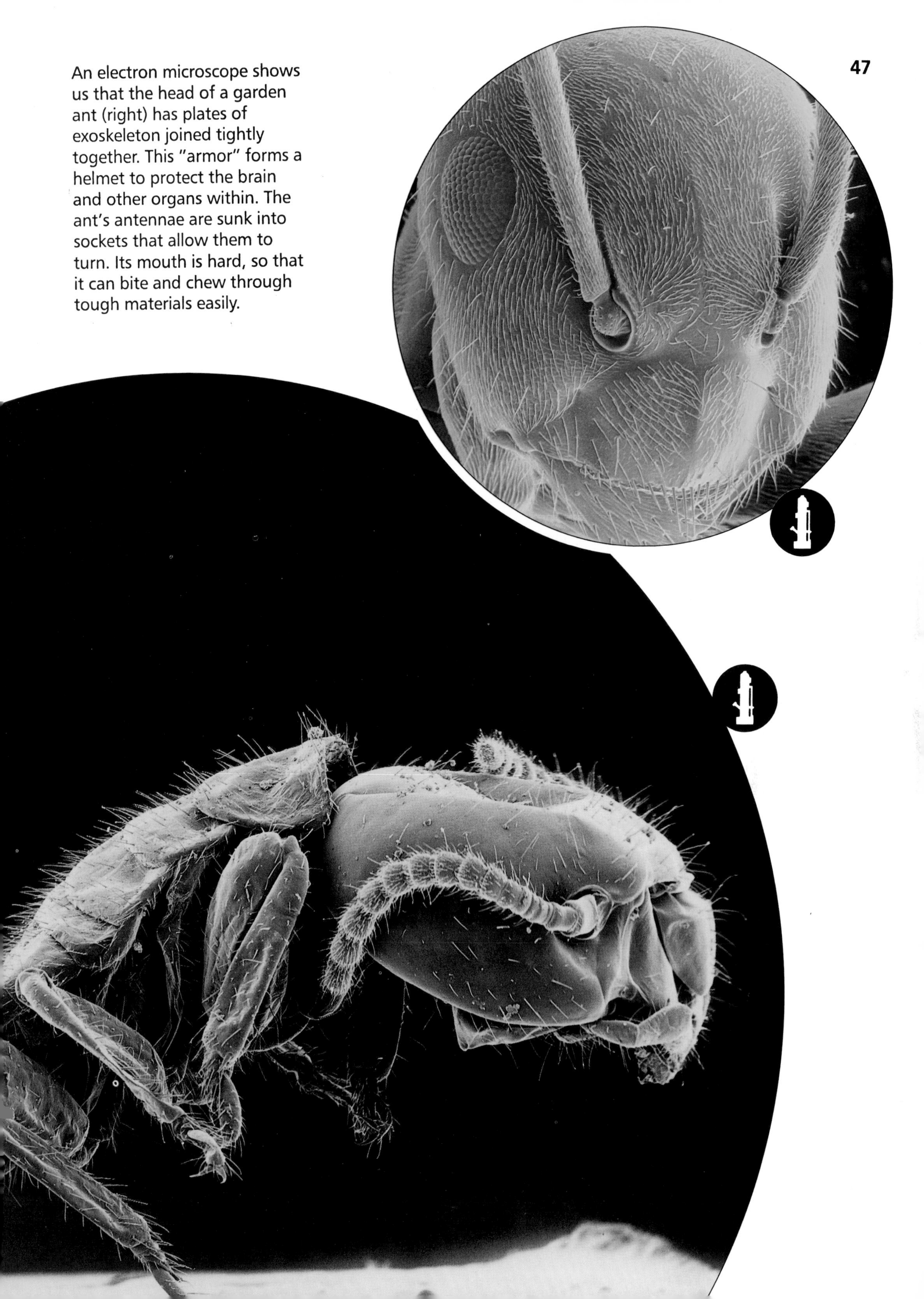

LEGS AND FEET

The legs of all adult insects are made the same way, with five main sections. There are two small sections close to the body, then a femur and tibia which are often long. At the end is the foot, or tarsus. But if you look closely at several types of insects you will see that their legs are shaped for different jobs. A locust or grasshopper, for example, is a jumper. The back legs are very long, and can be straightened suddenly. This enables the creature to leap. Some swimming beetles have wide legs with long setae that work as paddles in the water. Bees have special patches of setae on their legs to gather and hold pollen. These details on insect legs can be seen best with either a magnifying glass or a standard microscope.

The feet of most insects end in a pair of claws which often have a pad between them. On the fly's foot illustrated below we can see two sticky pads (called pulcilli) which help it to climb glass or walk upside down on a ceiling. The caterpillar (above-right) has five pairs of pro-legs, on its abdomen, each with a hook at the end, as well as the three true legs on its thorax.

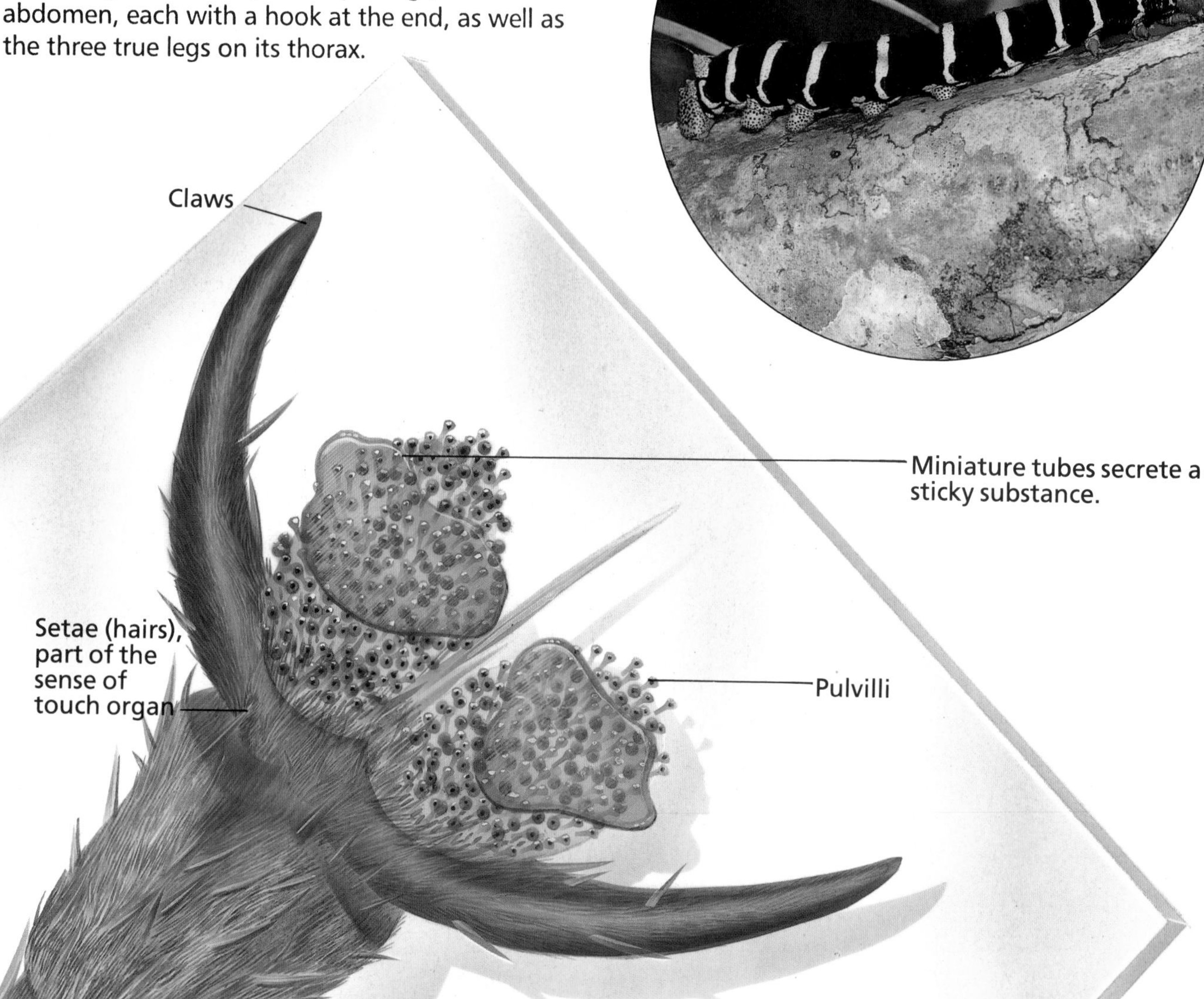

The housefly's foot (above) has two strong claws on the end, and between them two suction pads called pulvilli. There is a spine between the pulvilli, which in some kinds of fly can become a gripping pad as well. These pads allow the fly to perform some of its most amazing feats – such as climbing glass or crawling across a ceiling upside-down. Fleas live on animals and suck their blood. On the flea's foot (right) we can see the two long claws it uses to hang on to an animal's fur. Other spines on its foot and the rest of the body stop it slipping in the fur.

WINGS

The wings of all adult insects have the same basic structure.They are made of thin skin stretched over hollow but strong tubes called veins. Most insects have two pairs of wings which flap together at the same time. Some even have hooks to connect them, as can be seen on certain moths. However, a dragonfly uses each pair of wings separately so that it can hover. Beetles and cockroaches, on the other hand, have front wings which are more like stiff leather covers for their rear ones. They do not flap, but stick out in flight and steady their heavy bodies (see below). Houseflies are different again, and use only their front wings to fly. The rear ones look like pins but are sense organs used to keep them flying level.

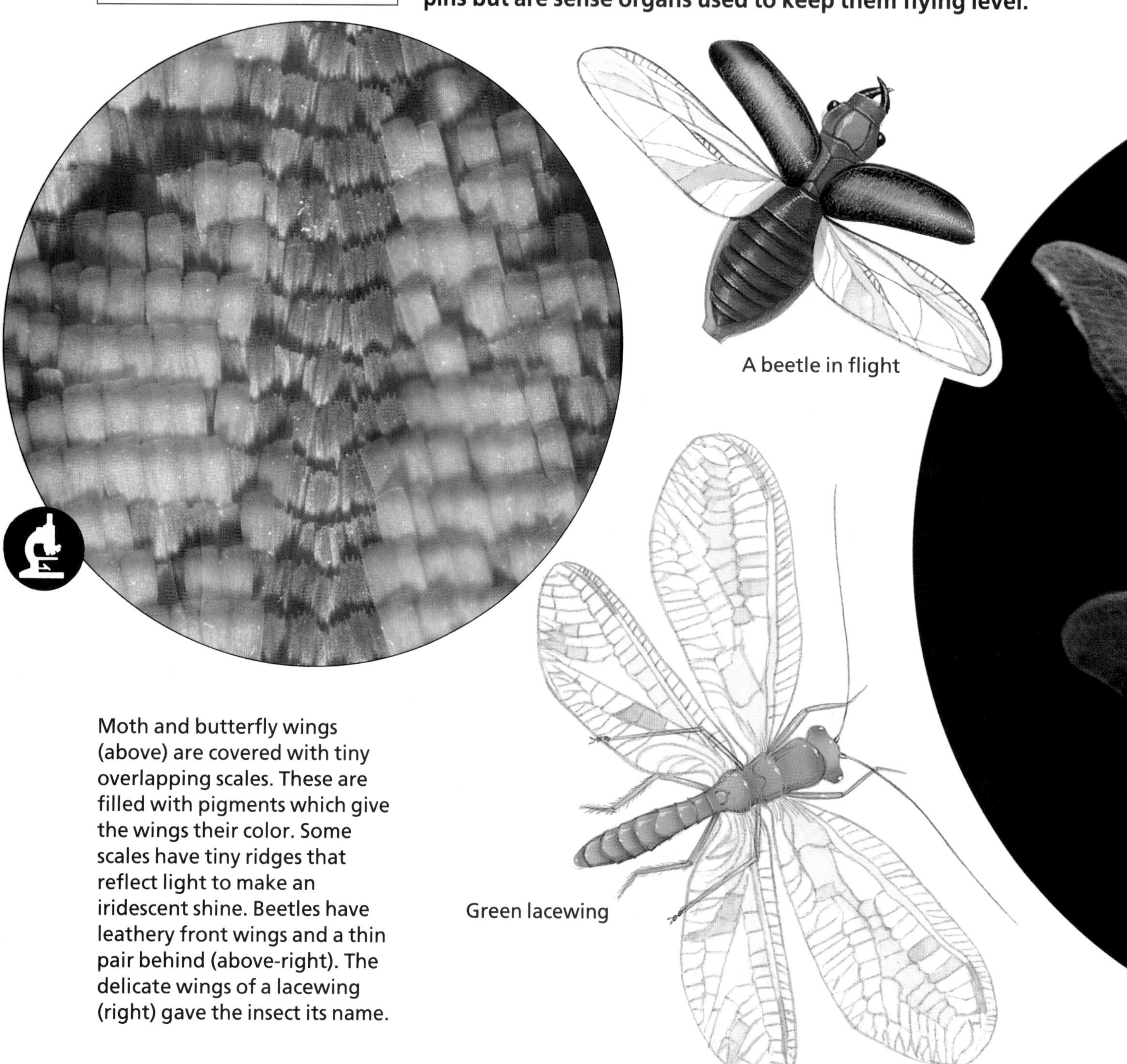

A beetle in flight

Green lacewing

Moth and butterfly wings (above) are covered with tiny overlapping scales. These are filled with pigments which give the wings their color. Some scales have tiny ridges that reflect light to make an iridescent shine. Beetles have leathery front wings and a thin pair behind (above-right). The delicate wings of a lacewing (right) gave the insect its name.

Each kind of insect has a special pattern of veins in its wings. The tip of a dragonfly's (right) shows a dense network which lets the wings bend as they flap. This same quality gives the lacewing (picture below-left) more control in flight. One of the most skilled flying insects is the dragonfly. It has muscles which pull directly at the base of the wings (see below). Other insects have muscles which work on their sides to make the wings beat.

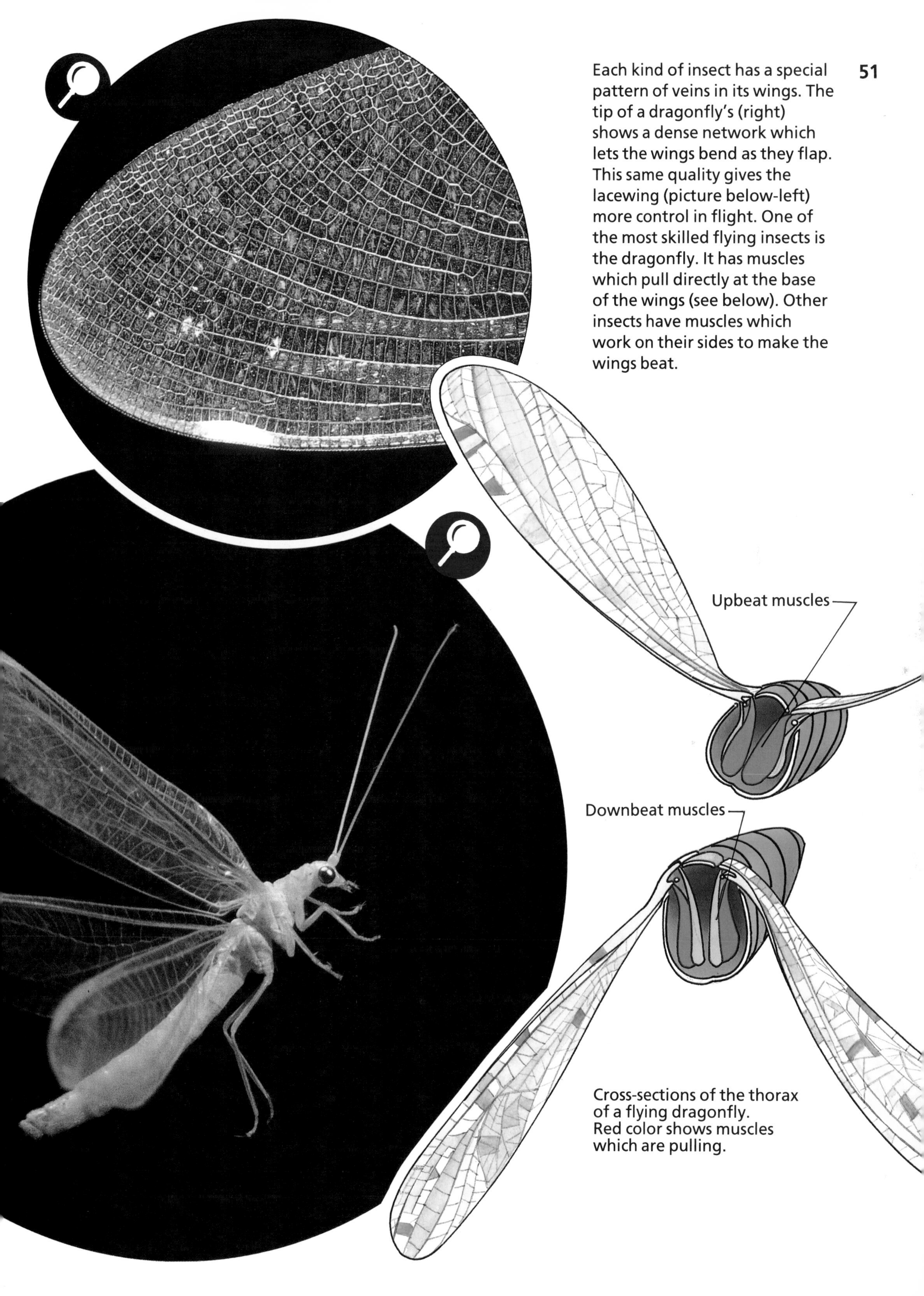

Cross-sections of the thorax of a flying dragonfly. Red color shows muscles which are pulling.

THE BREATHING SYSTEM

Since an insect's body has an exoskeleton covered with waxy layers it cannot "breathe" through its skin as other animals do. It does not carry oxygen in its bloodstream either. Instead, insects have a system of air-pipes, called tracheae, which allow them to breathe (see illustration below-left). These tracheae branch into smaller tracheoles, or air-tubes, which carry oxygen to the muscles and other organs. They are lined with a thin skin of chitin, the same material which makes up the exoskeleton, to protect them. Each also has spirals inside to strengthen it (see illustration lower-right). The tracheae form a complicated, branched breathing system throughout the insect's body and keep it alive.

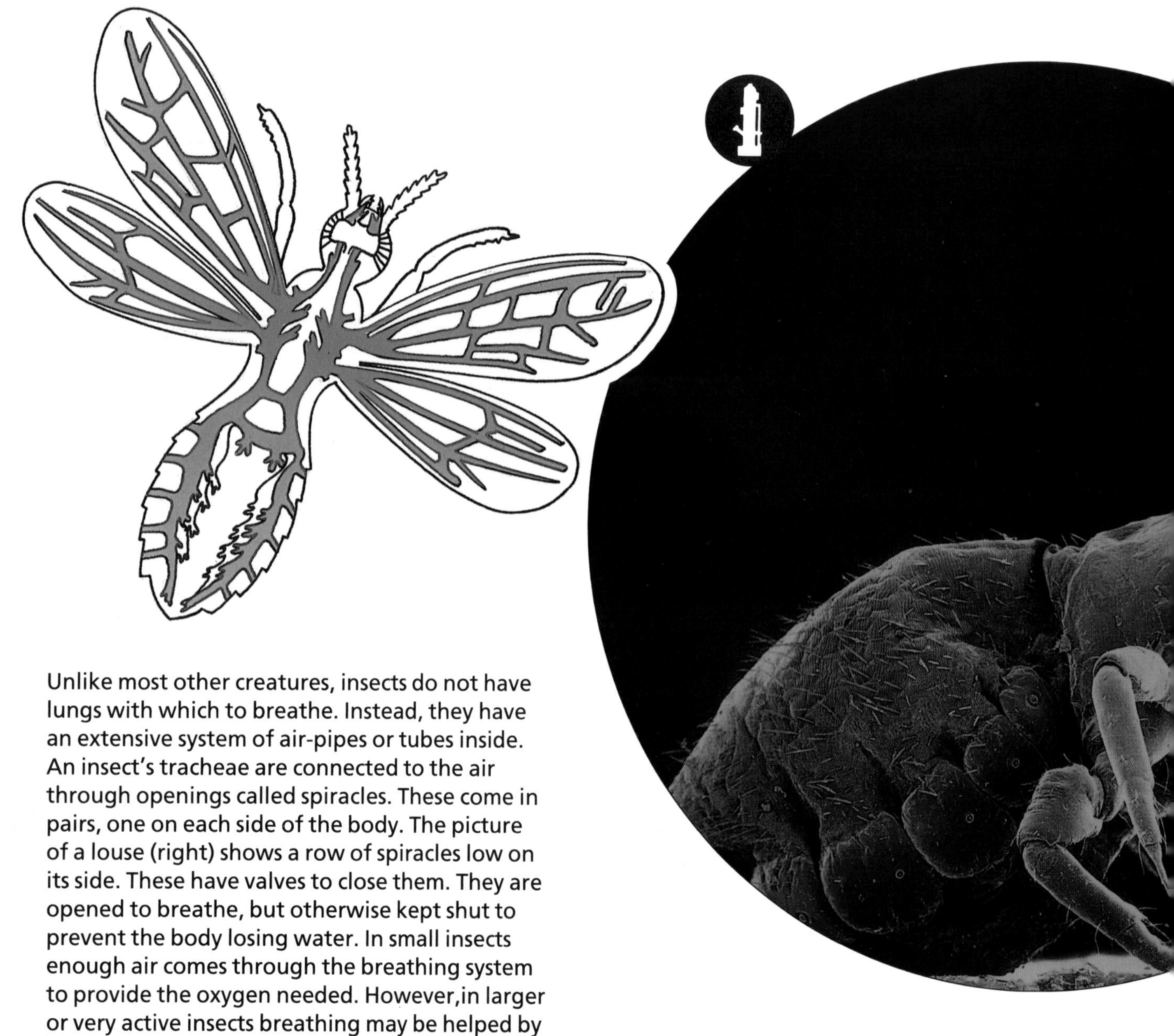

Unlike most other creatures, insects do not have lungs with which to breathe. Instead, they have an extensive system of air-pipes or tubes inside. An insect's tracheae are connected to the air through openings called spiracles. These come in pairs, one on each side of the body. The picture of a louse (right) shows a row of spiracles low on its side. These have valves to close them. They are opened to breathe, but otherwise kept shut to prevent the body losing water. In small insects enough air comes through the breathing system to provide the oxygen needed. However,in larger or very active insects breathing may be helped by pumping actions in the abdomen which suck in extra air.

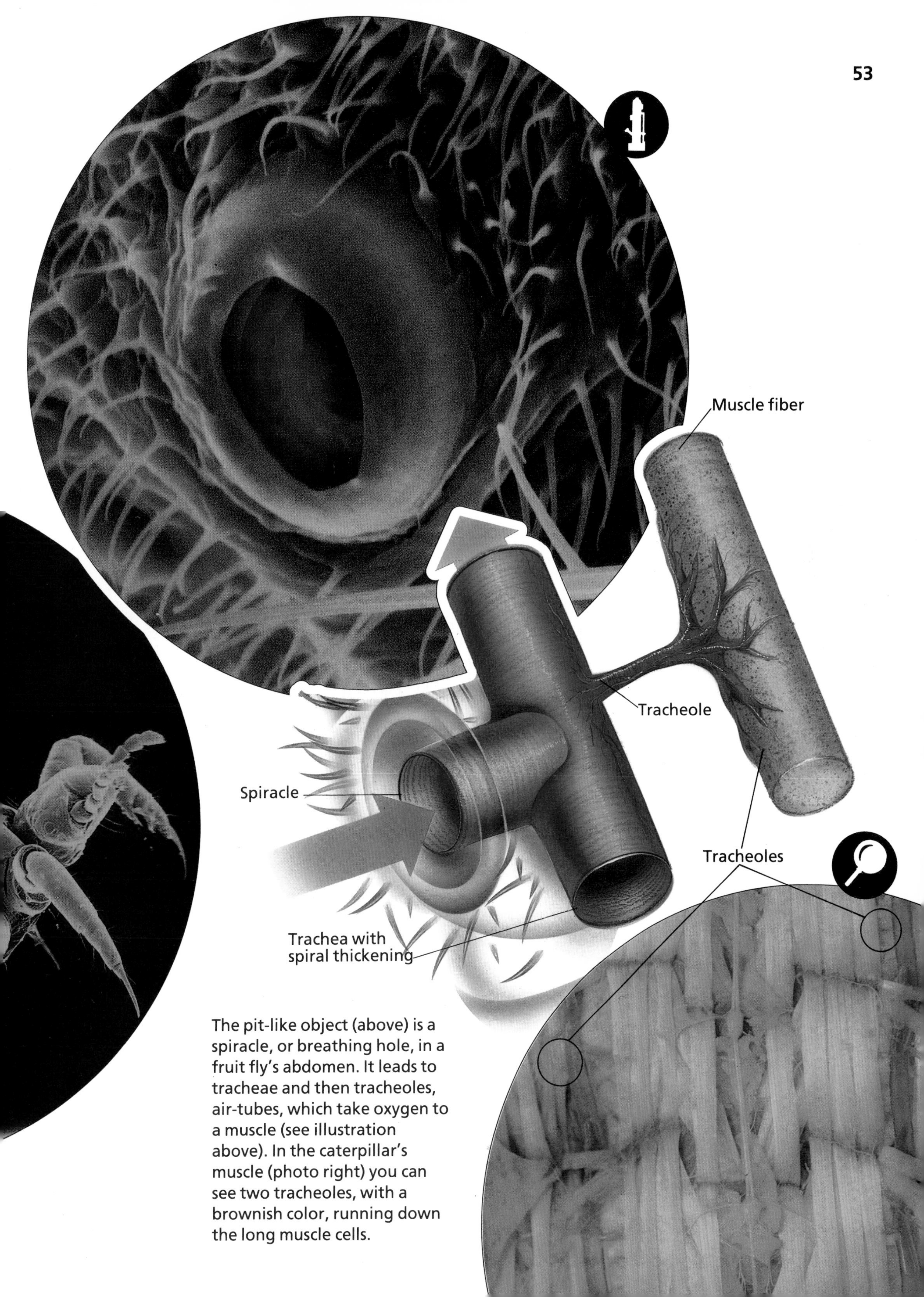

The pit-like object (above) is a spiracle, or breathing hole, in a fruit fly's abdomen. It leads to tracheae and then tracheoles, air-tubes, which take oxygen to a muscle (see illustration above). In the caterpillar's muscle (photo right) you can see two tracheoles, with a brownish color, running down the long muscle cells.

SUCKING MOUTHPARTS

Some insects only feed on liquids. They have mouths shaped like drinking straws which they use to suck their food through. Butterflies and moths are good examples of this. They both have a pair of mouthparts called maxillae. These zip together to form a long tube which can be pushed into a flower to suck up nectar. When not in use this tube is curled up under the head. If you watch butterflies you may see it in action. It is usually as long as the insect's favourite food flower. The worker honeybee also has mouthparts which form a tube for sucking nectar. The tip is wider and can move around, so it is called the "honey-spoon." However, the most common insects with sucking mouthpaths are flies.

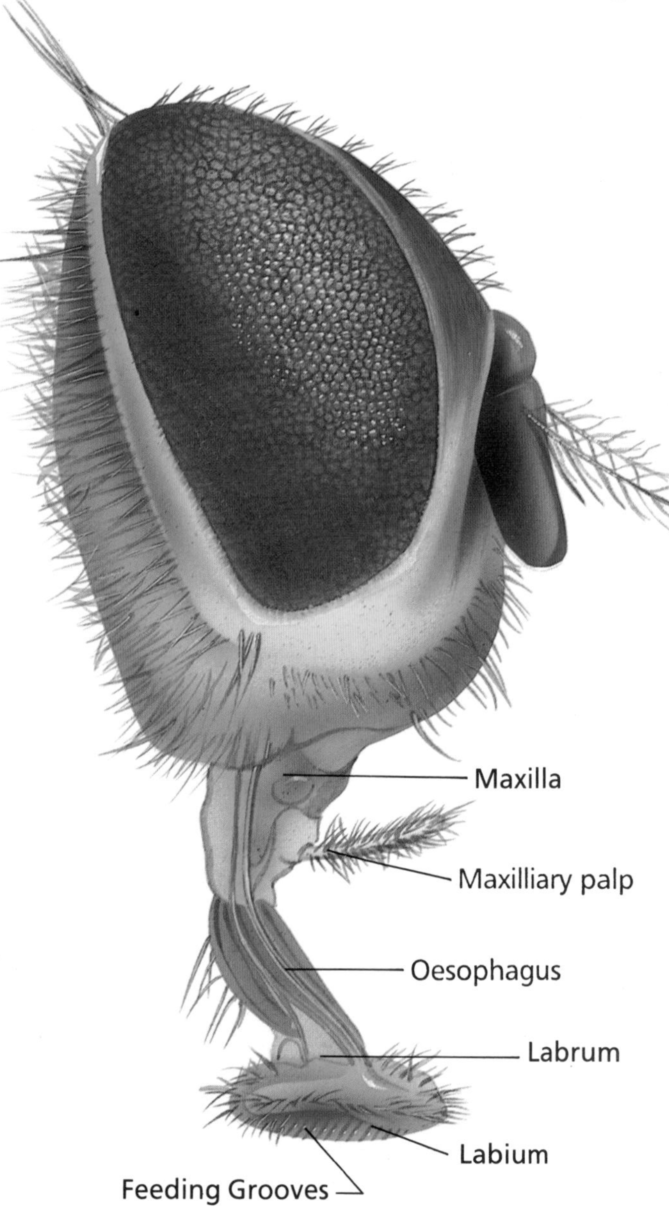

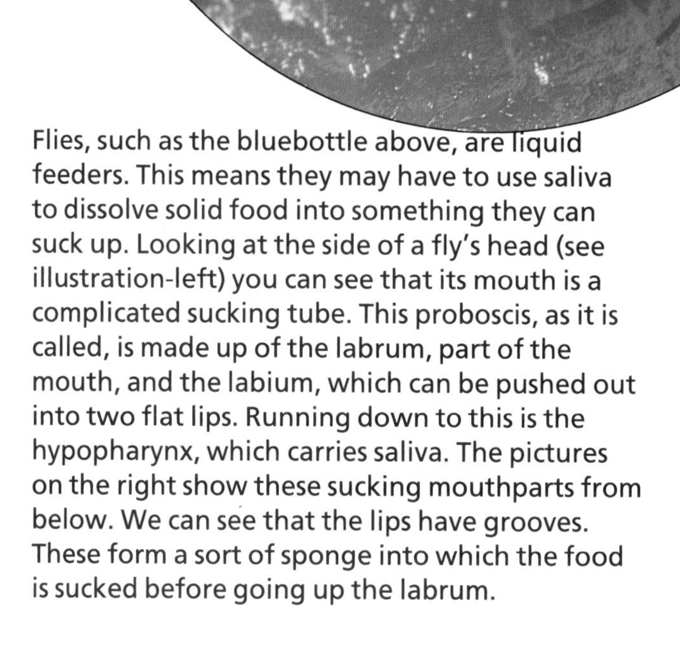

Flies, such as the bluebottle above, are liquid feeders. This means they may have to use saliva to dissolve solid food into something they can suck up. Looking at the side of a fly's head (see illustration-left) you can see that its mouth is a complicated sucking tube. This proboscis, as it is called, is made up of the labrum, part of the mouth, and the labium, which can be pushed out into two flat lips. Running down to this is the hypopharynx, which carries saliva. The pictures on the right show these sucking mouthparts from below. We can see that the lips have grooves. These form a sort of sponge into which the food is sucked before going up the labrum.

Labrum
Labium

PIERCING AND BITING MOUTHPARTS

Several kinds of insects have mouthparts that pierce. These include blood-hunters,like mosquitoes and gnats, and plant-suckers like aphids. They have needle-like jaws called mandibles and maxillae, covered by the labium (see illustration below-left). Inside of this tube two channels run down. One takes saliva down the maxilla while the insect can suck food up through the other one. But biting mouthparts are more common. Cockroaches, wasps, grasshoppers and dragonflies, for example, all bite their food. Some insects can even bite through wood or metal. Leg-like "palps" work around the mouth to feel and taste food, or to push it towards chewing jaws.

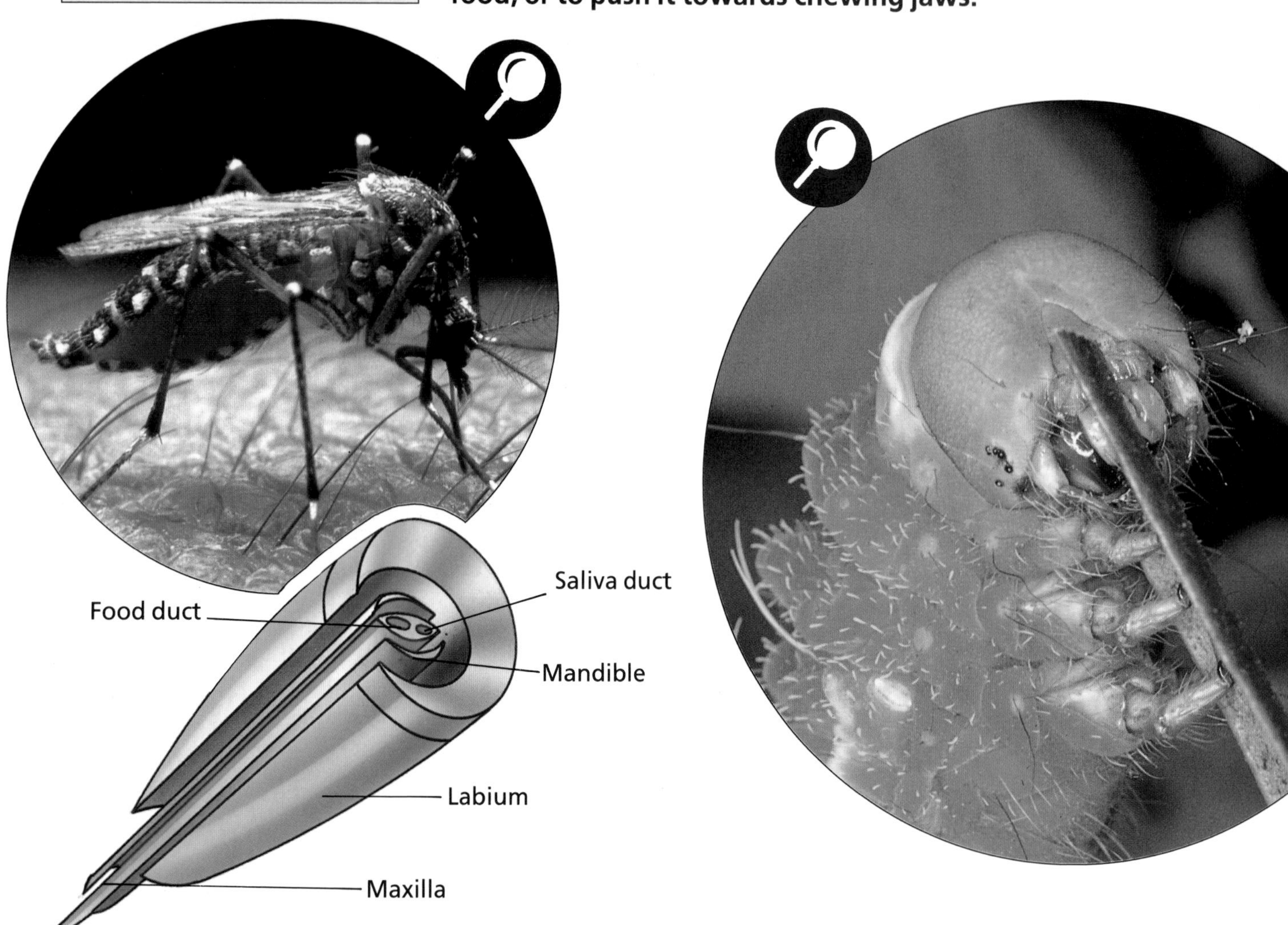

A female mosquito, see picture above, can have piercing mouthparts up to 1/8th inch (3mm) long. This is strong enough to get through an animal's hide so that the insect can suck blood. Male mosquitos have smaller mouthparts and cannot do this. They have to feed off the nectar in flowers.

Caterpillars, like the one in the picture above, may have soft bodies but their mouthparts are so good at biting and chewing that they are often thought of as a garden pest. Some eat their own eggshell after they hatch, but all kinds will consume large amounts of greenery as they grow.

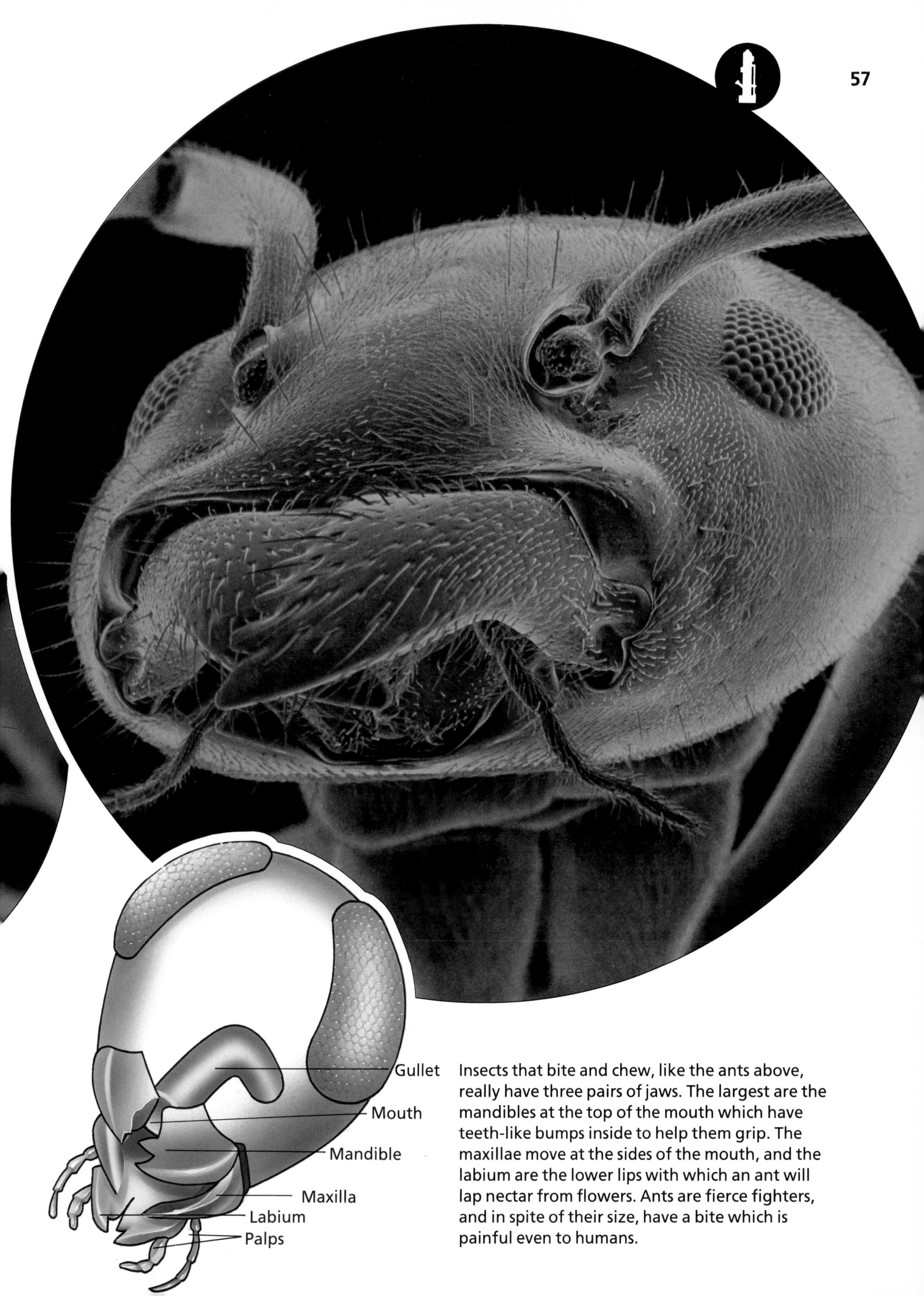

Insects that bite and chew, like the ants above, really have three pairs of jaws. The largest are the mandibles at the top of the mouth which have teeth-like bumps inside to help them grip. The maxillae move at the sides of the mouth, and the labium are the lower lips with which an ant will lap nectar from flowers. Ants are fierce fighters, and in spite of their size, have a bite which is painful even to humans.

INSECT SENSES

Insects have the same five senses that we do, but their organs of touch, taste, smell, sight and hearing look very different from ours. For example, the ears of a cricket are like tiny drums on its front legs, and the antennae of a moth, illustrated on the left, resemble feathers. Some insects, such as butterflies, can taste with their feet. When they land on a surface they taste it to tell whether it is worth staying to feed. Often the sense organs are "tuned in" to only those things that are vital for survival. On the other hand, some insects can see things that we cannot. For example, bees can see ultraviolet light. This helps them gather nectar since certain flowers are easier for them to spot that way.

A fly has hundreds of eyes in its head (picture-left). They notice everything that moves nearby.

The antennae of an insect are one of its most important organs since they are used for smelling and feeling their surroundings. The male moth, pictured on the right, has impressive-looking, feathery antennae which can detect the scent of a female from over half a mile (a kilometer) away. These antennae also help the insect find food.

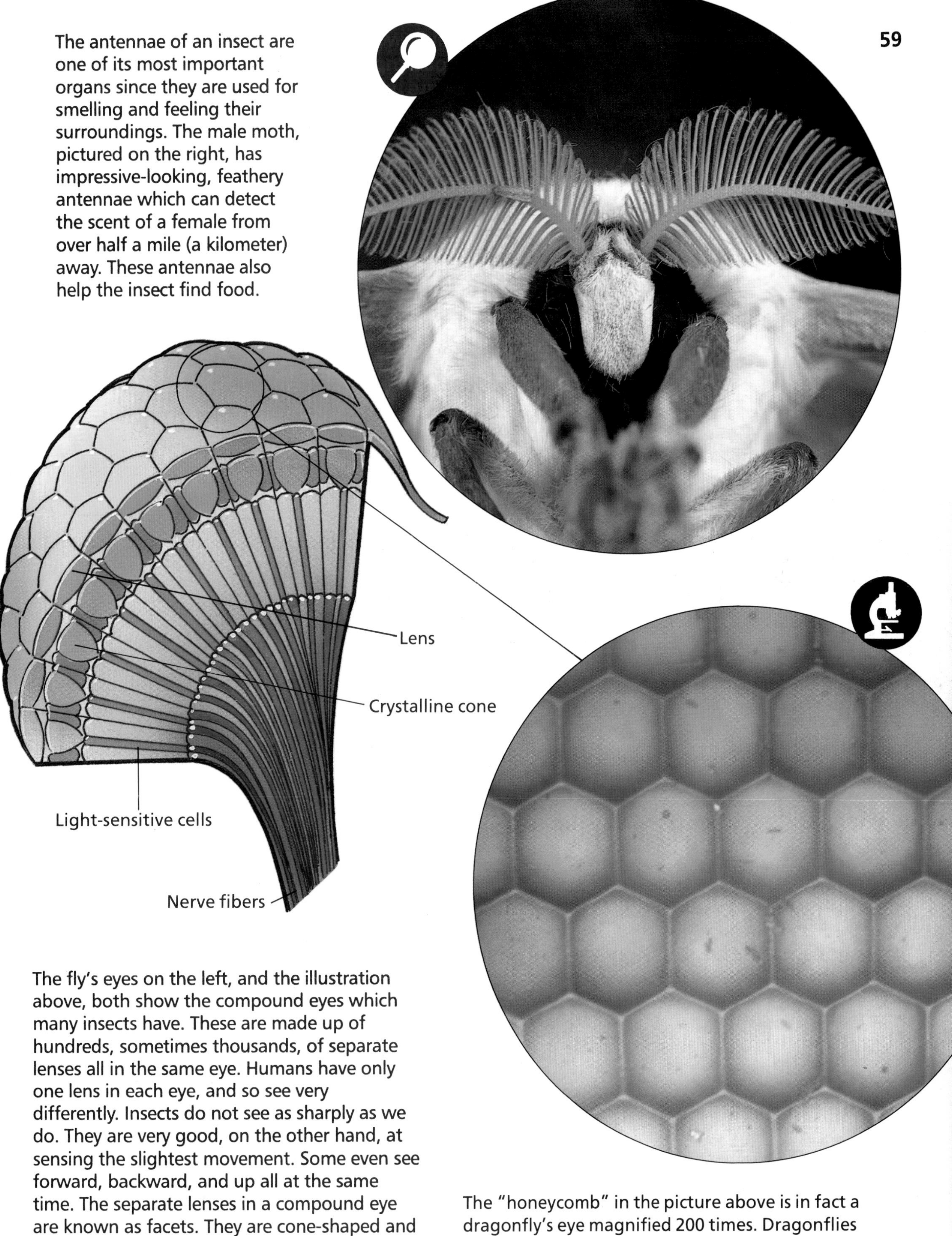

The fly's eyes on the left, and the illustration above, both show the compound eyes which many insects have. These are made up of hundreds, sometimes thousands, of separate lenses all in the same eye. Humans have only one lens in each eye, and so see very differently. Insects do not see as sharply as we do. They are very good, on the other hand, at sensing the slightest movement. Some even see forward, backward, and up all at the same time. The separate lenses in a compound eye are known as facets. They are cone-shaped and packed tightly together. Light passes down each through its crystalline cone onto nerve fibers which send signals to the insect's brain.

The "honeycomb" in the picture above is in fact a dragonfly's eye magnified 200 times. Dragonflies are fierce hunters, and have some 30,000 facets in each compound eye. These help then to pounce on their prey with deadly accuracy.

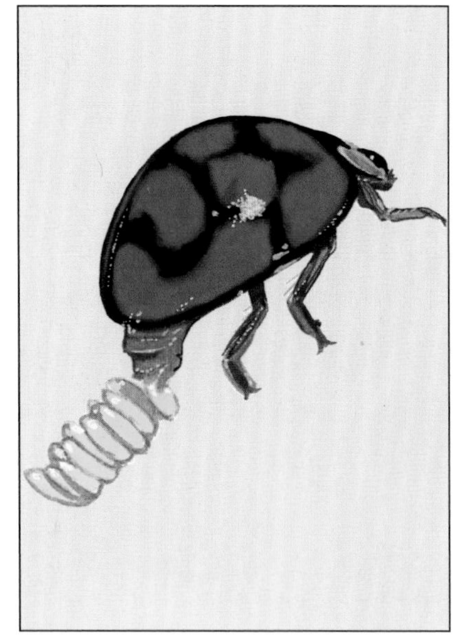

REPRODUCTION AND GROWTH

The adult life of many insects is short, only a few days or weeks long. The main task of the adults is to find a mate and to produce young. After mating, the female lays her eggs (see the ladybird illustrated on left), which have a tough shell and are waterproof to help them survive harsh conditions. The insect that hatches usually looks very different from its parents. It will not have wings and has to go through a process of change (called metamorphosis) before it becomes an adult. It also has to grow, which is difficult because its exoskeleton cannot expand as it gets bigger. So an insect must shed its old skin when it grows, stretching quickly before the new one, waiting underneath, has time to harden.

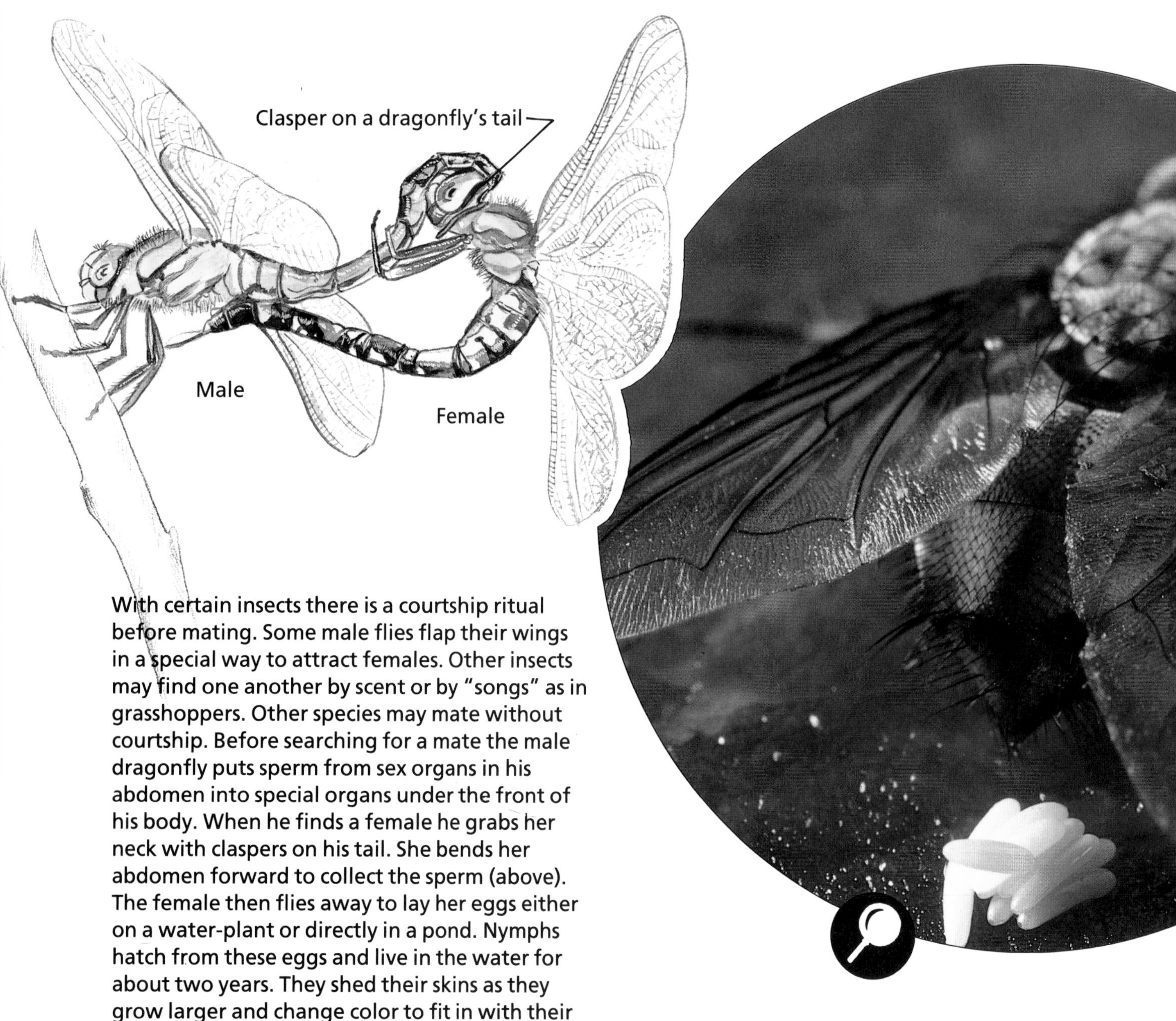

With certain insects there is a courtship ritual before mating. Some male flies flap their wings in a special way to attract females. Other insects may find one another by scent or by "songs" as in grasshoppers. Other species may mate without courtship. Before searching for a mate the male dragonfly puts sperm from sex organs in his abdomen into special organs under the front of his body. When he finds a female he grabs her neck with claspers on his tail. She bends her abdomen forward to collect the sperm (above). The female then flies away to lay her eggs either on a water-plant or directly in a pond. Nymphs hatch from these eggs and live in the water for about two years. They shed their skins as they grow larger and change color to fit in with their surroundings until they emerge as adults.

The picture (above-left) shows a female bluebottle fly laying her eggs on some meat. The young that hatch (called maggots) must have have plenty of food close by. They are not able to travel very far, unlike their parents, and will feed on this flesh for the first stage of their lives.

On the surface of a nasturtium leaf (above) you can see the sculptured eggshells of a large white butterfly. The eggs are laid in batches of up to 100, and hatch after 5 to 20 days. You can see where the caterpillar has chewed its way out of one egg. It will feed and grow for about 30 days.

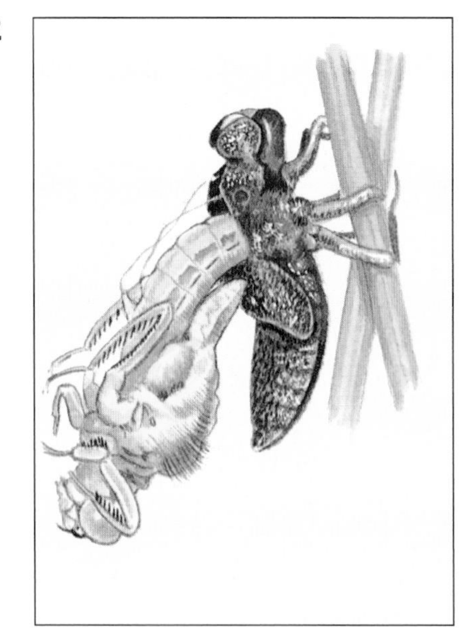

INCOMPLETE METAMORPHOSIS

Most insects hatch from eggs and will go through stages of growth. Some do not change their shape as much as others, only their size. Cockroaches and grasshoppers, for example, go through what is known as an incomplete metamorphosis. As they grow they have to shed their old skin. This is called molting. As you can see in illustrations below, an aphid changes size and shape gradually with each molt. Even before it is a full adult the wing-buds can be seen. Finally, the wings grow to full size, and the insect is ready to reproduce. Insects that grow in this way usually live in the same sort of place, and feed on the same type of food, throughout their lives. Young insects of this kind are known as nymphs.

The photograph on the right shows on adult female aphid with some aphid nymphs. All of these bugs suck juices from the plants they live on. Many kinds of aphid lay eggs in spring which grow into wingless adults by the summer. These can give birth to live young instead of laying eggs. Millions of nymphs are produced in this way, and aphids become a pest in our gardens. If you look closely at a leaf infested with aphids (a rosebush would be good example) you will observe the insects in many different sizes. You might also see empty cast skins (photo above-right) which have been molted by nymphs. They may still be attached to the leaf by their mouthparts. You might even see large females giving birth. Only when fall comes are winged adults that lay eggs produced again, and the numbers of aphids around will start to decline.

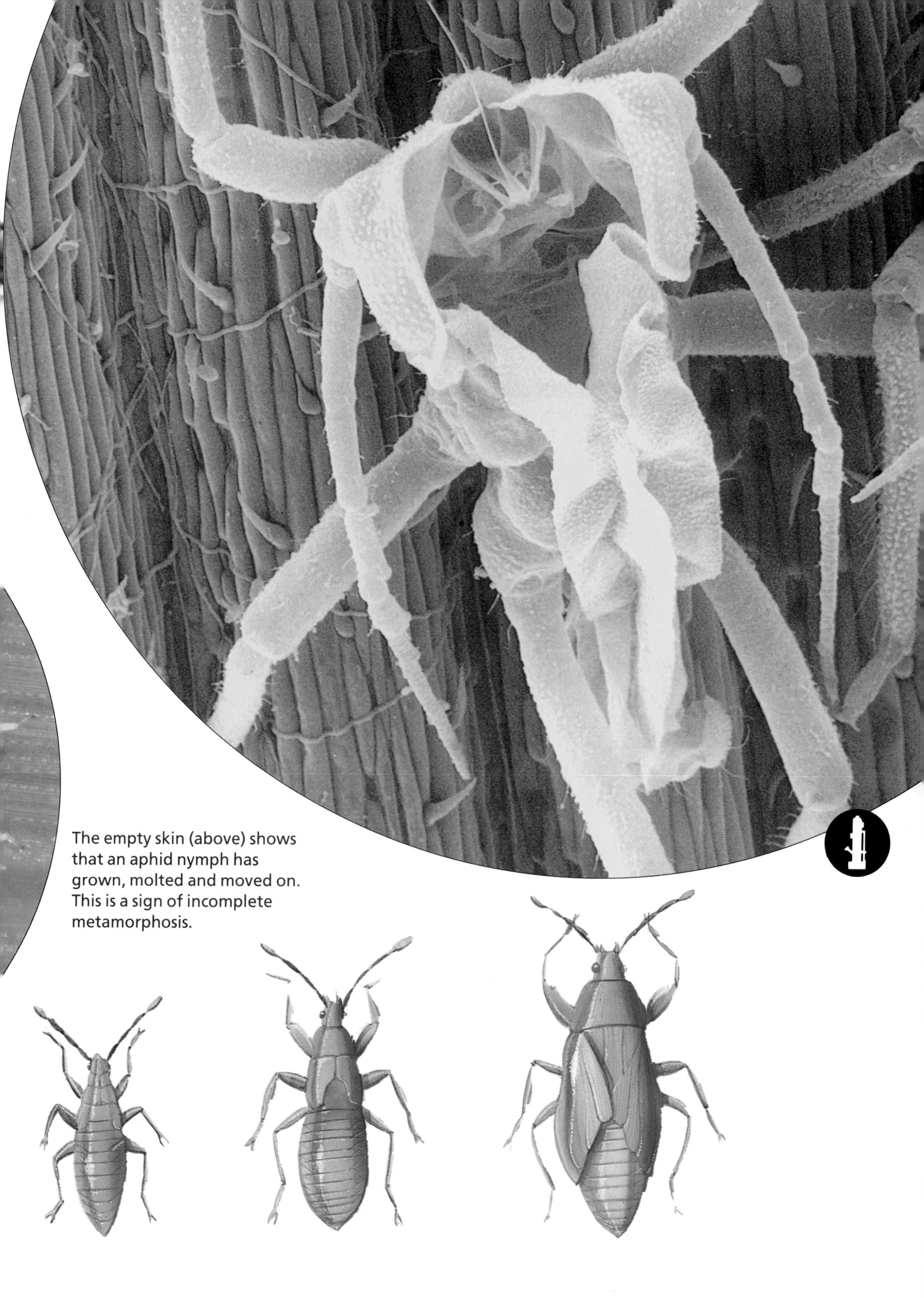

The empty skin (above) shows that an aphid nymph has grown, molted and moved on. This is a sign of incomplete metamorphosis.

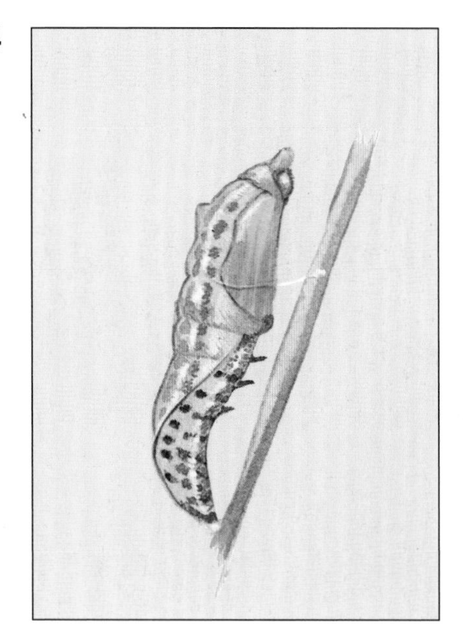

COMPLETE METAMORPHOSIS

Insects that undergo complete metamorphosis have offspring which look completely different from their parents. The young live apart and even feed on other types of food. Also, their wings do not normally appear until they can emerge as adults. However, most important of all, these creatures have to progress to a stage where they appear to be resting in a silky cocoon or chrysalis. During this period, called pupation, they do not move anywhere but a tremendous change takes place inside. The insect's body is completely broken down and rebuilt into a new form. Many insects, such as ants, moths, flies, butterflies, bees, and beetles undergo complete metamorphosis.

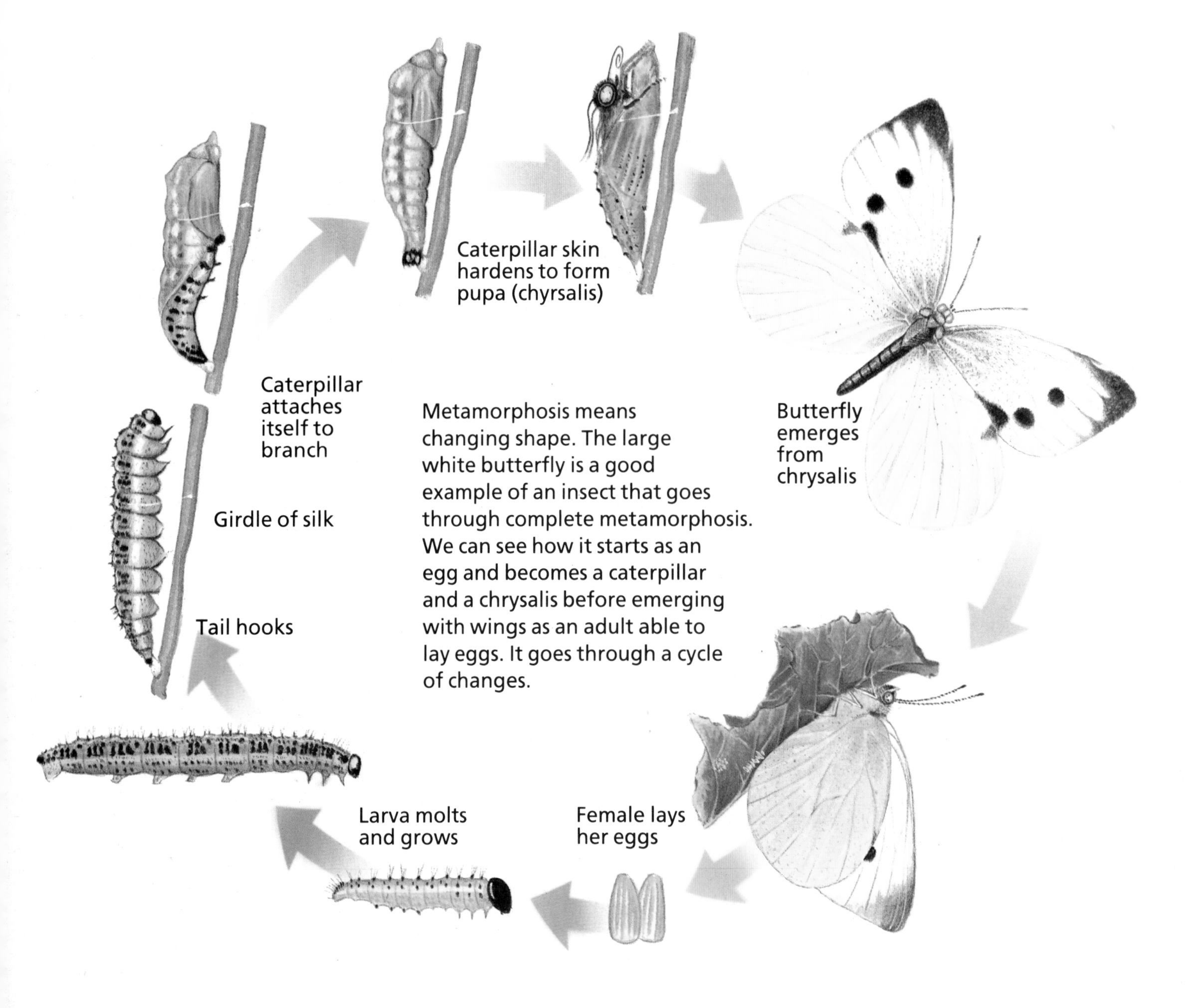

Metamorphosis means changing shape. The large white butterfly is a good example of an insect that goes through complete metamorphosis. We can see how it starts as an egg and becomes a caterpillar and a chrysalis before emerging with wings as an adult able to lay eggs. It goes through a cycle of changes.

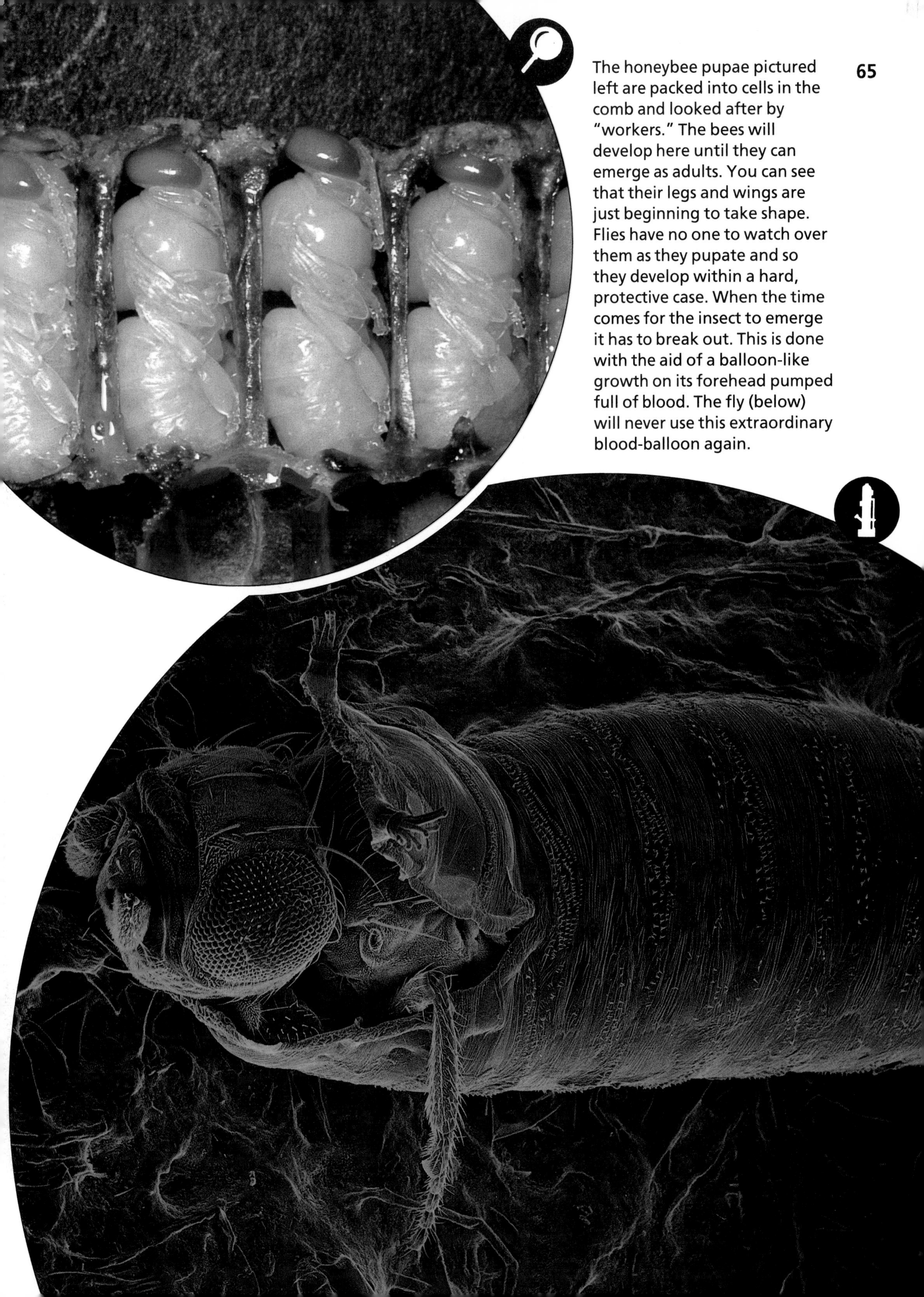

The honeybee pupae pictured left are packed into cells in the comb and looked after by "workers." The bees will develop here until they can emerge as adults. You can see that their legs and wings are just beginning to take shape. Flies have no one to watch over them as they pupate and so they develop within a hard, protective case. When the time comes for the insect to emerge it has to break out. This is done with the aid of a balloon-like growth on its forehead pumped full of blood. The fly (below) will never use this extraordinary blood-balloon again.

INSECTS AS PESTS

There are millions of different kinds of insect in the world. Most do not bother us at all but some can cause harm and are known as pests. Some insects like horseflies, mosquitoes and fleas (shown on the left), not only bite, but live by sucking blood and can sometimes spread disease. Many insect pests, such as caterpillars or aphids, do not harm people directly, but cause damage when they feed in our gardens by chewing away at leaves or sucking the life our of growing plants. Other insect pests eat crops once they have been gathered and put in storage. Beetles cause trouble in this way, particularly those known as weevils. Some pests can even attack our homes since they eat wood and will weaken roofs, floors and stairs.

Woodworm are the larvae, or young , of a beetle. They tunnel into and feed on wood before they pupate. In the photo on the right we can see an adult beetle emerging from its telltale hole after complete metamorphosis.

There are two types of human louse. One lives on the head (see photo below) and can be an itchy nuisance if it lays its sticky eggs (called nits) in your hair. The other kind of louse lives on the body and can spread serious diseases when it bites you.

An adult weevil, above, emerges from a grain of wheat. Weevil larvae can get into and feed on seeds and cereals. They have been known to ruin an entire crop and cause poverty and even famine. The mosquito, left, is one of the world's most common pests. They can carry malaria which kills thousands of people every year.

CONTENTS

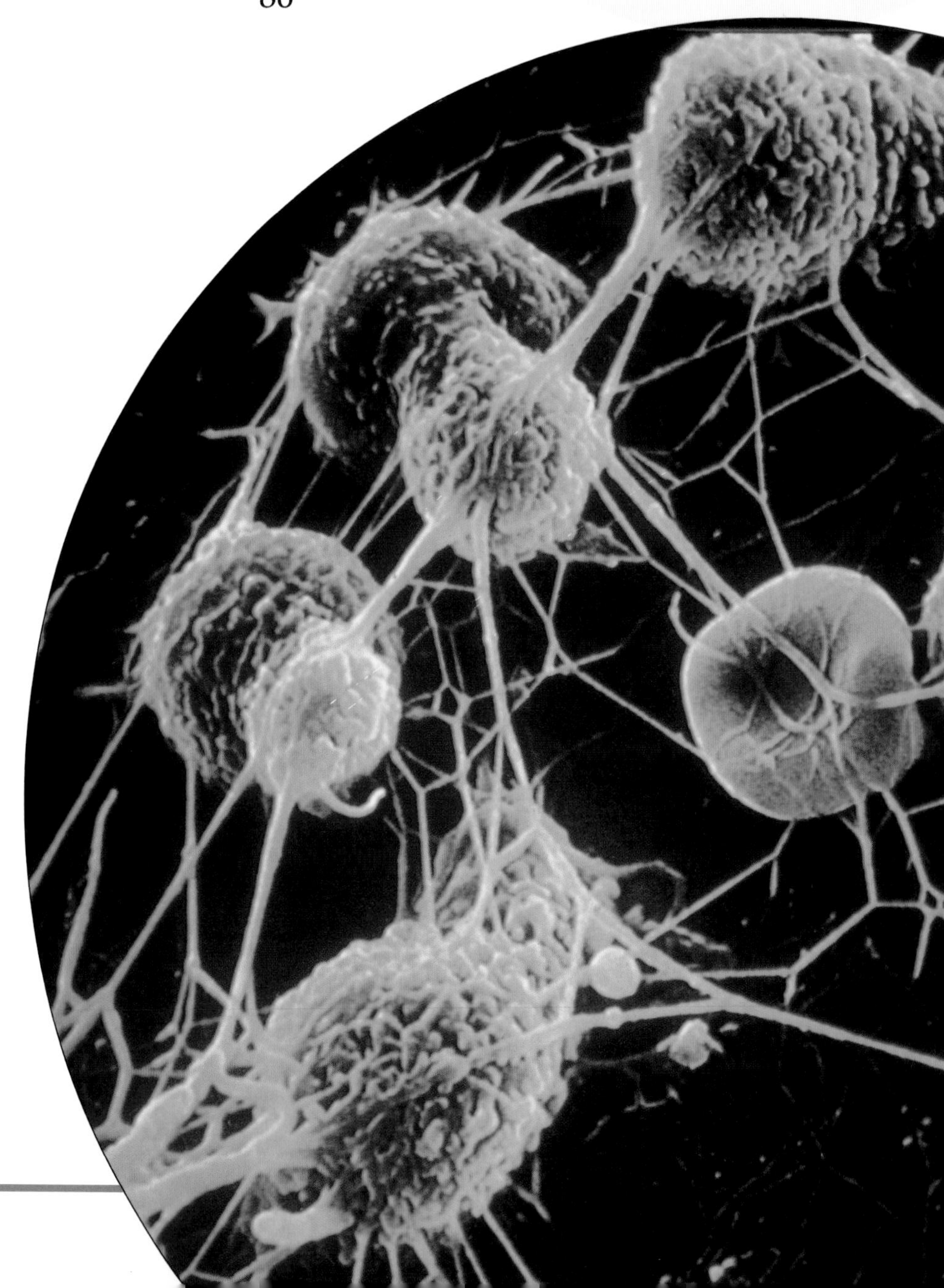

The Body

Lionel Bender

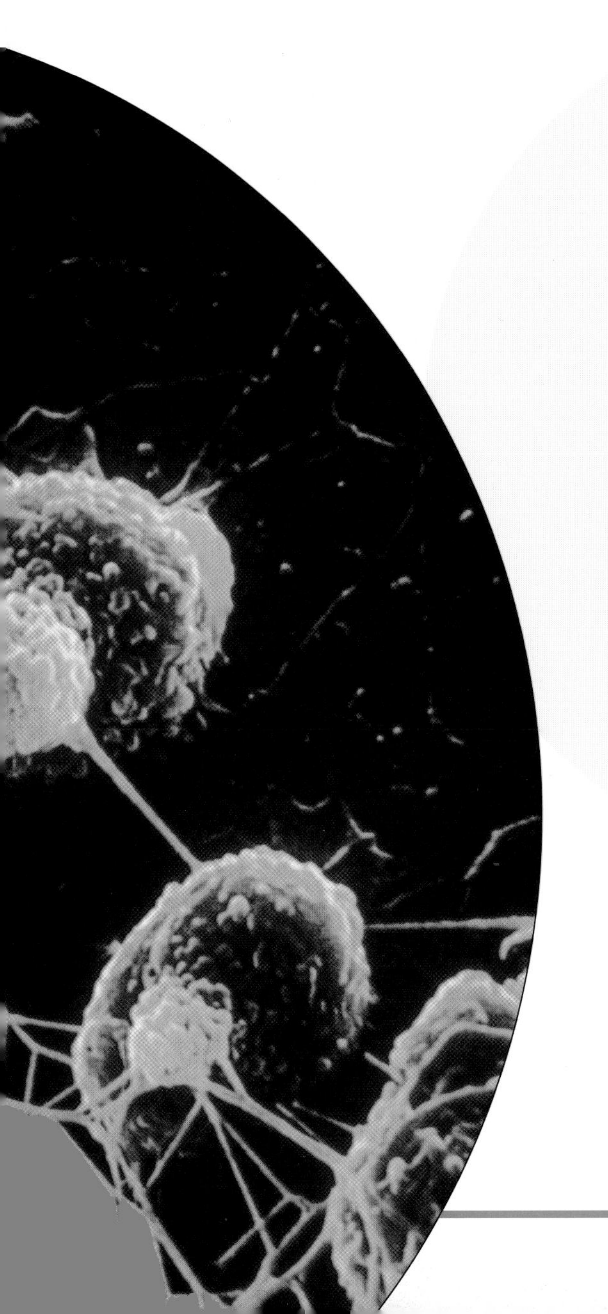

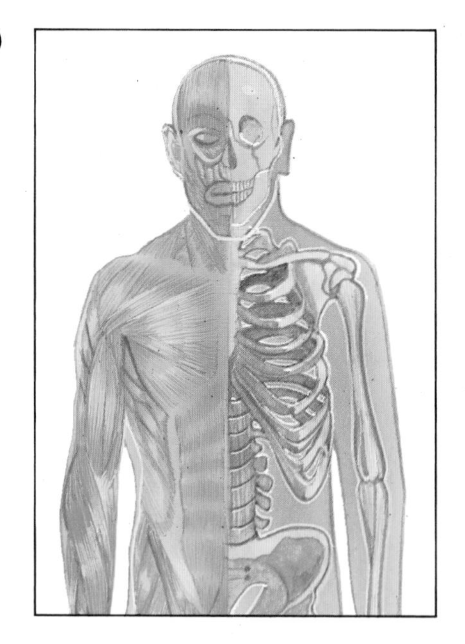

MUSCLE AND BONE

There are over 650 muscles in your body. A muscle is a fleshy bundle of fibers usually attached to a bone. Every movement we make is the work of muscles. Even your heartbeat is a muscular action. When you move an arm or leg, one muscle shortens to pull two bones closer while another muscle relaxes to let it go. About 200 bones form the skeleton which supports your body. Its most important organs, like the brain and the heart, are protected by the skull and rib bones. Bones have a hard, white coating but are almost hollow. They are filled with marrow which makes most of the blood cells for your body. Far from being dry and brittle objects, bones are living structures.

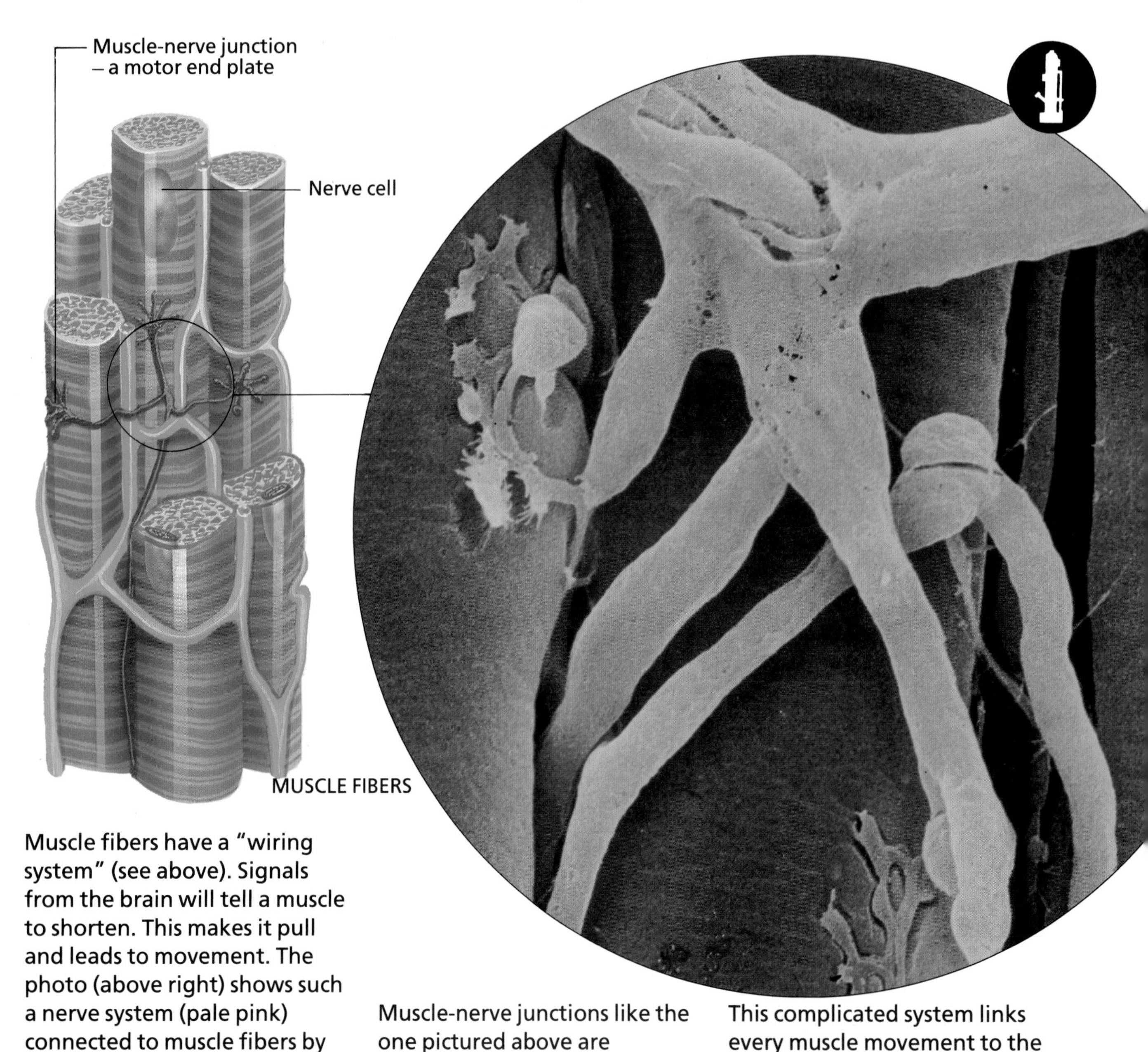

Muscle fibers have a "wiring system" (see above). Signals from the brain will tell a muscle to shorten. This makes it pull and leads to movement. The photo (above right) shows such a nerve system (pale pink) connected to muscle fibers by two motor end plates.

Muscle-nerve junctions like the one pictured above are repeated all over your body.

This complicated system links every muscle movement to the brain.

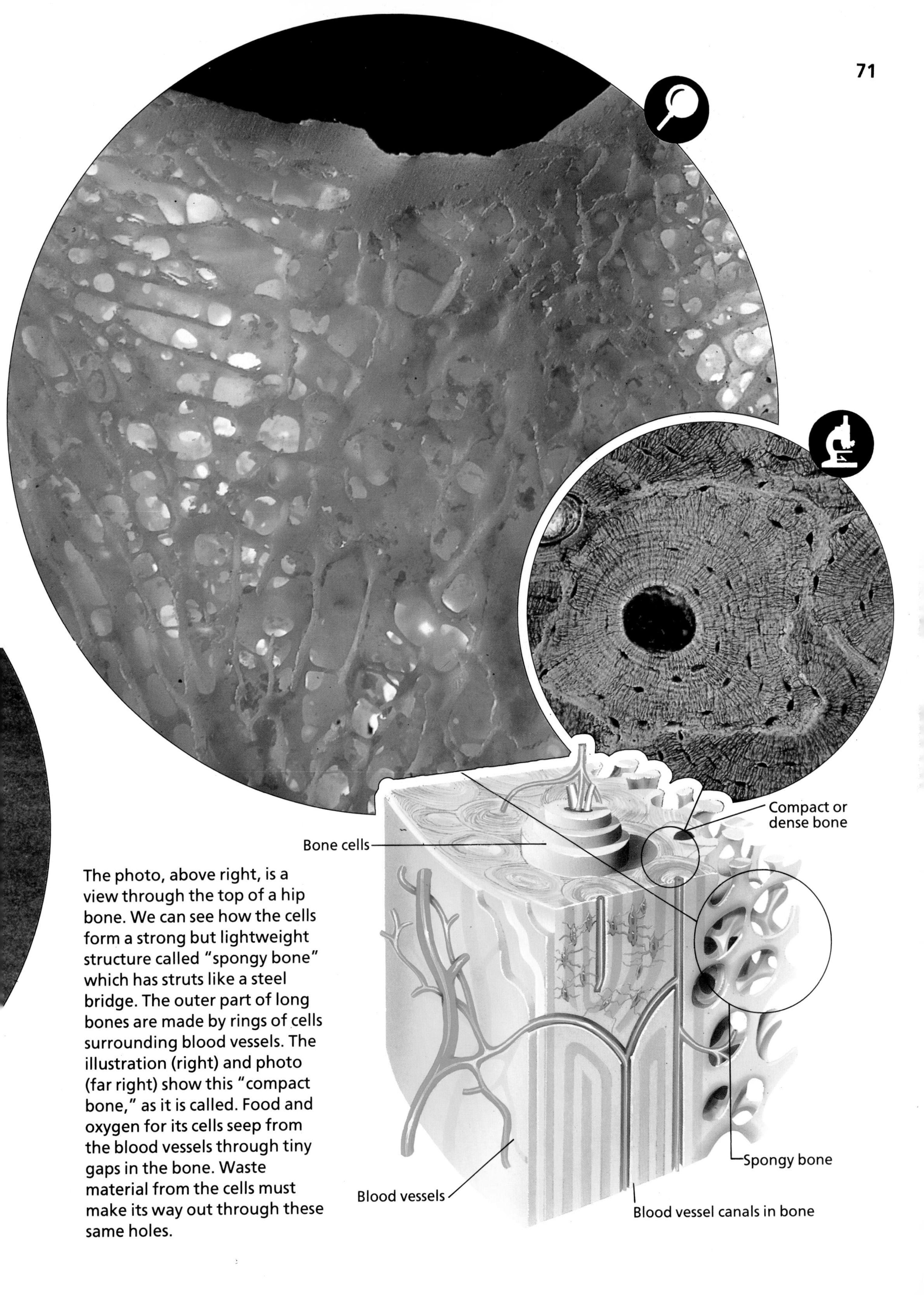

The photo, above right, is a view through the top of a hip bone. We can see how the cells form a strong but lightweight structure called "spongy bone" which has struts like a steel bridge. The outer part of long bones are made by rings of cells surrounding blood vessels. The illustration (right) and photo (far right) show this "compact bone," as it is called. Food and oxygen for its cells seep from the blood vessels through tiny gaps in the bone. Waste material from the cells must make its way out through these same holes.

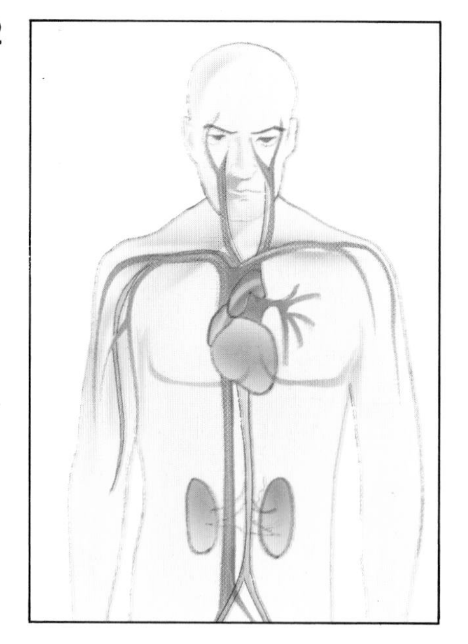

BLOOD AND BLOOD VESSELS

Our hearts are continually pumping blood through the 50,000 miles (80,000km) of blood vessels in our bodies (see illustration left). Blood circulates within the body and carries food materials, heat, and special chemicals called hormones to all our tissues and organs. It also takes away waste products like carbon dioxide and urea, to be dealt with by other main organs. Under a microscope we can see that blood consists of a yellowish, sticky fluid called plasma which has red and white cells called corpuscles. The red blood cells are colored by hemoglobin, which carries oxygen from the lungs to the tissues. White cells attack and destroy germs whenever they enter the bloodstream.

The largest vessel of the blood system are the veins and arteries. The smallest are capillaries (see illustration below). The widest artery is only about 3/4 inch (2cm) across, but this quickly divides into smaller arterioles. Blood flows though these and into tiny capillary "nets" within tissues. These are only a fraction of an inch wide. Here red cells tumble freely through while the white cells, which are much larger, have to squeeze by. The picture on the right shows red cells packed into a blood capillary.

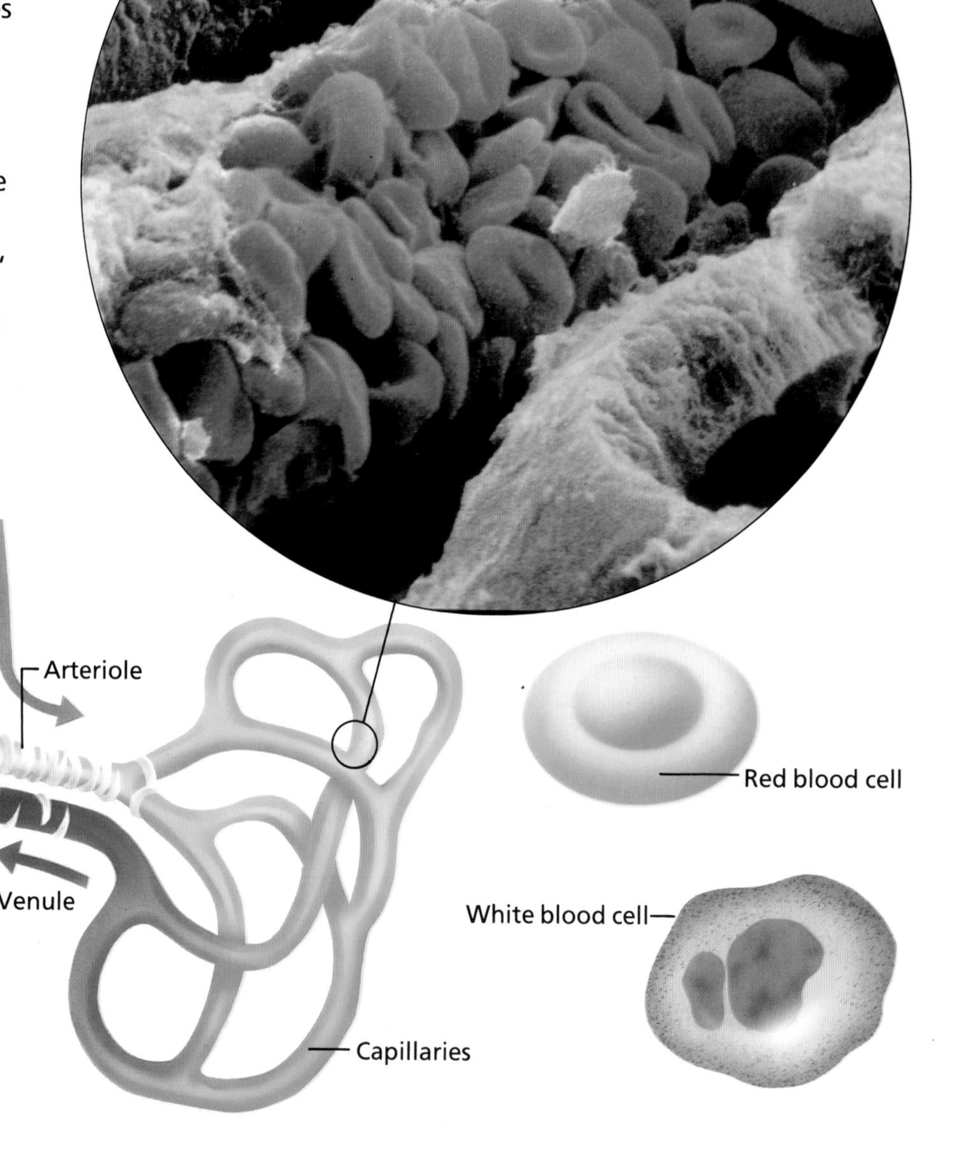

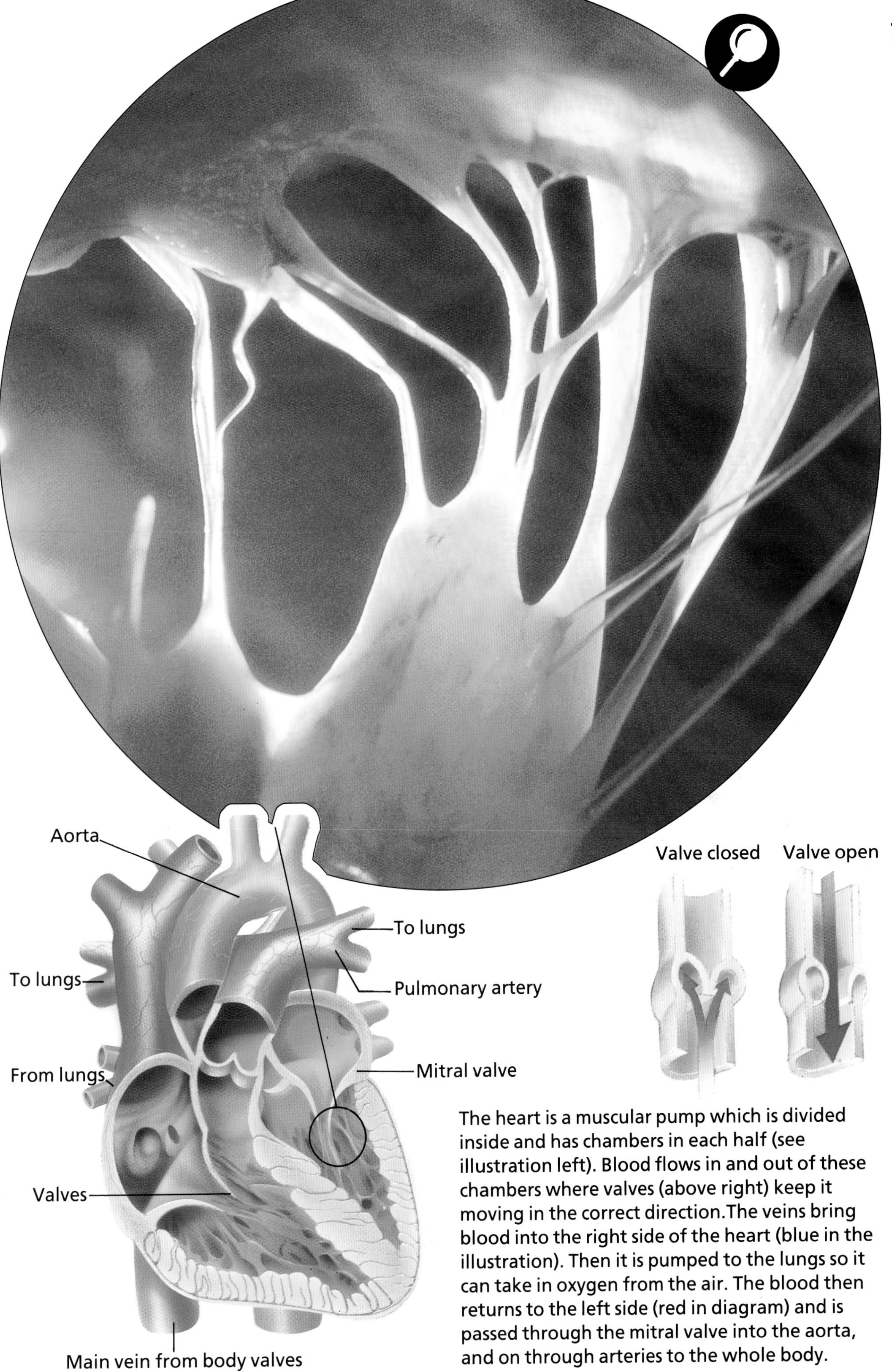

The heart is a muscular pump which is divided inside and has chambers in each half (see illustration left). Blood flows in and out of these chambers where valves (above right) keep it moving in the correct direction. The veins bring blood into the right side of the heart (blue in the illustration). Then it is pumped to the lungs so it can take in oxygen from the air. The blood then returns to the left side (red in diagram) and is passed through the mitral valve into the aorta, and on through arteries to the whole body.

LUNGS AND BREATHING

Every cell in your body needs oxygen and without it each would die in only 4 minutes. Oxygen helps change our food into energy. However, at the same time, a waste gas called carbon dioxide is produced which we need to get rid of. The lungs are the organs which deal with the exchange of these two gases. They are made of millions of air sacs surrounded by capillaries full of blood. Each time we breathe in, they expand like balloons and allow oxygen to pass through their thin walls into the bloodstream. When we breathe out, they contract so that the carbon dioxide waste is expelled. Whenever your body needs more oxygen, when you are running, for example, you start breathing more quickly and deeply.

Hairs line the inside of the nose and are covered in a sticky fluid called mucus. These hairs trap any dust and germs which may enter when you breathe in. Air gets into the lungs through a tree-like arrangement of pipes.

The trachea, or windpipe, is like the trunk. This is lined with yellow, grass-like cilia (photo below). The windpipe branches into tiny twigs within each lung called bronchioles. See illustration on the right.

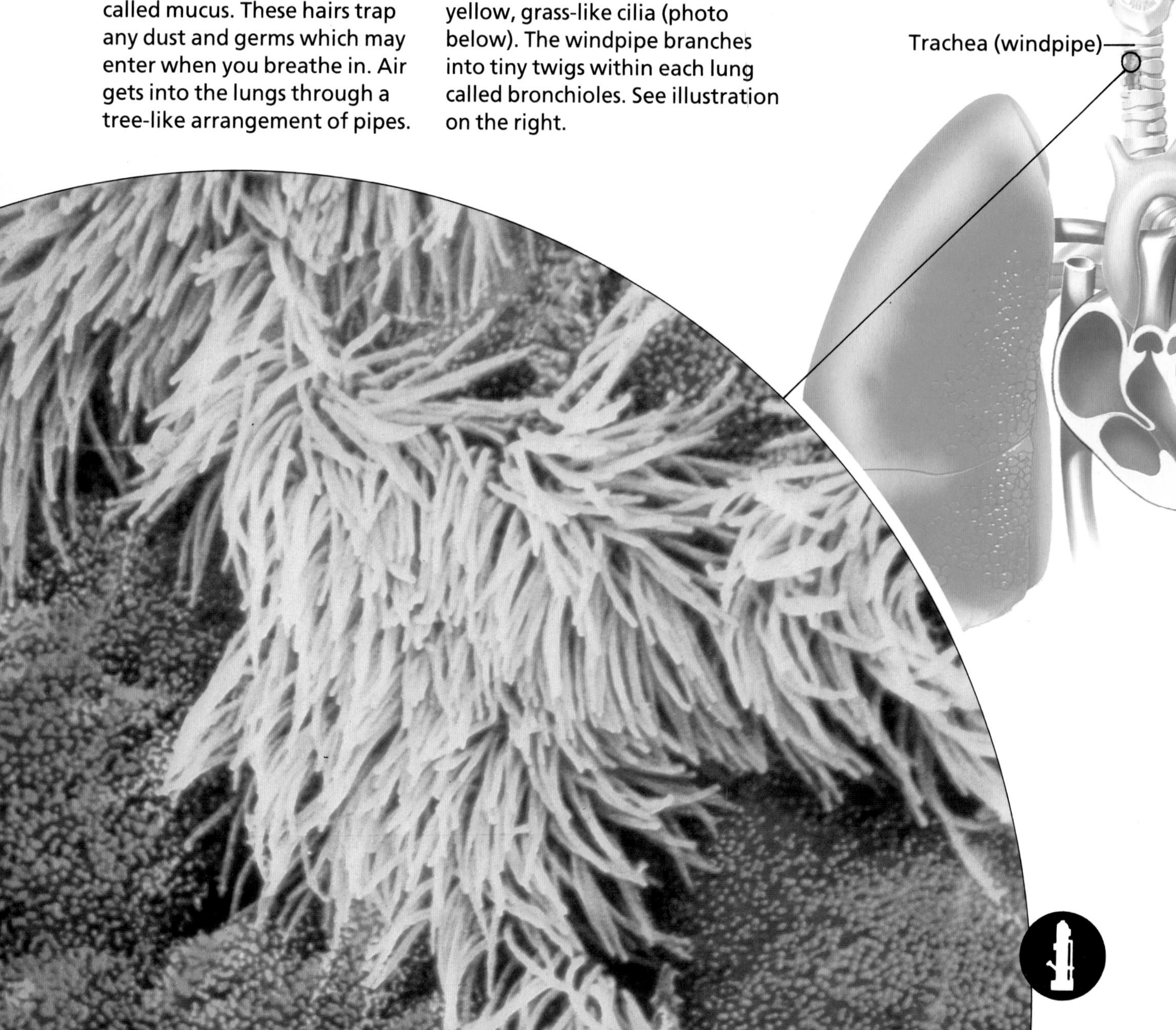

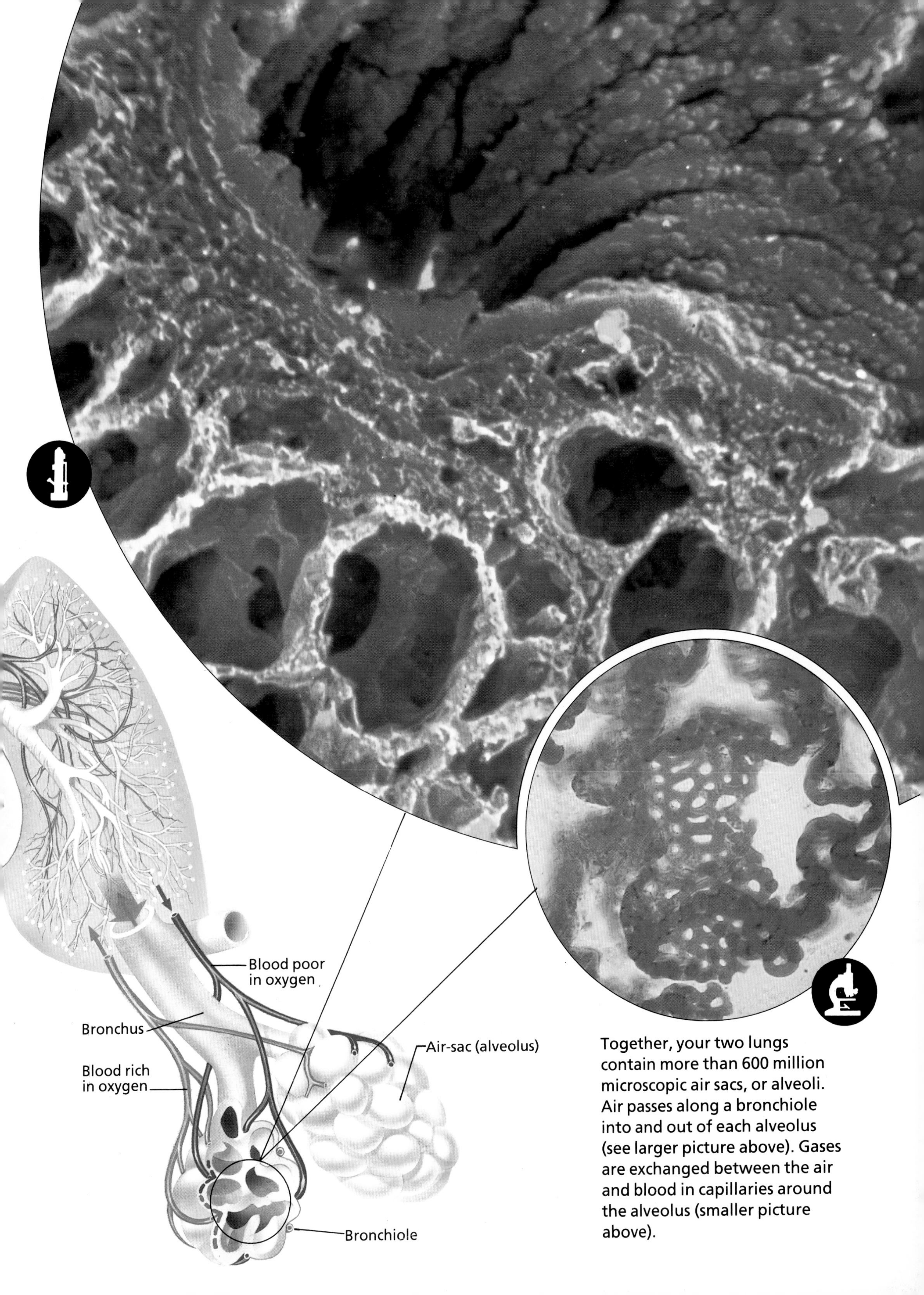

Together, your two lungs contain more than 600 million microscopic air sacs, or alveoli. Air passes along a bronchiole into and out of each alveolus (see larger picture above). Gases are exchanged between the air and blood in capillaries around the alveolus (smaller picture above).

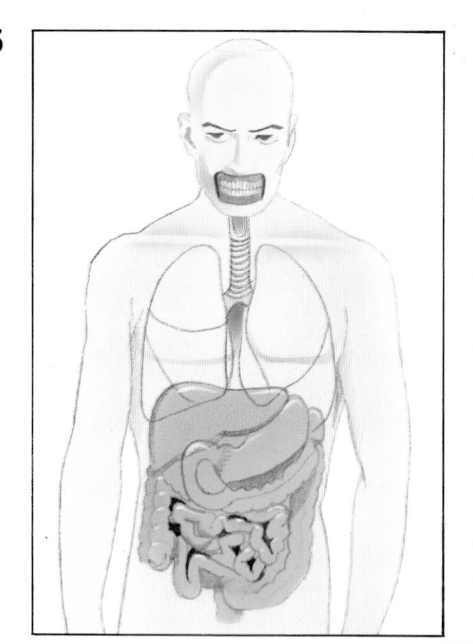

THE DIGESTIVE SYSTEM

The human body is like a machine built from and fuelled with food. But for our cells to use the food, it must first be converted into simple chemicals which will enter the bloodsteam and so travel to where they are needed. This is the job of our digestive system. Think of it as a 23 foot (7m) long tube winding through your body, changing food into fuel. First food is softened in your mouth by chewing. Once swallowed, it is attacked by acids in you stomach and intestines until it is so broken-down that the chemicals can pass though the walls of the tube (or digestive tract) into the blood, or lymph system. Finally, whatever the body cannot digest is excreted as feces.

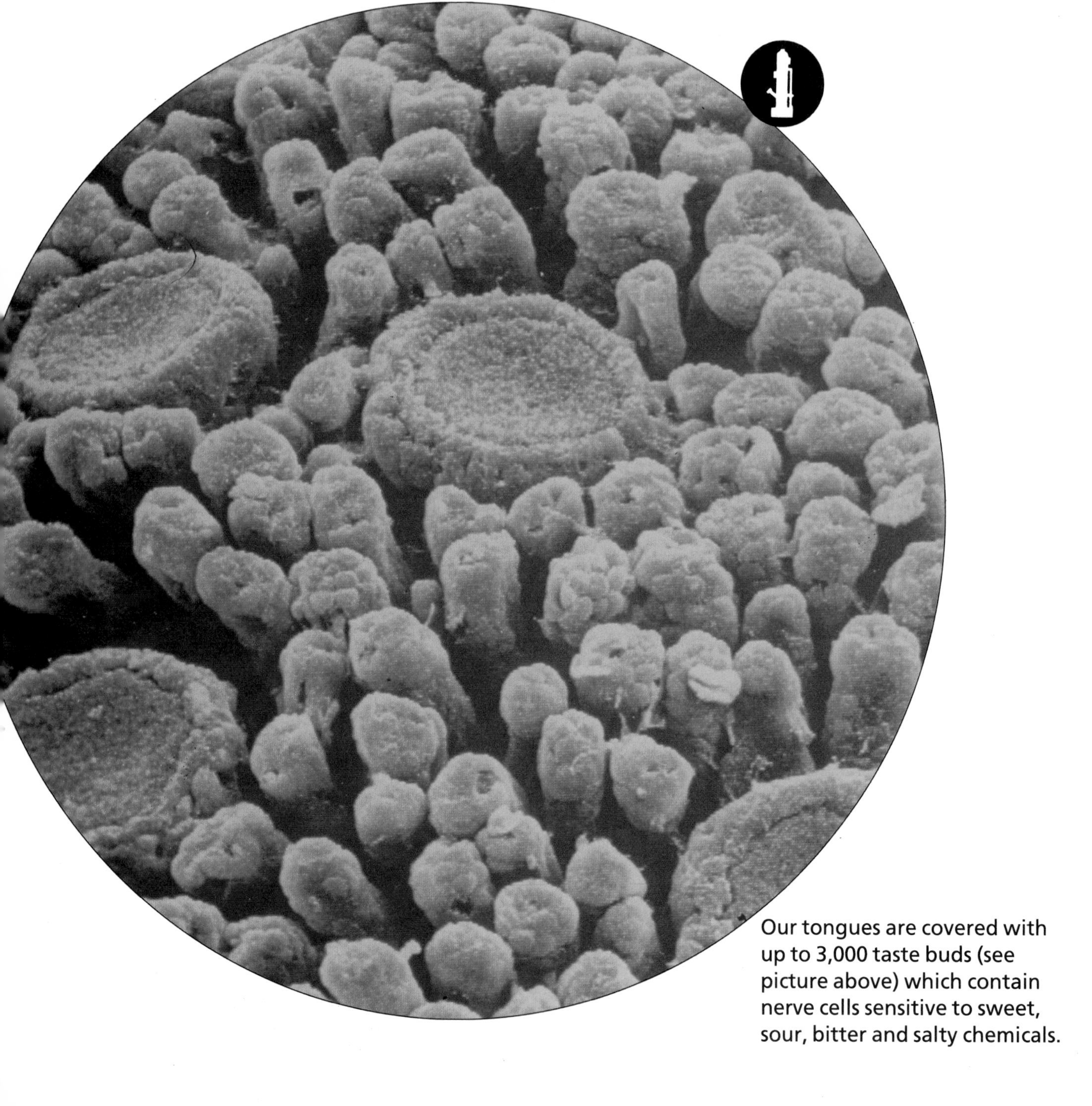

Our tongues are covered with up to 3,000 taste buds (see picture above) which contain nerve cells sensitive to sweet, sour, bitter and salty chemicals.

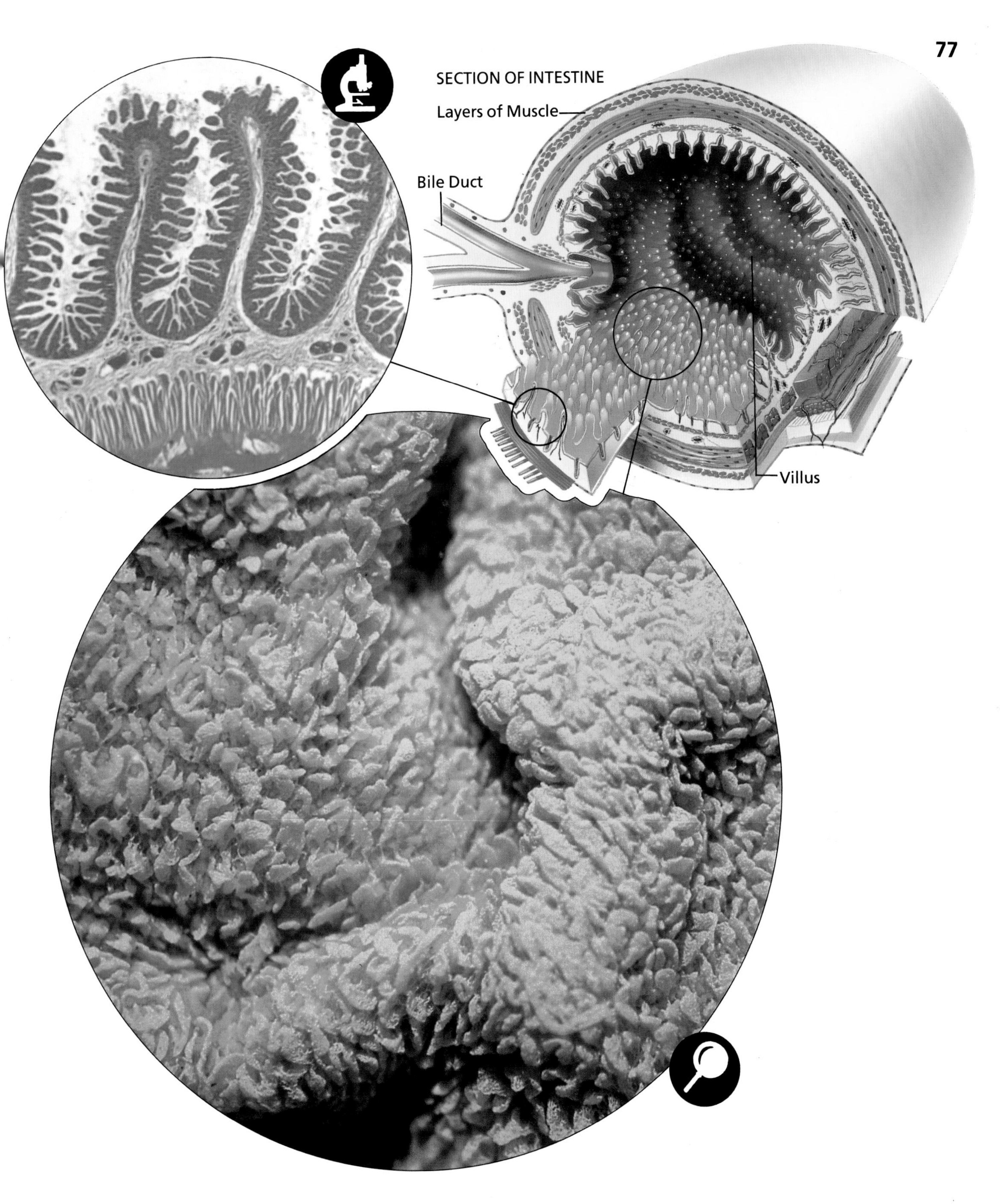

Each day, your digestive system will handle about 18 pints (10 liters), of food and drink from your stomach and intestines. Only about one pint (125ml) of this leaves your body as feces. The rest is absorbed into capillaries and lymph vessels in the walls of the intestines (see photo and illustration uppermost on this page). Most absorption takes place in the duodenum (photo above). The walls of your intestines are so highly folded that they have a surface area that would be larger than a tennis court if they were to be spread out flat.

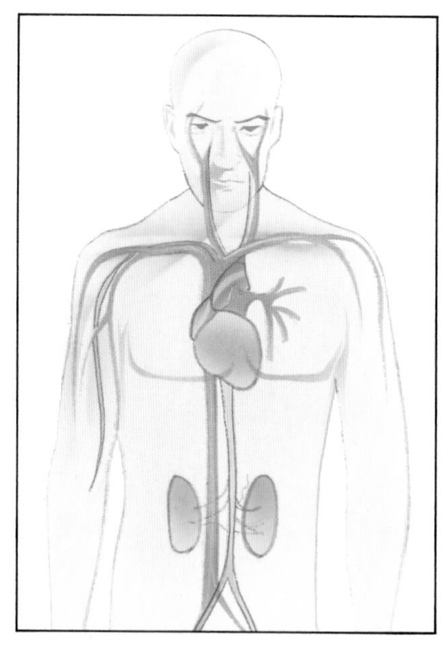

THE EXCRETORY SYSTEM

Your blood contains many substances that the body does not need and a few that can actually be harmful to you. These include excess water and minerals from food, dead or damaged cells, and waste products of cell activity. They must be eliminated from your body if you are to stay healthy. Your kidneys are the organs that filter your blood and remove the chemicals and water. One quarter of all the blood your heart pumps is sent straight to your kidneys. This means that every day your heart pumps about 2,500 pints of blood through your kidneys. Small materials are squeezes out of blood capillaries into microscopic filter unit to form a trickle of unwanted water and waste products known as urine.

Each kidney contains a million filter units called nephrons. At the top of every nephron is a cup-like collector called the Bowman's capsule. This surrounds a knot of blood capillaries (photo far right). Hundreds of cup-and-knot pairs are packed into the outer cortex of a kidney (right).

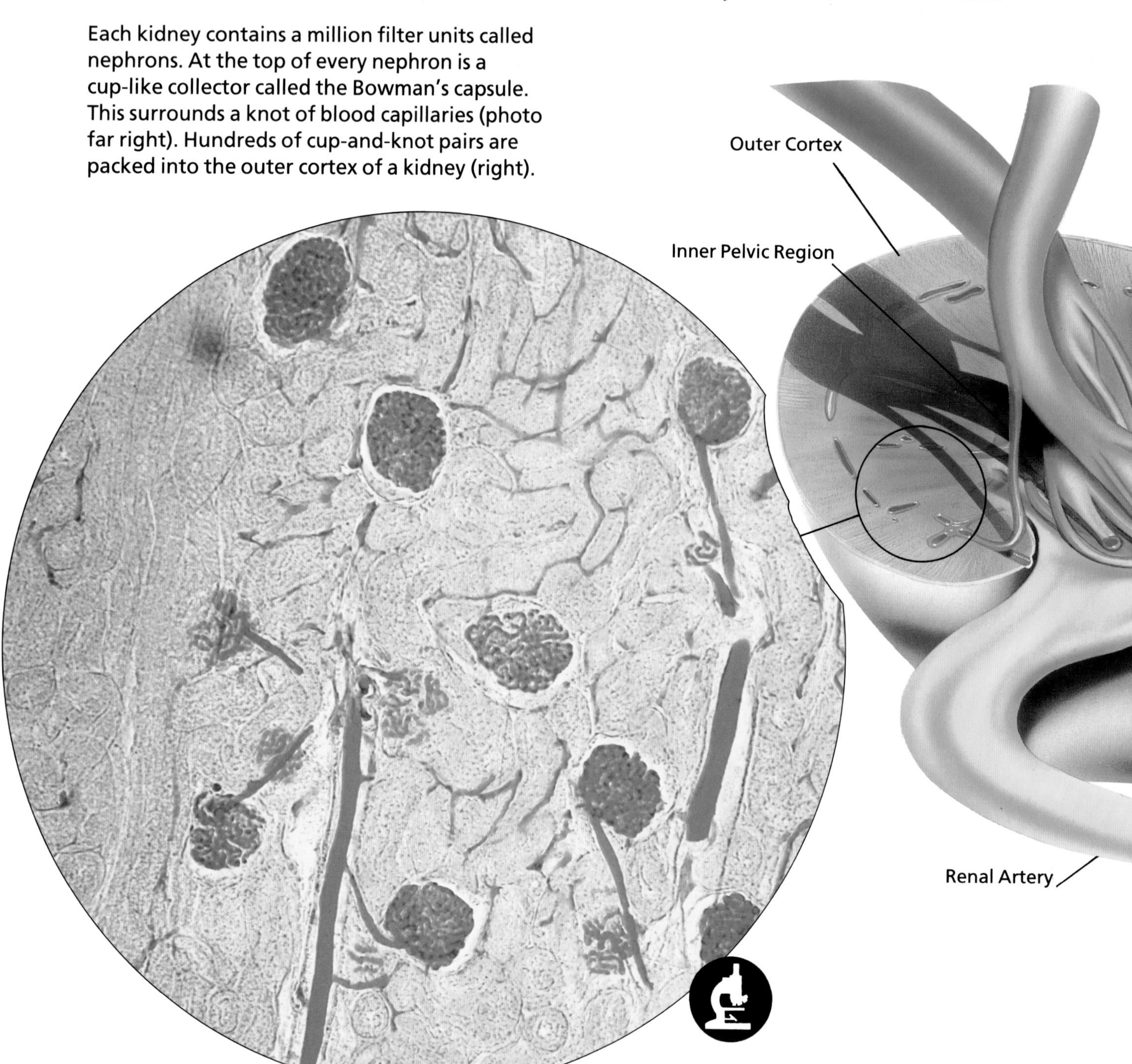

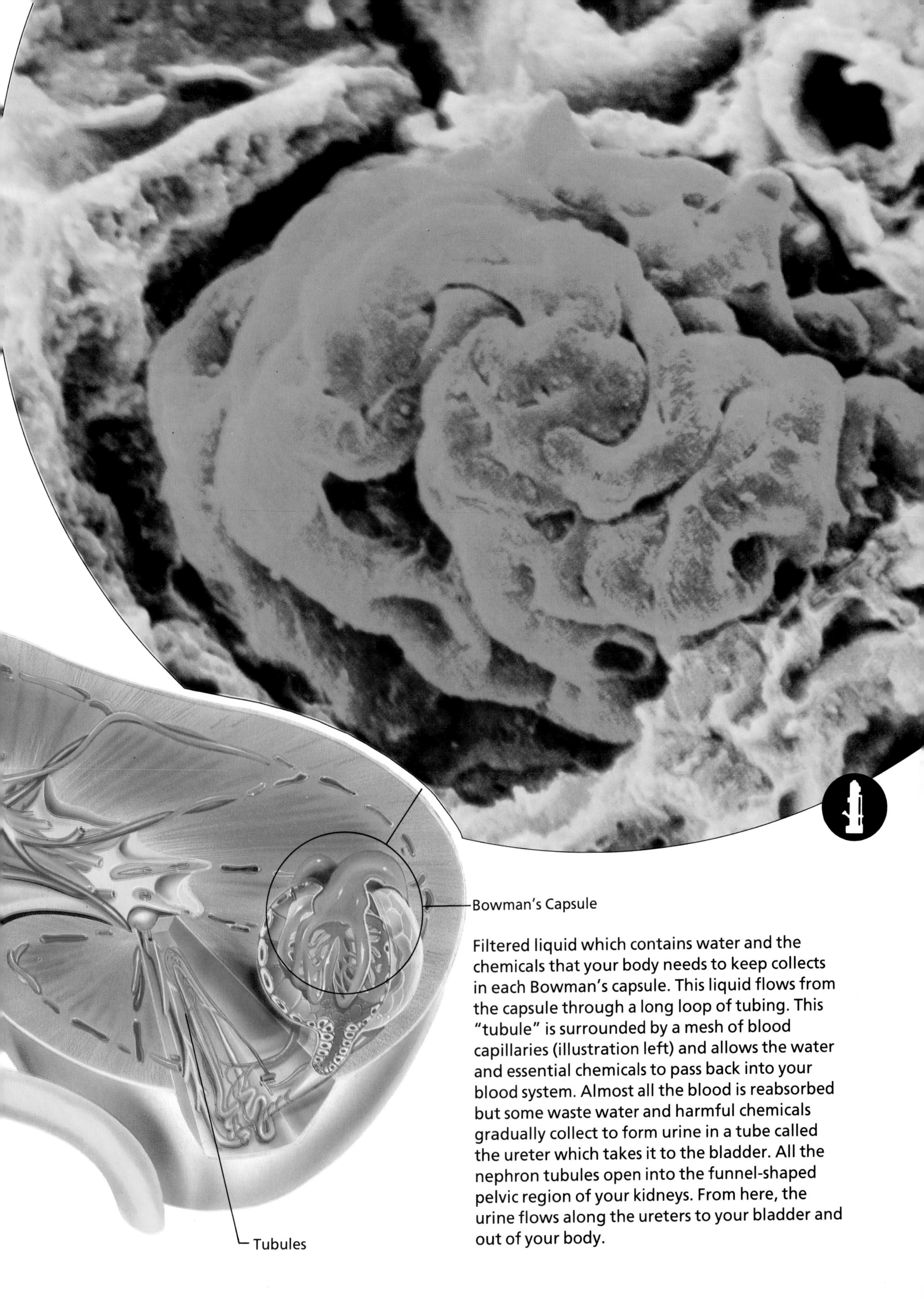

Filtered liquid which contains water and the chemicals that your body needs to keep collects in each Bowman's capsule. This liquid flows from the capsule through a long loop of tubing. This "tubule" is surrounded by a mesh of blood capillaries (illustration left) and allows the water and essential chemicals to pass back into your blood system. Almost all the blood is reabsorbed but some waste water and harmful chemicals gradually collect to form urine in a tube called the ureter which takes it to the bladder. All the nephron tubules open into the funnel-shaped pelvic region of your kidneys. From here, the urine flows along the ureters to your bladder and out of your body.

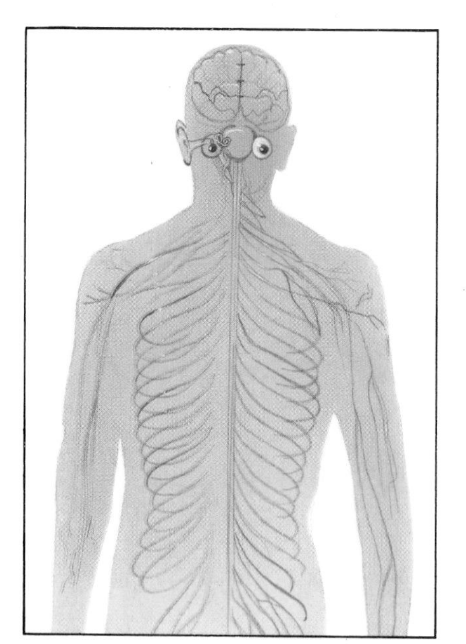

THE NERVOUS SYSTEM

Your body has a communication and control network called the nervous system. Its headquarters is the brain where 12,000 million cells are constantly sending and receiving messages. Tiny nerve fibers act like telephone wires and carry signals throughout the body. Some of these fibers branch out from the base of the brain, others from your spinal cord. Information about our surroundings is sent to the brain from our sense organs (the nose, eyes, ears and tongue), as well as from the nerves embedded in our skin and muscles. The brain receives all the information and decides how we should act. All the pictures on these two pages show details of the brain and your body's nervous system.

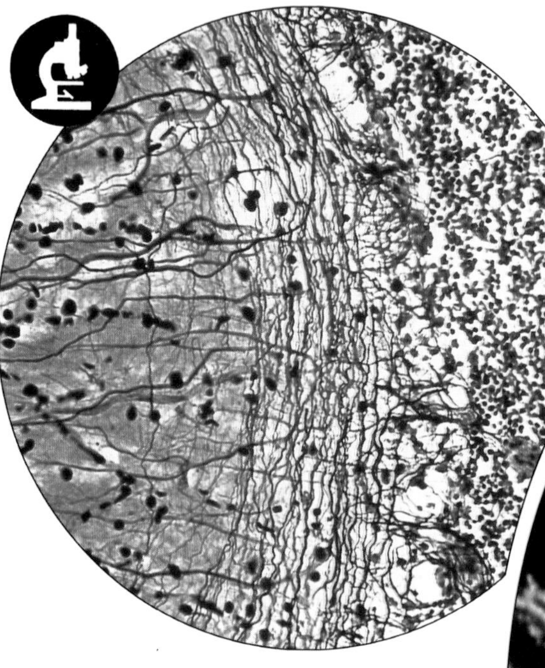

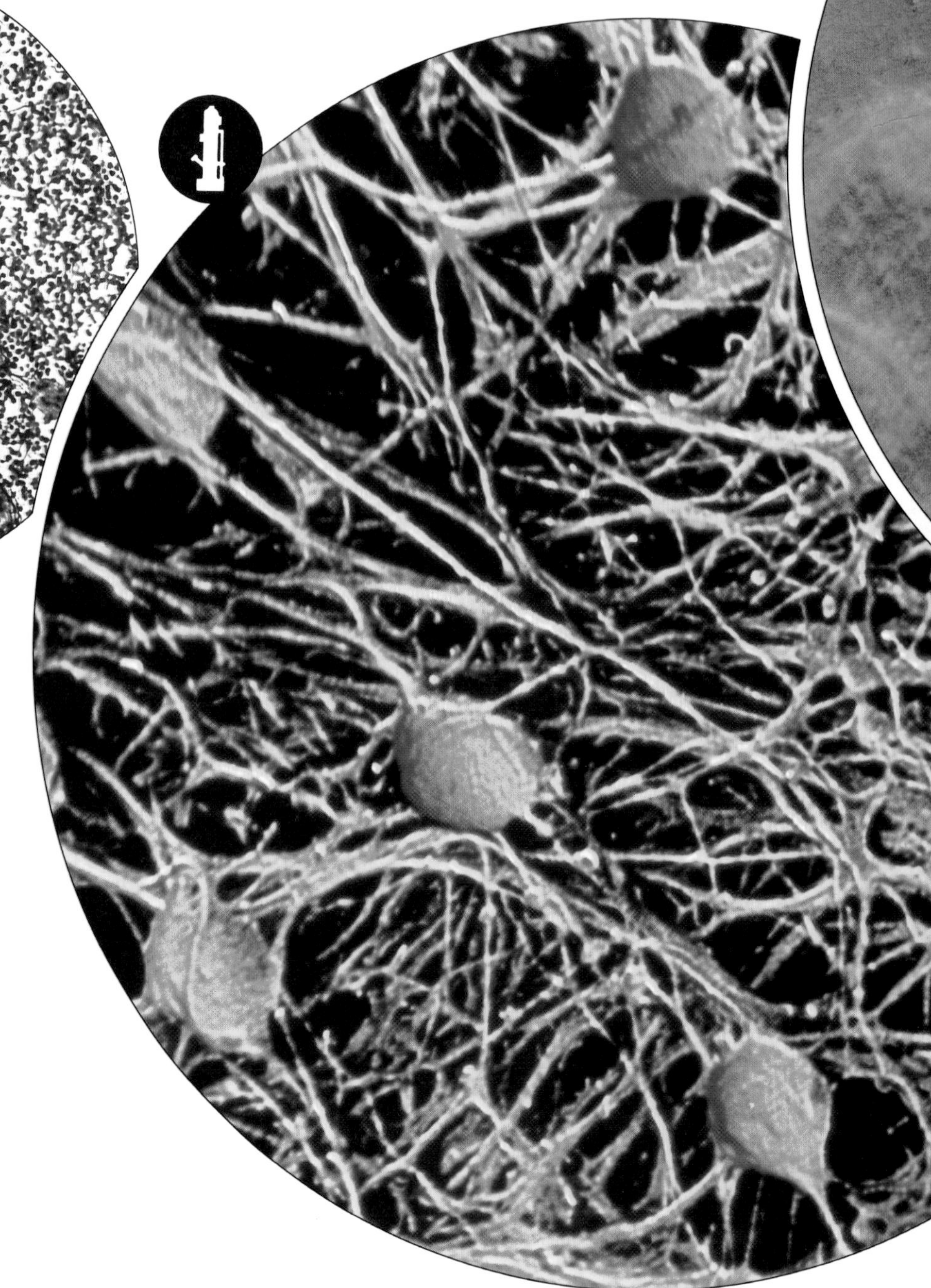

A view through the very folded outer layers of the brain (above) shows a tightly packed area of nerve cells. Each is connected to thousands of others by tree-like "dendrites" (see illustration far right). These form a mass of strands which carry messages or "nerve impulses" – short bursts of electricity. The dendrites are so densely packed in the brain that they resemble the wires of a complicated telephone exchange. Millions of signals pass along them every minute, which the brain decodes as hot or cold, soft or hard, for example.

The picture below is an electron microscope's view of a synapse, a junction between two nerve fibers in the outer part of a human brain. The colors are false, the brain is in fact gray.

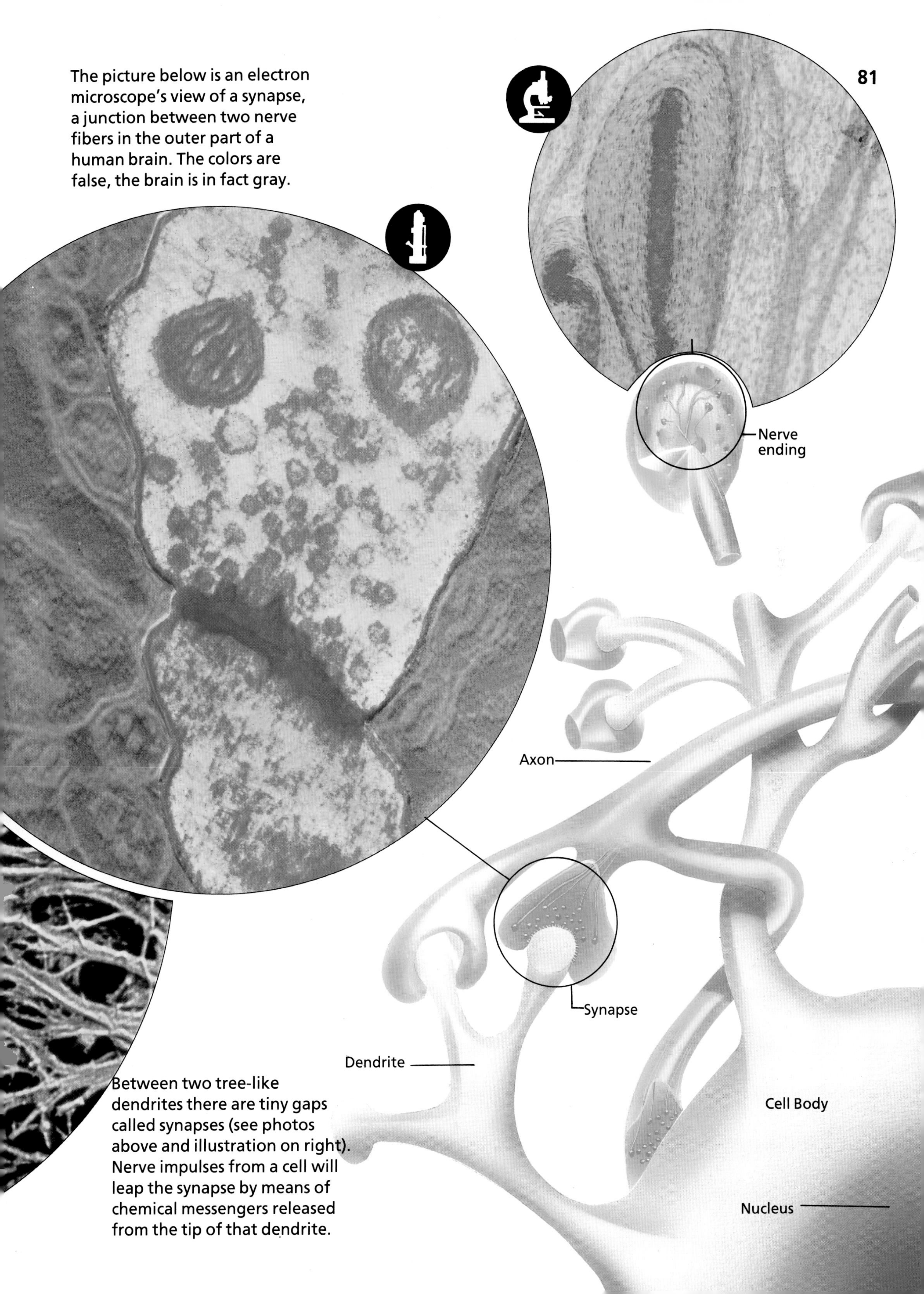

Between two tree-like dendrites there are tiny gaps called synapses (see photos above and illustration on right). Nerve impulses from a cell will leap the synapse by means of chemical messengers released from the tip of that dendrite.

EYES AND EARS

The five senses are touch, taste, smell, sight and hearing. Each makes us aware of our surroundings by using microscopic nerve cells. Just as your skin has nerves which are sensitive to hot and cold, so we see, hear, smell and taste with groups of cells called receptors. Their special job is to report changes of the nerves they are attached to. In our eyes these work by noticing changes in the light falling on them. In our ears receptors sense changes in sound. Receptors operate our sense of smell in the same way, by sending nerve signals to our brains to be interpreted. For example, our eyes see upside down but the brain decodes this information so that we know which is the right way up.

Each of your eyes is like a miniature camera. At the front is a clear, curved window called the cornea. The colored area, the iris, see picture on the right, is a ring of muscle that controls the amount of light shining on the lens . This lens forms a sharp picture on receptor cells within the retina at the back of the eye. These signal the brain via the optic nerve (see illustration below), so that the optic nerve carries a picture to the brain where it can be studied.

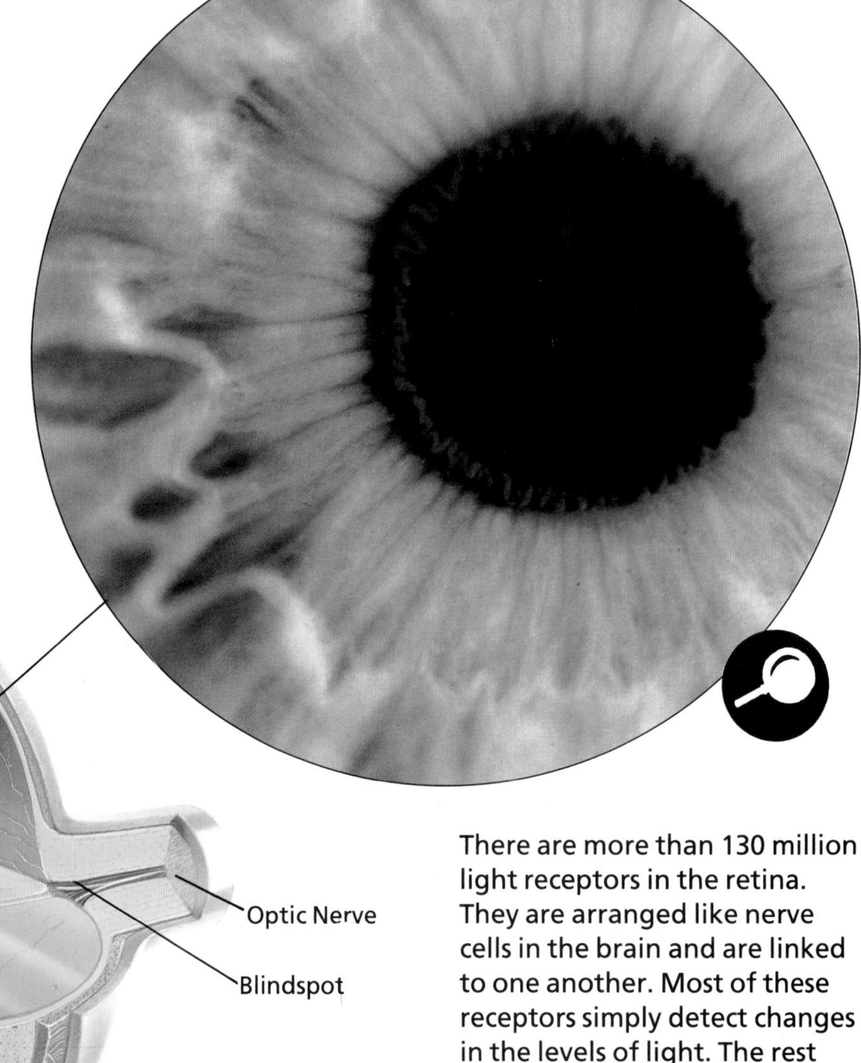

Cornea
Iris
Optic Nerve
Blindspot
Retina
Lens
Muscle

There are more than 130 million light receptors in the retina. They are arranged like nerve cells in the brain and are linked to one another. Most of these receptors simply detect changes in the levels of light. The rest are sensitive to color and allow your brain to build up information which will produce a realistic image of what is being viewed.

Sounds are really vibrations in the air. The outer ear, or pinna, funnels these down the bony canal to the ear-drum which trembles and moves three connected earbones in the middle ear. They pass vibrations to the inner ear where the cochlea, or hearing organ, a shell-like tube, receives them. Within it are receptors with hairs sticking into a jelly-like mass (see below right). Sounds make fluid in the cochlea move and cause the hairs to send signals to your brain along the auditory nerve.

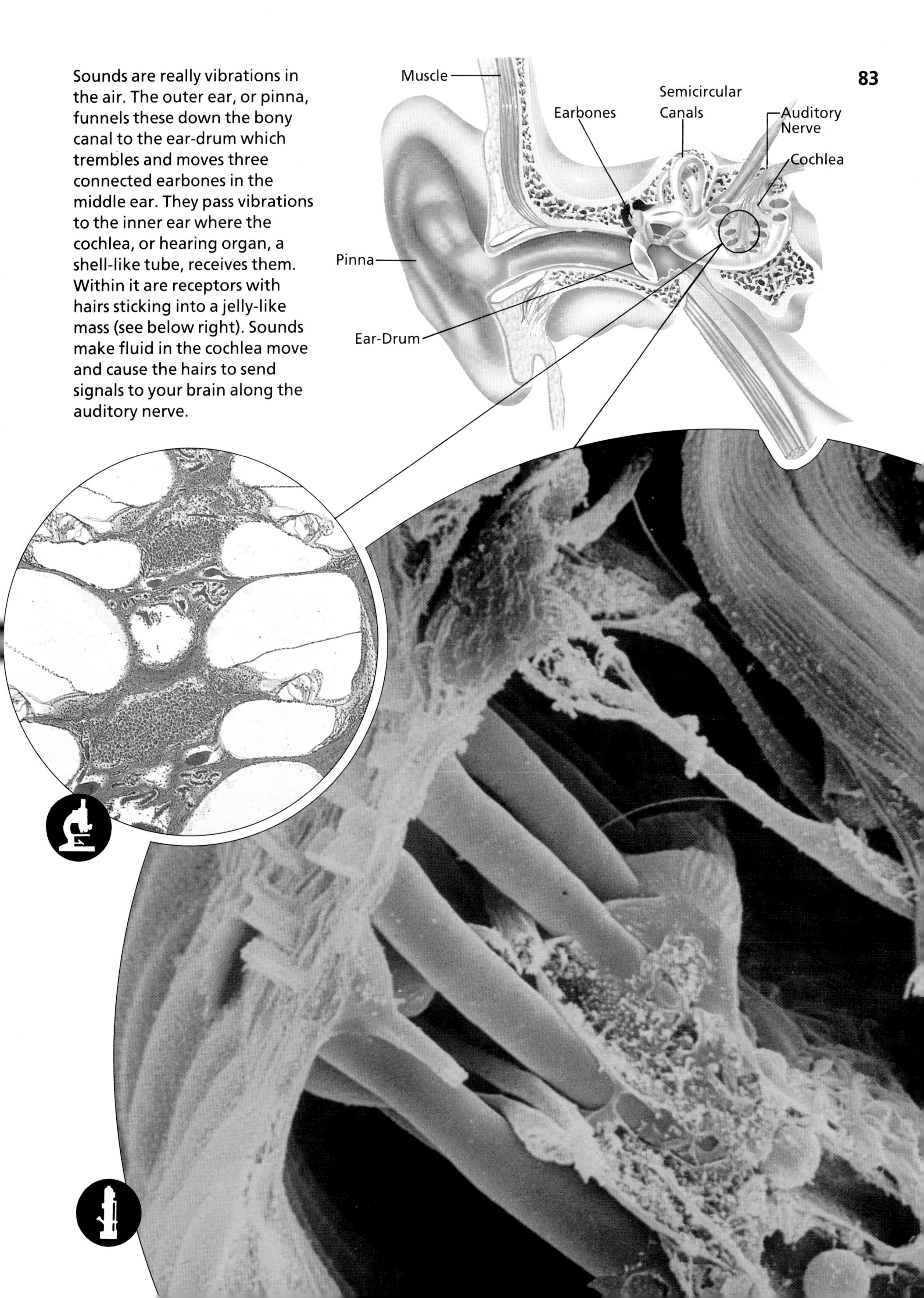

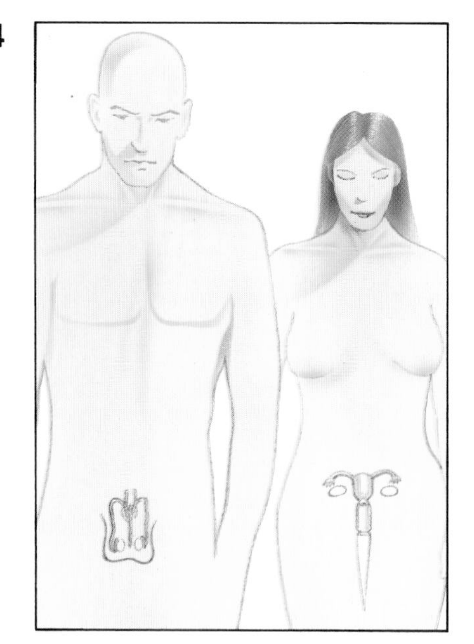

THE REPRODUCTIVE SYSTEM

Human life goes on because we are able to produce more humans like ourselves. This is called reproduction and every sex plays its part. An adult male produces about 200 million seed-cells, or sperm, in his testes every day. Sperm are so tiny that several hundred would easily fit onto a pin-head. A female's ovaries make one egg-cell, or ovum, each month. The ovum is the largest human cell and is just visible to the naked eye. Despite their minute sizes, a sperm and an ovum together contain all the information needed to produce a new human being. Following sexual intercourse, millions of sperm come into contact with an ovum. But just one sperm combines with, or fertilizes, the ovum to make an embryo.

The testicles, a cross-section of one is illustrated below, are two sperm-making organs attached to a male body.

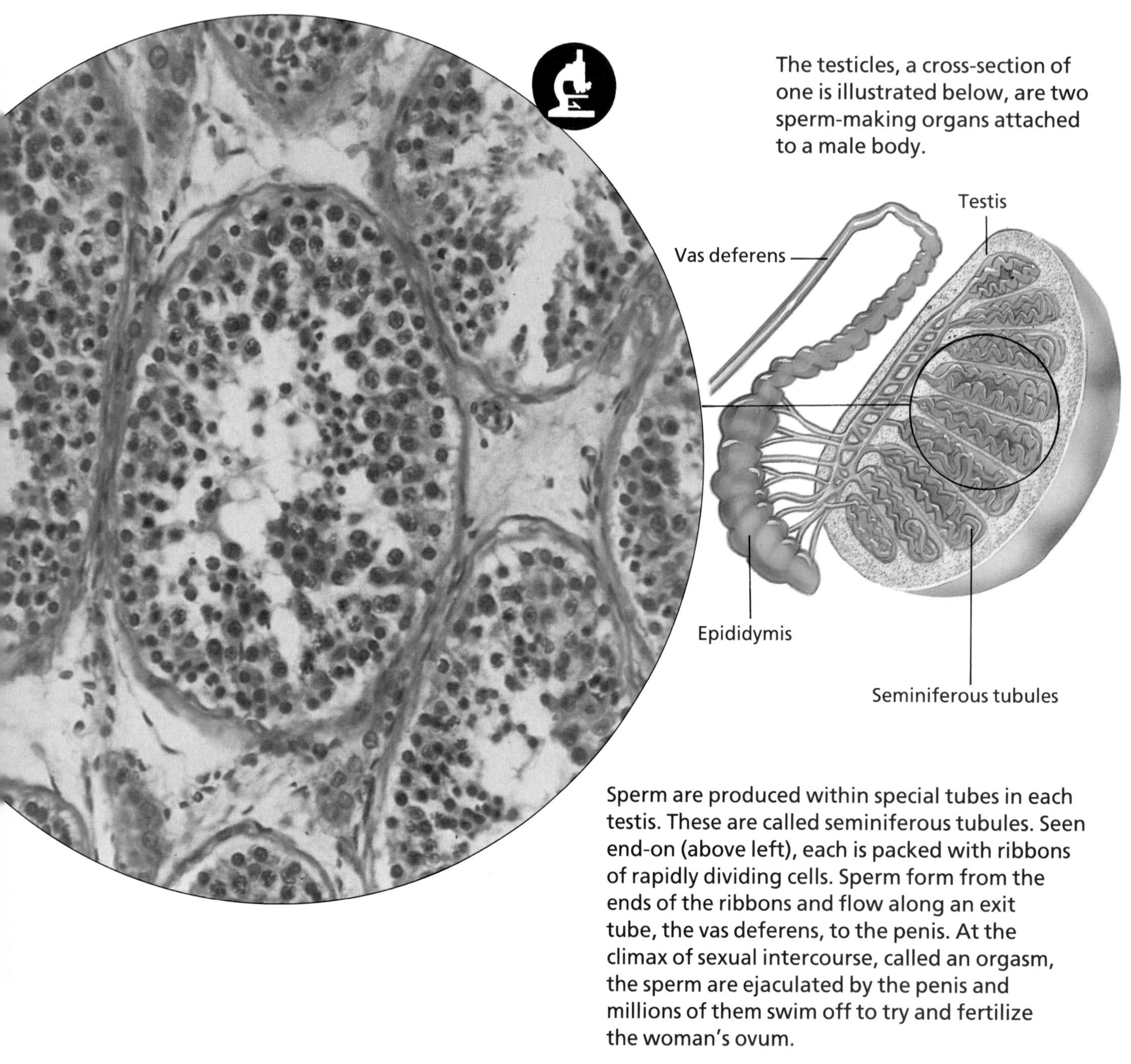

Sperm are produced within special tubes in each testis. These are called seminiferous tubules. Seen end-on (above left), each is packed with ribbons of rapidly dividing cells. Sperm form from the ends of the ribbons and flow along an exit tube, the vas deferens, to the penis. At the climax of sexual intercourse, called an orgasm, the sperm are ejaculated by the penis and millions of them swim off to try and fertilize the woman's ovum.

At any one moment, there are cells at different stages of development in each of a woman's two ovaries (see photo right). When these become mature ovum they are released into the fallopian tubes (see below left). The ovum is pushed toward the womb by muscles in the wall of this tube. Along the way it may encounter sperm which have swum up from the vagina. Cells lining the walls of the ovum sac produce chemicals called hormones to control this entire process. Once an ovum is fertilized by a single sperm the egg divides and its cells begin to multiply. Within three weeks it will become an embryo, and after nine months a baby will be born, if all goes well.

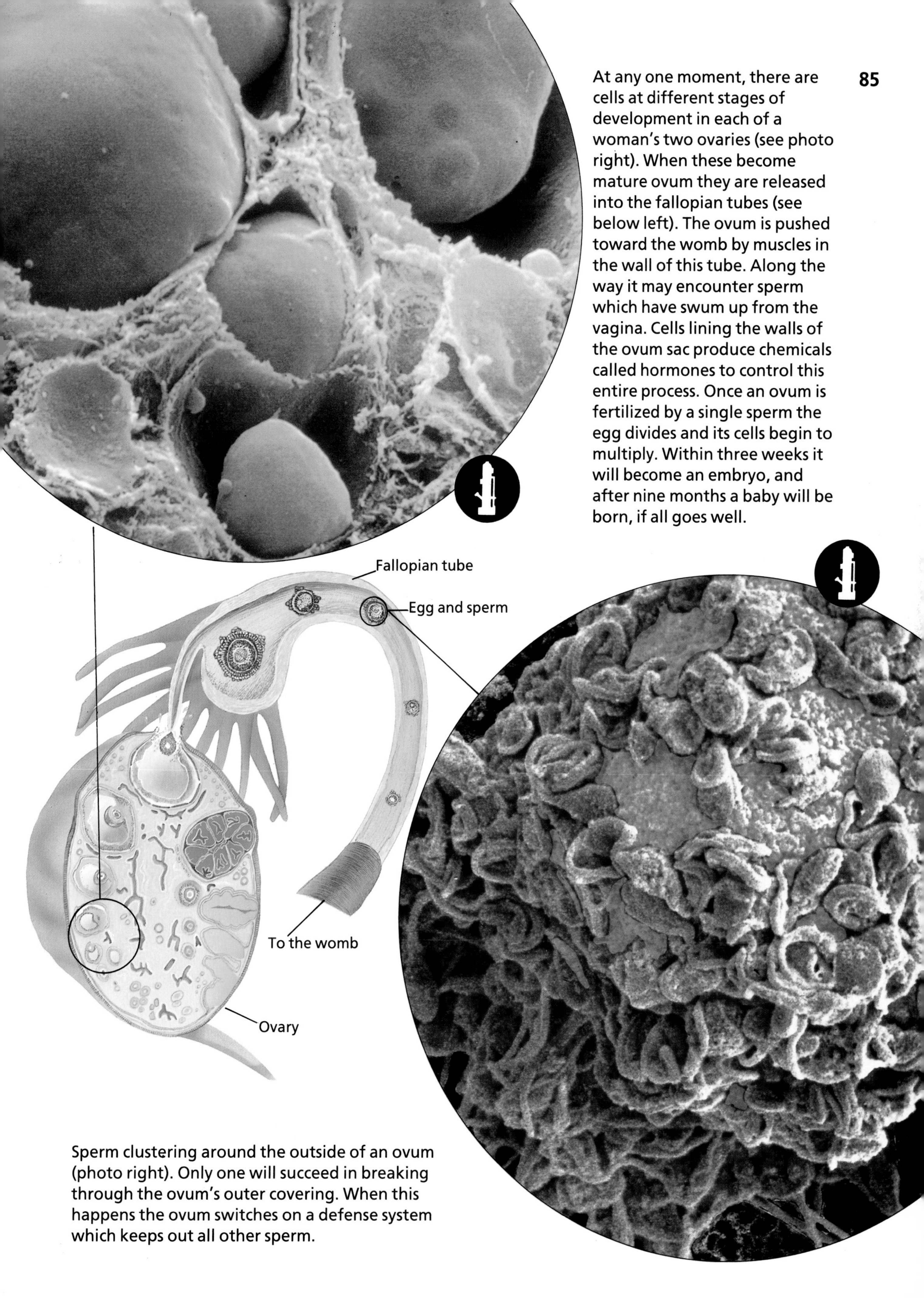

Sperm clustering around the outside of an ovum (photo right). Only one will succeed in breaking through the ovum's outer covering. When this happens the ovum switches on a defense system which keeps out all other sperm.

THE EMBRYO

No matter how different we all look from one another, we all started life in our mother's body as a ball of cells less than 1/16th inch (1mm) wide. This ball, or blastocyst, was formed by the fertilized egg dividing four of five times. With some 30 more cell divisions, the blastocyst develops into an embryo, or growing baby. Only seven weeks after a sperm and ovum join together the embryo measures about one inch (25mm) long. Most parts of its body are formed and working. The embryo receives food and oxygen from the placenta. This is an organ that develops in the womb and is connected to the embryo by the umbilical cord. Nine months after fertilization, the baby is ready to leave the mother's body.

The blastocyst is made up of about 100 cells arranged as an outer ring and an inner mass. But soon different types of cells – nerve, muscle, blood and digestive – start to develop.

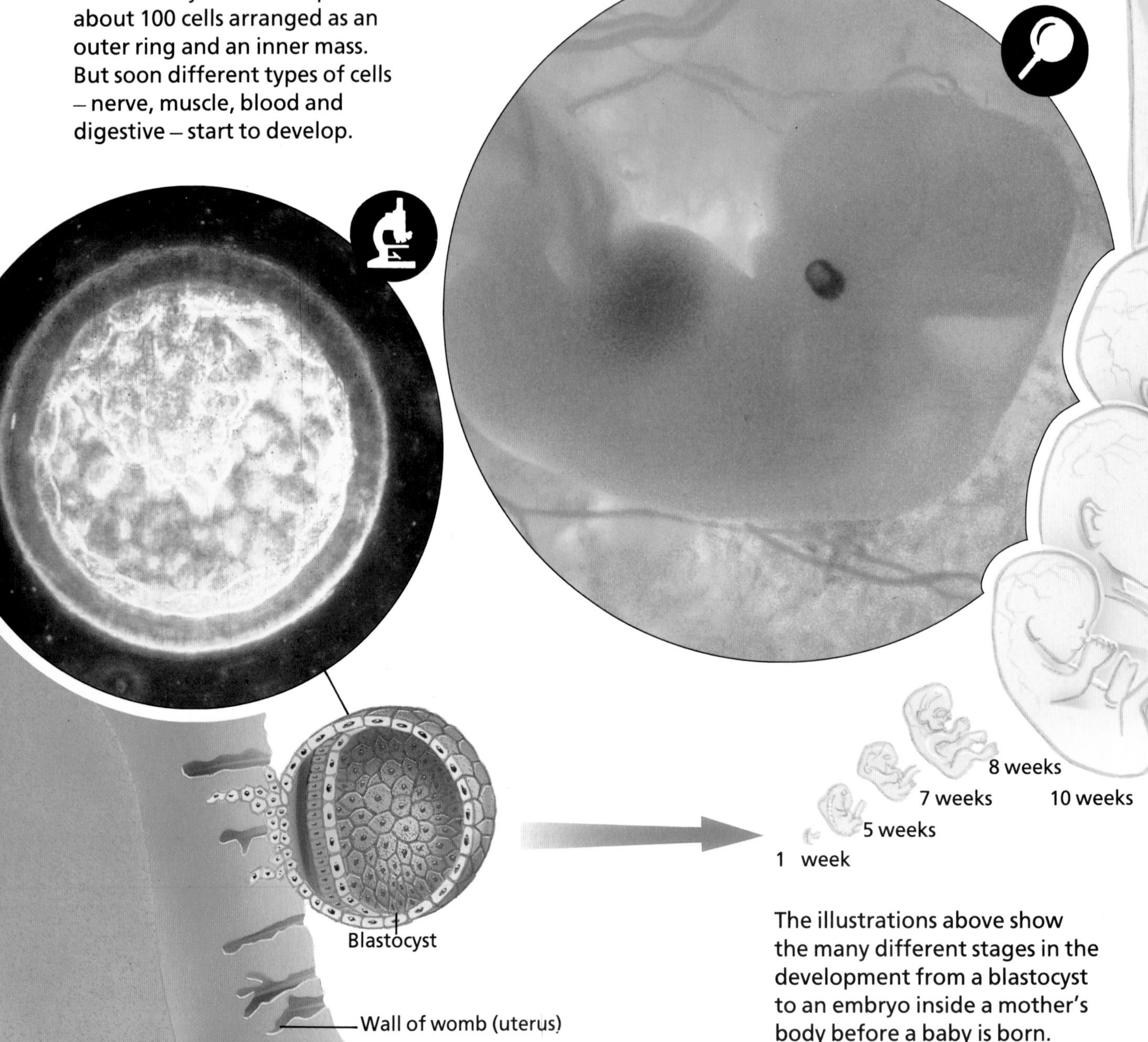

The illustrations above show the many different stages in the development from a blastocyst to an embryo inside a mother's body before a baby is born.

A fertilized ovum, called a zygote, travels slowly down the fallopian tube dividing, so that when it reaches the uterus 7 days later, it consists of many hundreds of cells. On arrival in the uterus it attacks the walls, digesting its cells and burrowing-in until it is firmly attached. After only 3 weeks the basic plan of the body has developed – the head, the skin, the digestive tube, muscle, and bone are all in place. By 7 weeks, the embryo has arms and legs and looks like a tiny person (photo below). After 5 months, the infant is 1 foot (30cm) long from top to toe, and weighs 1.5 pounds (681g). It can now grip with its hands, wriggle its toes, and open and close its eyelids. At the age of 9 months it consists of 20,000 million cells, measures 20 inches (50cm) long and weighs 7 pounds (3.3kg).

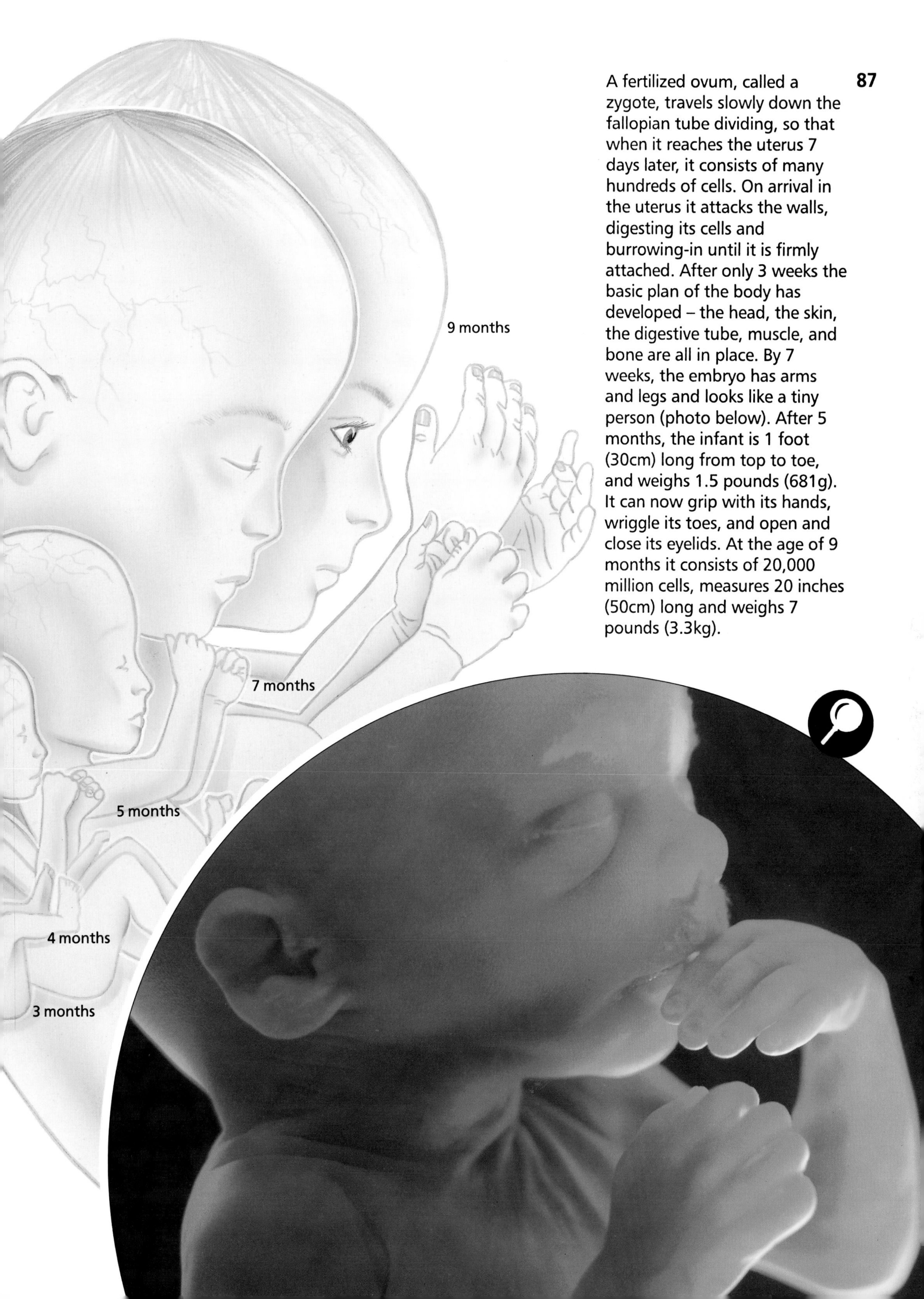

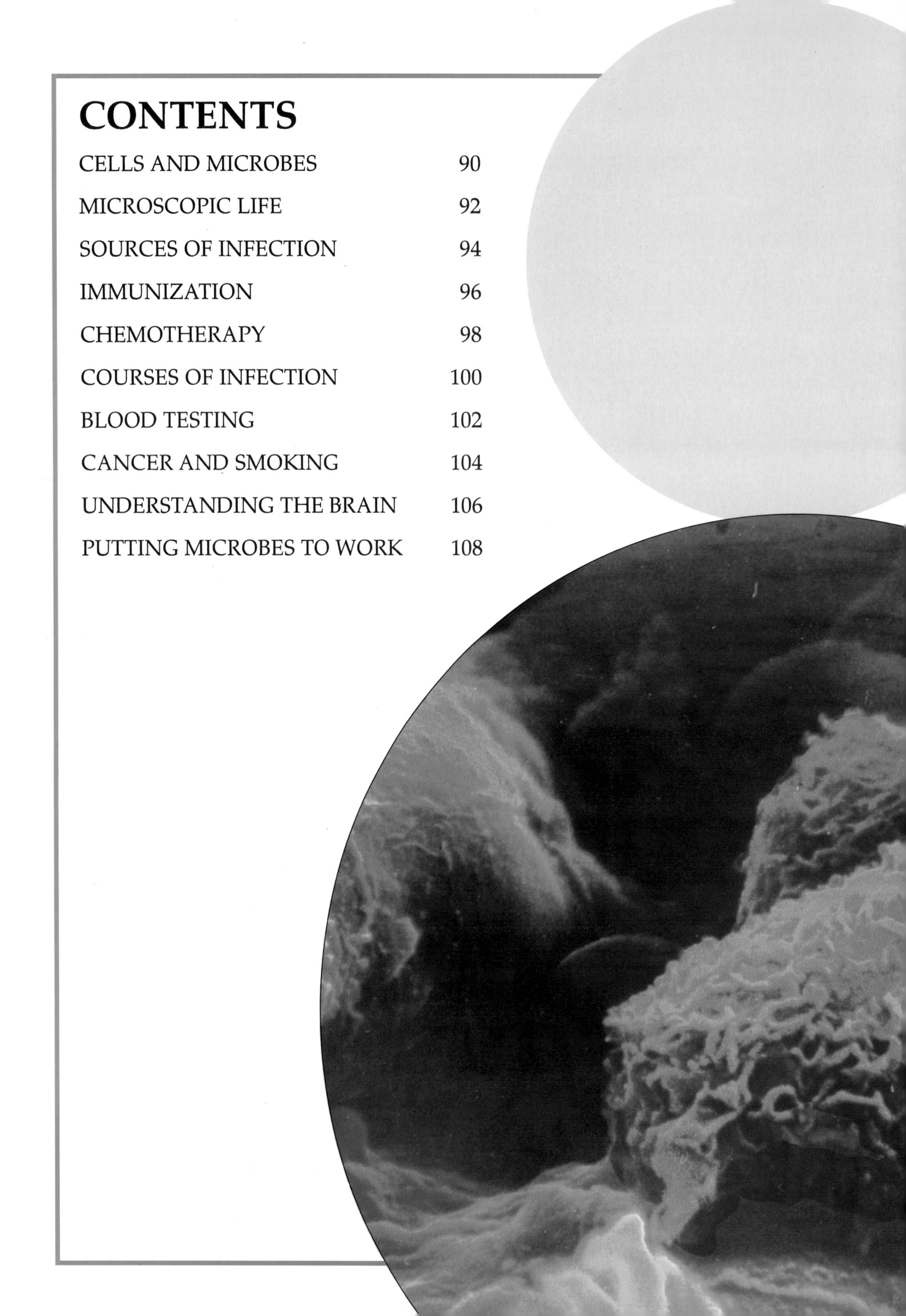

CONTENTS

Frontiers of Medicine

Lionel Bender

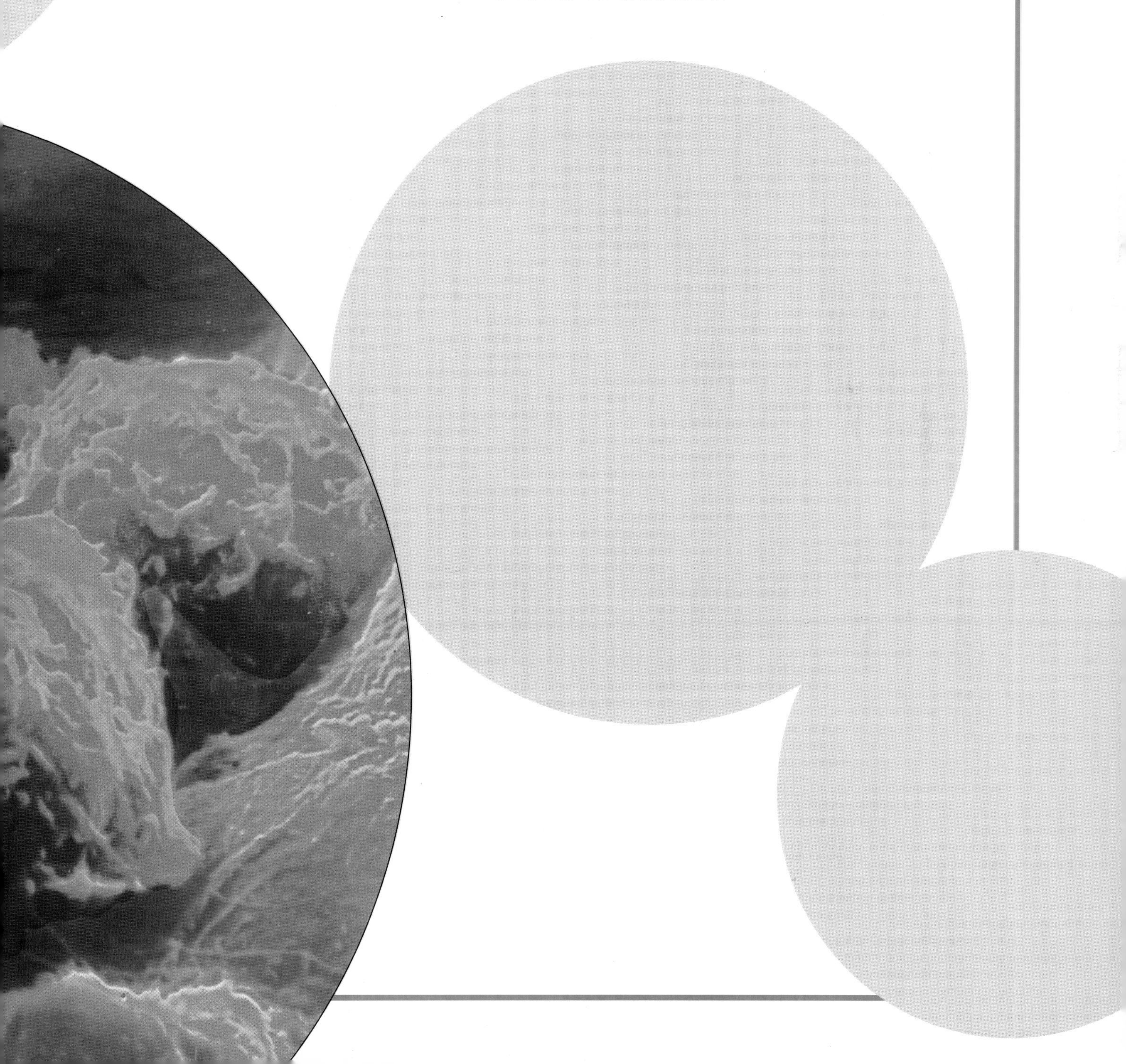

CELLS AND MICROBES

The foundations of modern medicine were laid in ancient Greece when Hippocrates (460-377 B.C.) developed a system called "diagnosis." This is the way doctors use examination and reason to decide what is wrong with a patient. But it was not until a Dutchman named Antonie van Leeuwenhoek (1632-1723) studied tiny creatures from his mouth with a single-lens microscope that microbes, some of which cause diseases, were recorded (see diagram on left). Soon afterward, an Englishman, Robert Hooke (1635-1703), used more elaborate microscopes to prove that all living things are made up of tiny cells; and an Italian, Marcello Malpighi (1629-64), made the first microscopic studies of human body organs.

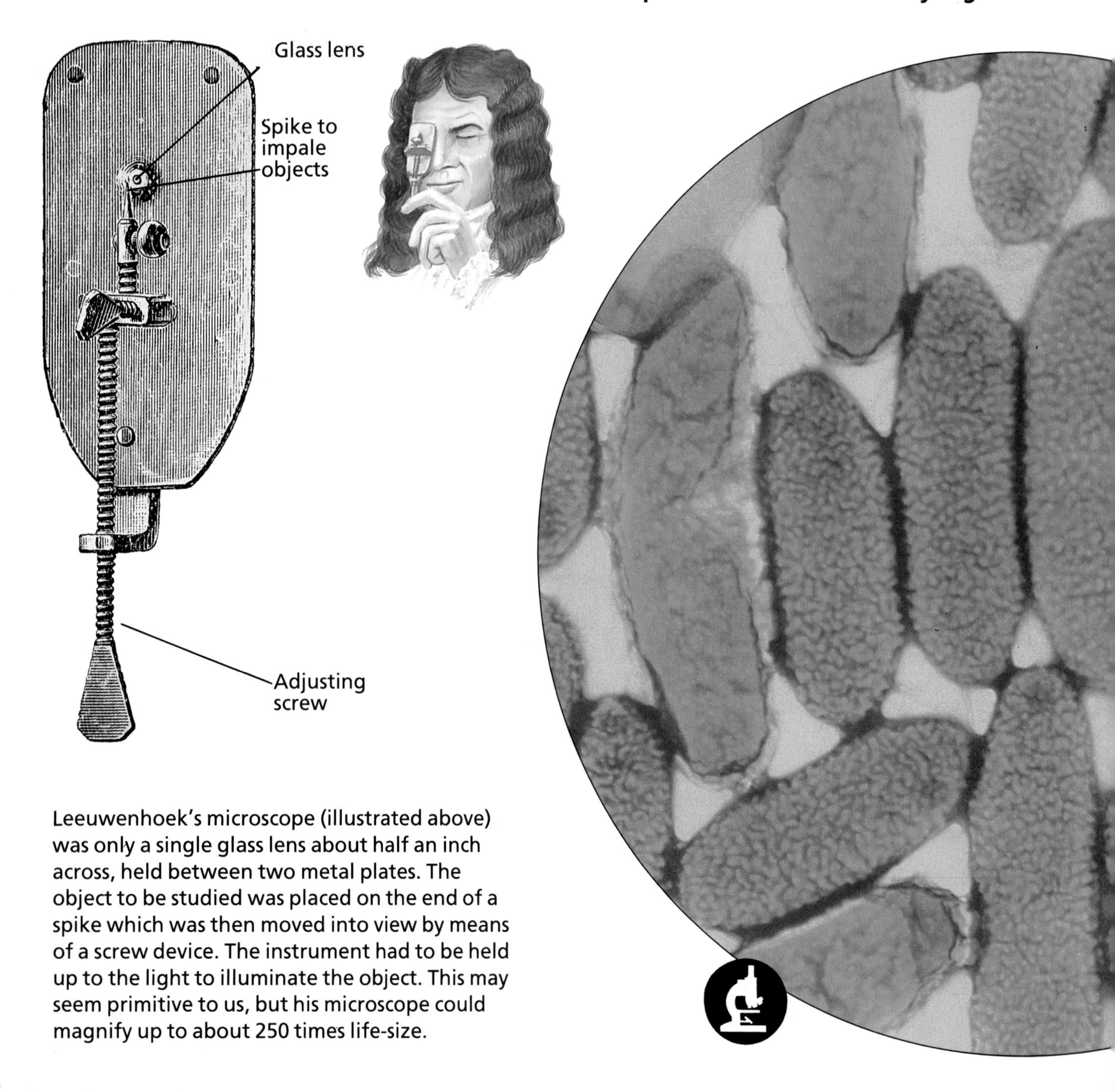

Leeuwenhoek's microscope (illustrated above) was only a single glass lens about half an inch across, held between two metal plates. The object to be studied was placed on the end of a spike which was then moved into view by means of a screw device. The instrument had to be held up to the light to illuminate the object. This may seem primitive to us, but his microscope could magnify up to about 250 times life-size.

Antonie van Leeuwenhoek was one of the first people to make a microscopic study of the everyday world. The photo below-left shows the cells of a fern plant seen through a modern copy of Leeuwenhoek's simple microscope.

Robert Hooke studied plant cells and tiny bacteria like those in the photo below-right, magnified × 5,270. The bacteria shown here cause Legionnaires' disease. However, neither Leeuwenhoek nor Hooke realized the importance of their observations to medical science.

Robert Hooke's "compound" microscope (below) had three lenses. A "condenser" concentrated light onto the object, which was magnified by a small "objective" lens. The magnified image was viewed with the "eyepiece" lens.

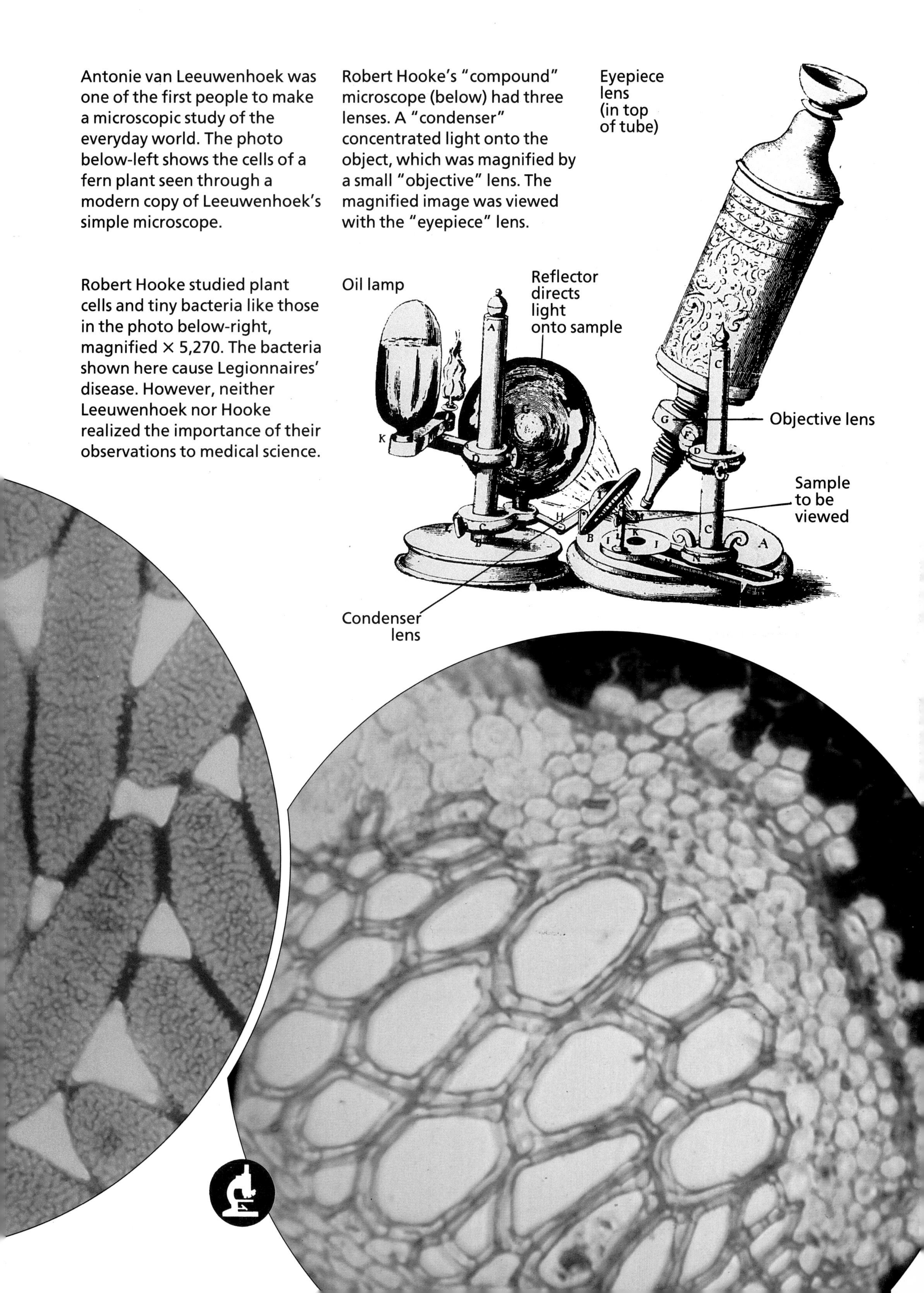

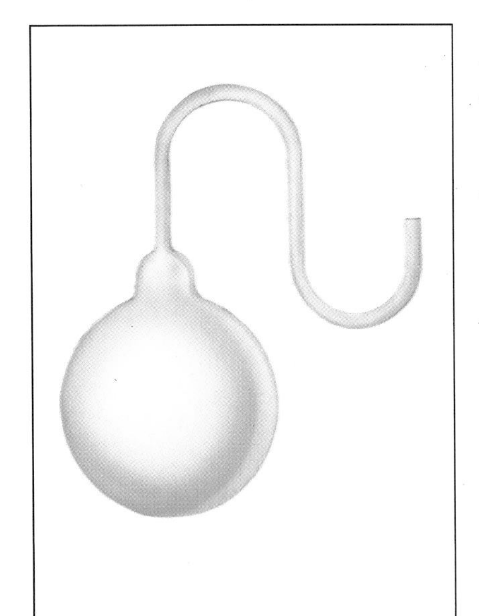

MICROSCOPIC LIFE

For over 100 years after the discoveries made with the first microscopes, people still believed that small creatures just sprang to life in soil, air or water. So it was thought that maggots, one stage in the life cycle of houseflies, simply grew out of meat. It took the great French scientist Louis Pasteur (1822-1895) to confirm that tiny living things come from existing ones. He did this by heating broth, which bacteria would normally have spoiled within a few days, inside a "gooseneck" flask (see diagram left). The heat killed off any bacteria, and the shape of the neck prevented any new ones from entering in the air. A similar process, called pasteurization, is still used to kill harmful bacteria in the milk we drink.

The life cycle of the housefly (illustrated right) was first established by an Italian called Francesco Redi (1626-1697). He proved that the adult flies laid microscopic eggs in meat and that maggots (magnified ×3,000 below) hatch from them.

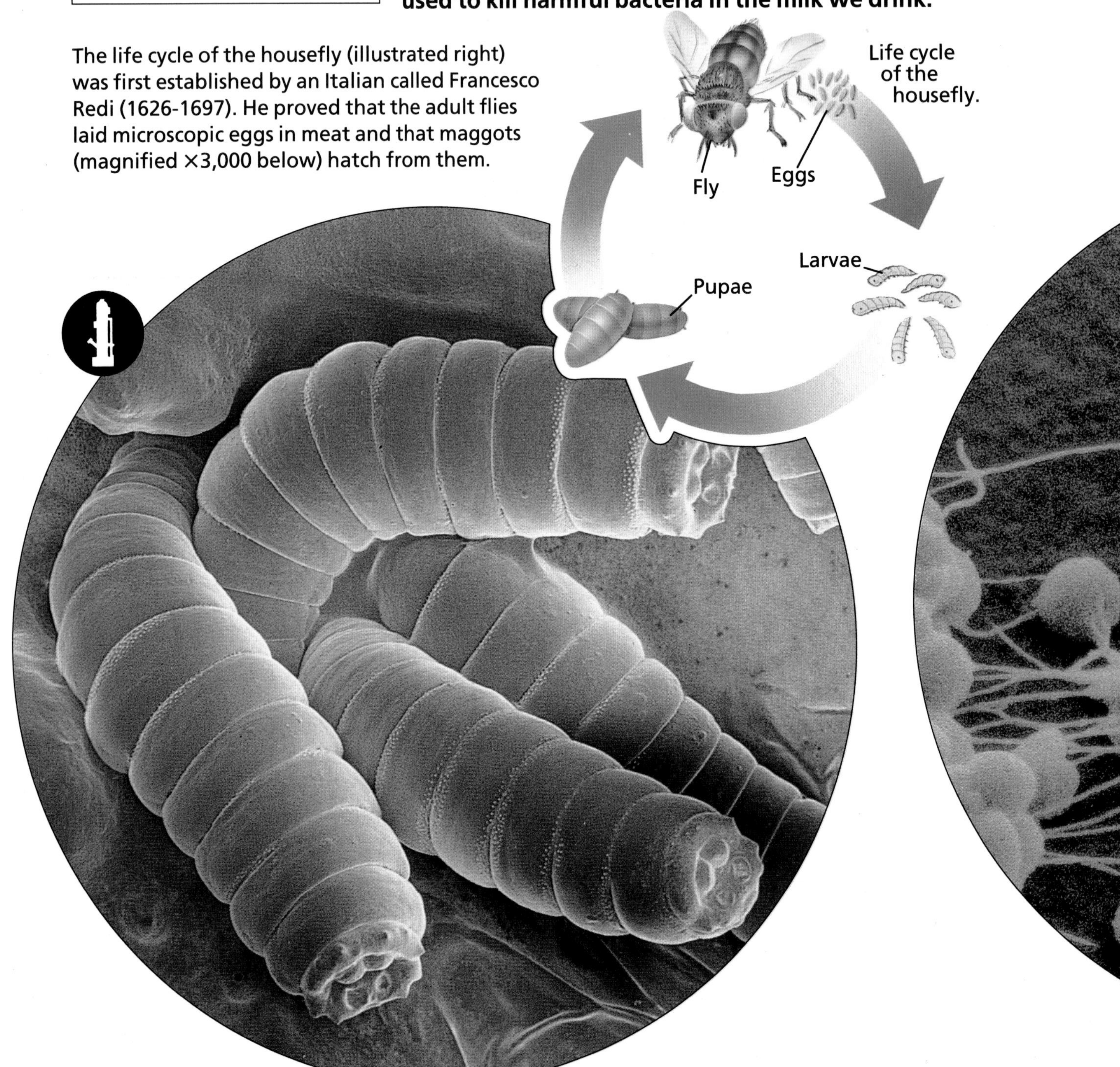

In medical laboratories where the cause of a disease is sought, saliva, urine, or blood from the patient is spread on a layer of food material in a glass or plastic dish. The food and dish are first sterilized (heated to a high temperature to kill all microbes) and allowed to cool. The chosen body fluid is then placed on the food, where any bacteria present grow, multiply in their millions, and form colonies like those on the right. The bacteria shown here cause the disease anthrax. If no bacteria are put on the food and no air – which may carry bacteria – is allowed to enter the dish, no colonies appear.

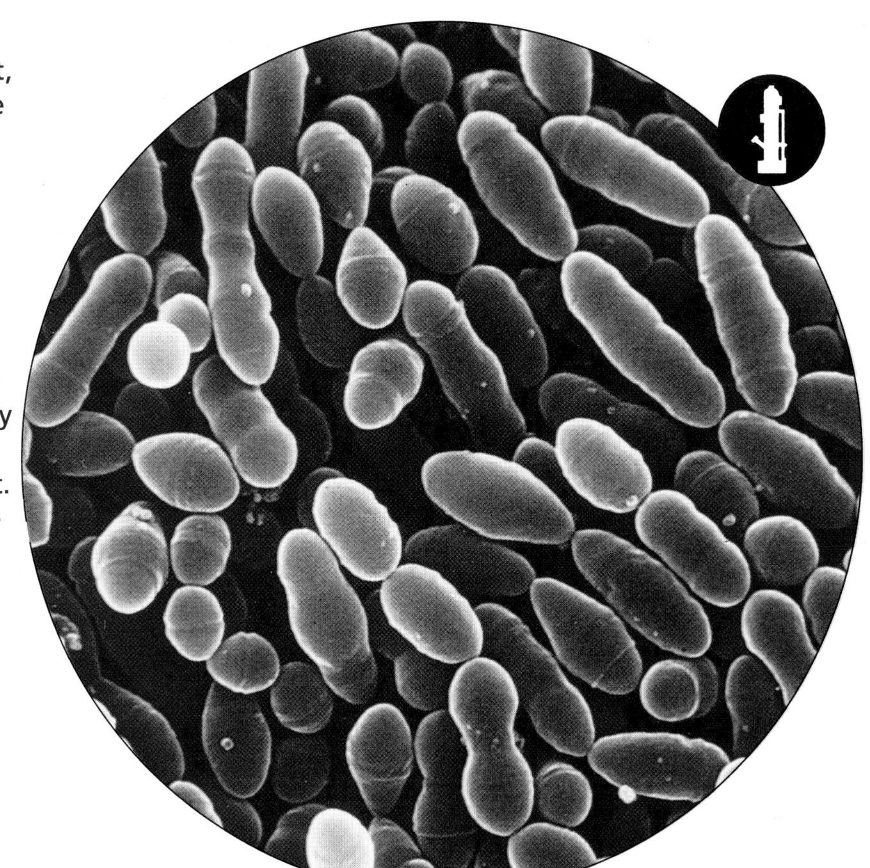

A German scientist, Theodor Schwann (1810-1882), used the experiment below to prove that air would not cause fermentation in grape juice all by itself. His microscope showed that the growth of tiny yeast cells in the juice caused fermentation. Louis Pasteur used a similar experiment to show that bacteria exist in the air. The bacteria shown left (× 16,500) are often present in air and can cause throat infections.

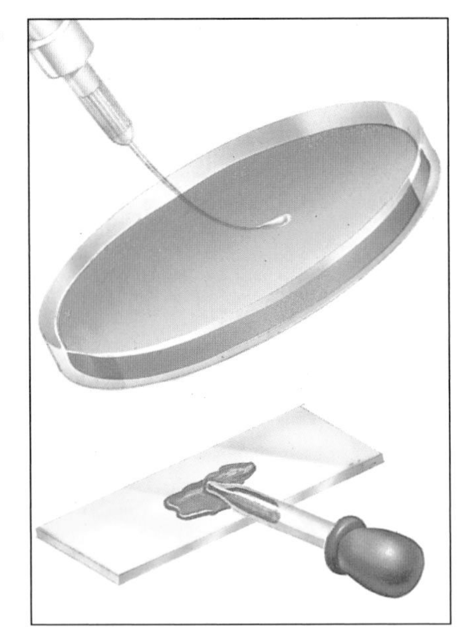

SOURCES OF INFECTION

In the 1790s an English doctor named Edward Jenner (1749-1823) experimented with inoculating people with a small quantity of cowpox virus in order to prevent infections of smallpox. However, like most people of his day, he never thought that microscopic creatures, which we call germs, were the cause of disease. Louis Pasteur was the first to prove their involvement. He also used a microscope to discover that some microbes survived by living in or on others. These creatures, known as parasites, can produce dangerous diseases such as anthrax, which kills people as well as other animals. Another example of a parasite is the rat-flea, which can carry the germs that cause bubonic plague in its gut.

Bacteria, which grow in colonies on food material (photo right), are just one type of microbe or microorganism. Others include viruses, protozoa and some fungi and algae. "Germs" are disease-producing microbes. Viruses are tiny organisms which can only survive inside the cells of other creatures.

The image below shows the bacterium *Treponema pallidum* (magnified × 8,700) which causes the disease known as syphilis.

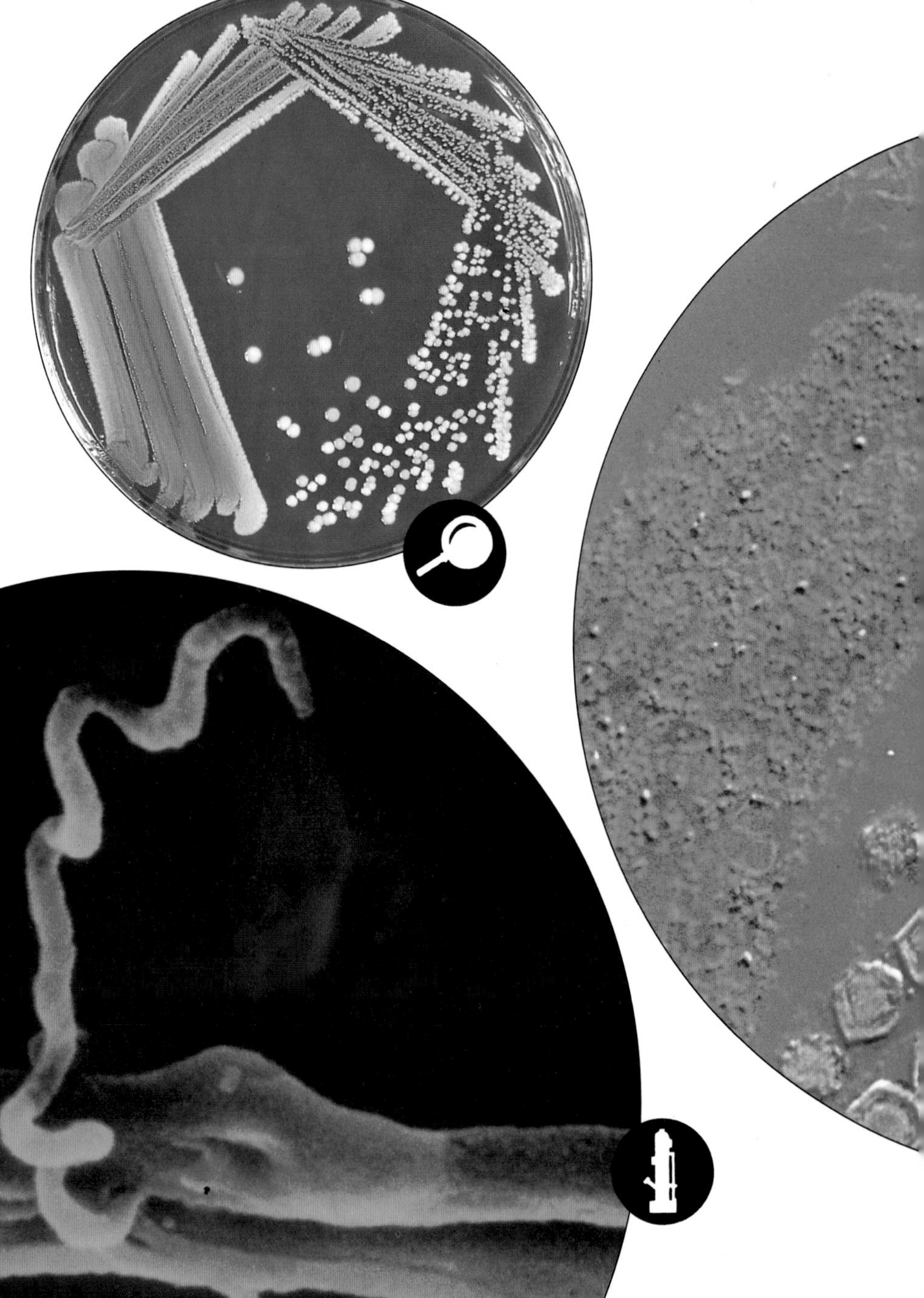

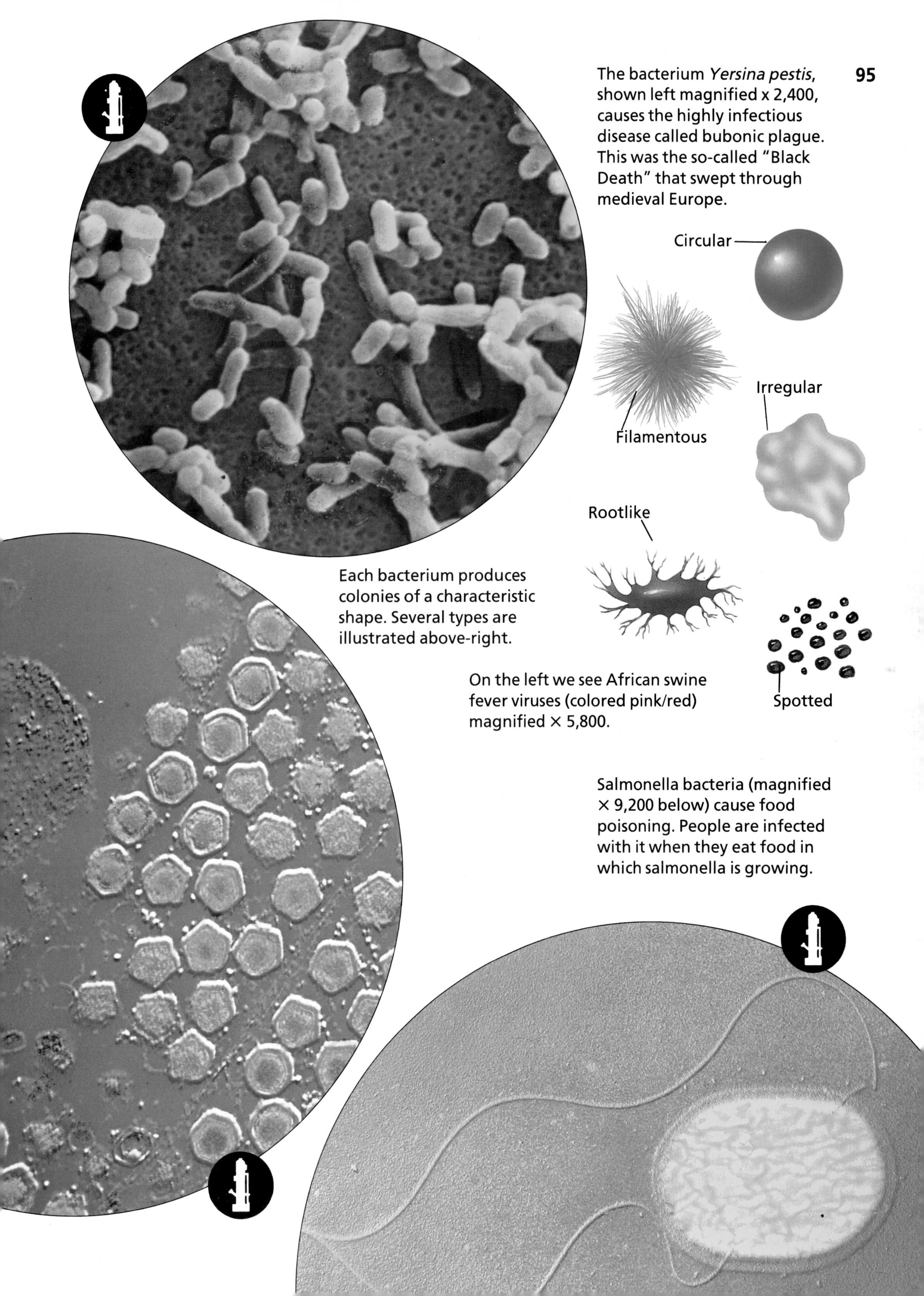

The bacterium *Yersina pestis*, shown left magnified x 2,400, causes the highly infectious disease called bubonic plague. This was the so-called "Black Death" that swept through medieval Europe.

Each bacterium produces colonies of a characteristic shape. Several types are illustrated above-right.

On the left we see African swine fever viruses (colored pink/red) magnified × 5,800.

Salmonella bacteria (magnified × 9,200 below) cause food poisoning. People are infected with it when they eat food in which salmonella is growing.

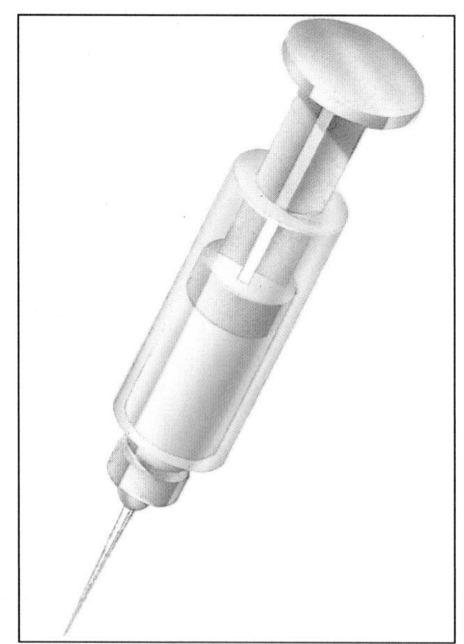

IMMUNIZATION

In spite of Pasteur's discovery of germs, 19th-century doctors were not sure why Edward Jenner's inoculations against smallpox worked. But they understood that the body has a natural defense, or "immune," system that can be improved. When a weak solution of a germ is injected into the body using a syringe (shown left) it gives the body the ability to combat the disease later on. This "immunization" was obvious even though microscopes at the time were not powerful enough to show the viruses. A German doctor called Robert Koch (1834-1910) made great progress in the battle against the diseases anthrax, cholera and tuberculosis. Koch grew their bacteria in his laboratory and proved how they caused the diseases.

Rabies, shown left magnified × 36,700, is a deadly virus that spreads from animals to people.

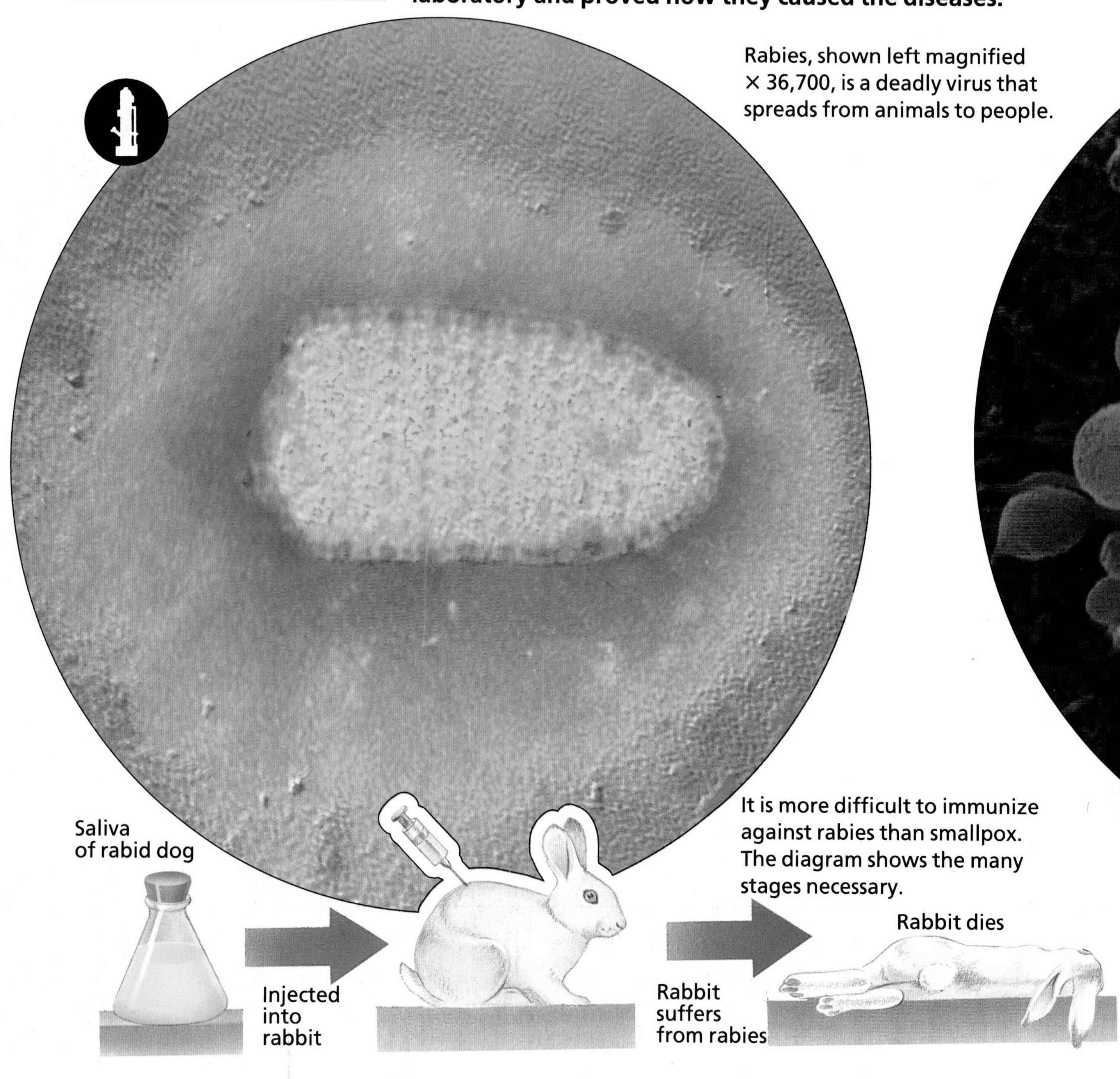

It is more difficult to immunize against rabies than smallpox. The diagram shows the many stages necessary.

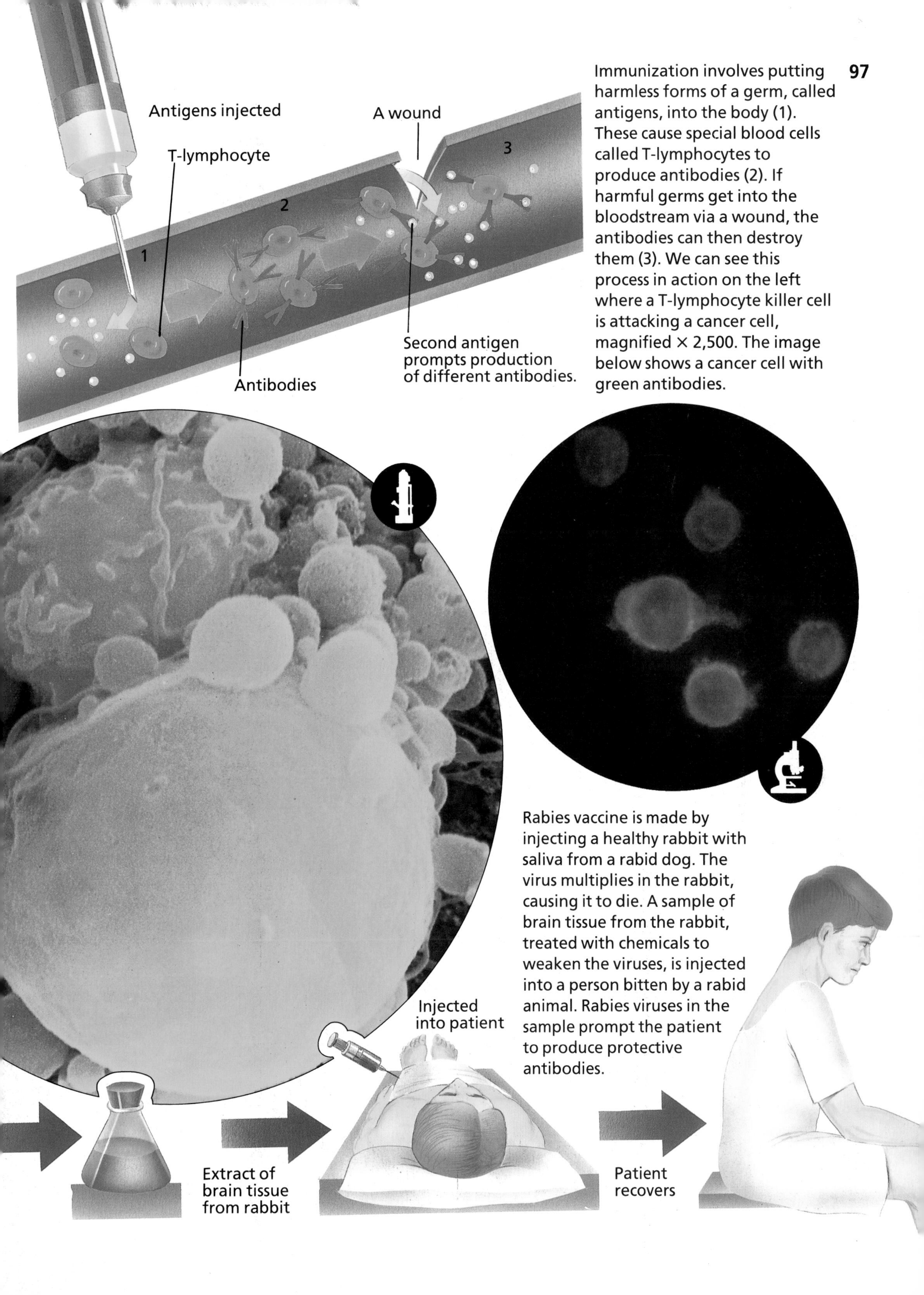

Immunization involves putting harmless forms of a germ, called antigens, into the body (1). These cause special blood cells called T-lymphocytes to produce antibodies (2). If harmful germs get into the bloodstream via a wound, the antibodies can then destroy them (3). We can see this process in action on the left where a T-lymphocyte killer cell is attacking a cancer cell, magnified × 2,500. The image below shows a cancer cell with green antibodies.

Rabies vaccine is made by injecting a healthy rabbit with saliva from a rabid dog. The virus multiplies in the rabbit, causing it to die. A sample of brain tissue from the rabbit, treated with chemicals to weaken the viruses, is injected into a person bitten by a rabid animal. Rabies viruses in the sample prompt the patient to produce protective antibodies.

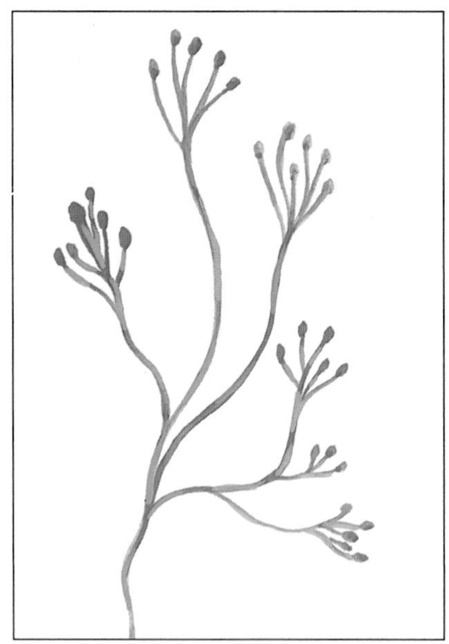

CHEMOTHERAPY

Chemotherapy, the treatment of diseases with chemicals, began in the 1900s. Scientists discovered the bacteria that cause tetanus, typhoid and syphilis, and looked for ways of destroying germs in patients without harming healthy tissues and organs. In 1910, German scientist Paul Ehrlich (1854-1915) made the first such "magic bullet," Salvarsan, a chemical that kills the bacteria causing syphilis. In 1928, Scottish scientist Alexander Fleming (1881-1955) accidentally discovered an antibiotic – a chemical produced by one type of microbe that destroys others – when he noticed that a fungus, *Penicillium* (shown left), had contaminated samples of bacteria grown on dishes and killed the bacteria.

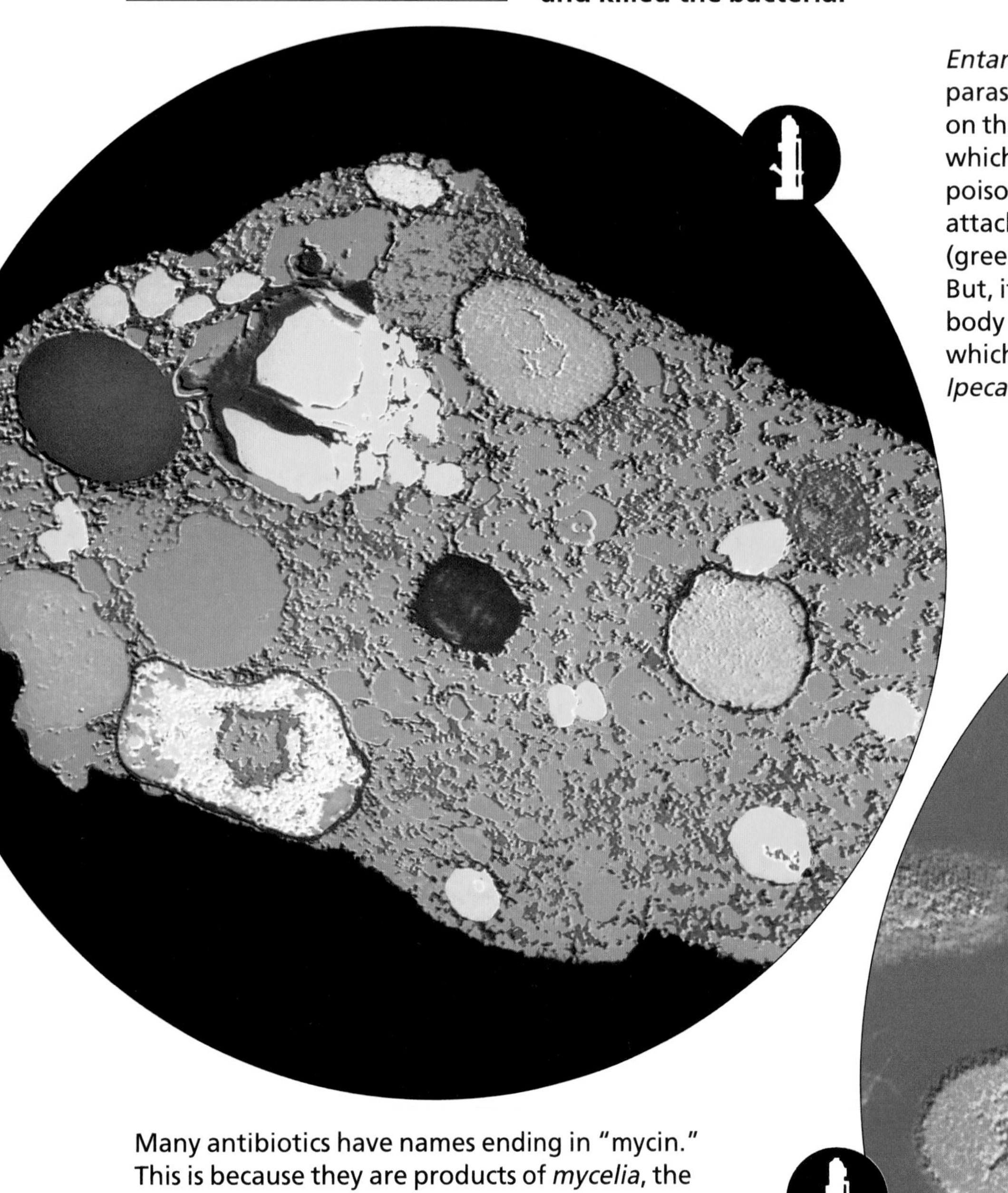

Entamoeba histolytica is a parasite (shown as yellow spots on the left magnified x 880) which causes a type of food poisoning. Inside the body, it attacks and eats red blood cells (green ovals in the the photo). But, it can be destroyed in the body by the chemical *emetine*, which is made from a plant, *Ipecacuanha*.

Many antibiotics have names ending in "mycin." This is because they are products of *mycelia*, the threadlike structures of fungi. One of these, *streptomycin*, is used to combat the bacteria which cause bubonic plague (right x 10,500).

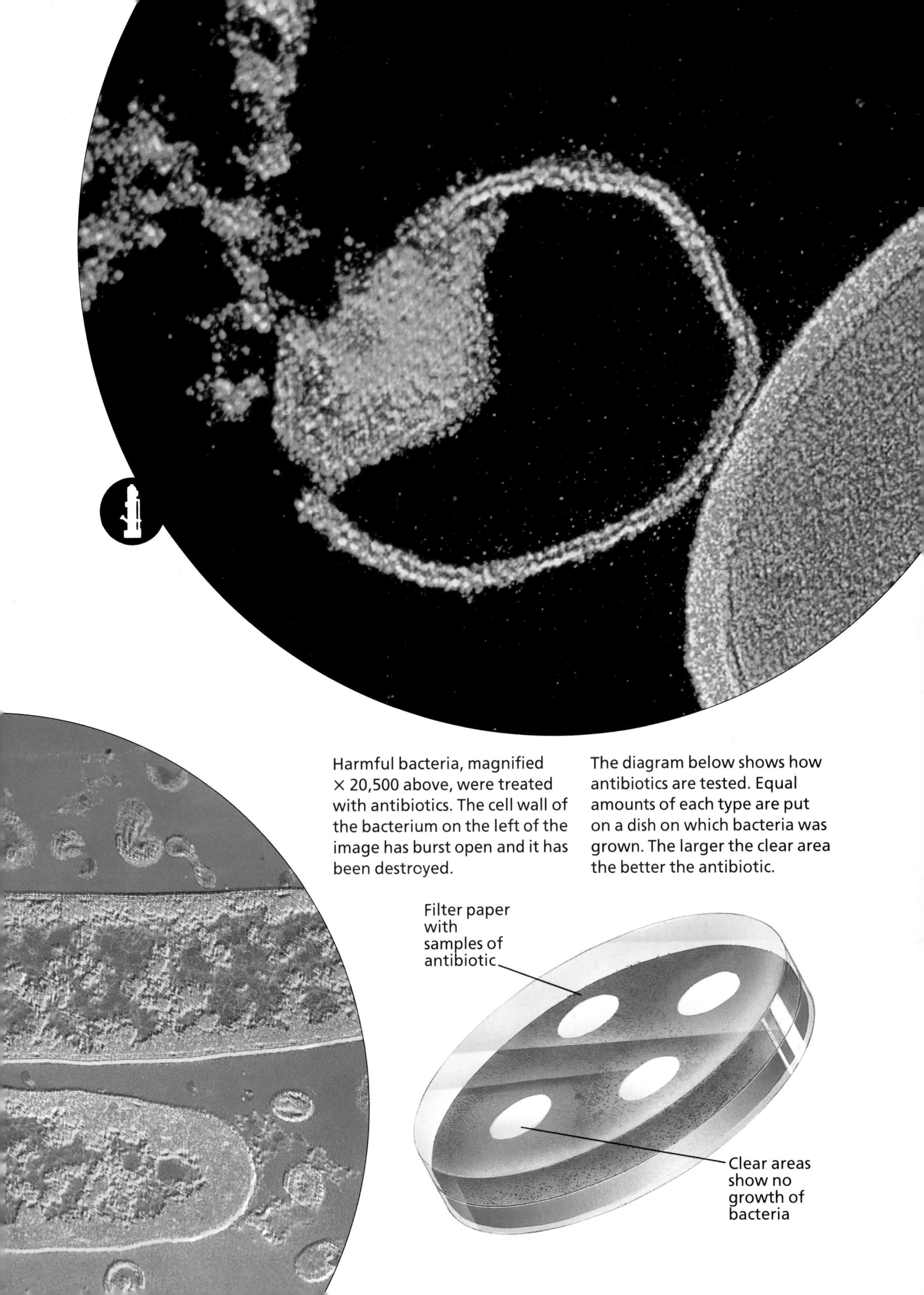

Harmful bacteria, magnified × 20,500 above, were treated with antibiotics. The cell wall of the bacterium on the left of the image has burst open and it has been destroyed.

The diagram below shows how antibiotics are tested. Equal amounts of each type are put on a dish on which bacteria was grown. The larger the clear area the better the antibiotic.

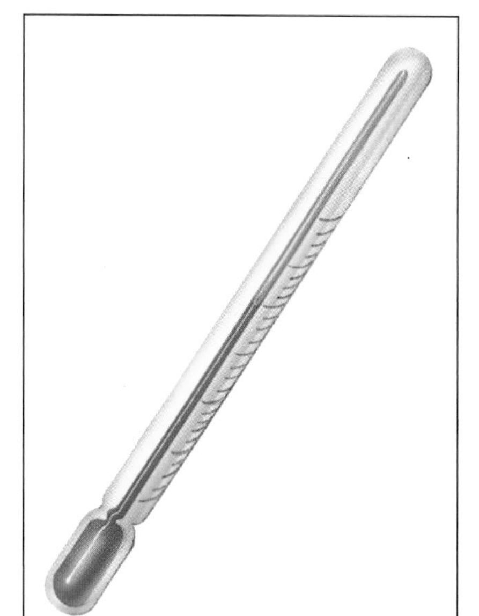

COURSES OF INFECTION

As the diagram below shows, germs can enter the body in a variety of everyday ways. Once inside, they may grow and multiply. For the first few hours or days of infection the person shows no symptoms (signs) of the disease. Then, as the microbes reach high numbers and produce more of their own chemicals, the person could develop a high temperature, headache, upset stomach, and so on. The body's natural defenses combat the germs and usually overcome them after a few days, but sometimes the microbes can go on to cause serious harm. Using a thermometer, a doctor can check how well the body's natural defenses, or the medicines which have been taken, are keeping down the patient's temperature.

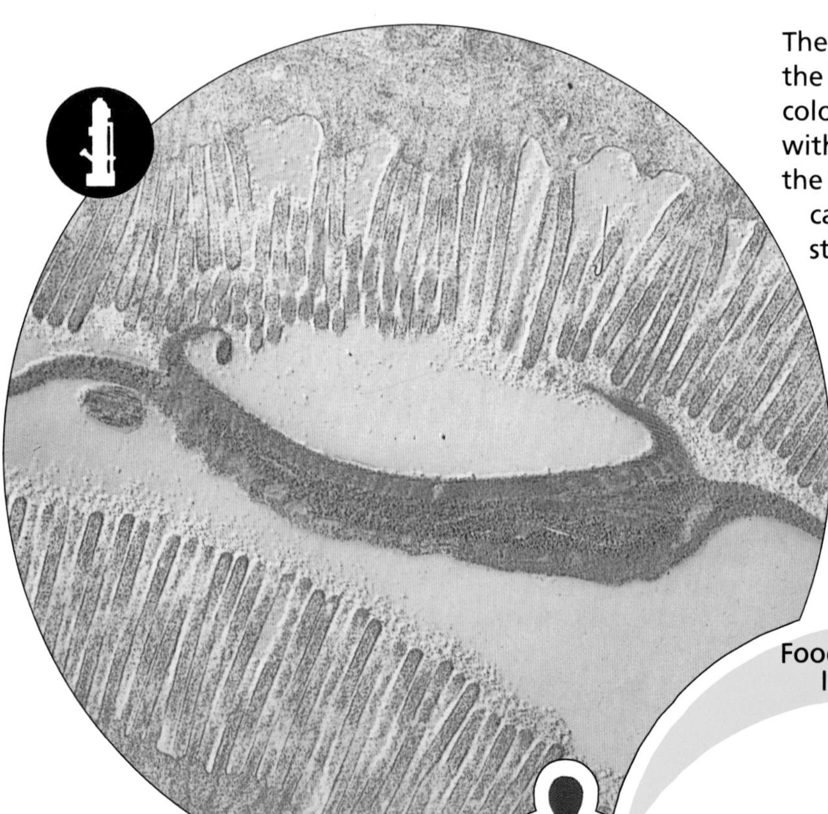

The protozoan in the image on the left, magnified × 1190 and colored green, enters the body with food. It attaches itself to the inside of the intestines and can cause a nasty stomachache.

Food and water – Indirect

Direct contact Touching, kissing and sneezing

Insects and microscopic organisms

Infected person

Healthy person

Animal source

The diagram right shows the three main ways in which disease-causing microbes pass from an infected person to a healthy one. It also shows how diseases pass from wild animals to people. Diseases transmitted, or passed on, in food and water include cholera and salmonella. Some microbes multiply within insects and are passed on. Others are carried on the insect's body.

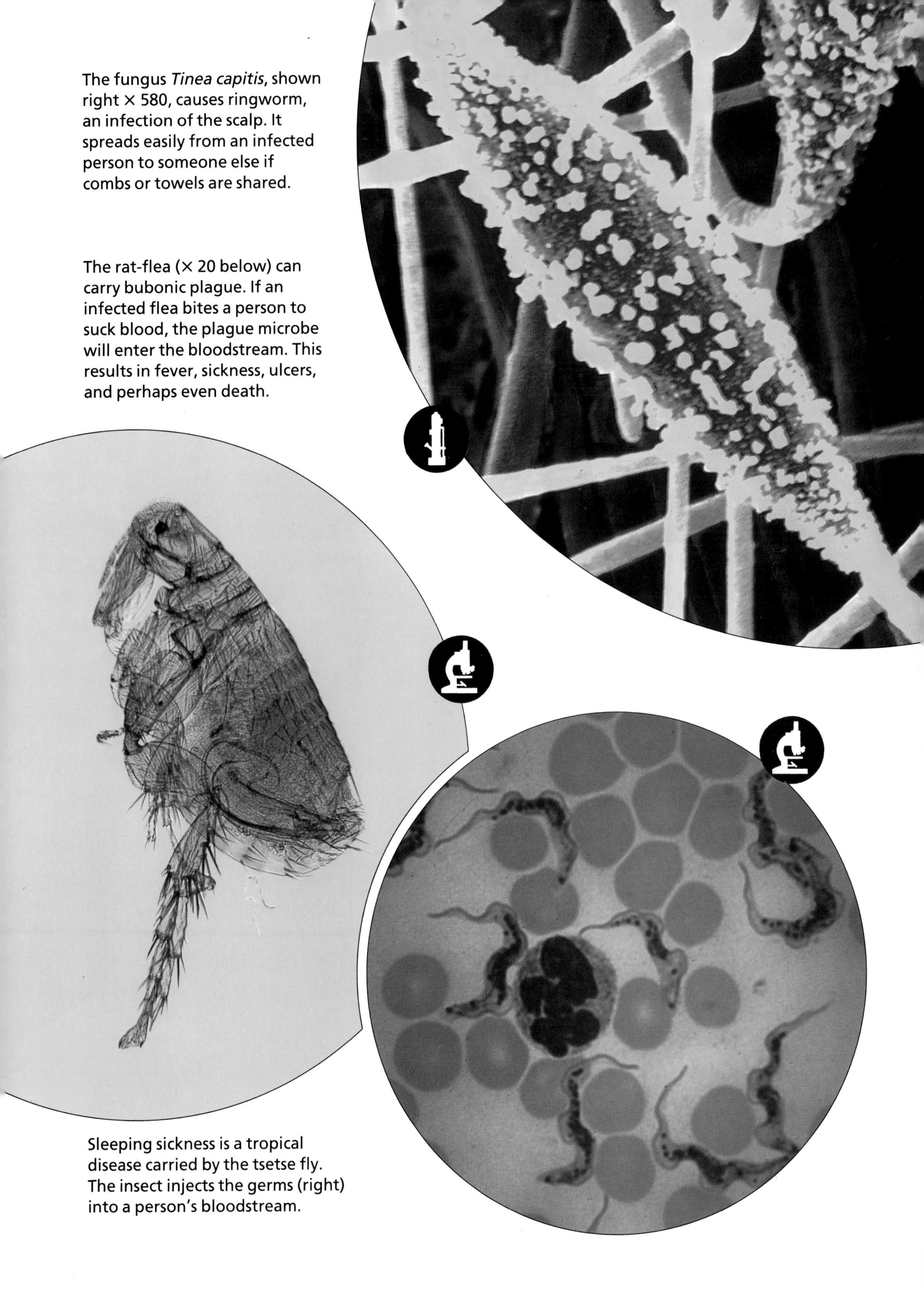

The fungus *Tinea capitis*, shown right × 580, causes ringworm, an infection of the scalp. It spreads easily from an infected person to someone else if combs or towels are shared.

The rat-flea (× 20 below) can carry bubonic plague. If an infected flea bites a person to suck blood, the plague microbe will enter the bloodstream. This results in fever, sickness, ulcers, and perhaps even death.

Sleeping sickness is a tropical disease carried by the tsetse fly. The insect injects the germs (right) into a person's bloodstream.

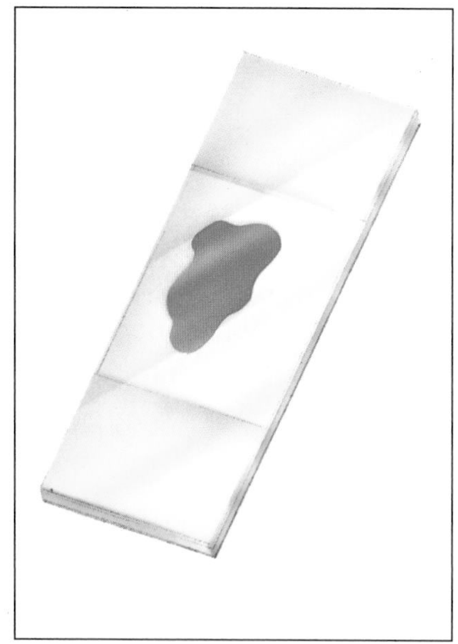

BLOOD TESTING

Blood testing is used to search for the cause of a disease, or to determine the correct type of blood for transfusions. Transfusions are needed to give blood to a sick person or to one who has lost blood due to an injury or during surgery. The donor's and the recipient's blood must match. To look for microbes in blood, a small sample – from a pin-prick – is smeared onto a microscope slide, as shown left. Doctors may then be able to see the protozoan responsible for malaria or the bacterium causing typhoid. They may also find clues about a patient's ill health. For example, a low number of red blood cells shows the patient may be suffering from lack of vitamin B or iron in their diet.

White blood cells ×3,450 (colored dark-blue in the computer image below) travel in the bloodstream. They gobble up invading microbes and produce antibodies.

A healthy person has up to 10,000 white cells in each cubic millimeter of blood. A person with leukemia, a cancer of the blood, may have up to 600,000.

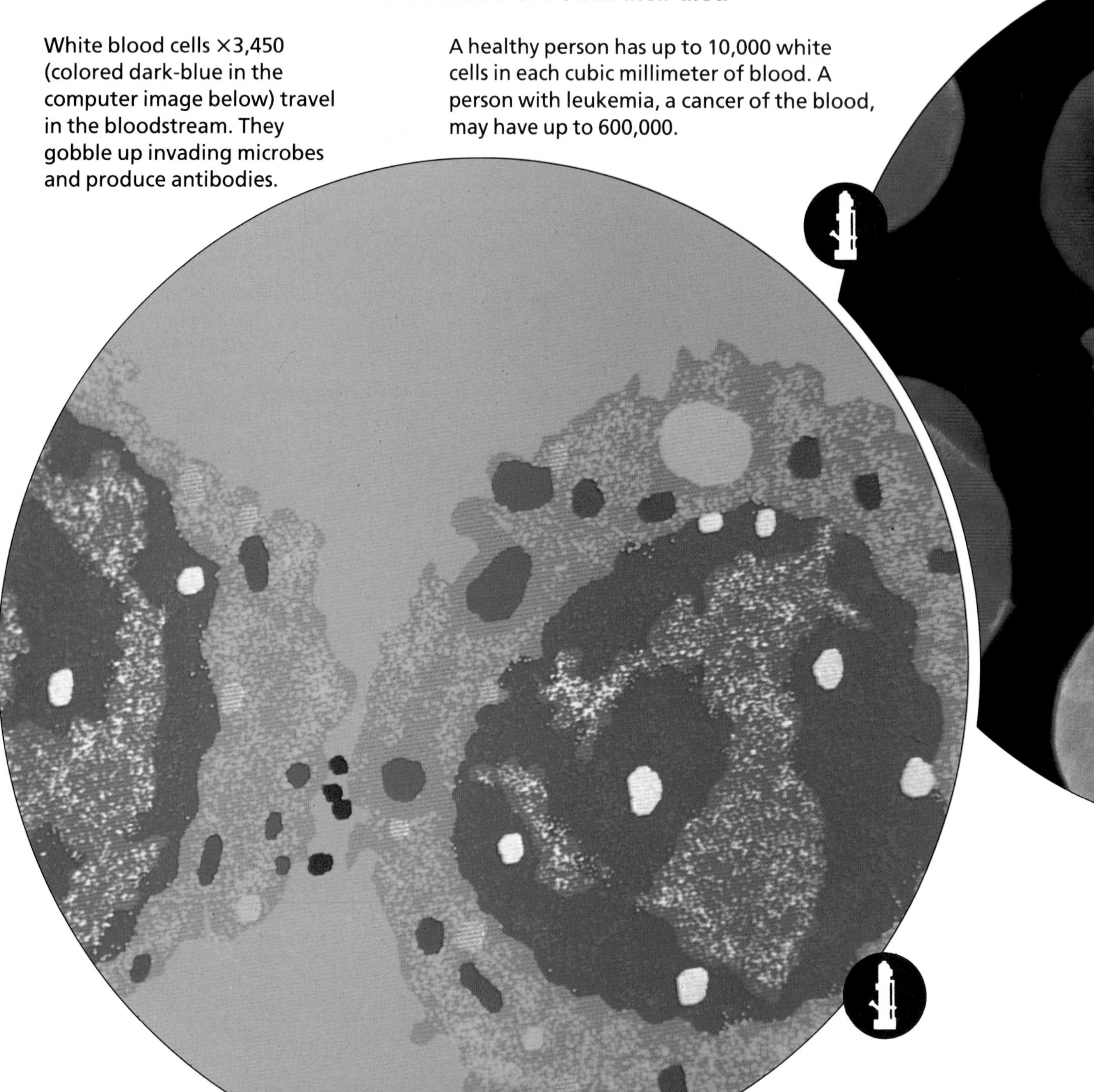

Red blood cells (x1,000 below) carry chemicals on their surface that act like antigens (see page 97). In the normal ABO blood groups, each serum, or blood fluid, is different. Some possess antibodies against the antigens, but others do not. The test for blood grouping is recorded in the diagram on the right. If a blood sample tested with anti-A serum results in blood cells clumping, the person is group A, and so on with each group.

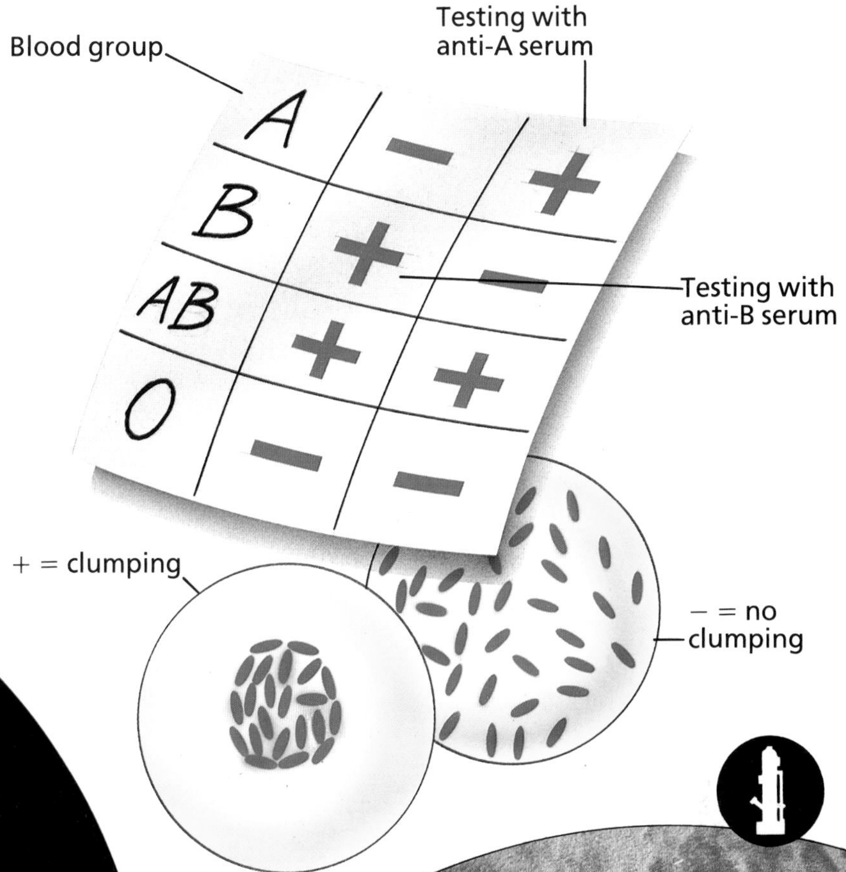

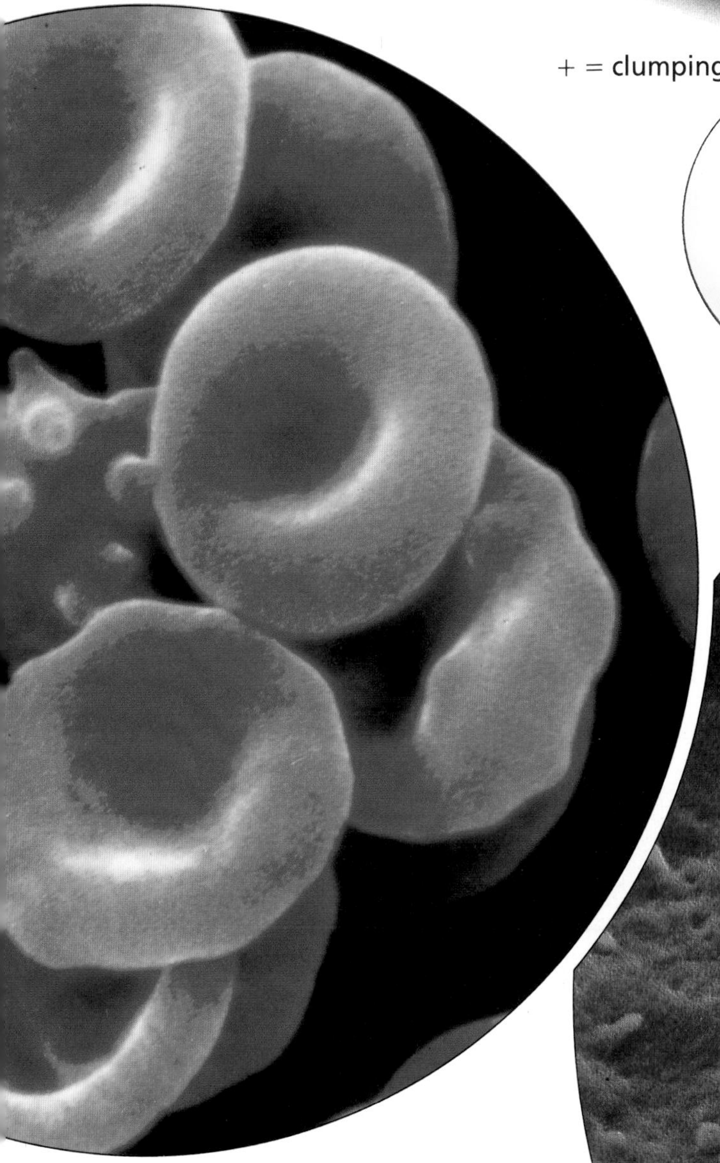

Under an electron microscope, a white blood cell (× 3,450 in the image on the right) can be seen squeezing through the wall of a vein in order to attack an invading microbe.

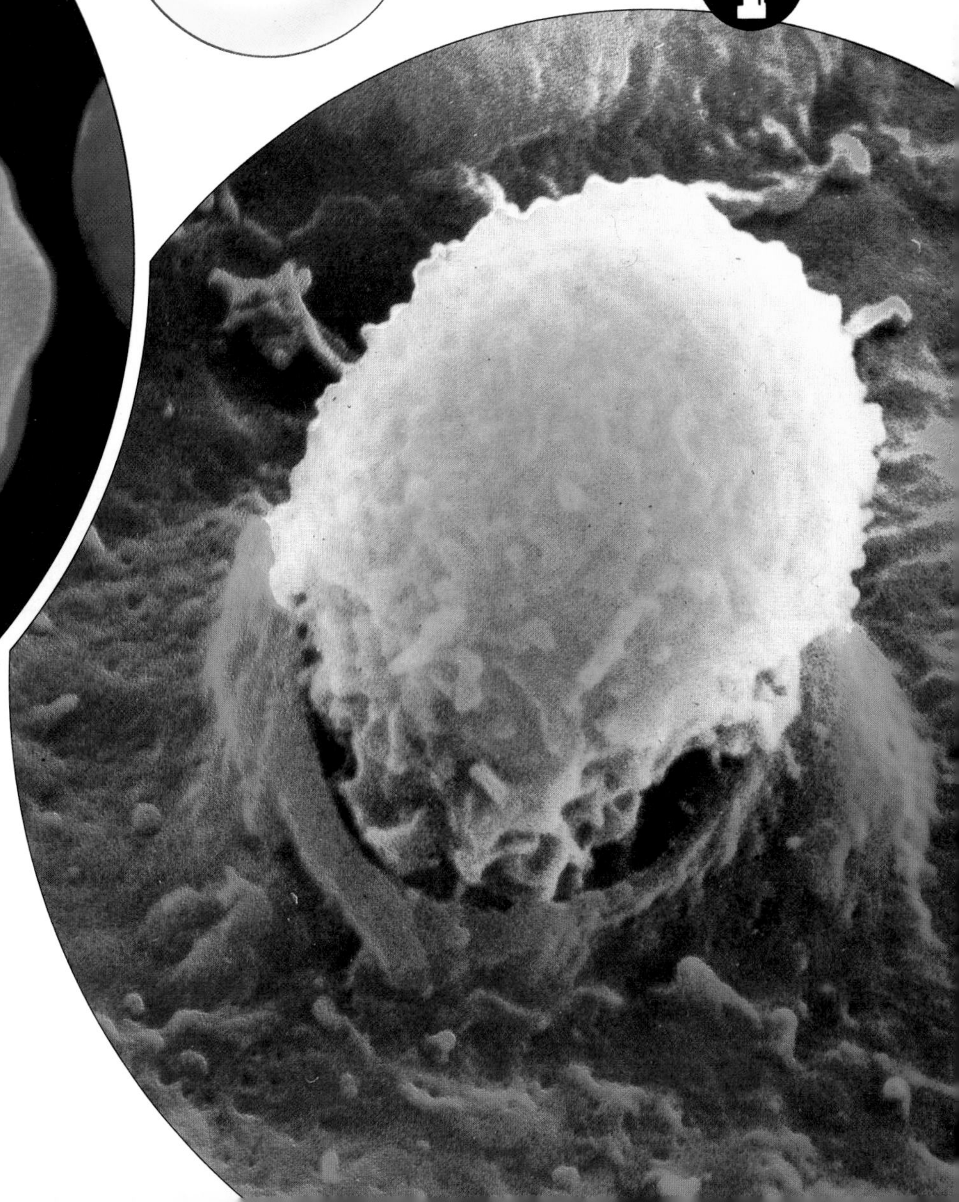

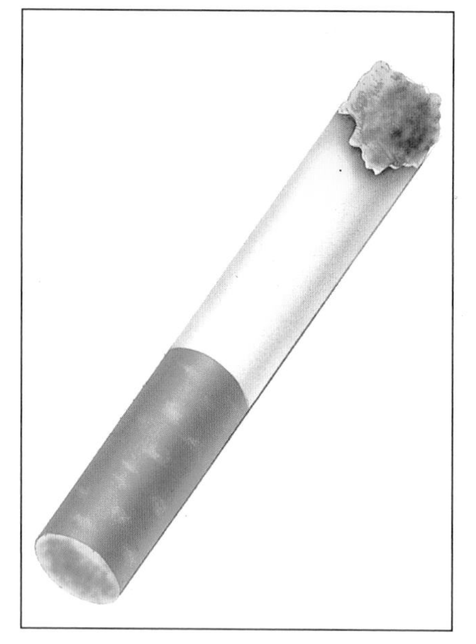

CANCER AND SMOKING

Cancer cells are cells which were once healthy but have become abnormal. They grow rapidly, causing damage. As well as lung cancer, there are cancers of the skin, stomach, blood, and so on. Smoking tobacco is partly responsible for a wide range of serious illnesses, including cancer. Microscopic studies of diseased lungs, heart, and blood vessels have proved this time after time. Tobacco smoke contains poisonous chemicals, some of which can cause cancer. Smoking also produces large amounts of tar. This consists of millions of dust-like particles which stick to and irritate the linings of the breathing tubes. Tar also clogs the delicate air-sacs within the lungs, which makes breathing difficult and puts a strain on the heart.

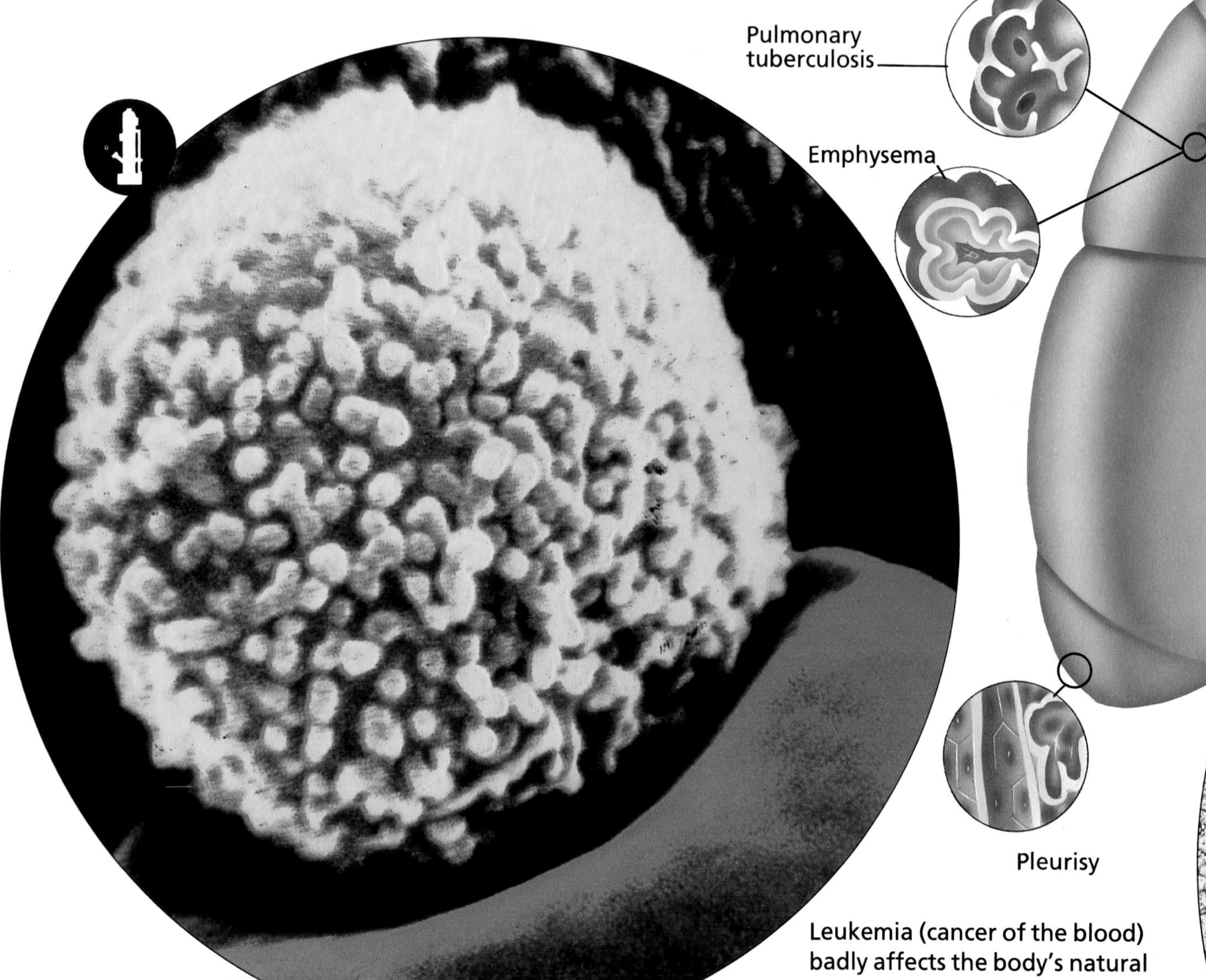

Leukemia (cancer of the blood) badly affects the body's natural production of red and white blood cells. This increases the chances that microbes will invade the person. They will then be able to multiply, which can cause other diseases.

The white cell in the image above, seen here × 4,860, is from a person with leukemia.

The diseased cell has lots of tiny surface projections not present on healthy white cells.

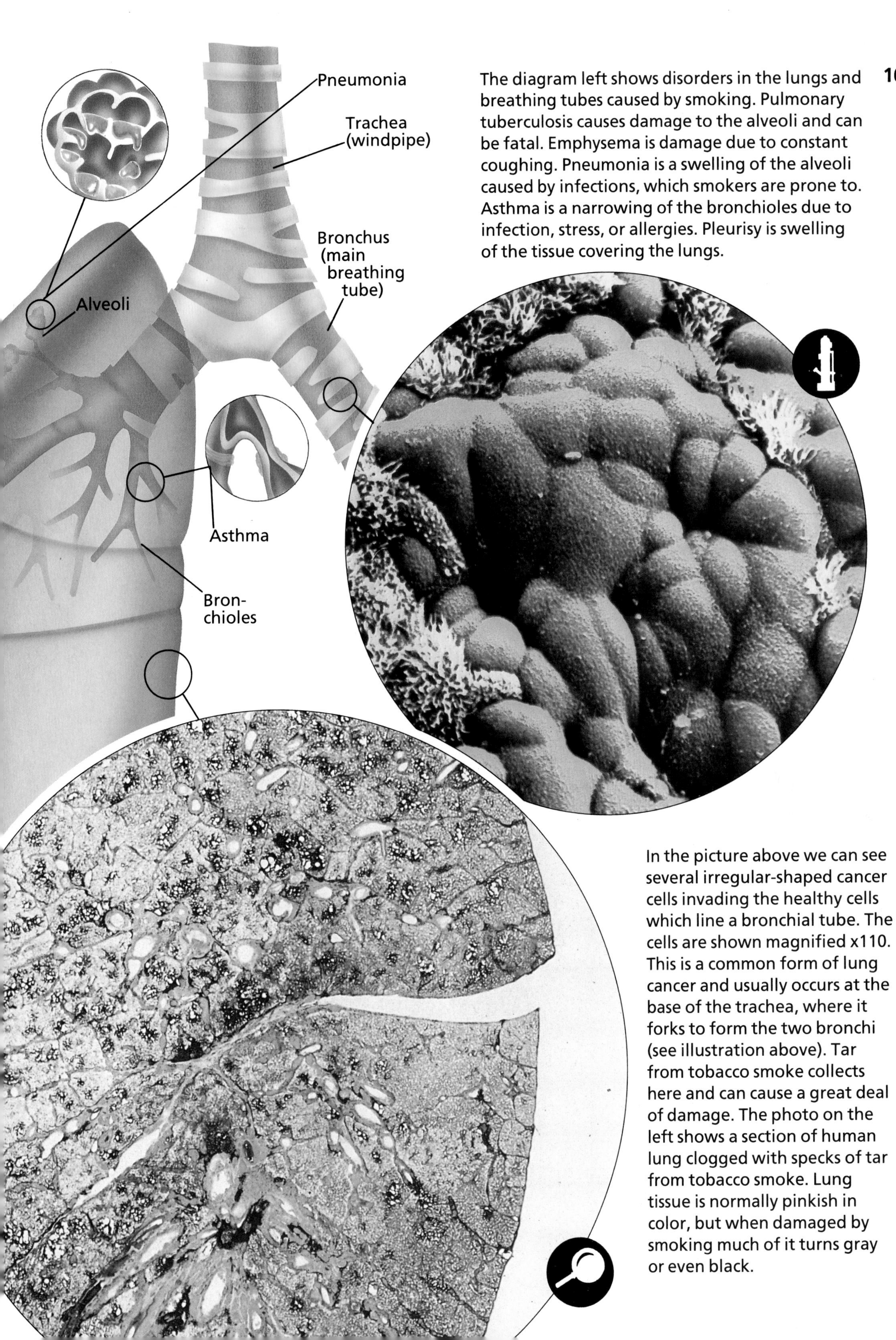

The diagram left shows disorders in the lungs and breathing tubes caused by smoking. Pulmonary tuberculosis causes damage to the alveoli and can be fatal. Emphysema is damage due to constant coughing. Pneumonia is a swelling of the alveoli caused by infections, which smokers are prone to. Asthma is a narrowing of the bronchioles due to infection, stress, or allergies. Pleurisy is swelling of the tissue covering the lungs.

In the picture above we can see several irregular-shaped cancer cells invading the healthy cells which line a bronchial tube. The cells are shown magnified x110. This is a common form of lung cancer and usually occurs at the base of the trachea, where it forks to form the two bronchi (see illustration above). Tar from tobacco smoke collects here and can cause a great deal of damage. The photo on the left shows a section of human lung clogged with specks of tar from tobacco smoke. Lung tissue is normally pinkish in color, but when damaged by smoking much of it turns gray or even black.

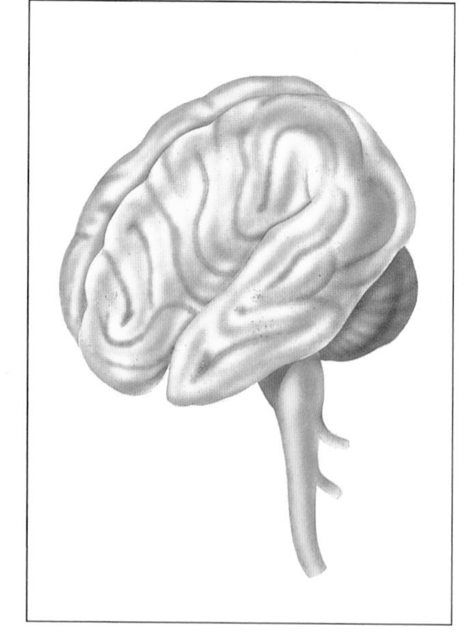

UNDERSTANDING THE BRAIN

The microscope has also played an important role in discovering and understanding the detailed structure of the brain and how nerves carry millions of messages between it and the rest of the body every second. Microscopic research has helped scientists and doctors understand how the brain can sometimes repair itself following injury; and also how it can be affected by various medicines and drugs. The brain is the body's control center. It functions like a computer, collecting information from sense organs – the eyes, ears, nose, tongue and skin – sorting the information, then sending out signals to muscles and other tissues, and to organs such as the heart, lungs, liver, kidneys, nose, and eyes.

Nerve cells in the brain are magnified × 160 below. Each is connected to the others by thousands of branchlike dendrites. A fingerlike fiber, the axon, is also visible in each.

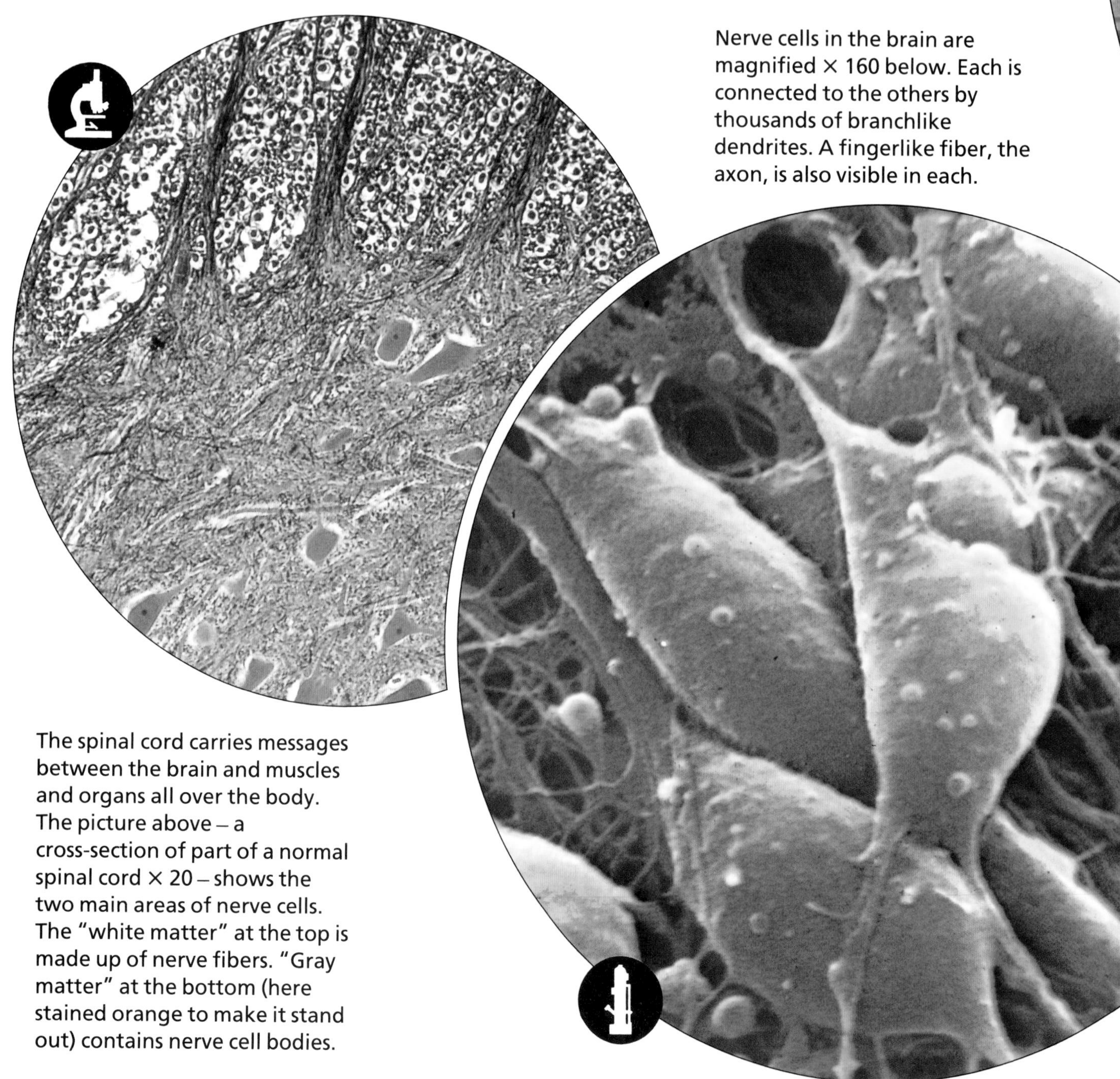

The spinal cord carries messages between the brain and muscles and organs all over the body. The picture above – a cross-section of part of a normal spinal cord × 20 – shows the two main areas of nerve cells. The "white matter" at the top is made up of nerve fibers. "Gray matter" at the bottom (here stained orange to make it stand out) contains nerve cell bodies.

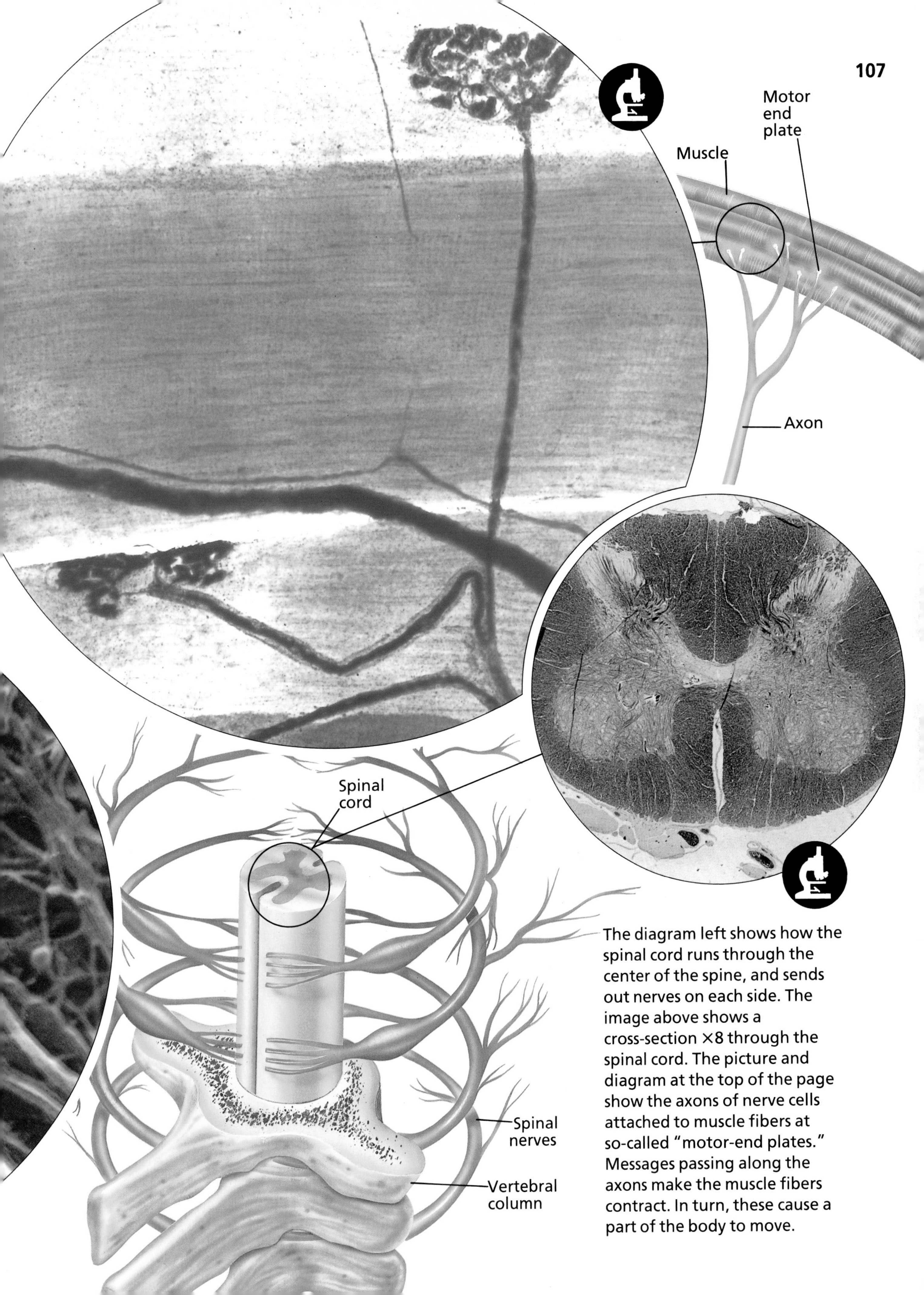

The diagram left shows how the spinal cord runs through the center of the spine, and sends out nerves on each side. The image above shows a cross-section ×8 through the spinal cord. The picture and diagram at the top of the page show the axons of nerve cells attached to muscle fibers at so-called "motor-end plates." Messages passing along the axons make the muscle fibers contract. In turn, these cause a part of the body to move.

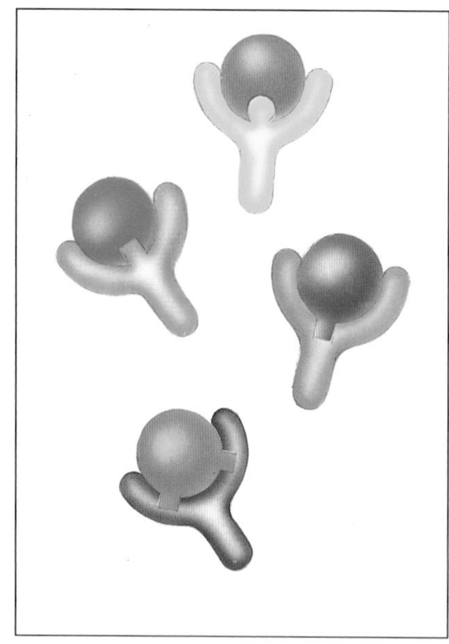

PUTTING MICROBES TO WORK

Many microbes do not cause disease and are helpful to us. The fungi *Pencillium, Streptomyces*, and *Aspergillus* produce antibiotics. Many protozoa, algae, fungi, and bacteria break down natural substances in sewage and so help cleanse water for drinking. In the past 20 years scientists have used the natural chemical activities of microbes to make new types of medicines. One microbe in particular, *Escherichia coli* (see top right), has been put to good use. It can be grown and made to produce the hormones and enzymes usually made only by human cells in tiny amounts. Scientists have also used cancer cells from mice to make antibodies, like the ones illustrated below, against harmful microbes.

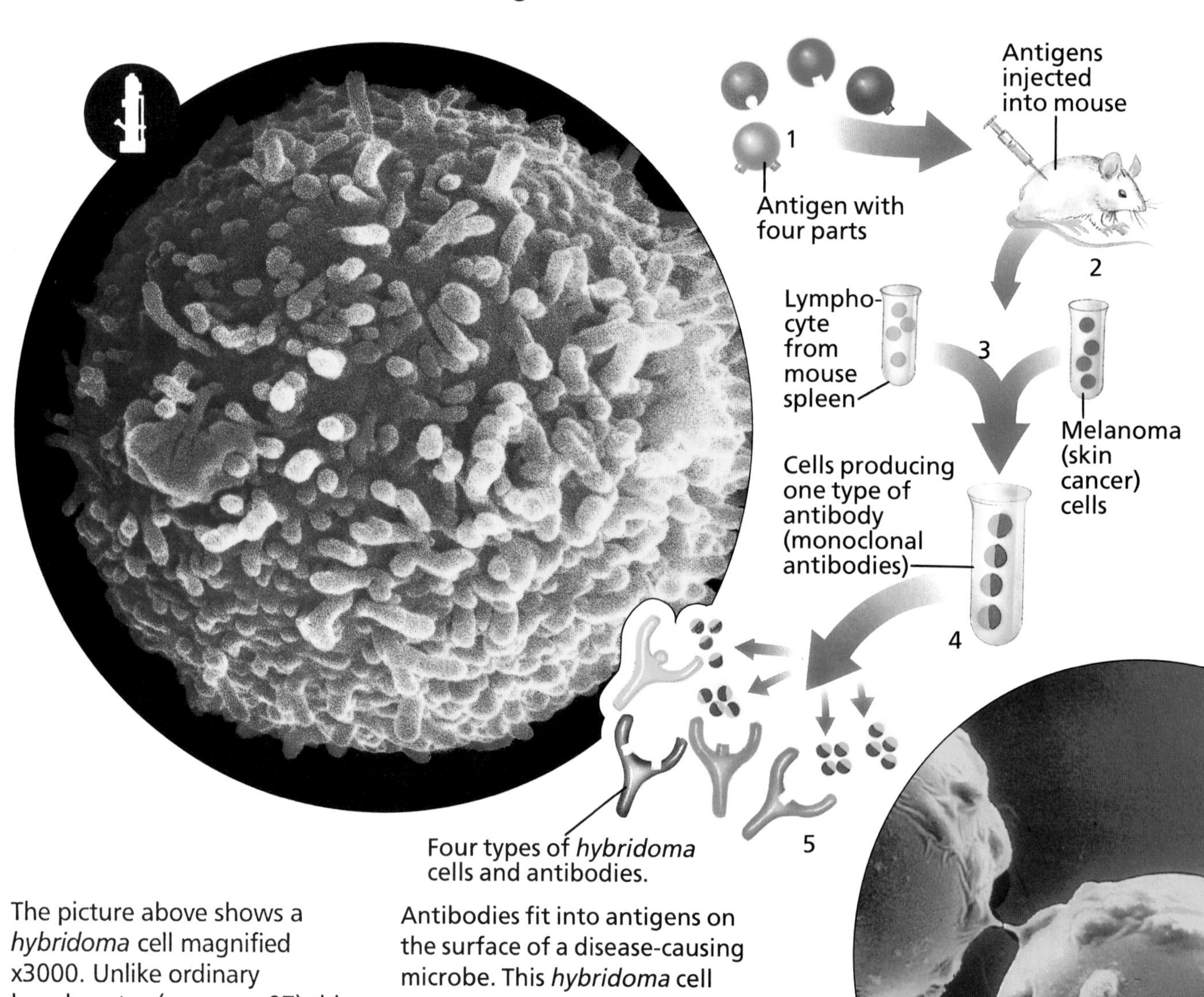

Four types of *hybridoma* cells and antibodies.

The picture above shows a *hybridoma* cell magnified x3000. Unlike ordinary lymphocytes (see page 97) this produces only one type of antibody and, as it multiplies, makes exact copies if itself called "clones." It can be made to mass-produce antibodies against a bacterium or virus.

Antibodies fit into antigens on the surface of a disease-causing microbe. This *hybridoma* cell was made by joining a white blood cell from a mouse with a mouse's cancer cell. The diagram above shows the five stages in making *hybridoma* cells, each producing antibodies against one of the four antigens.

The bacterium *Escherichia coli* (right × 14,700) grows in the human digestive system and usually does no harm. In it is a ring-shaped cell structure called a "chromosome" which contains a series of genes, each producing chemicals needed by the cell. Using other natural chemicals called enzymes, scientists can cut open the chromosome, insert genes from human cells, and then seal it (see below).

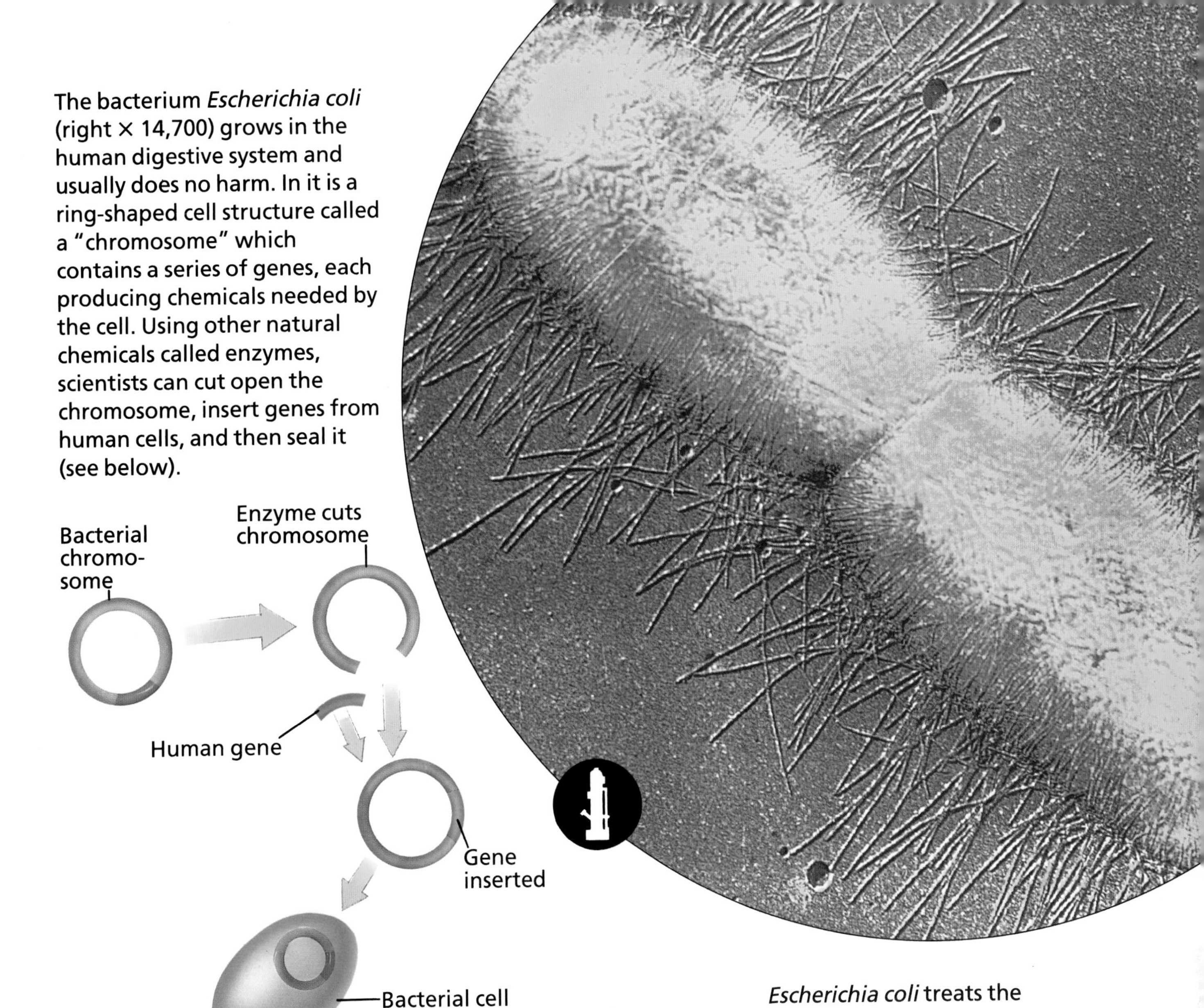

Escherichia coli treats the human genes as its own and makes them produce human chemicals. This is known as "genetic engineering." Among the useful substances made in this way is interferon, which stops viruses from reproducing and so allows white blood cells to destroy them. It may also combat cancer cells. Human insulin and growth-factor are hormones which some people are unable to make enough of. Producing them by genetic engineering and injecting them into patients helps to solve this problem. The image far left shows cells used for genetic engineering after five hours of growth on tiny glass beads in the laboratory. The image left shows the same cells after 48 hours growth.

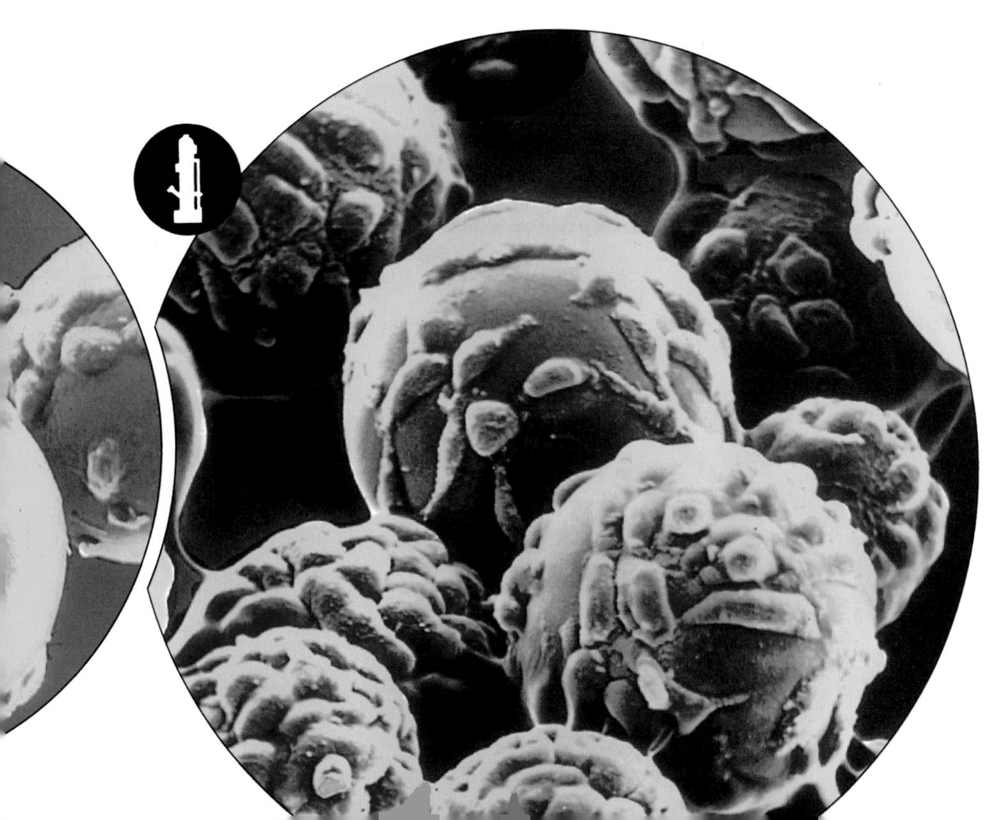

CONTENTS

Around the Home

Lionel Bender

LIFE IN THE KITCHEN

With the invention and use of powerful light microscopes in the 1880s, scientists were able to discover why food rots and how it can sometimes poison us. Both problems are caused by tiny living creatures which are present in even the cleanest of kitchens. Microscopic animals lurk in cracks, on walls, inside closets, and sometimes on food itself. Usually, they do no harm and go about their lives entirely unnoticed by people. Similarly, molds are tiny fungi that release spores which float through the air. They are likely to be present in almost any kitchen, ready to colonize pieces of bread, cheese, or other food that are left lying about. More visible visitors, like common houseflies, often bring harmful bacteria with them.

The photo below (magnified x6) shows mold on part of a lemon skin. Most fungi consist of branching threads that spread through and over their food, taking in nourishment. But often the most obvious parts of a fungus are the fruiting bodies (*sporangia*) they send up. These release spores into the air which float away to land on a new food source.

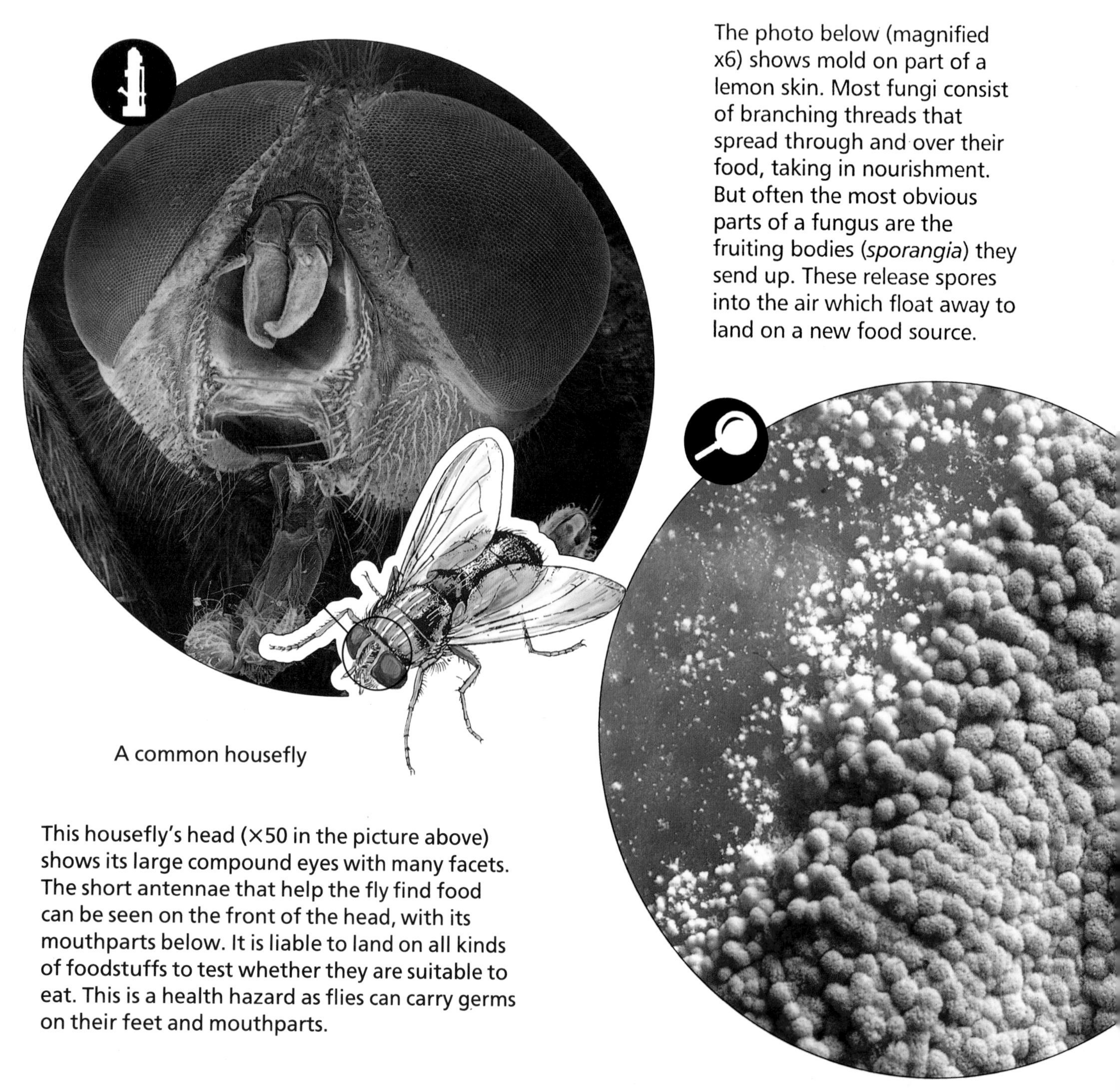

A common housefly

This housefly's head (×50 in the picture above) shows its large compound eyes with many facets. The short antennae that help the fly find food can be seen on the front of the head, with its mouthparts below. It is liable to land on all kinds of foodstuffs to test whether they are suitable to eat. This is a health hazard as flies can carry germs on their feet and mouthparts.

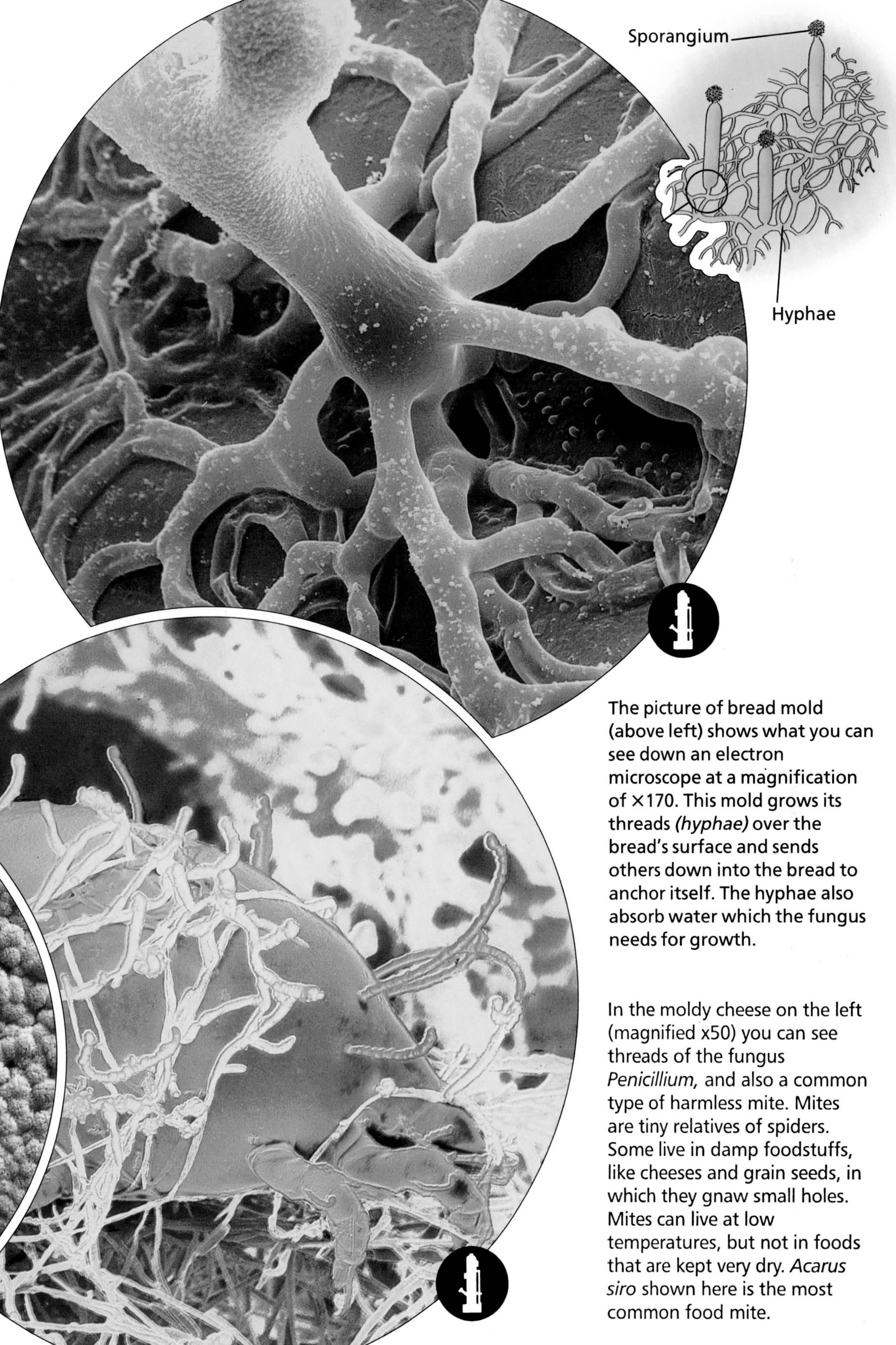

The picture of bread mold (above left) shows what you can see down an electron microscope at a magnification of ×170. This mold grows its threads *(hyphae)* over the bread's surface and sends others down into the bread to anchor itself. The hyphae also absorb water which the fungus needs for growth.

In the moldy cheese on the left (magnified x50) you can see threads of the fungus *Penicillium,* and also a common type of harmless mite. Mites are tiny relatives of spiders. Some live in damp foodstuffs, like cheeses and grain seeds, in which they gnaw small holes. Mites can live at low temperatures, but not in foods that are kept very dry. *Acarus siro* shown here is the most common food mite.

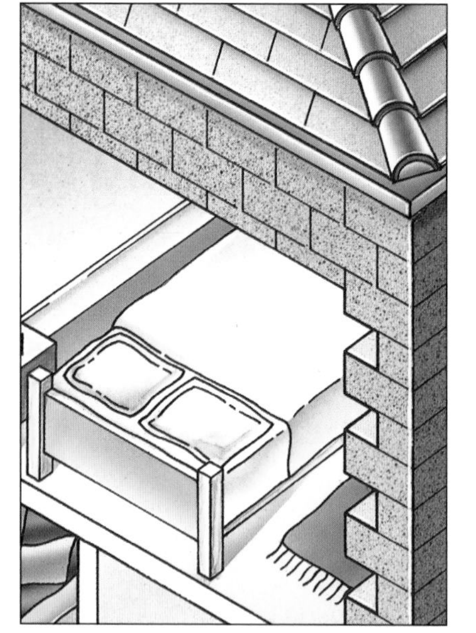

FABRICS IN THE BEDROOM

Fabrics are an essential part of our lives. Clothes keep us warm by day and sheets, blankets and bedspreads do the same at night. Drapes and carpets add to our comfort, while clean towels and linen contribute to our personal hygiene. In general, fabrics are woven from threads or long strands a fraction of a millimeter thick. For example, wool comes from sheep, cotton from the seeds of a bush, rayon from the bark of trees, and the delicate threads of real silk are spun by tiny worms. The microscopic study of natural fibers and fabrics has led to the production of new synthetic ones. These "artificial" fibers are normally much cheaper to produce in the large quantities that modern manufacturers want.

The image (right) shows part of a pair of panty hose magnified ×110. These are made of the artificial fiber, nylon. The yarn for such stockings comes in various thicknesses, the thinnest giving the sheerest stockings when woven. Nylon is a strong fiber, and when woven into a mesh, makes even lightweight stockings reasonably long-lasting. As with many electron microscope images, the color here is not that of the original object, but has been tinted by a computer.

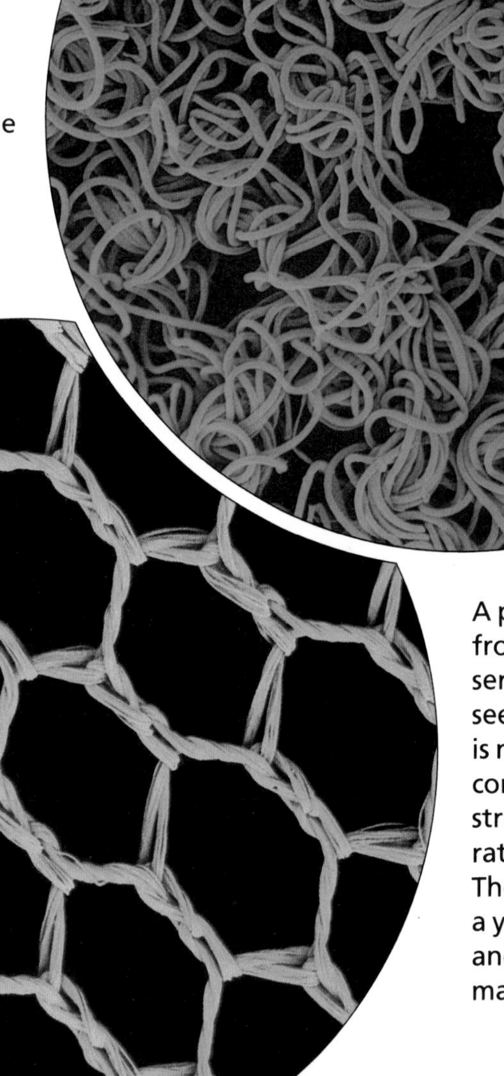

A piece of machine-made lace from a curtain (left) shows a series of very even "cells" as seen magnified ×160. Each cell is made up of a succession of complicated knots, and its even structure is typical of machine- rather than hand-made fabrics. The lace seen here is made from a yarn that includes both cotton and polyester fibers in its many-stranded threads.

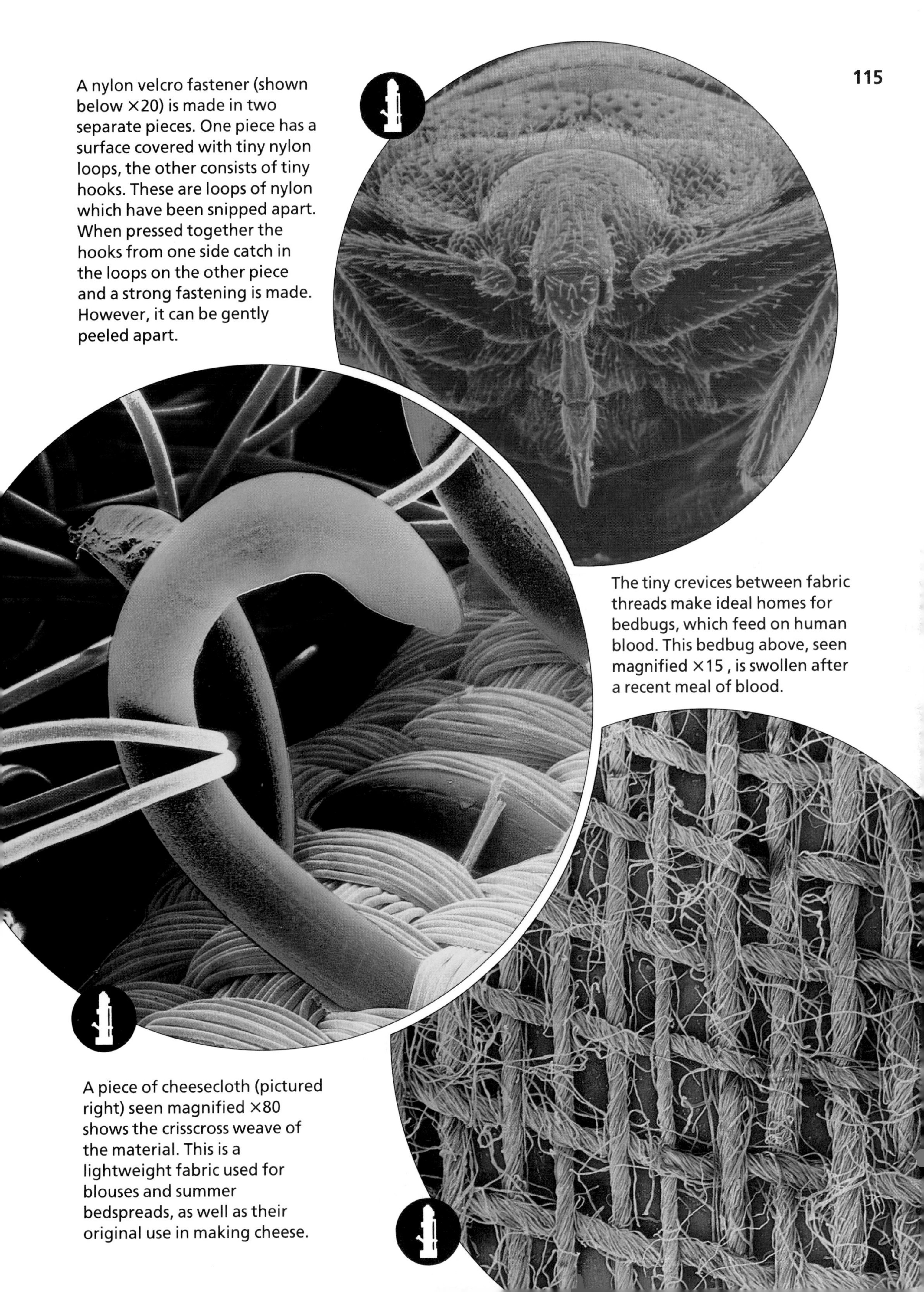

A nylon velcro fastener (shown below ×20) is made in two separate pieces. One piece has a surface covered with tiny nylon loops, the other consists of tiny hooks. These are loops of nylon which have been snipped apart. When pressed together the hooks from one side catch in the loops on the other piece and a strong fastening is made. However, it can be gently peeled apart.

The tiny crevices between fabric threads make ideal homes for bedbugs, which feed on human blood. This bedbug above, seen magnified ×15 , is swollen after a recent meal of blood.

A piece of cheesecloth (pictured right) seen magnified ×80 shows the crisscross weave of the material. This is a lightweight fabric used for blouses and summer bedspreads, as well as their original use in making cheese.

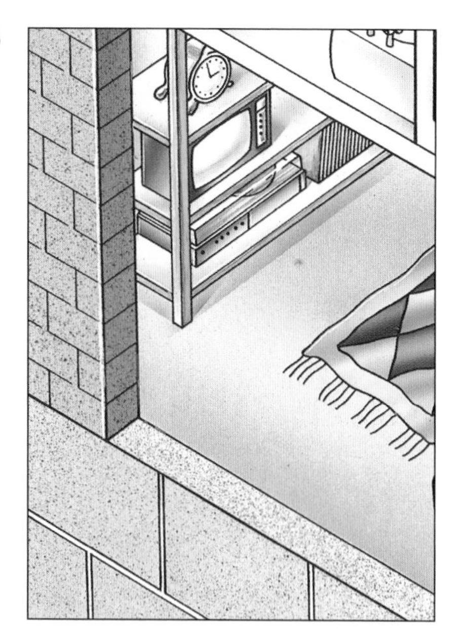

ELECTRONICS IN THE LIVING ROOM

Modern technology has made an ever-increasing range of gadgets and devices available to us today. Many of these items have minute working parts that cannot be seen properly with the unaided eye. This is because they were actually designed and manufactured with the aid of microscopes. On these pages we can see what some of these amazingly intricate structures look like close up. The wires and hand-soldered connections of an electrical circuit used to take up a great deal of space. Today, many thousands of circuits can be fitted into a fraction of the same space within a micro-chip.

Unlike records, the surface of a compact disk (×143 in the picture below) is well protected, and is not worn by playing. A coating of transparent plastic covers the "music." Here the coating is removed to show the playing surface. The flat areas and pits are pressed in the plastic disk and then coated with aluminum which will reflect a laser beam. A sensor reads the flashes made by these reflections and translates them into music.

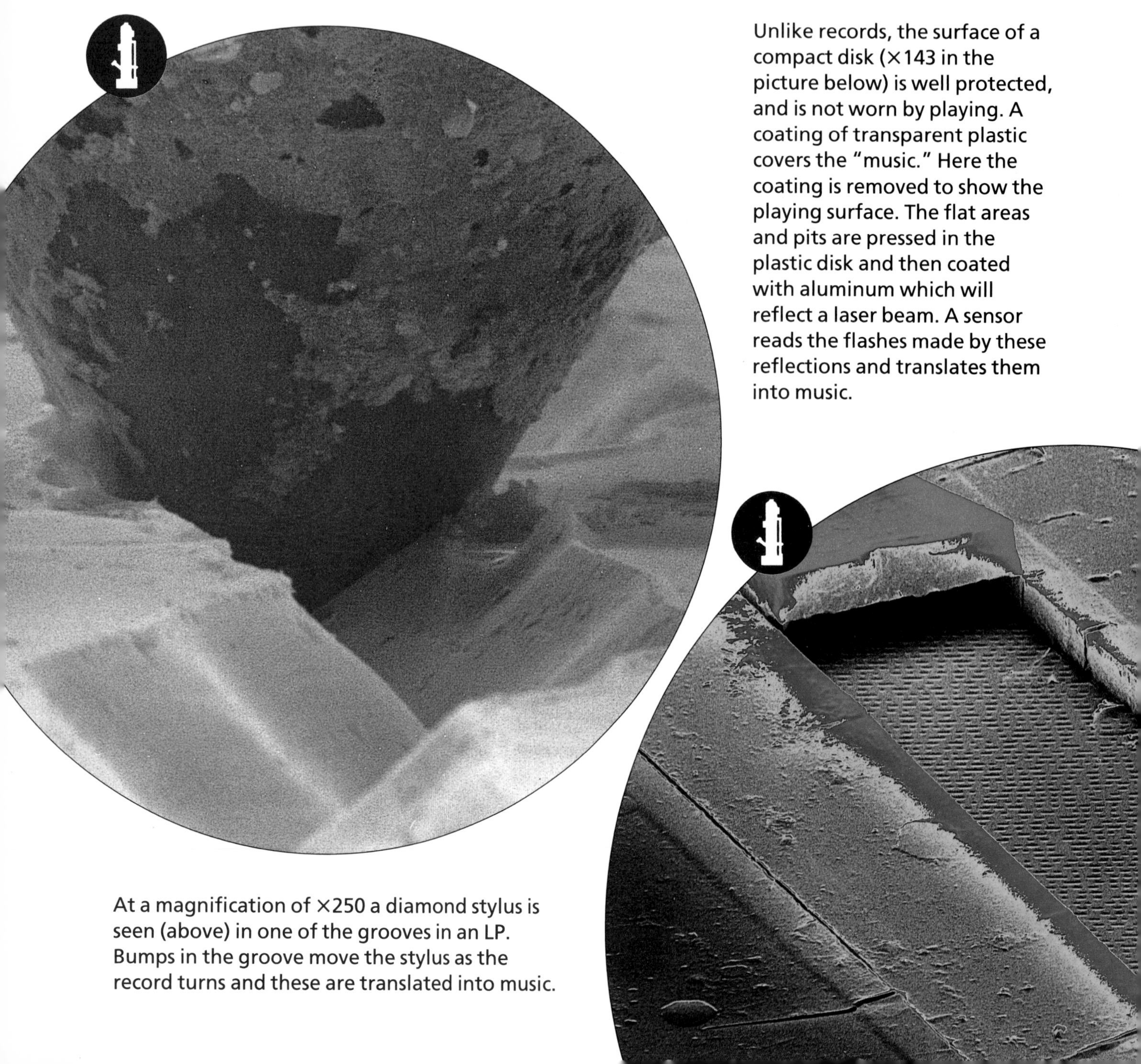

At a magnification of ×250 a diamond stylus is seen (above) in one of the grooves in an LP. Bumps in the groove move the stylus as the record turns and these are translated into music.

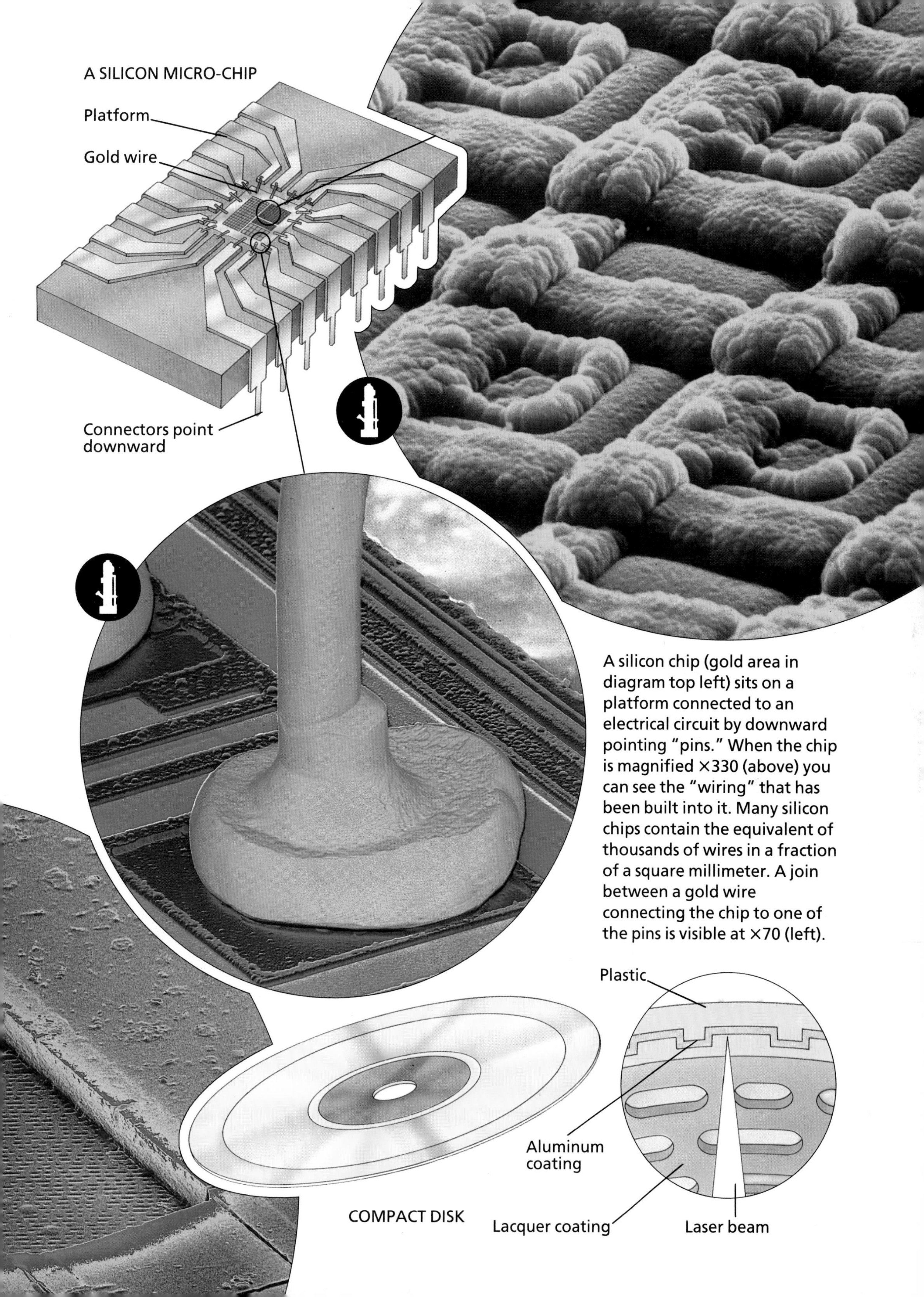

A silicon chip (gold area in diagram top left) sits on a platform connected to an electrical circuit by downward pointing "pins." When the chip is magnified ×330 (above) you can see the "wiring" that has been built into it. Many silicon chips contain the equivalent of thousands of wires in a fraction of a square millimeter. A join between a gold wire connecting the chip to one of the pins is visible at ×70 (left).

FOOD IN THE DINING ROOM

Microscopic studies have helped nutrionalists, dieticians and food technologists to understand what is important in the things that we eat. As a result we now have a wide range of artificial sweeteners and flavorings, and even meatlike products processed from fungi grown in factory conditions. Most food consists of a mixture of fibers, starch, sugars, fats and water. Cooking makes it tastier, as well as easier to chew and swallow. However, cooking also releases some of the substances within the raw components at the same time as it destroys others. Our bodies can only process and use certain combinations of the food we swallow. There is always much more to food than meets the unaided eye.

Looking at a slice of raw potato (enlarged ×25 below) we can see the regular structure of the cells and egg-shaped grains of starch within. When the potato is cooked (right) the cell walls break down. Notice how the starch inside has turned into a gluey mass.

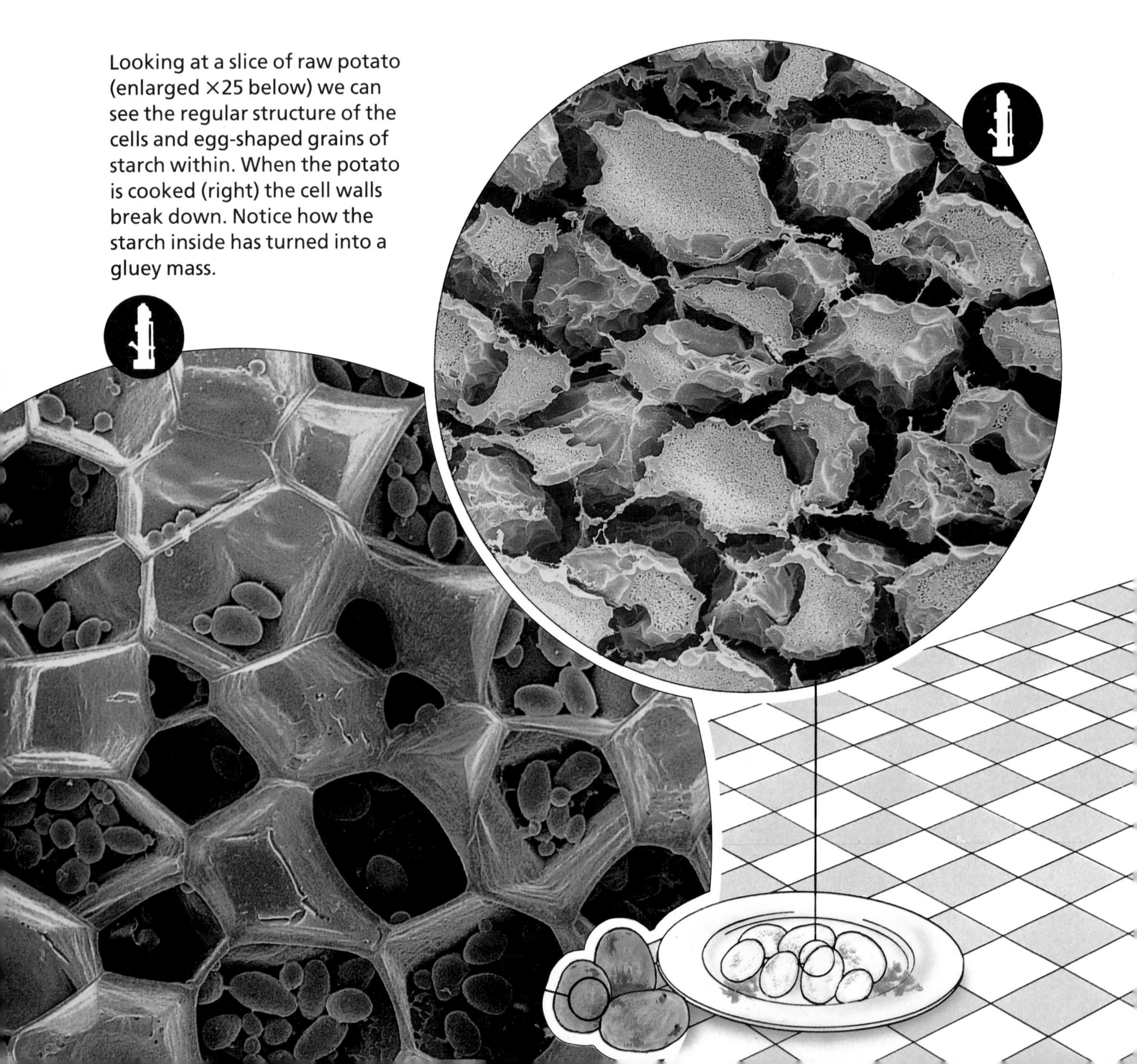

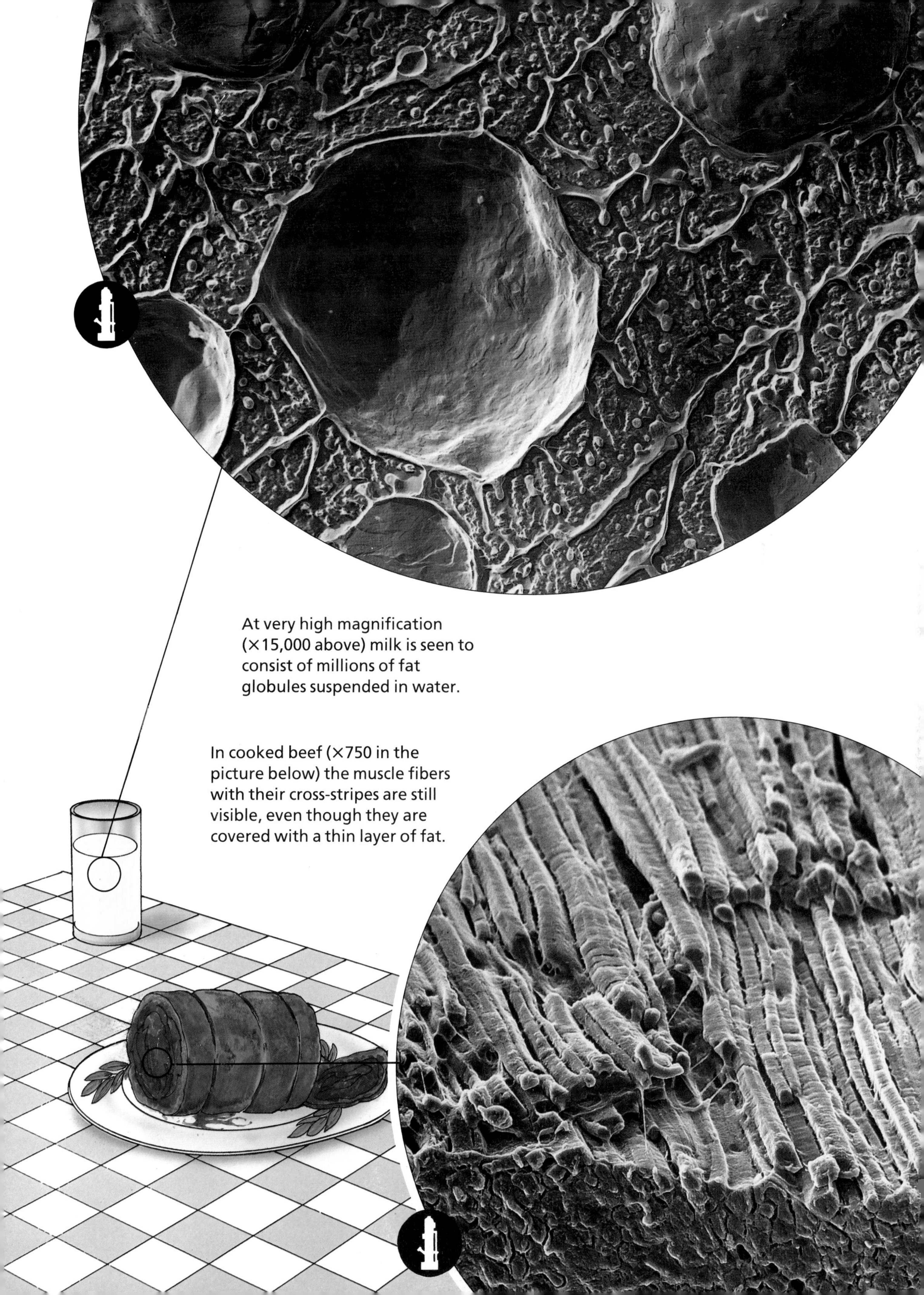

At very high magnification (×15,000 above) milk is seen to consist of millions of fat globules suspended in water.

In cooked beef (×750 in the picture below) the muscle fibers with their cross-stripes are still visible, even though they are covered with a thin layer of fat.

CLEANING UP IN THE BATHROOM

Bathrooms tend to have shiny surfaces of porcelain and tiles that show up dirt and grime and are easy to scrub down. As long as the floor, walls, toilet, sink and tub in a bathroom are regularly cleaned, there is no danger from germs. However, no matter how clean and shiny surfaces look to the unaided eye, microscopic examination shows how much mess we ourselves create. Splashes of water leave behind a residue of chemicals that can harden and become difficult to shift. Flakes of skin and fallen hairs clog combs, brushes, and even drains. Small wonder that some people always seem to be cleaning the bathroom!

A scan of the surface of a bar of soap (magnified ×16 below) reveals a flaky texture that is not apparent to the unaided eye. Used bars such as this accumulate microscopic grit on and between the flakes.

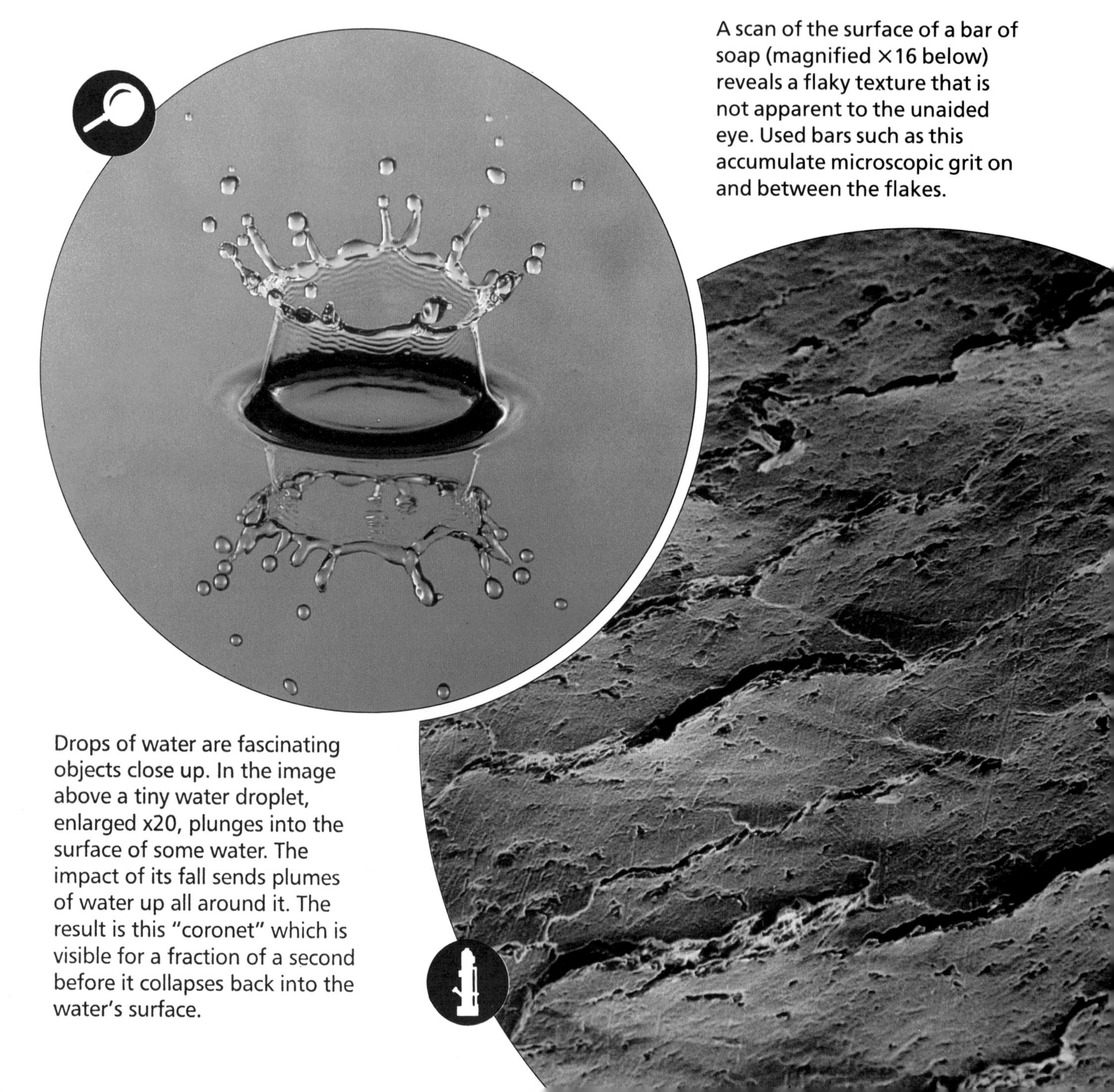

Drops of water are fascinating objects close up. In the image above a tiny water droplet, enlarged x20, plunges into the surface of some water. The impact of its fall sends plumes of water up all around it. The result is this "coronet" which is visible for a fraction of a second before it collapses back into the water's surface.

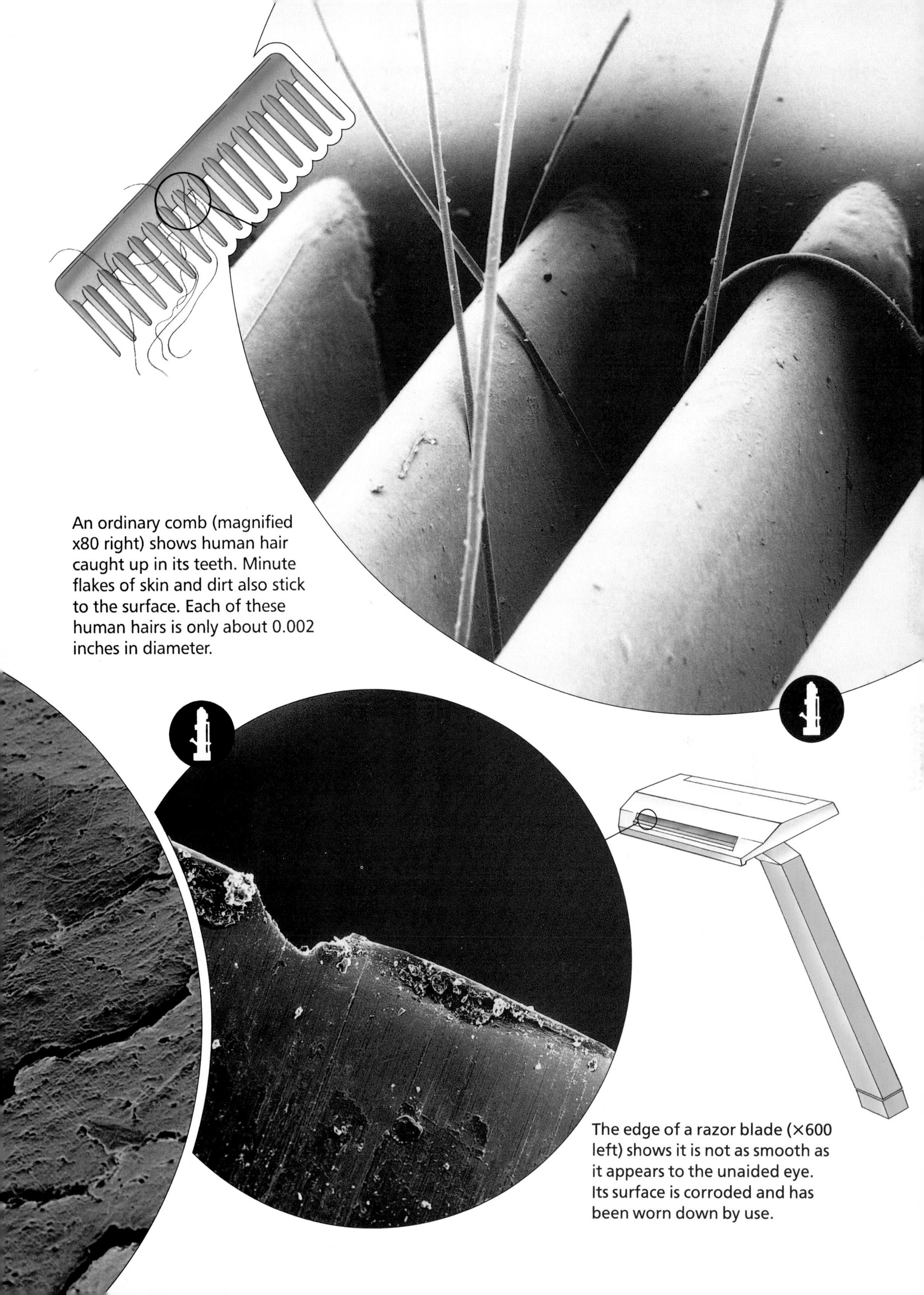

An ordinary comb (magnified x80 right) shows human hair caught up in its teeth. Minute flakes of skin and dirt also stick to the surface. Each of these human hairs is only about 0.002 inches in diameter.

The edge of a razor blade (×600 left) shows it is not as smooth as it appears to the unaided eye. Its surface is corroded and has been worn down by use.

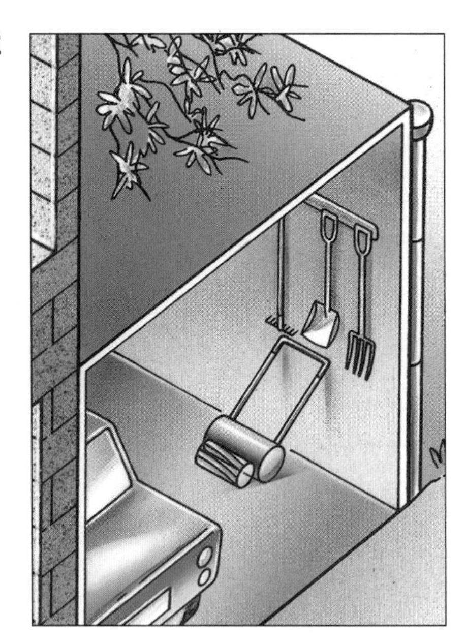

METALS, PLASTICS AND PAINTS IN THE GARAGE

The garage is often home to a host of other items as well as the family car. Many of these are either made of metals that rust or corrode, or have coverings of plastic that eventually harden and crack. The surface of metals and plastics is always interesting when looked at under a microscope. Even the paintwork that covers a car is special and unique to that vehicle when portions of it are viewed microscopically. This has been dramatically proven by forensic scientists who have been able to establish a connection between a car-owner and a crime by matching samples of chipped paintwork.

The joint shown below (x20) has been made with two different metals, aluminum and nickel. Such welds are found on car body panels. They have been welded by rotating the two bars of metal end to end at high speed to produce heat and then forcing the bars together while they are still hot.

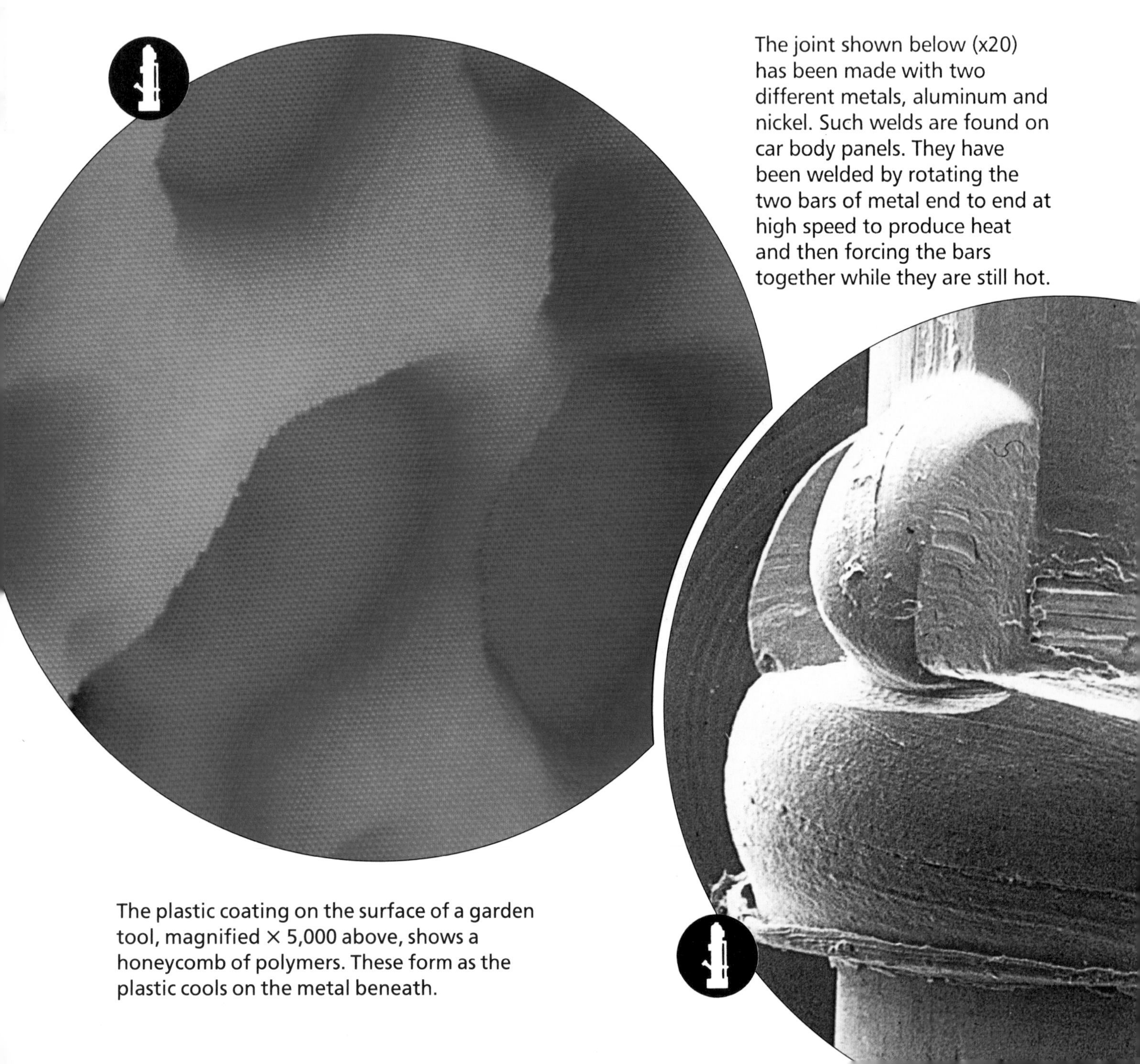

The plastic coating on the surface of a garden tool, magnified × 5,000 above, shows a honeycomb of polymers. These form as the plastic cools on the metal beneath.

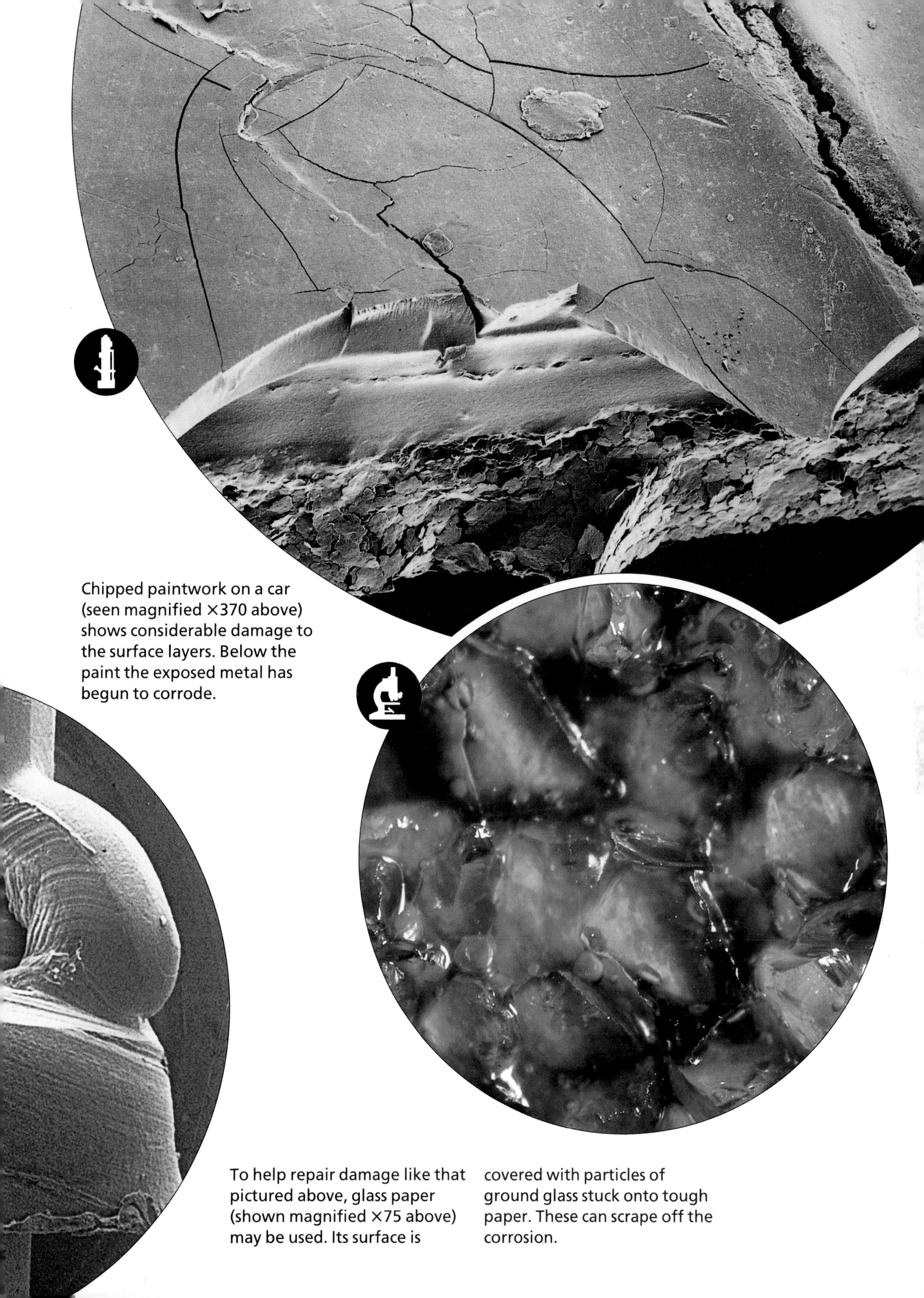

Chipped paintwork on a car (seen magnified ×370 above) shows considerable damage to the surface layers. Below the paint the exposed metal has begun to corrode.

To help repair damage like that pictured above, glass paper (shown magnified ×75 above) may be used. Its surface is covered with particles of ground glass stuck onto tough paper. These can scrape off the corrosion.

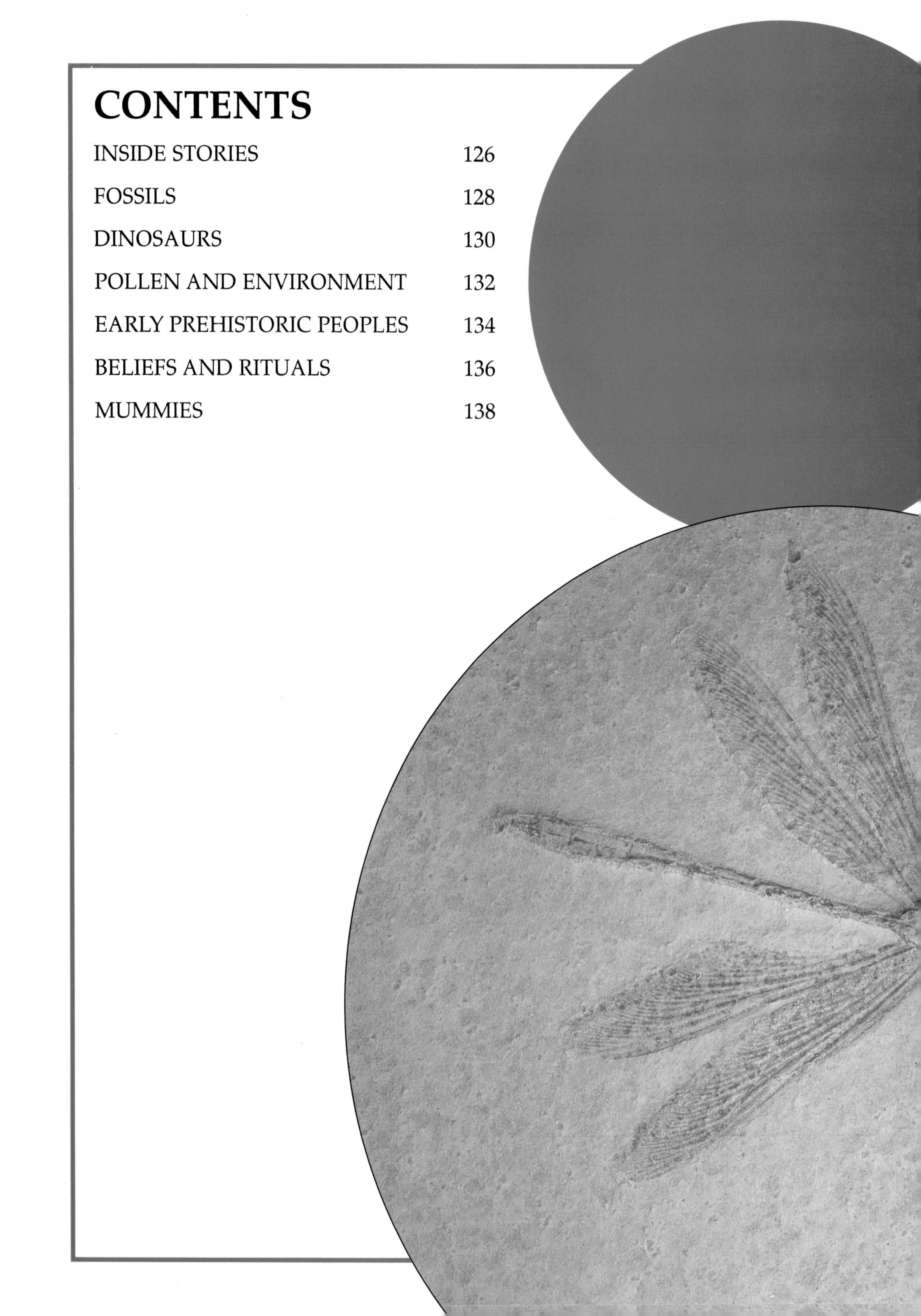

CONTENTS

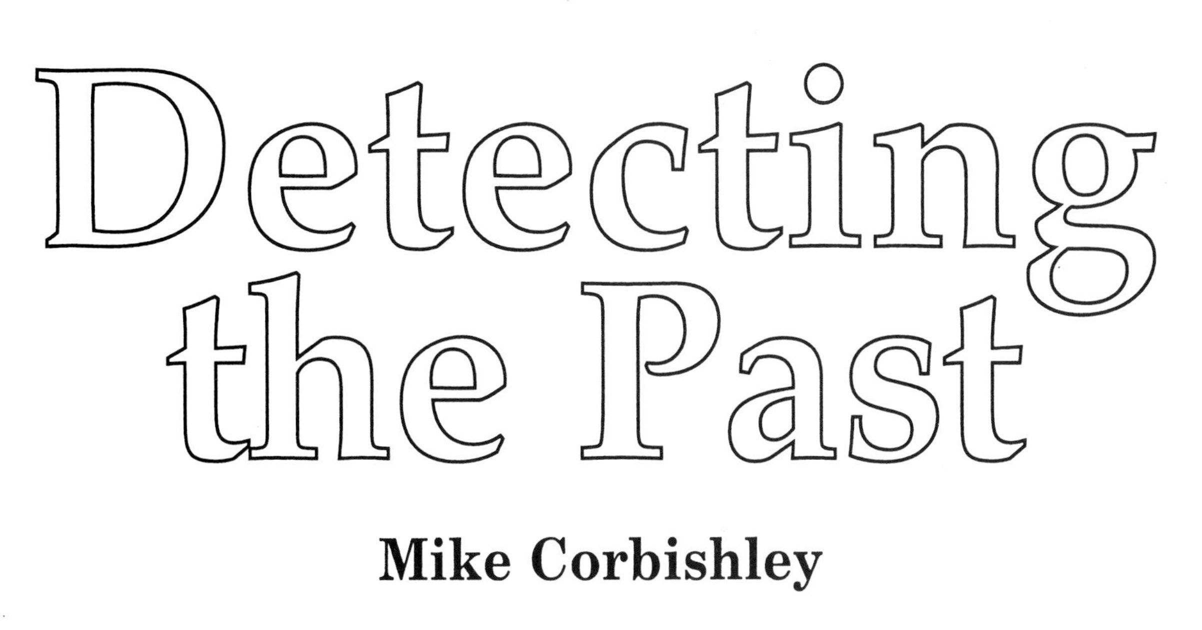

Mike Corbishley

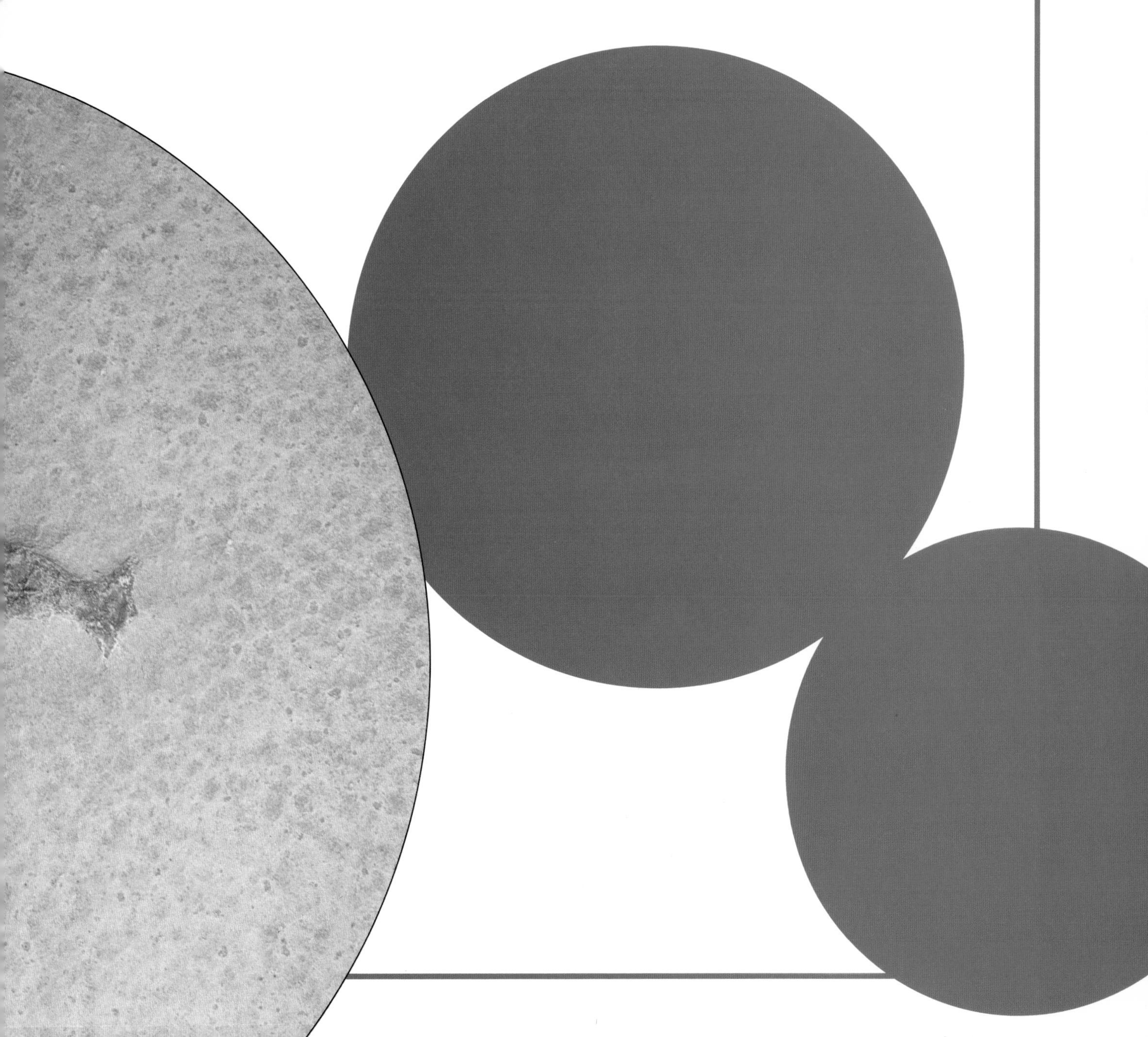

INSIDE STORIES

Four and a half thousand million years ago the Earth was a molten mass. Gradually its surface cooled and formed a crust. This crust is still on the move as layers of rock push against each other or drift apart. Different kinds of rock have been formed on the crust which we can study today. Some were once molten material squeezed up from beneath the crust; others have been built up from layers of sand and mud (see illustration – left), others have undergone enormous change. They are called igneous, sedimentary and metamorphic rock respectively. However, geologists can tell us more than just how our planet was made. They use their understanding to detect the mineral resources and fuel deposits essential to our way of life.

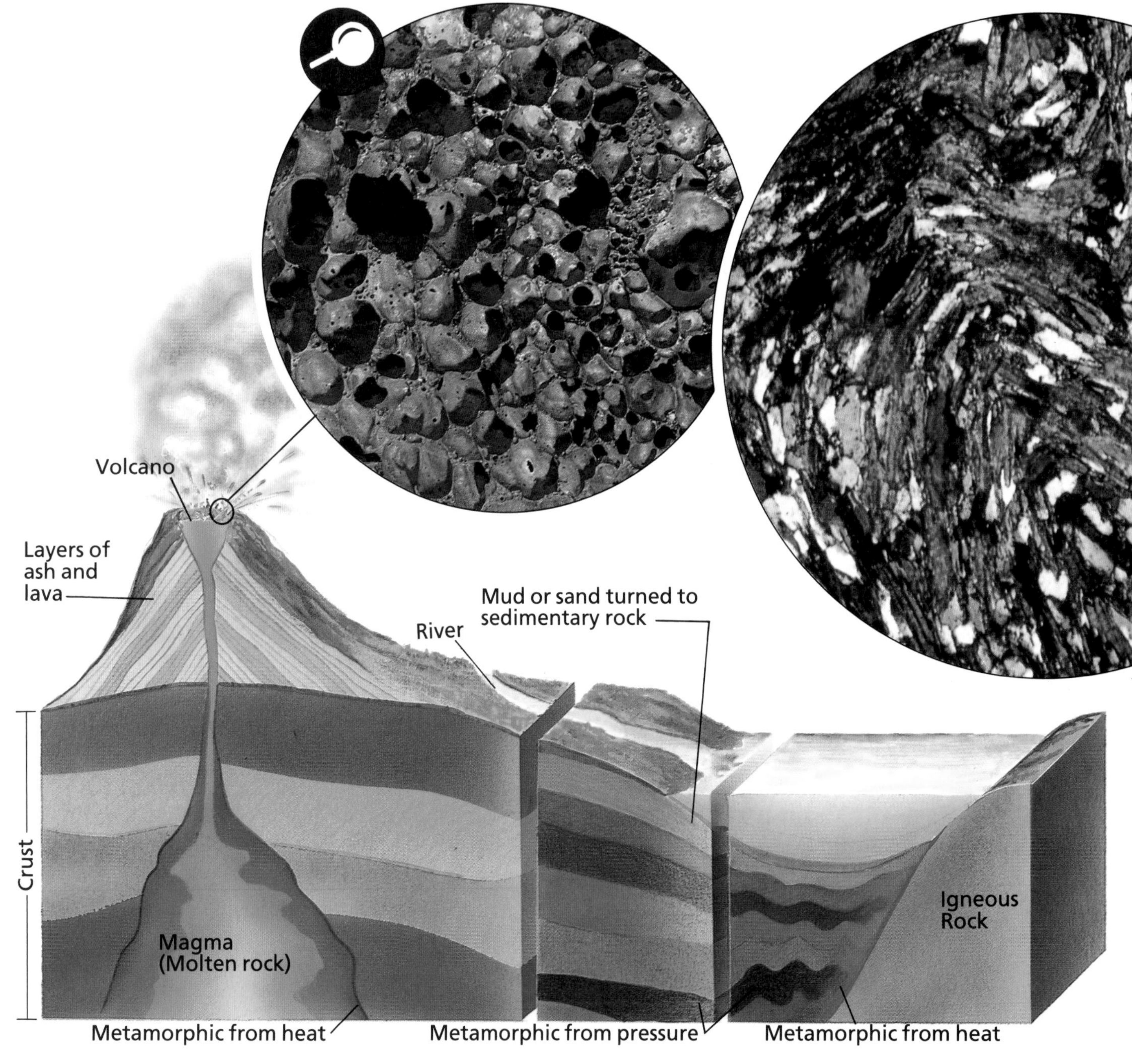

Geologists can often identify different types of rock by eye, but a magnifying glass or microscope is sometimes essential. On the left is a piece of sandstone (a sedimentary rock), made up of small particles of different types of quartz and shown here magnified × 25. Below is a piece of limestone (magnified × 4) which has been metamorphosed, or changed, by tremendous heat or pressure. Sometimes igneous rock, which solidified from molten rock called magma, is forced onto the surface of the earth. Two examples of this are the basalt rock (far left magnified at × 8) which was blown out of a volcano and the schist to its right which has fragments of crystal to be seen when magnified at × 30.

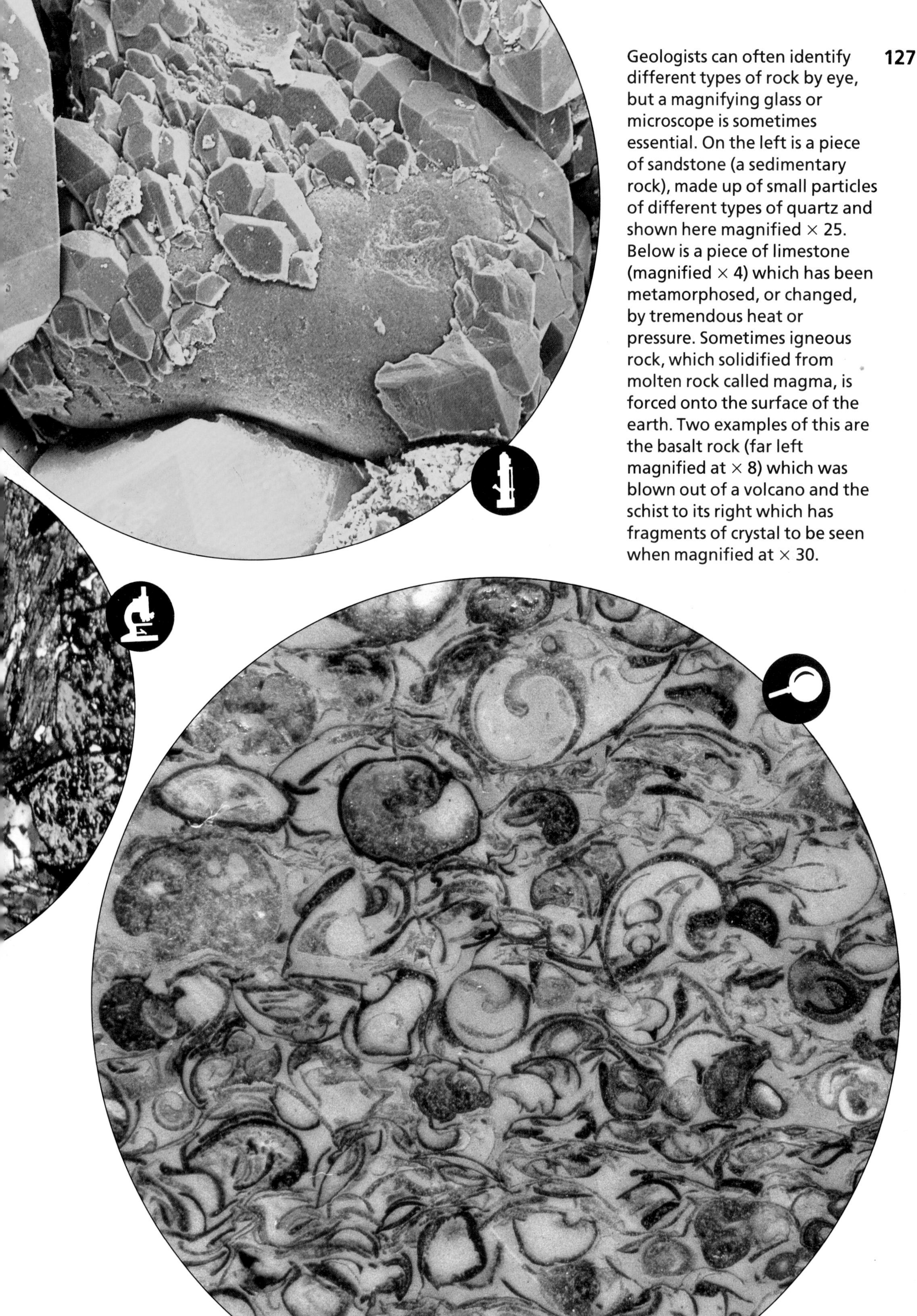

FOSSILS

Fossil is the word we use for the remains of animals or plants which have been preserved in or on the ground. Fossils are usually made of stone, but sometimes a whole insect is trapped, like the moth in amber, shown bottom right. Often the creature or plant is replaced by stone leaving a "petrified" object. Sometimes the hardest parts actually survive, such as the bones of an animal. Another type, illustrated on the left, shows the print of a leaf, surviving only as a film of carbon. "Trace" fossils can be anything from a dinosaur's footprint to a worm hole in what was once mud. Some rocks are made up entirely of fossils. Coal, for instance, is mainly composed of compressed plants that lived 300 million years ago.

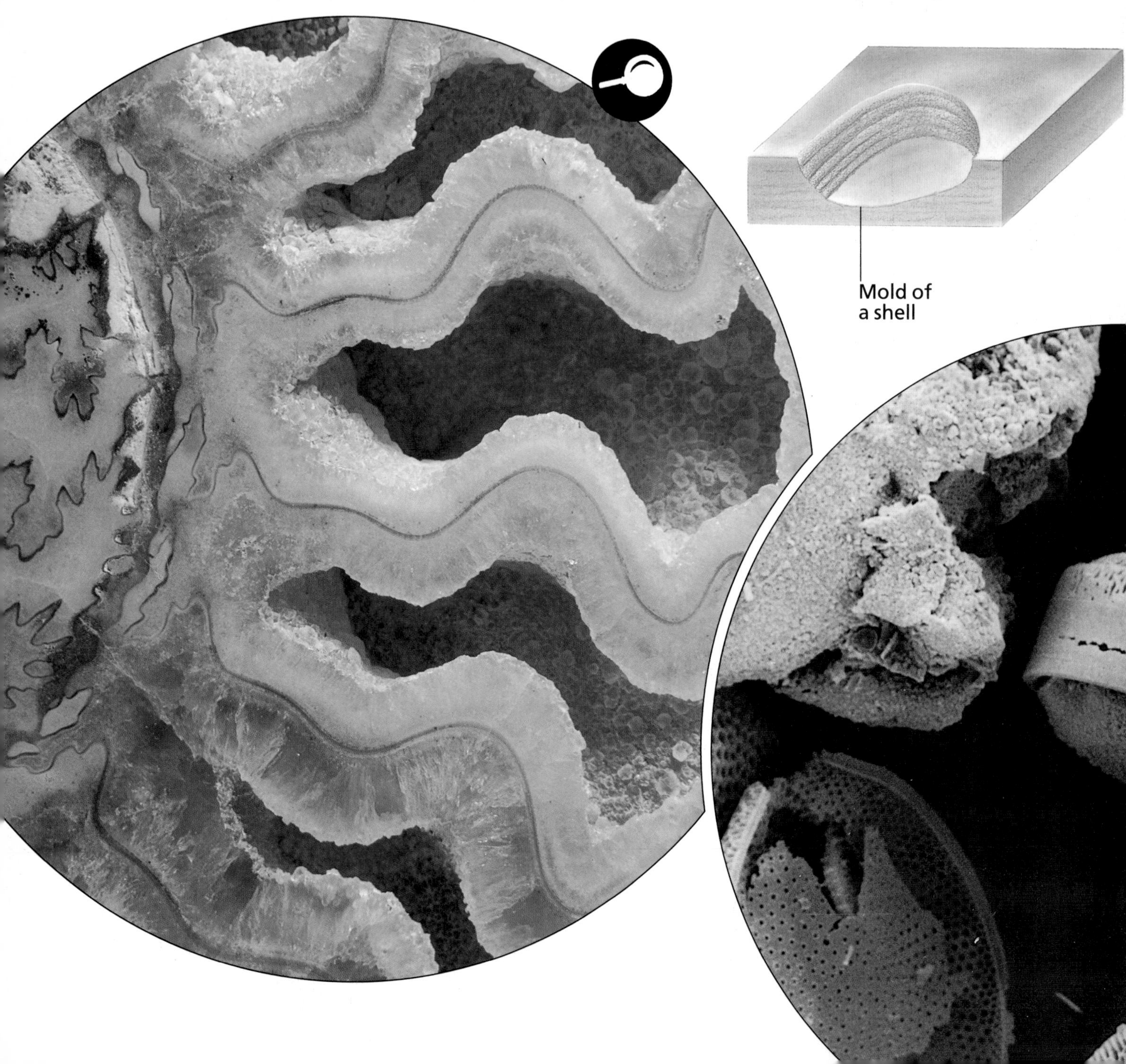

Geologists say that the oldest known rocks are 3,800 million years old. Fossils of single-cell algae 2,000 million years old (see center photo of diatoms × 700) have been found which can only be seen through a microscope. Fossils also show that humans evolved from apelike creatures over some 5-10 million years. The drawings on the left show different types of fossils. Below is an example of fossil bark. Fossil ammonites (far left) are to be found in many areas. These creatures died out 65 million years ago, about the same time as the last dinosaur.

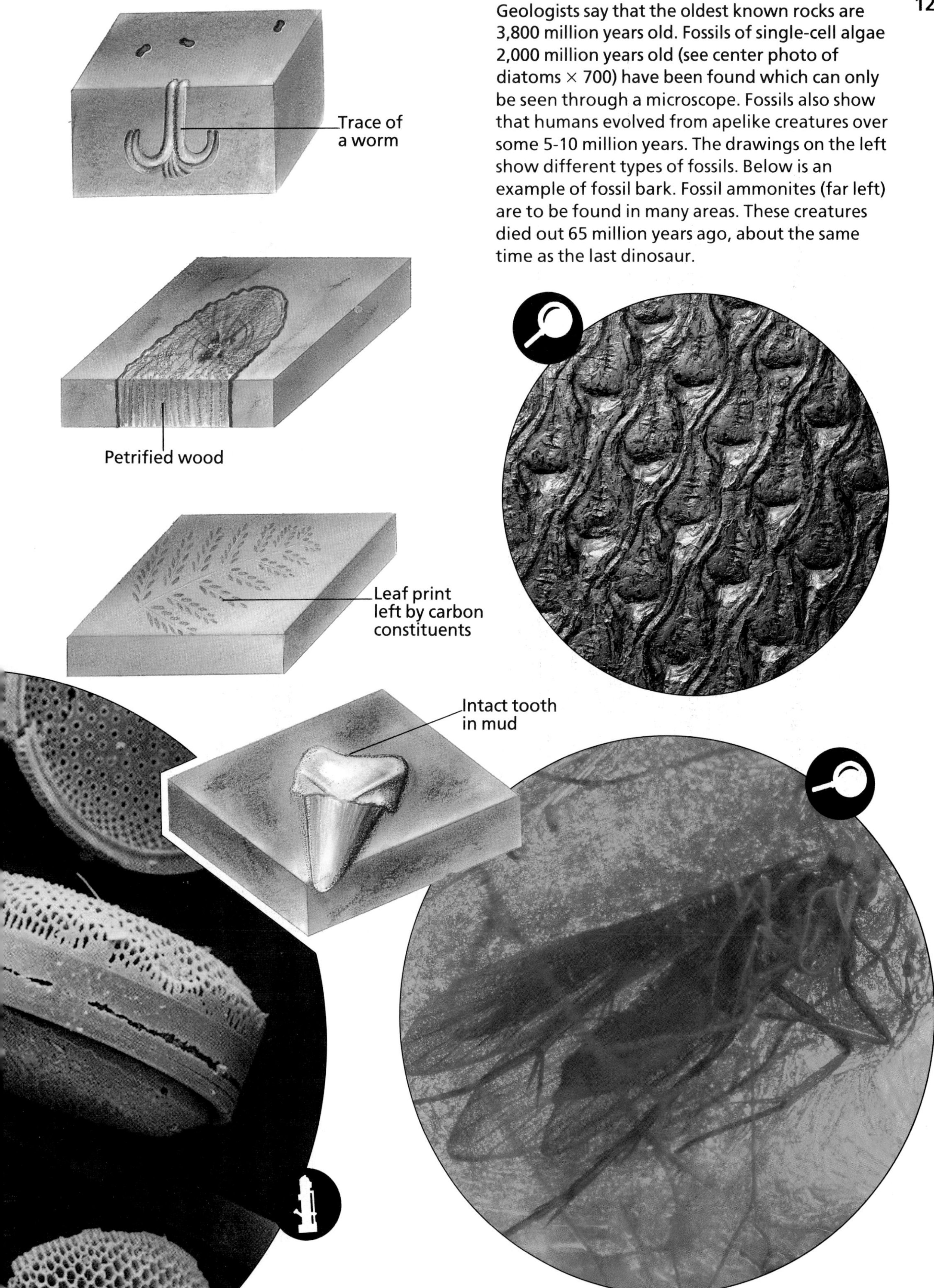

DINOSAURS

Dinosaurs, the word means "terrible lizards," were reptiles which became extinct about 65 million years ago. They lived on the earth for over 140 million years, but the last ones suddenly died out. This was possibly due to a rapid cooling of the planet's climate. Before that time most of the earth was warm and damp so that even in the Arctic Circle there were tropical plants and dinosaurs that ate them. Dinosaurs vanished from the earth millions of years before people evolved. We have to reconstruct what they might have looked like from their fossils. Today the animals that are related most closely to them are crocodiles and birds. Up to now scientists have discovered many hundreds of species of dinosaur.

Protoceratops, when fully grown to 5 feet (1.8m) in length, had horns. The discovery of a complete nest of fossil eggs (below) told scientists how dinosaurs looked after their young. Baby *Protoceratops* was about 1 foot (30cm) long. The size of dinosaurs varied a lot. *Brachiosaurus*, for example, was 70 feet (23m) long and weighed 80 tonnes. *Cynognathus*, from which the tooth (below right) came, was only 4 feet long (1.5m). This reptile lived 200 million years ago.

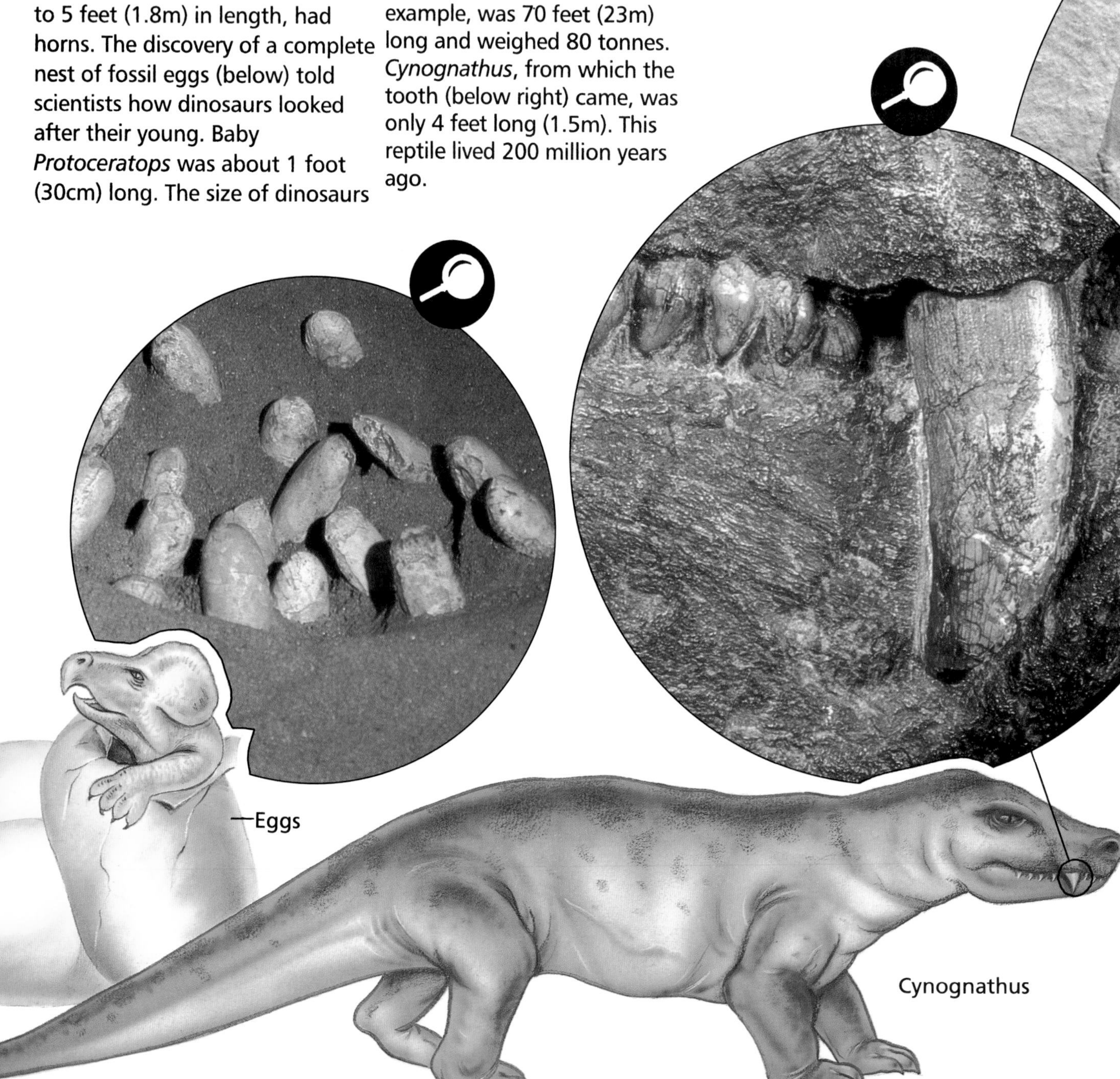

Not all creatures that lived during the "Age of the DInosaurs" were dinosaurs. Dinosaurs lived on the land. In the air were flying reptiles called *Pterosaurs*, and in the sea were various types of swimming reptiles including *Plesiosaurs* and *Ichthyosaurs.*

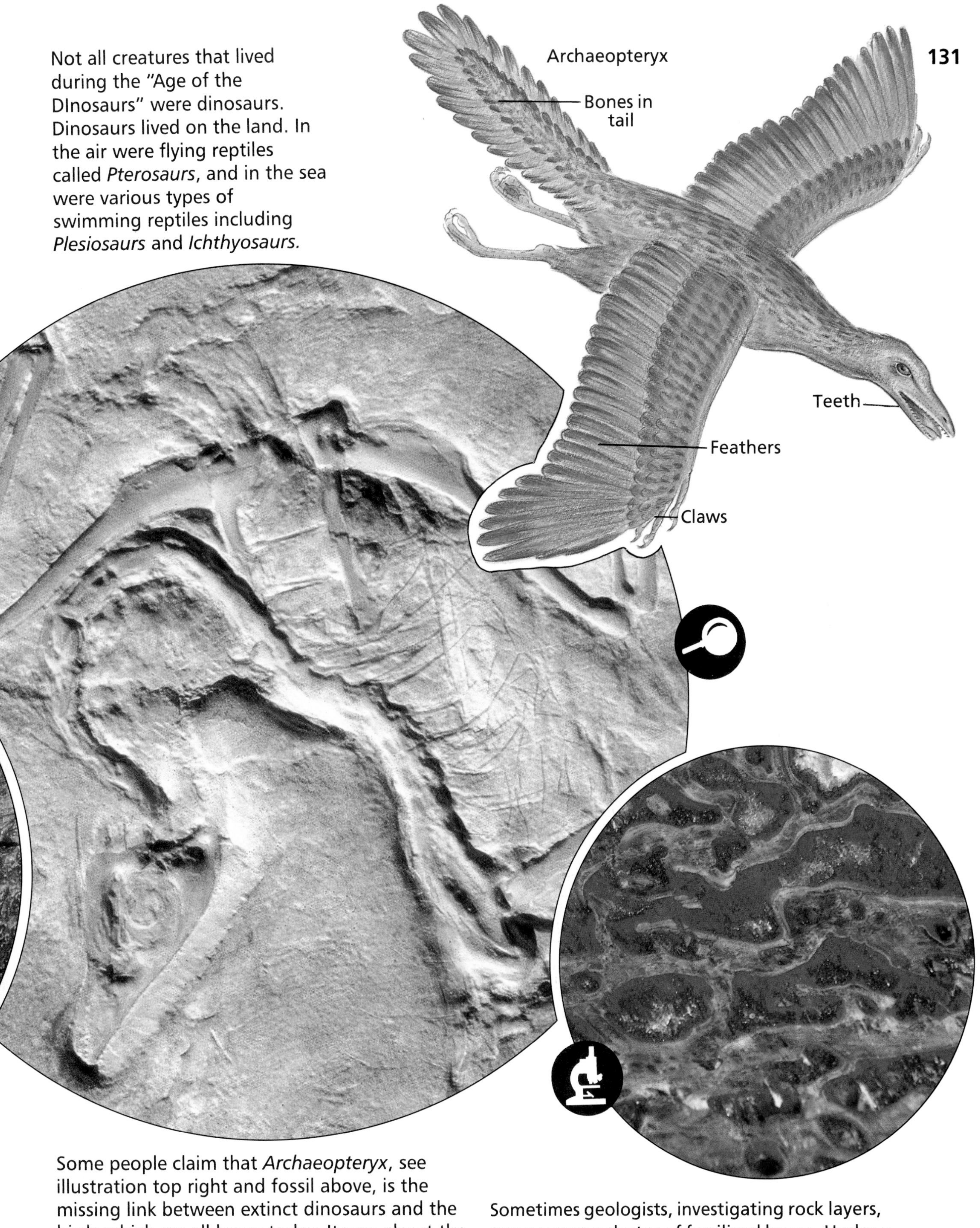

Some people claim that *Archaeopteryx*, see illustration top right and fossil above, is the missing link between extinct dinosaurs and the birds which we all know today. It was about the same size as a modern crow and ate insects and small reptiles. These strange flying animals had feathers, jaws with sharp teeth, wing claws for climbing trees, and a long bony tail.

Sometimes geologists, investigating rock layers, come across a cluster of fossilized bones. Under a microscope (see above) these can appear to be very beautiful. Paleontologists, scientists who specialize in fossils, will often have to study these finds in detail.

POLLEN AND ENVIRONMENT

Pollen is found in the anthers of any plants or trees which flower. It is like powder and the individual grains can only be seen through a microscope. Each pollen grain is a single cell with two coatings. The inner one, called the intine, is thin, but the outer one, the exine, is thicker and very resistant to decay or damage. This helps preserve the pollen for a long period of time. During the flowering season millions of pollen grains are constantly in the air. Many of these are trapped in places where they can be preserved, such as peat bogs. Samples can be collected by archaeologists during an excavation and studied. Pollen grains can be identified and so the types of plants and trees the pollen came from can be determined.

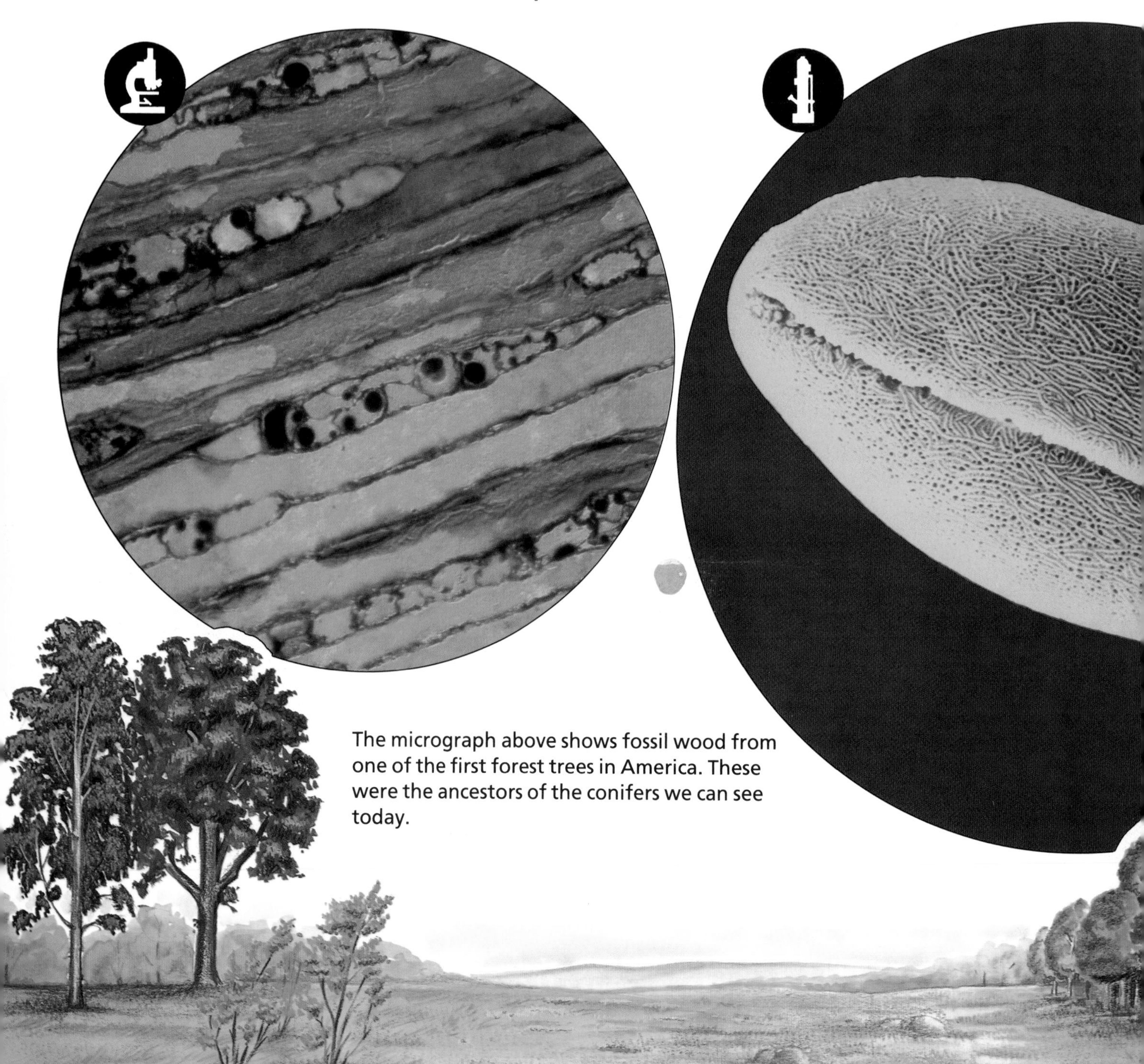

The micrograph above shows fossil wood from one of the first forest trees in America. These were the ancestors of the conifers we can see today.

Pollen grains travel only a short distance from the plants or trees they come from. We can therefore build up a good picture of a vanished environment by studying surviving pollen samples. Many kinds of prehistoric pollen grains resemble those of plants and trees alive today.

Each type of pollen grain can be recognized. The outer coatings of the two shown at the bottom of this page are different (Speedwell on the left magnified × 560, Cat's-Foot right × 486). In the middle is the pollen grain of a Hollyhock at × 665.

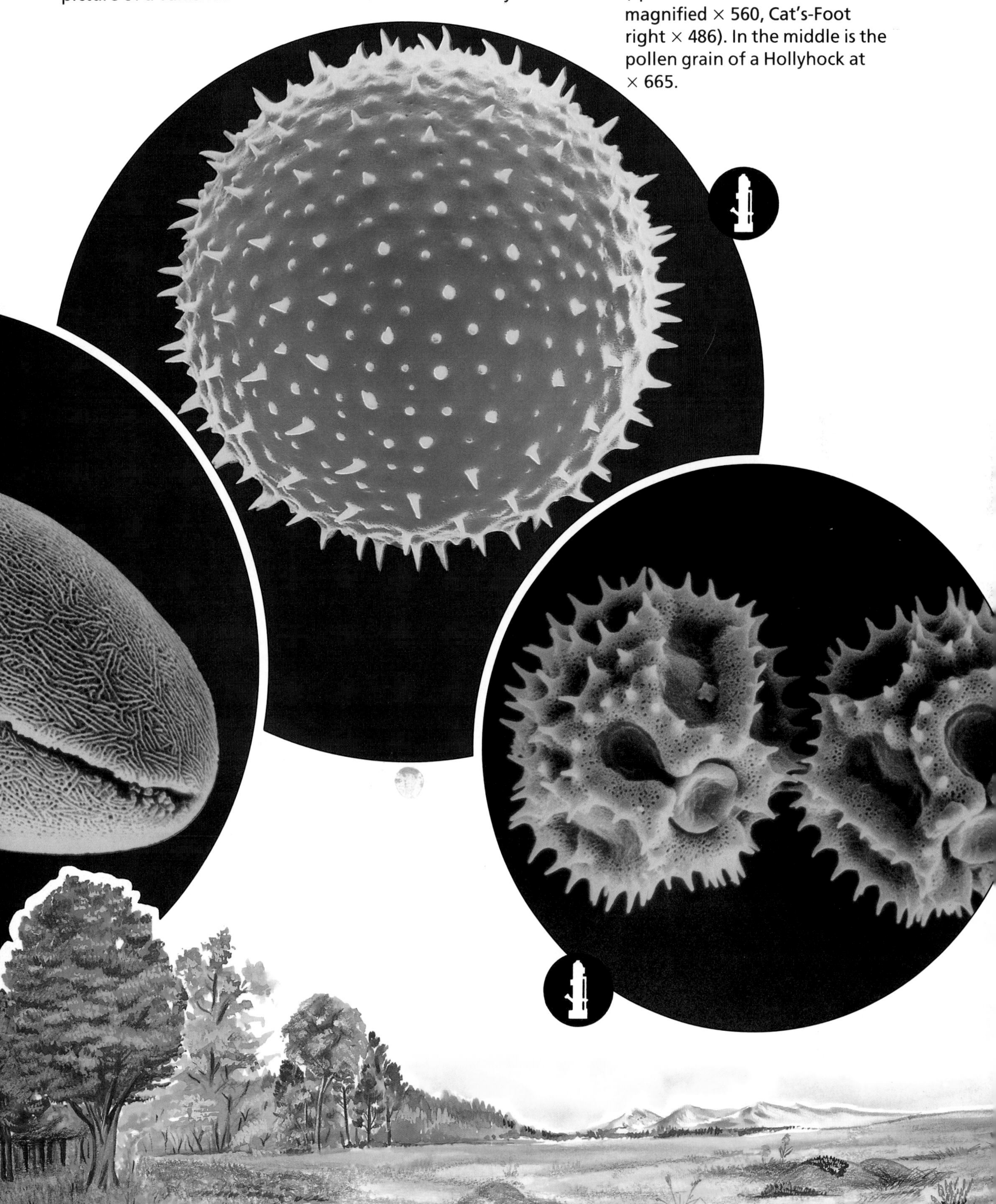

EARLY PREHISTORIC PEOPLES

There have been human beings on earth for at least 3 million years. Archaeologists have found fossil bones and the tools which people used. The most difficult job is to figure out the dates for the bones they found and the order in which we developed from these earliest peoples. On the right are the fossil bones of the jaw and teeth of one of our early relatives called Australopithecus afarensis, found in Ethiopia in Africa. Our human species (called Homo sapiens) probably spread out from Africa to Europe, Asia, and Australia. We now know that people reached Australia about 40,000 years ago. We call all these early people hunter-gatherers because they had to exist by hunting, gathering, and fishing for their food.

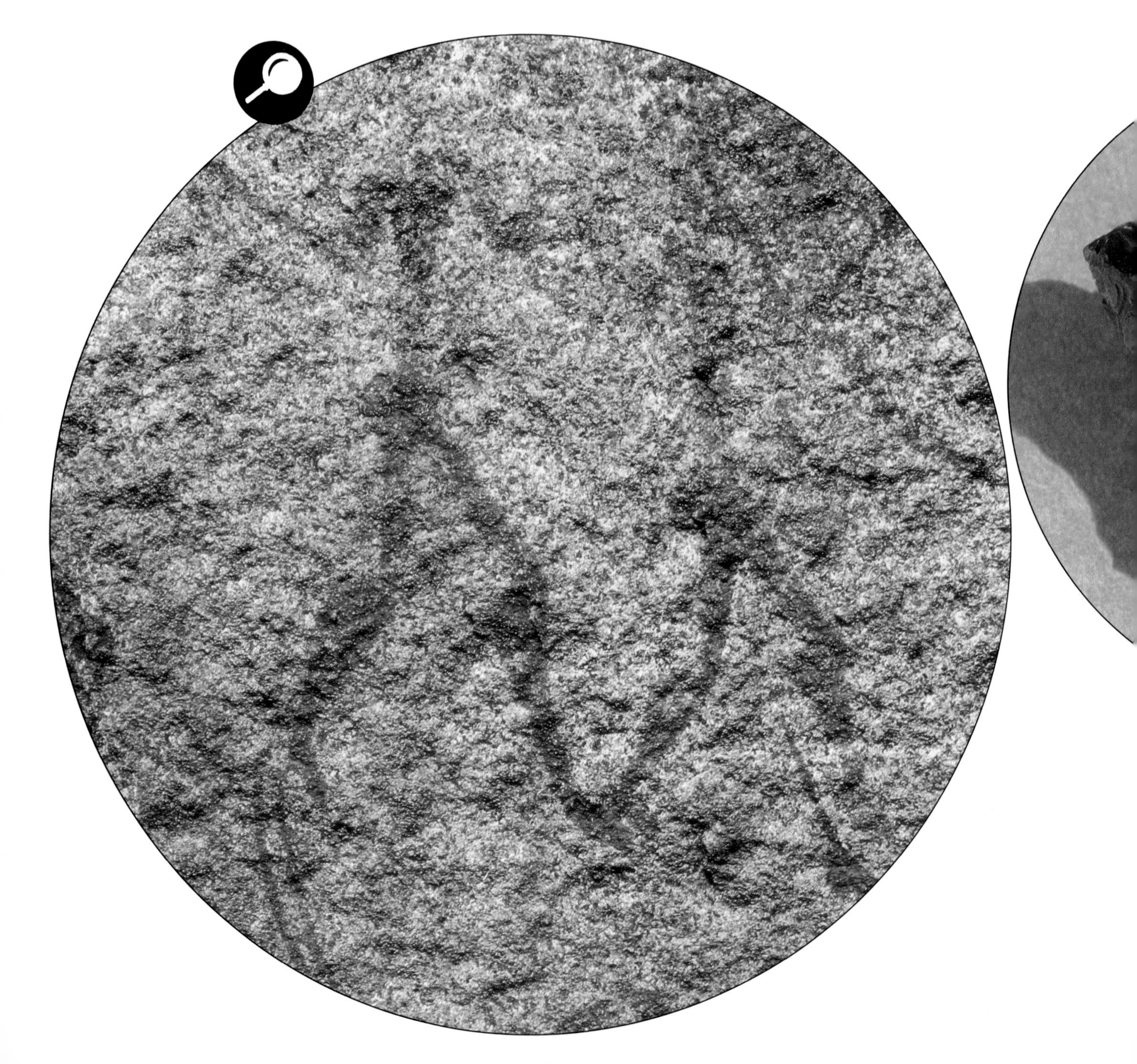

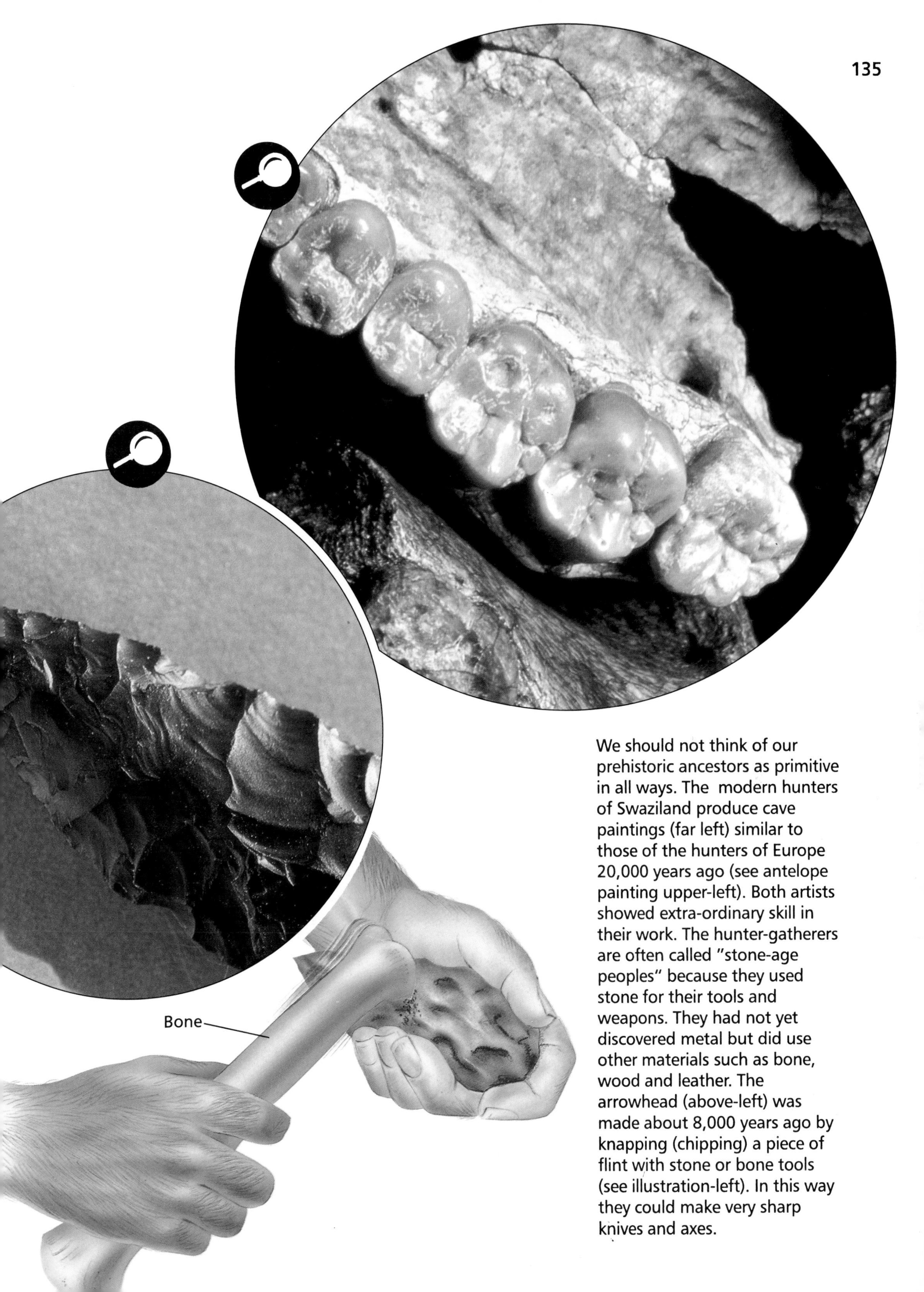

We should not think of our prehistoric ancestors as primitive in all ways. The modern hunters of Swaziland produce cave paintings (far left) similar to those of the hunters of Europe 20,000 years ago (see antelope painting upper-left). Both artists showed extra-ordinary skill in their work. The hunter-gatherers are often called "stone-age peoples" because they used stone for their tools and weapons. They had not yet discovered metal but did use other materials such as bone, wood and leather. The arrowhead (above-left) was made about 8,000 years ago by knapping (chipping) a piece of flint with stone or bone tools (see illustration-left). In this way they could make very sharp knives and axes.

BELIEFS AND RITUALS

The farmers of prehistory often worked together to build huge monuments of stone and earth. Some were great long or round burial mounds which have survived to this day and show they had beliefs about a life after death. Inside the burial mounds were chambers in which the bones of the dead were laid out. Sometimes pots were buried with the dead. Some monuments, especially standing stones (left) or circles like Stonehenge, showed that special rituals or ceremonies were involved in their religious worship. Building these monuments needed great effort on the part of the prehistoric peoples since there were no machines to help cut and lift the stones or to move vast quantities of earth.

The seeds below were found during the excavation of a huge mound called Silbury Hill in Wiltshire, England, built around 4,500 years ago. It has been estimated that it was originally over 165 feet high, and would have taken ten years to build if 500 people had worked on it every day! The seeds, grasses, beetles, and flying ants preserved under the mound showed that the work must have been started in summer. So we know when and how it was built – but not why.

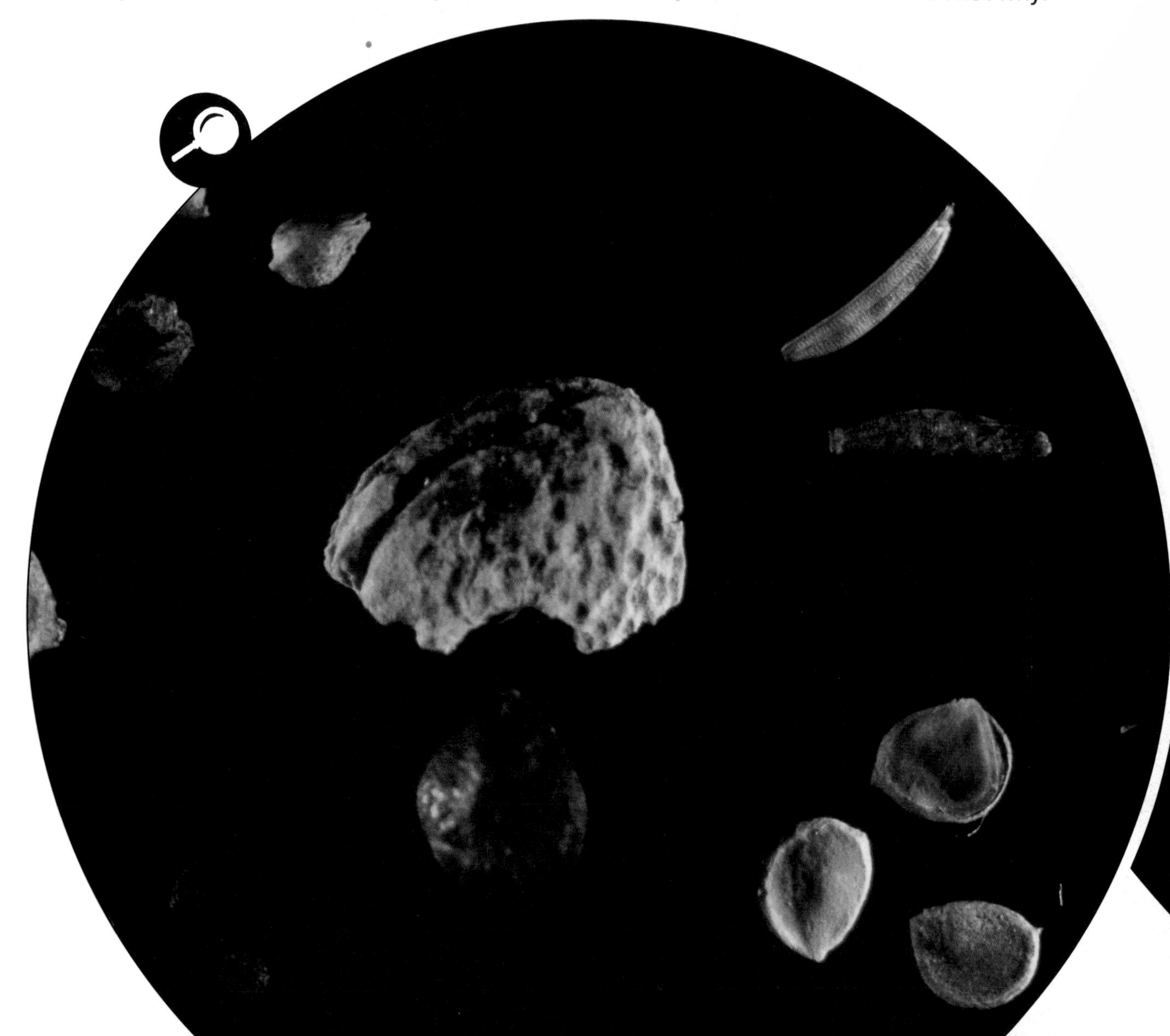

The Celts were people living in western Europe from about 700 BC. They were famous for their beautiful metalwork. The picture on the right is from a bucket decorated with helmeted heads, animals and designs. The Celts believed that gods and spirits were everywhere and needed offerings and sacrifices made to them. Below is the head of "Tollund Man," who was probably a sacrificial victim. He was either hanged or strangled and then thrown into a peat bog in Denmark. His body was so well preserved that archaeologists have been able to identify his last meal from various seeds found in his stomach.

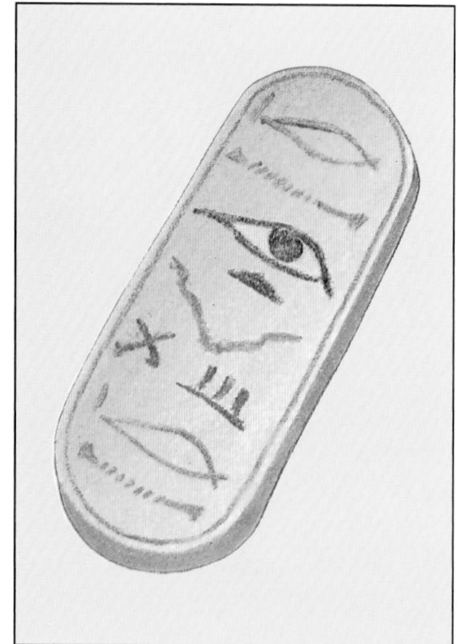

MUMMIES

The ancient Egyptians believed there was a life after death. They thought that the dead went on a journey to the underworld where they would continue their lives as before. Kings would continue to be kings, rich merchants would enjoy their usual luxuries, servants would still fetch and carry, and so on. We know all this because archaeologists have unraveled the meaning of their hieroglyphs, or writing, like that seen on the left. The Egyptians thought it important that the body itself, as well as the person's possessions, should reach the underworld in good condition. A complicated process of mummification, to dry out the body, was developed to preserve the bodies of their dead.

Making a mummy involved first removing the internal organs, which were placed in special jars. The body was dehydrated (dried out) using natron, a form of salt, to stop the flesh rotting. It was then wrapped in cloth and bandages (see right).

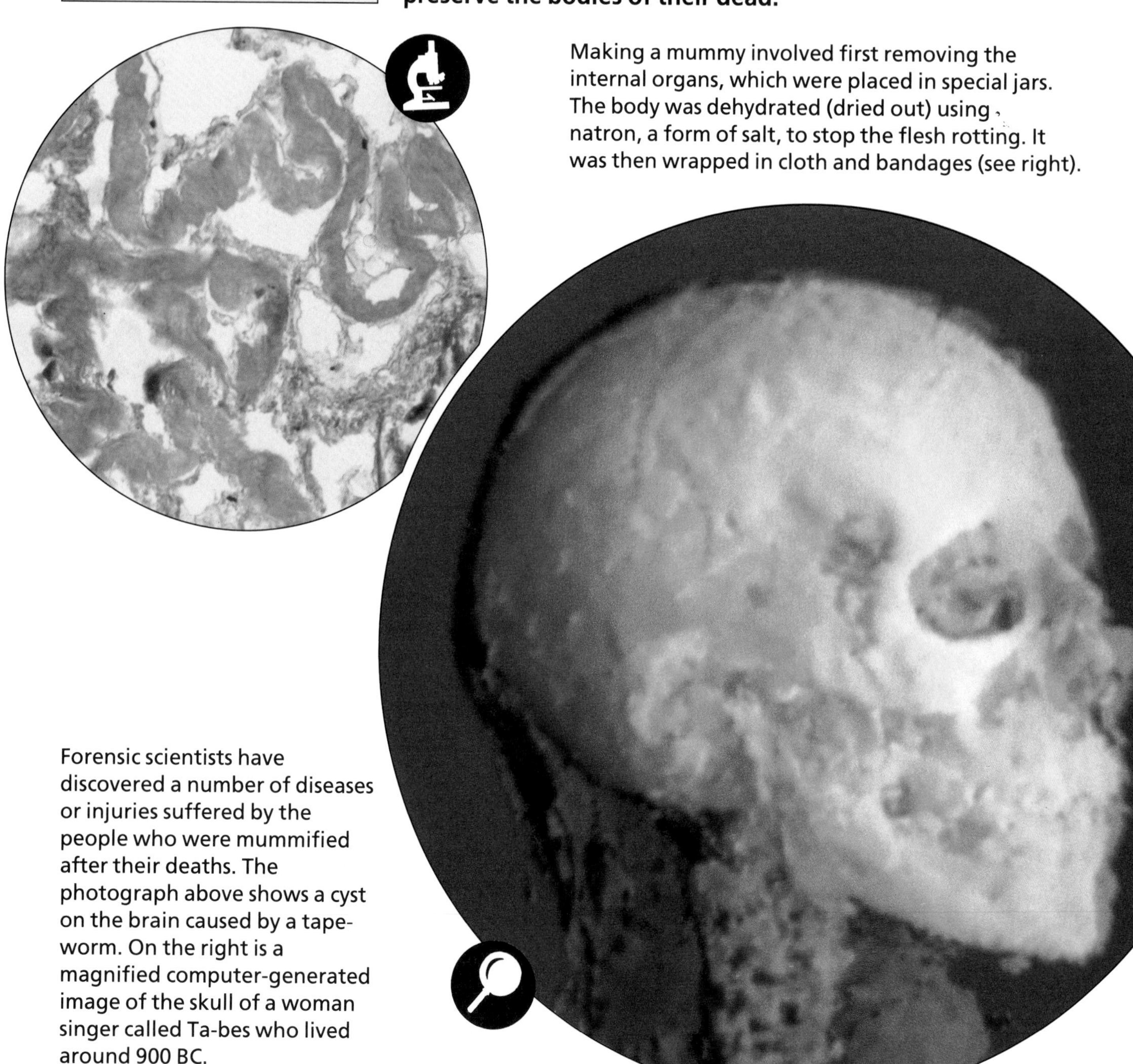

Forensic scientists have discovered a number of diseases or injuries suffered by the people who were mummified after their deaths. The photograph above shows a cyst on the brain caused by a tape-worm. On the right is a magnified computer-generated image of the skull of a woman singer called Ta-bes who lived around 900 BC.

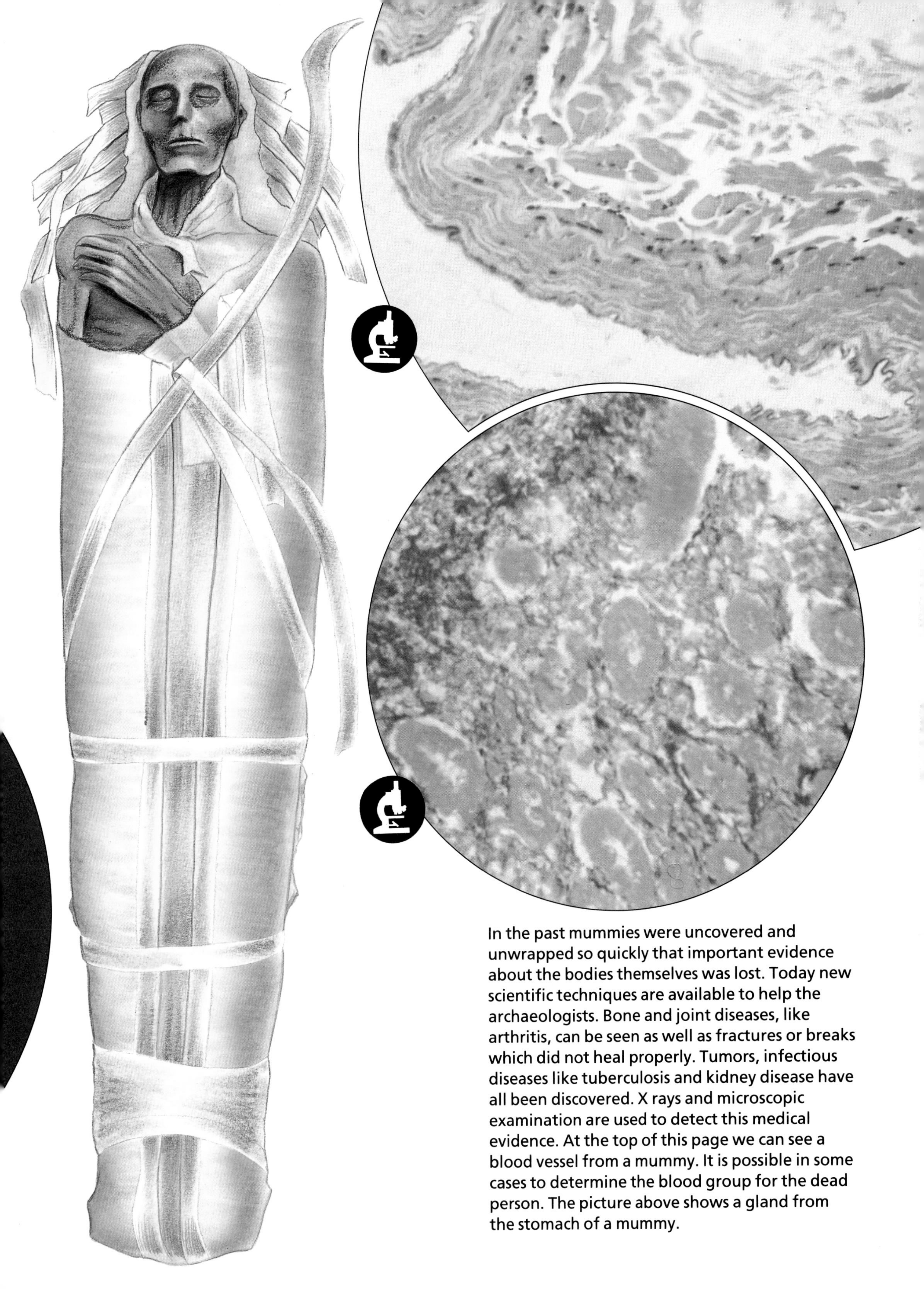

In the past mummies were uncovered and unwrapped so quickly that important evidence about the bodies themselves was lost. Today new scientific techniques are available to help the archaeologists. Bone and joint diseases, like arthritis, can be seen as well as fractures or breaks which did not heal properly. Tumors, infectious diseases like tuberculosis and kidney disease have all been discovered. X rays and microscopic examination are used to detect this medical evidence. At the top of this page we can see a blood vessel from a mummy. It is possible in some cases to determine the blood group for the dead person. The picture above shows a gland from the stomach of a mummy.

CONTENTS

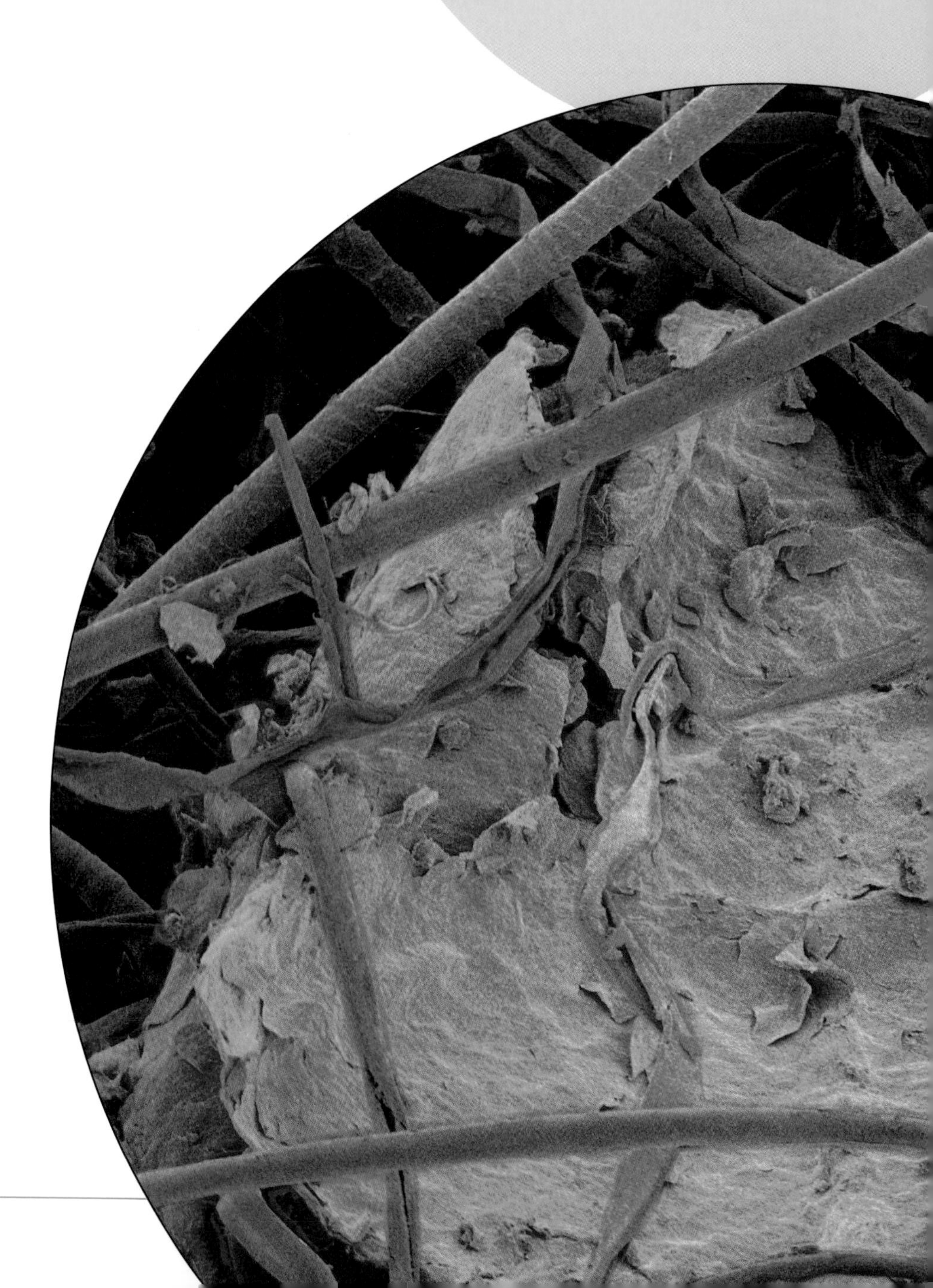

Forensic Detection

Lionel Bender

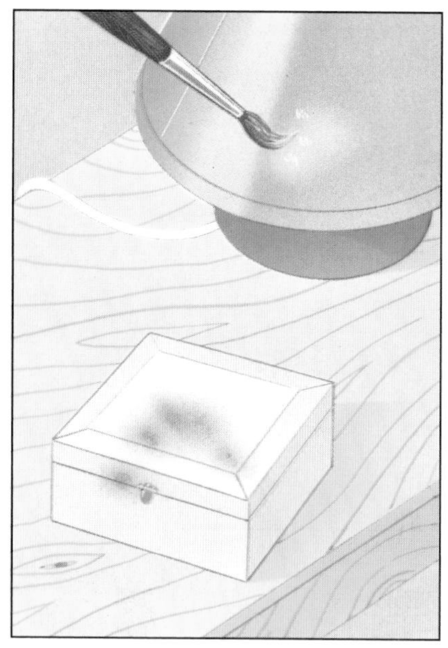

FINGERPRINTS AND FOOTPRINTS

A criminal, for example a burglar who breaks into a house to steal something, almost always leaves a trace of himself or his clothing at or around the house. It may be fingerprints on a table, or footprints in the garden or on a carpet. It could even be tire marks made by his getaway car. Some of these clues will be visible to the naked eye, but they all need to be examined closely with a hand-lens in order to make a positive identification. Fingerprints need to be developed and printed, and a plaster impression made of shoes or tire marks.

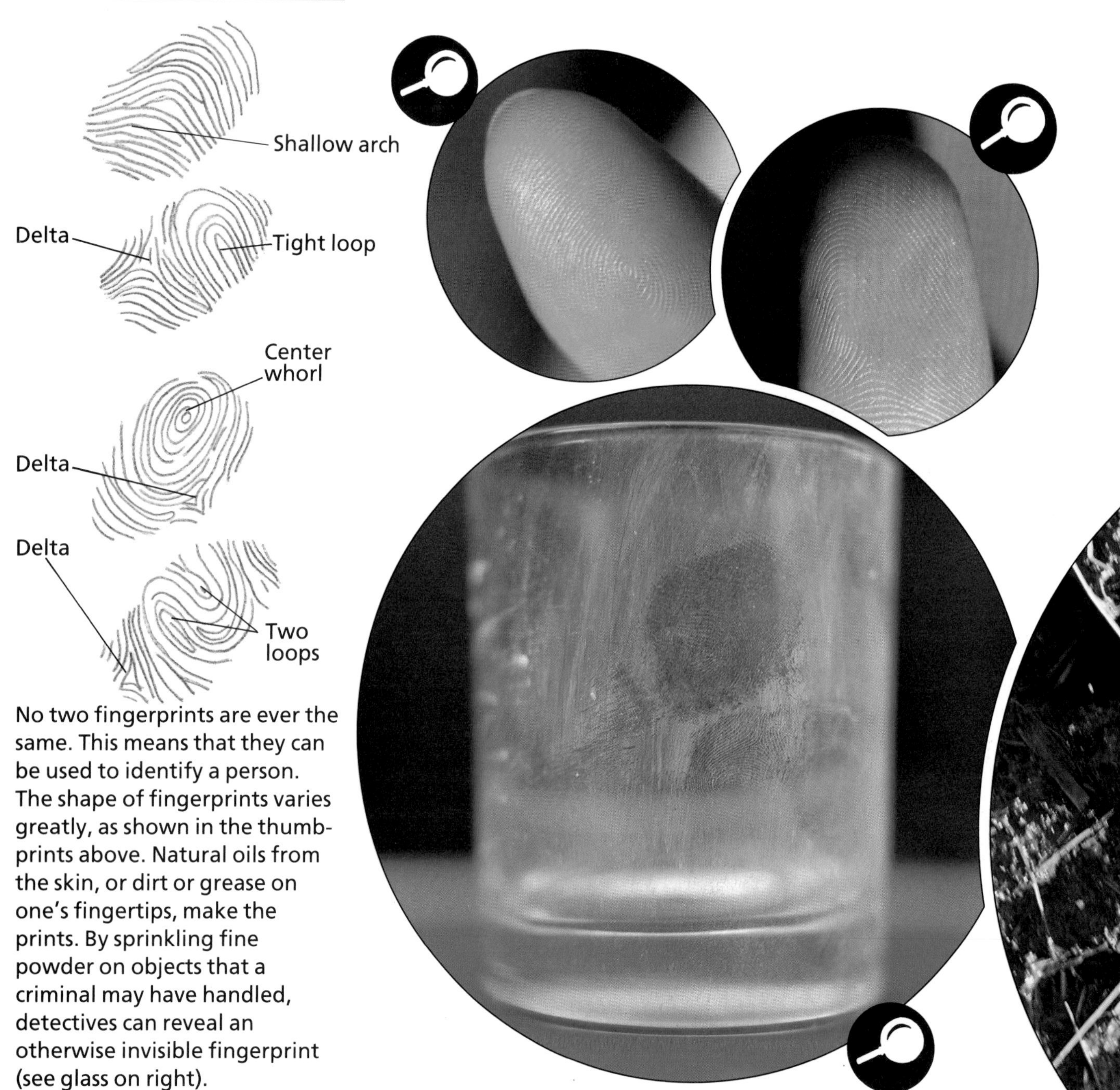

No two fingerprints are ever the same. This means that they can be used to identify a person. The shape of fingerprints varies greatly, as shown in the thumbprints above. Natural oils from the skin, or dirt or grease on one's fingertips, make the prints. By sprinkling fine powder on objects that a criminal may have handled, detectives can reveal an otherwise invisible fingerprint (see glass on right).

Take a look at a number of car tires and the soles of shoes of friends or relatives. You will notice that the cuts and grooves in the rubber, the tread, vary in shape, width and depth. On some tires and soles you may also see that the tread has worn away more on the inside than on the outside, or vice versa. A tire print in mud (see below and right) can reveal the make, model, and even the age or mileage of a car. The tread may also have trapped pieces of glass, grass or nails that can be matched with those found at the scene of an incident.

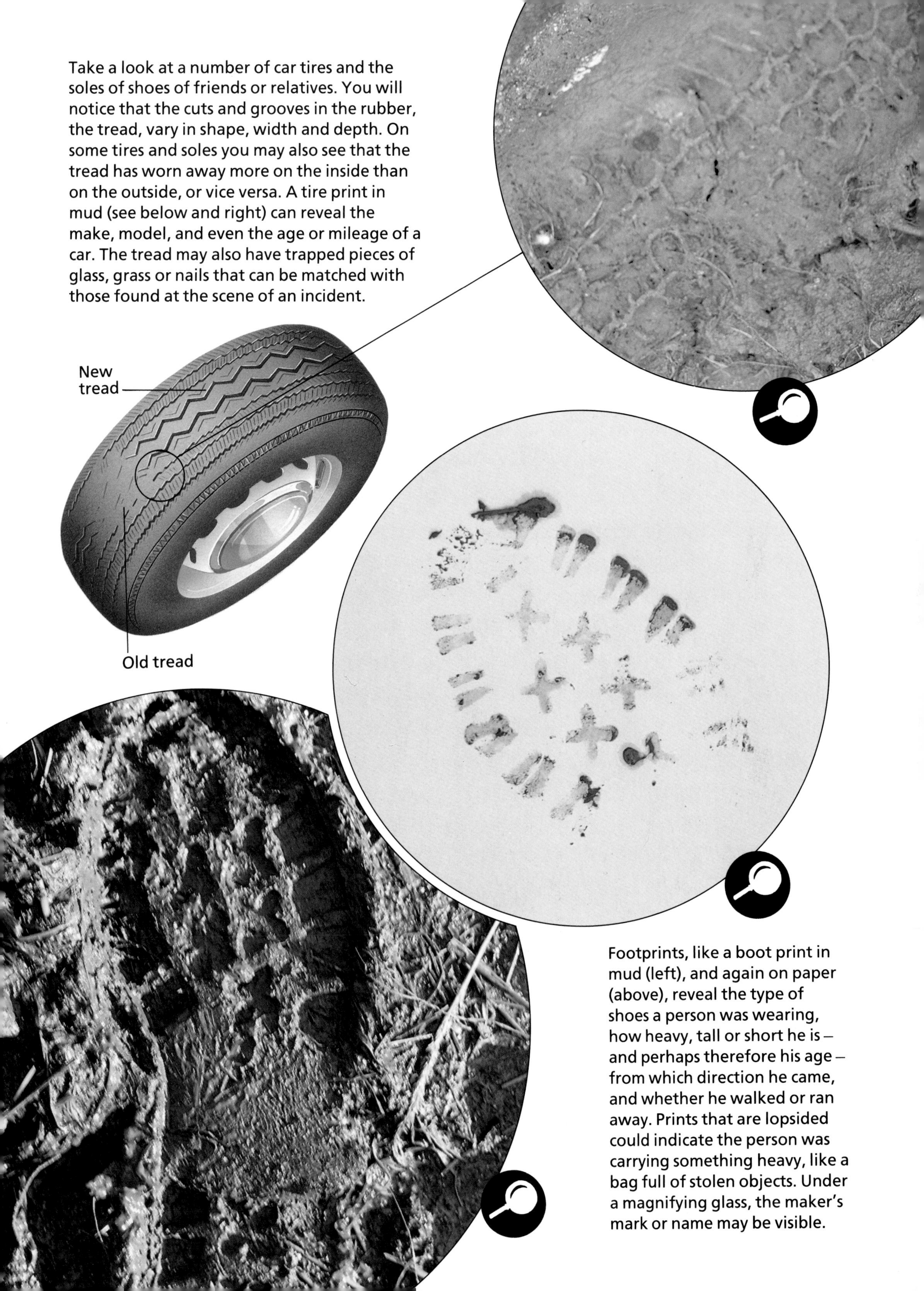

Footprints, like a boot print in mud (left), and again on paper (above), reveal the type of shoes a person was wearing, how heavy, tall or short he is – and perhaps therefore his age – from which direction he came, and whether he walked or ran away. Prints that are lopsided could indicate the person was carrying something heavy, like a bag full of stolen objects. Under a magnifying glass, the maker's mark or name may be visible.

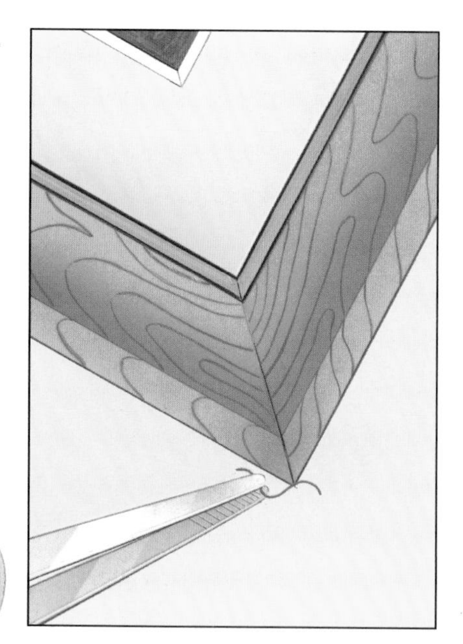

THREADS, FIBERS, WIRES

Whenever you brush up against a rough or sharp edge, such as the corner of a table, tiny threads or fibers from your clothing rub or are pulled off. Under a microscope these can often be seen to have characteristic shapes and smoothness, depending on whether they are natural fibers like cotton or silk, for example, or man-made, such as nylon, acrylic, or polyester. Each clothes manufacturer will usually keep a photographic record of the types of fibers it uses, and the police will have access to these. A forensic scientist can use these clues to match them to a suspect's clothing. Microscopic examination of cut rope fibers and wires can also reveal how, and with exactly which tool, the cuts were made.

Microscopic comparison of the ends of a length of rope can determine if the rope was severed with scissors (above) or cut by rubbing against a rough edge (below). It is even possible to detect whether the rope was cut by a right or left-handed person.

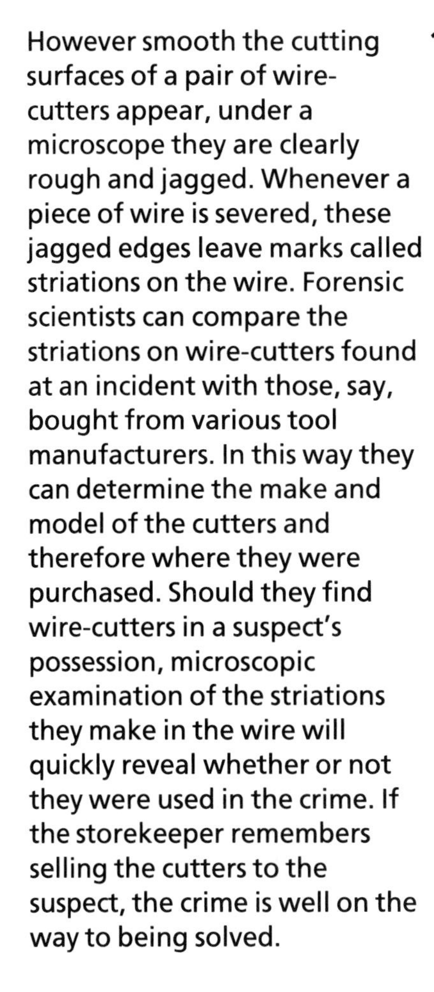

However smooth the cutting surfaces of a pair of wire-cutters appear, under a microscope they are clearly rough and jagged. Whenever a piece of wire is severed, these jagged edges leave marks called striations on the wire. Forensic scientists can compare the striations on wire-cutters found at an incident with those, say, bought from various tool manufacturers. In this way they can determine the make and model of the cutters and therefore where they were purchased. Should they find wire-cutters in a suspect's possession, microscopic examination of the striations they make in the wire will quickly reveal whether or not they were used in the crime. If the storekeeper remembers selling the cutters to the suspect, the crime is well on the way to being solved.

At a magnification of several hundred times life-size, silk threads (left) look quite different from those of pure cotton (above). The cotton threads, from a person's shirt collar, are coated with dirt and oils from the skin. Chemical studies of the oils can reveal who was wearing the shirt.

BULLETS AND KNIVES

An important part of forensic science is the study of weapons, especially firearms and the behavior of bullets or shot fired from them, which is known as ballistics. For example, scientists may be able to match the striations on a bullet found in the body of a murdered person with those on a bullet fired by a suspect's gun. By firing a revolver at sheets of cardboard from various distances and studying the different gunpowder stains and bullet hole shapes, they may be able to determine which of a group of armed criminals fired the lethal shot. A knife may be stained with blood that can be analyzed chemically. Or it may bear a unique manufacturer's mark which police can identify from a catalog or record file.

When a bullet is fired, marks are left on the end of the used cartridge by the firing pin and on the sides of the bullet by the spiraled groove, or rifling, in the barrel (see diagram). A pistol taken from the scene of a crime will be fired and the used cartridges examined. Comparisons of firing pin marks (photo below left) and rifling marks (below) will be made.

In the photo above, of two pieces of metal at a magnification of about x10, forensic scientists were able to match the scratch marks and jagged edge of a fragment of metal found in a victim's skull with the broken tip of the blade of a knife found on a suspect. Similar comparisons can be made between the ends of a used cartridge in a pistol and the bullet cap taken from a victim.

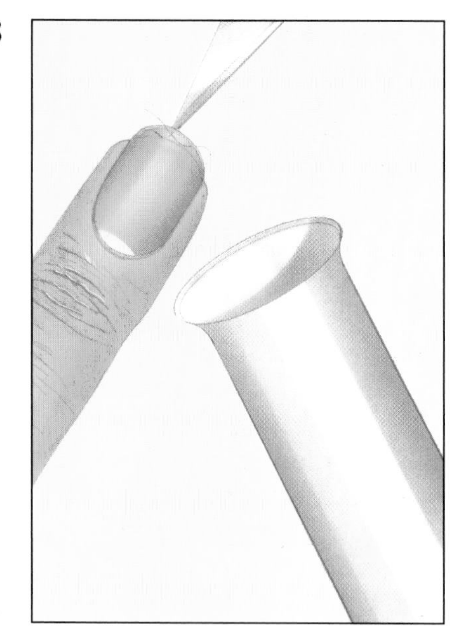

SKIN AND HAIRS

A murder victim is carefully wrapped in plastic and taken to police headquarters for examination. Care is taken to ensure that no possible clues or evidence on the body are disturbed, in this case skin cells and hairs caught under a fingernail. A pathologist, a specially trained doctor, will try to establish the cause of death. Scratches or bruises on the body, as shown in the two photographs below, indicate that the murder involved a scuffle or fight. Examination of the victim's hair may reveal unusual distortion of the individual strands, indicating poisoning by the chemical thallium. Forensic scientists will try and determine who was the murderer by microscopically examining the trapped skin cells and hairs.

This victim scratched the attacker while fighting for his, or her, life. The skin cells and hairs scratched off were later used by scientists for genetic fingerprinting. This involved studying the pattern made by separating the chemicals within DNA, the genetic or hereditary material in living cells which determines a person's characteristics. DNA exists in tiny chromosomes. The DNA pattern is different for everybody, with the exception of identical twins, so comparing DNA patterns from the suspect's cells and those from the victim can establish guilt.

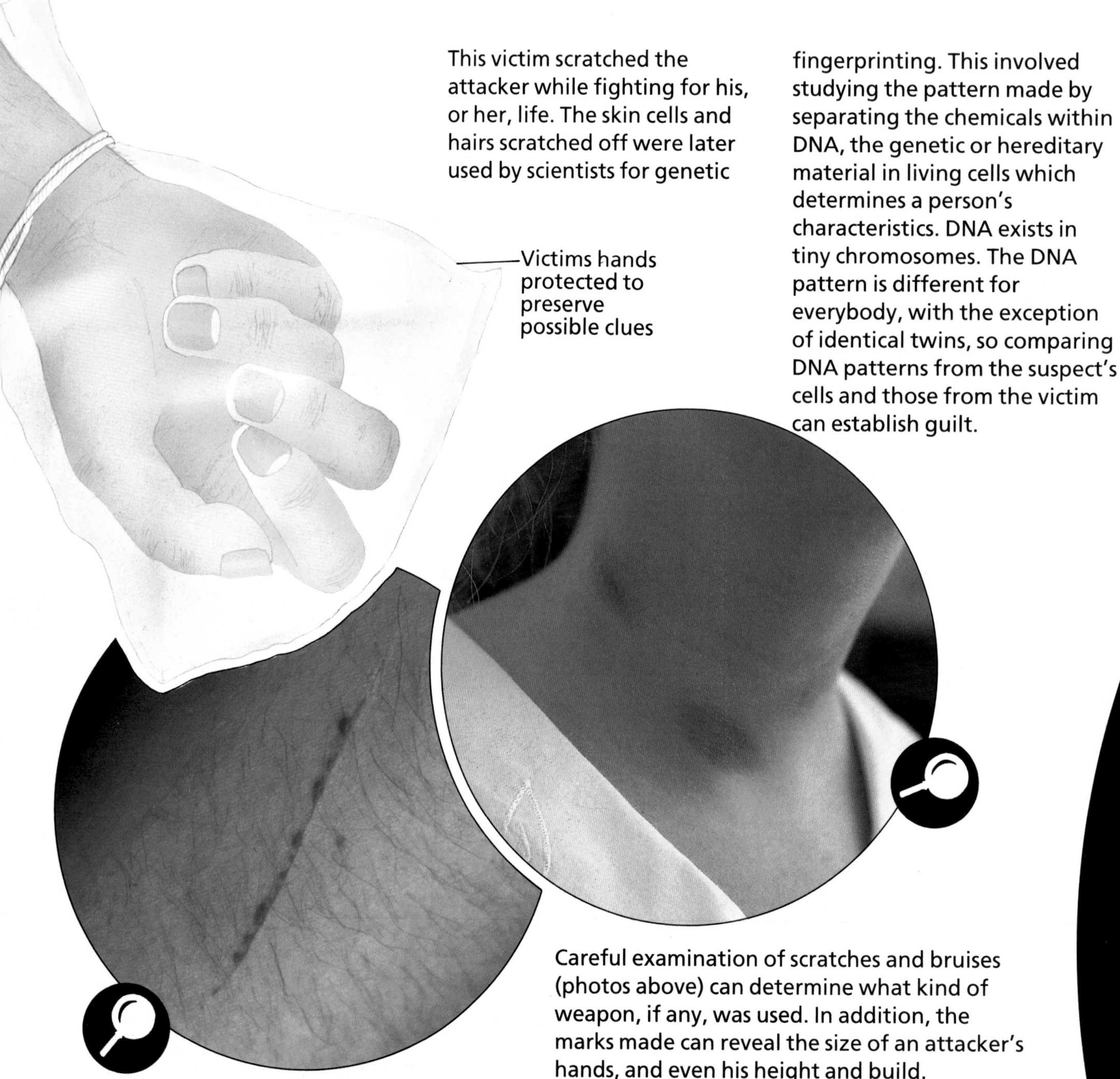

Victims hands protected to preserve possible clues

Careful examination of scratches and bruises (photos above) can determine what kind of weapon, if any, was used. In addition, the marks made can reveal the size of an attacker's hands, and even his height and build.

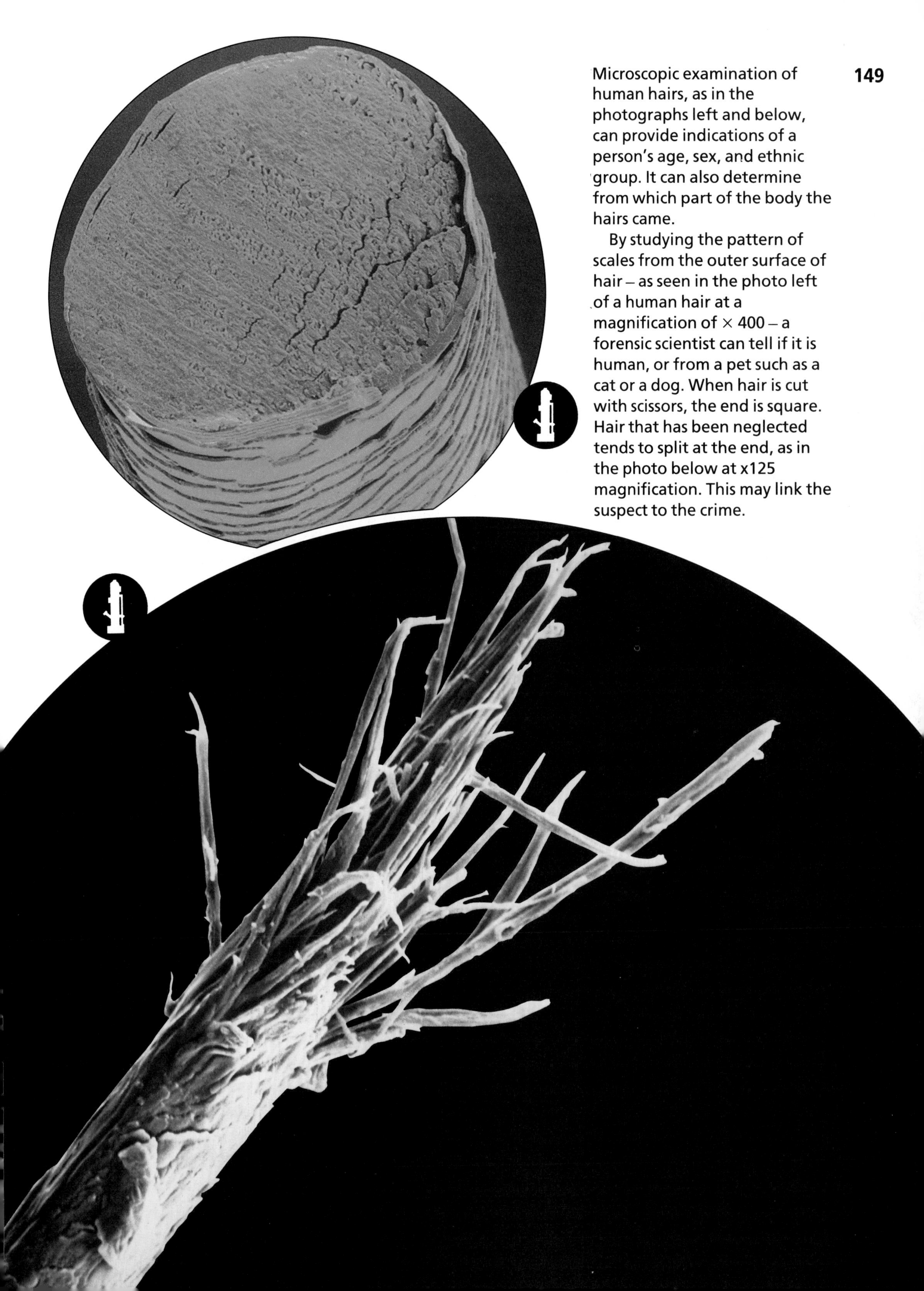

Microscopic examination of human hairs, as in the photographs left and below, can provide indications of a person's age, sex, and ethnic group. It can also determine from which part of the body the hairs came.

By studying the pattern of scales from the outer surface of hair – as seen in the photo left of a human hair at a magnification of × 400 – a forensic scientist can tell if it is human, or from a pet such as a cat or a dog. When hair is cut with scissors, the end is square. Hair that has been neglected tends to split at the end, as in the photo below at x125 magnification. This may link the suspect to the crime.

BODY CELLS

An obvious clue to a serious crime is a bloodstain on the victim's clothing. Microscopic studies of the victim's body cells can reveal if the stain also includes some blood from the attacker. The shape of blood splashes at the scene can show how a wound was inflicted and if the victim was moved after being stabbed or shot. In a sexual attack, traces of a man's sperm may be found on clothing. Or a severed arm or leg may be discovered and a sample of tissue removed for further analysis. Examination of the chromosomes in the cells can establish at least the sex of the victim. A pathologist will study these and many other types of cells, both chemically and under the microscope, for signs of poisons, drugs or bruising.

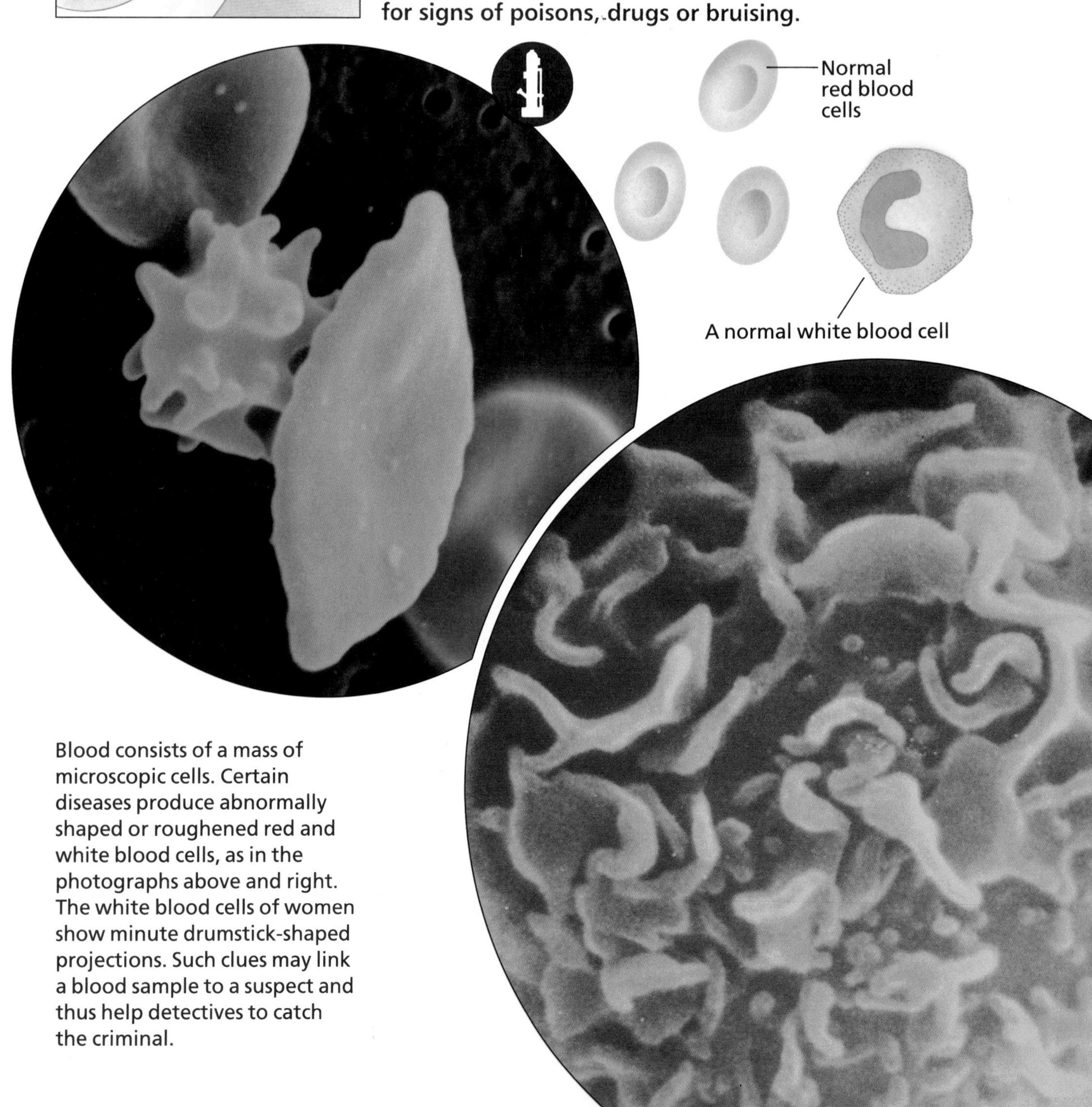

Blood consists of a mass of microscopic cells. Certain diseases produce abnormally shaped or roughened red and white blood cells, as in the photographs above and right. The white blood cells of women show minute drumstick-shaped projections. Such clues may link a blood sample to a suspect and thus help detectives to catch the criminal.

Sperm are a man's sex cells. An adult man produces about 200 million sperm a day. Sperm are so tiny that several hundred would easily fit onto a pinhead. The photograph, right, of human sperm, was taken at a magnification of x300. Clothing worn by a victim or suspect in an assault case is usually examined for sperm. Any found can be tested chemically to identify the man involved.

Human cells contain microscopic chromosomes. These are arranged in pairs. One special pair, the sex chromosomes, differ in males and females (see diagram below right). In females there are two large X chromosomes, and in males an X and a smaller Y chromosome. Microscopic studies of chromosomes taken from cells found at the scene of a crime, as in the photo below, can determine the sex of the person involved.

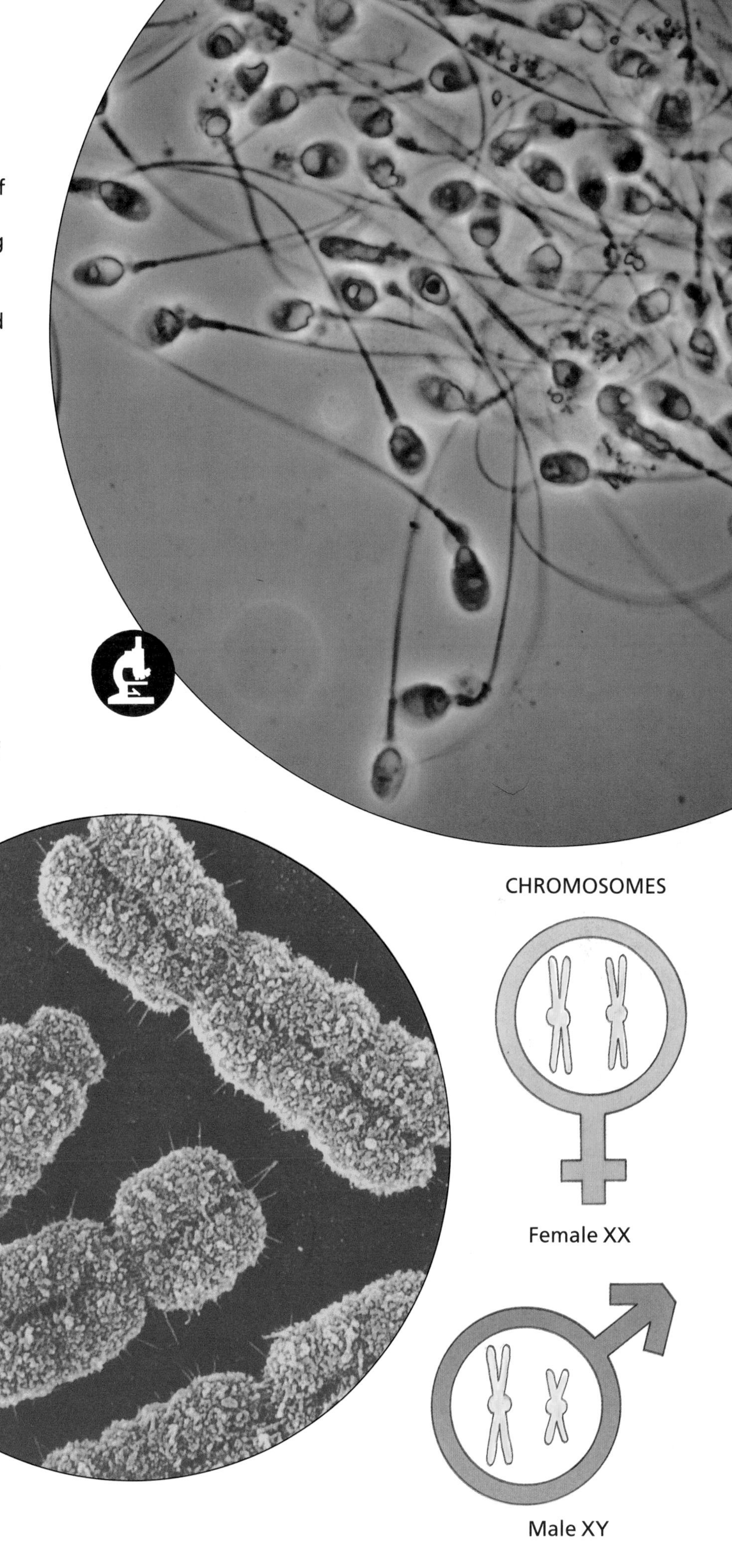

CHROMOSOMES

Female XX

Male XY

PRACTICAL PROJECTS

You can discover a great deal about how forensic scientists work with just a magnifying glass. But to see greater detail you will need a home microscope (see page 4). The objects you wish to study must be mounted on a glass slide. They must be thin enough to allow light to shine through them. You may need to cut very thin slices of material or to tease them out until they are very fine. To pick out different types of structures, you will need to stain your specimens. The way to do this is outlined below. If you are going to try something which is a bit tricky, it is worth getting help from an adult. You may be able to start your studies with some ready-made slides bought from a microscope supplier.

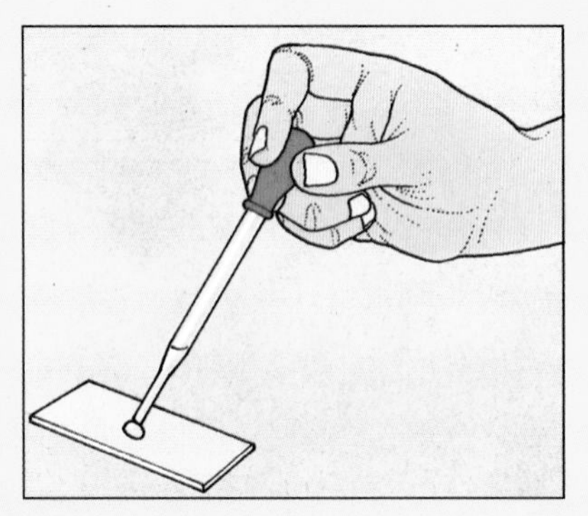

To prepare a cell slide, place a drop of clean water containing the cells on the glass.

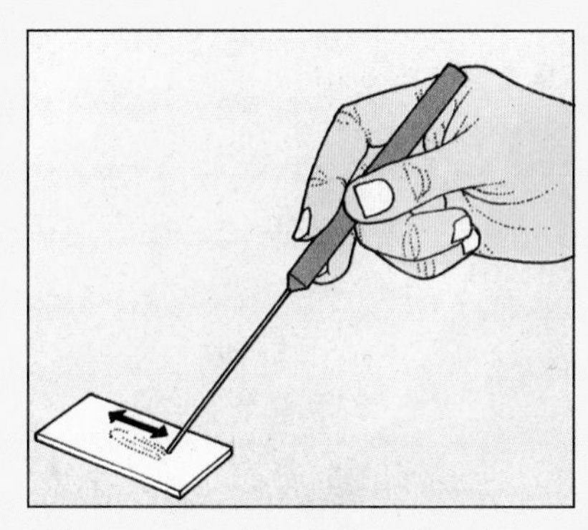

With a wire loop that has been sterilized in a flame, spread the fluid thinly and let it dry.

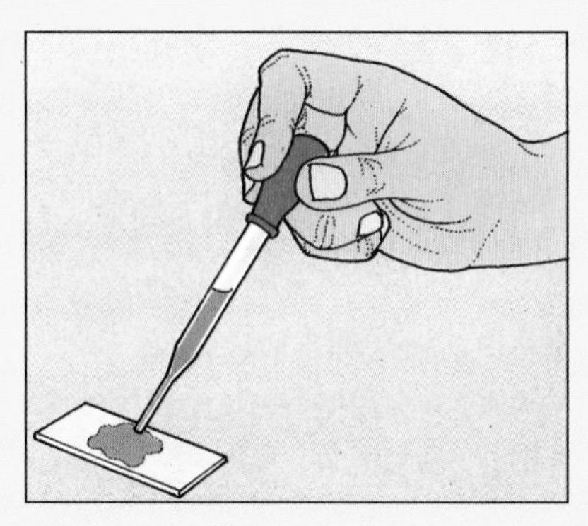

Add a small drop of staining dye to the cells and leave for a few minutes.

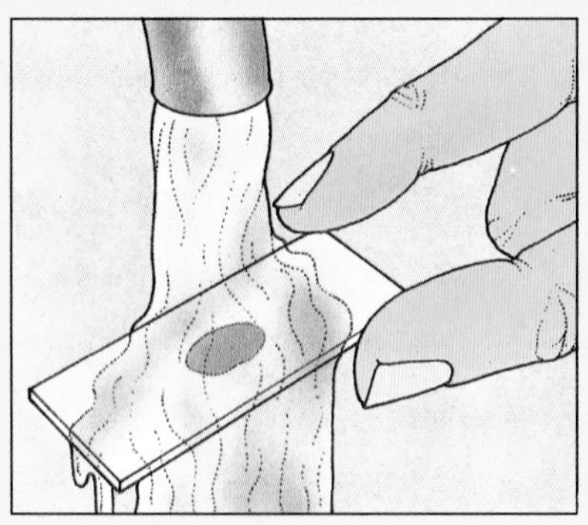

Wash off the dye with water or alcohol. You can stain with another, contrasting dye.

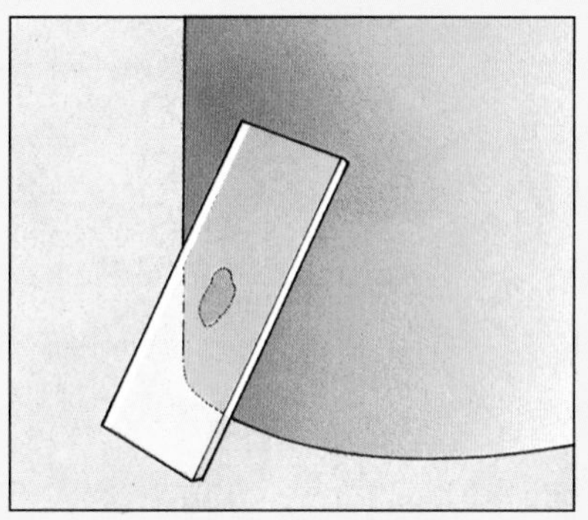

Leave the slide to dry. You can speed up drying by gently warming the slide over a flame.

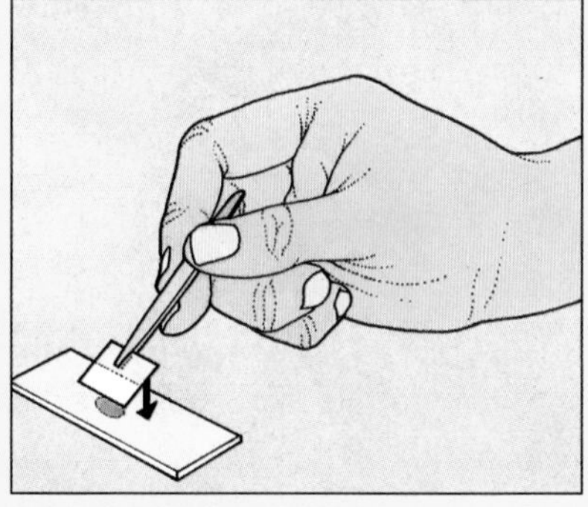

Place a cover slip (a thin square of glass) over the stained cells, using a pair of tweezers.

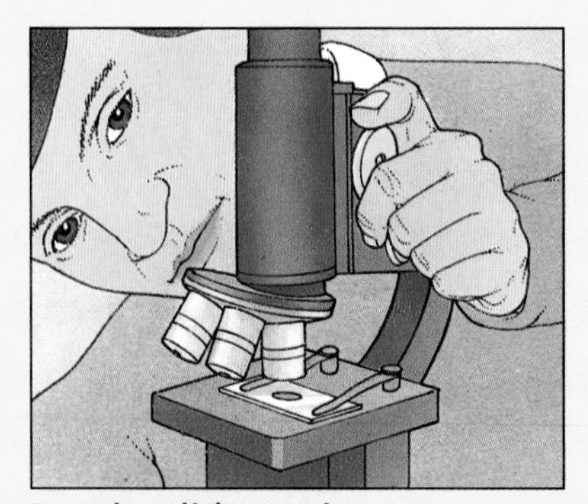

Put the slide on the microscope stage and position the mirror to give you good illumination.

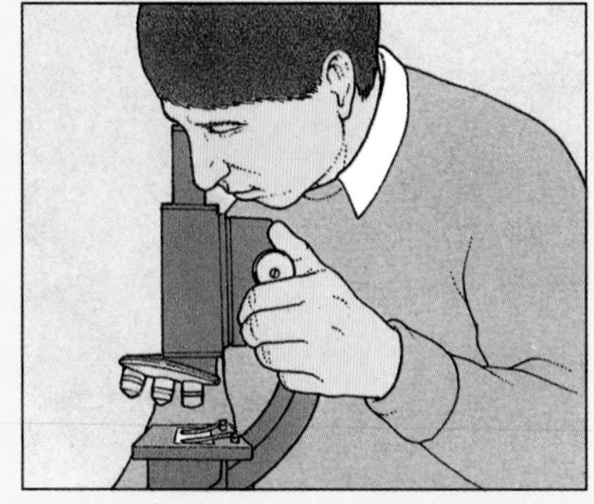

Select the objective lens you want, then move the eyepiece up and down to focus. Start at the lowest magnification.

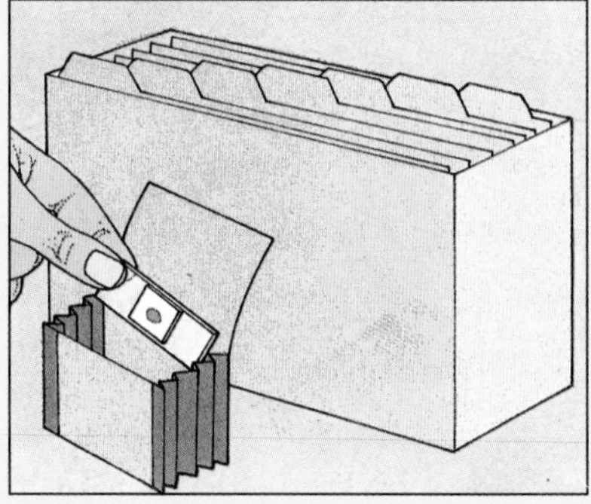

Keep your prepared slides in a wallet made from a folded sheet of cardboard, which will protect them from dust.

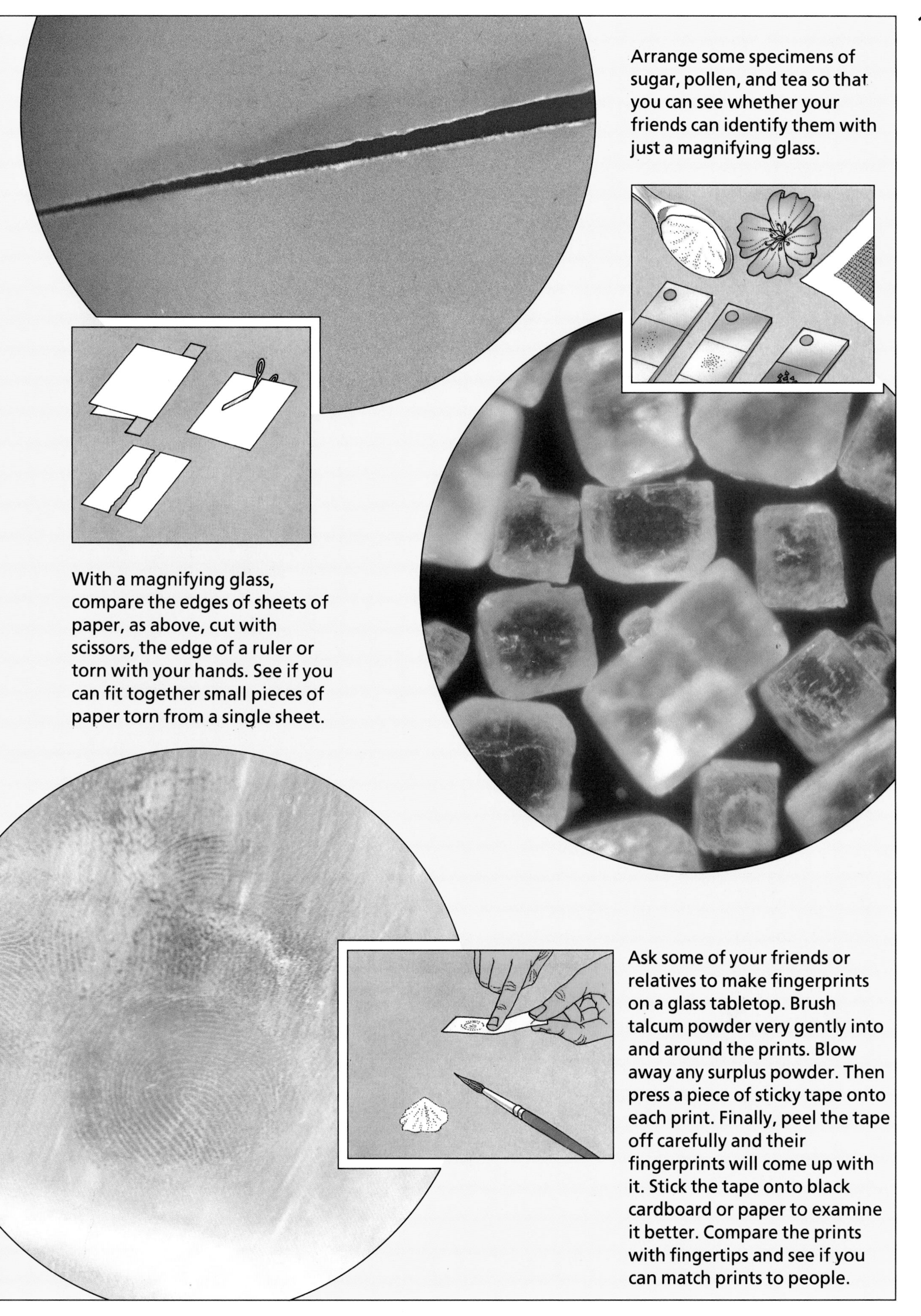

Arrange some specimens of sugar, pollen, and tea so that you can see whether your friends can identify them with just a magnifying glass.

With a magnifying glass, compare the edges of sheets of paper, as above, cut with scissors, the edge of a ruler or torn with your hands. See if you can fit together small pieces of paper torn from a single sheet.

Ask some of your friends or relatives to make fingerprints on a glass tabletop. Brush talcum powder very gently into and around the prints. Blow away any surplus powder. Then press a piece of sticky tape onto each print. Finally, peel the tape off carefully and their fingerprints will come up with it. Stick the tape onto black cardboard or paper to examine it better. Compare the prints with fingertips and see if you can match prints to people.

MICROPHOTOGRAPHY

Forensic scientists collect clues and evidence at the scene of a crime and take them back to the laboratory for further examination. They usually arrive at the scene of a crime with a box full of plastic collecting bottles, tubes and envelopes; tags for listing objects; a camera to photograph the position of items such as a dead body, bloodstains or weapons; a fingerprint kit; and scissors, tweezers etc. Back at the laboratory they photograph microscope slide images to check them against police records and for use as evidence in court. This is a long and hard job. However, the telltale evidence uncovered by such painstaking police procedures has helped put many a criminal behind bars.

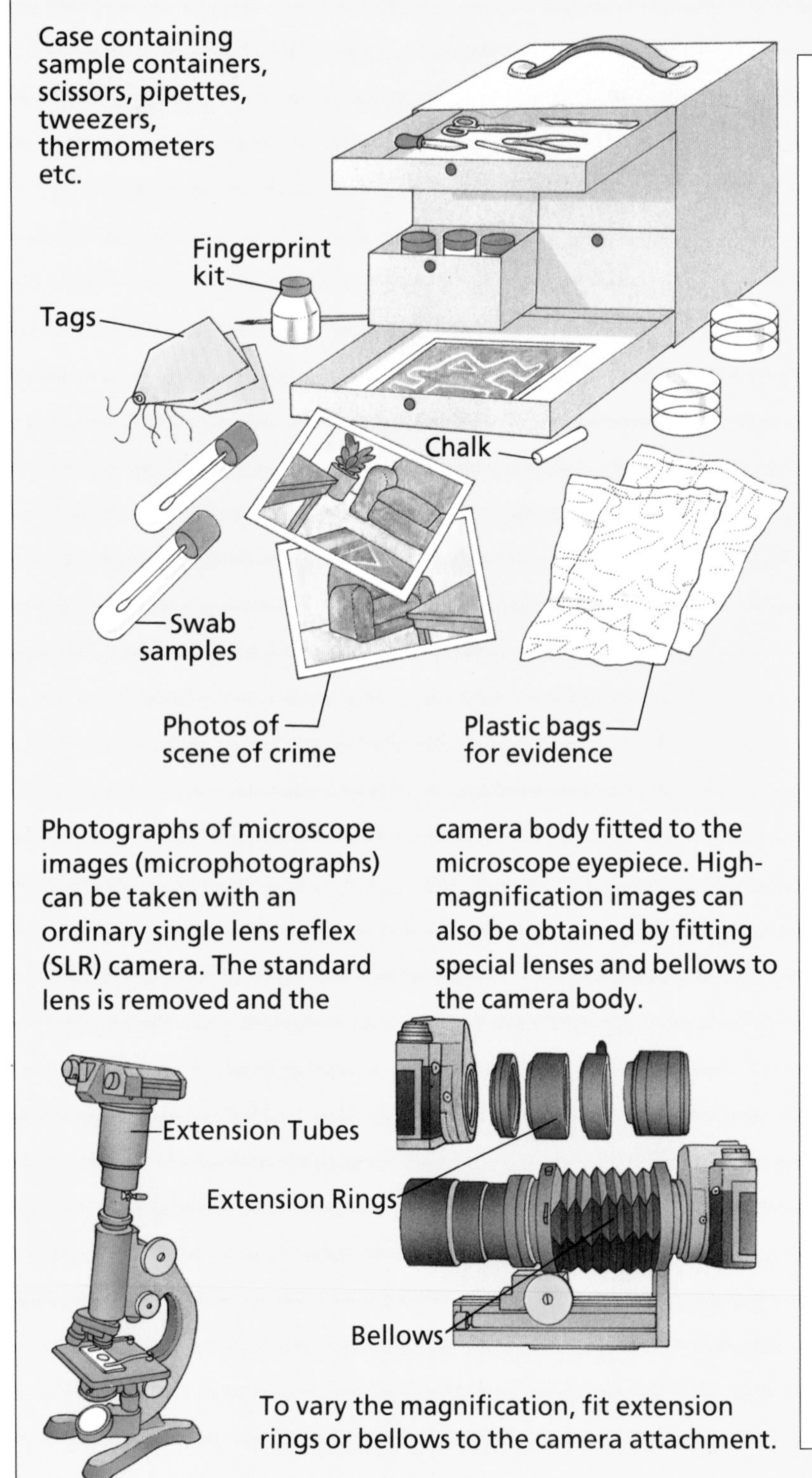

Photographs of microscope images (microphotographs) can be taken with an ordinary single lens reflex (SLR) camera. The standard lens is removed and the camera body fitted to the microscope eyepiece. High-magnification images can also be obtained by fitting special lenses and bellows to the camera body.

To vary the magnification, fit extension rings or bellows to the camera attachment.

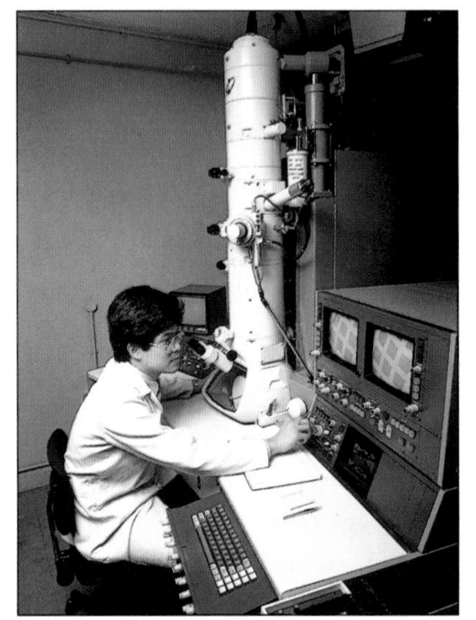

There are two main types of electron microscope. In a transmission type (TEM), a beam of electrons is passed through a very thin slice of tissue and an image is produced on a screen. In a scanning electron microscope (SEM), a fine beam of electrons is moved across the surface of the tissue for reflections to be collected and used to create an image on a television type of screen. Using an SEM, realistic 3-D images are produced. But as with all types of microscope specimens, the tissues and organs are no longer alive. The slide preparation process kills live cells. The colors on photos produced using an SEM are false colors added in processing.

antennae the feelers on an insect's head. They contain tiny sense organs concerned with touch and smell, for detecting temperature or moisture.

antibiotic a substance produced by one type of microbe – usually a fungus – that destroys or prevents the growth of another – most commonly a bacterium.

antibody a special type of chemical produced by white blood cells which combat the harmful effects of an antigen.

antigen any substance that the body regards as "foreign" or not part of itself.

atom the smallest particle that can exist. Normally, atoms are indivisible. All matter – solids, liquids and gases – is made up of atoms.

axillary the angle above where a leaf joins a stem.

bacteria small single-cell organisms without chlorophyll but with a cell wall and nucleus.

ballistics the study of the movement of objects, such as bullets, under the force of gravity.

biomolecule a type of molecule found in living things, such as sugars, fats and proteins.

blood a red fluid that travels around the body in the veins and arteries. Blood is made up of two types of blood cells, the red and white corpuscles, and a straw-colored liquid, the plasma. Blood is pumped round the body by the heart and gushes from a cut. The shape and size of bloodstains can tell forensic scientists something about how a cut or injury was sustained.

bone the tissue that forms the skeleton.

brain the organ within the skull which co-ordinates and controls the body; the headquarters of the nervous system.

capillaries microscopic blood vessels; tubes which carry blood to every cell in the body.

carbon dioxide one of the body's waste products; it is released by the cells into the bloodstream during the chemical breakdown of food.

cell the smallest unit or building block of living things. Most cells in the human body are about 0.03 mm across and can be seen only with a microscope. They differ greatly in shape and form and can reveal which part of the body a sample of flesh comes from.

chitin a tough substance related to sugar that makes up the cell wall of fungi.

chlorophyll the green pigment of plants and some simple single-cell creatures, that absorbs the energy of sunlight to produce sugars.

chromosome part of the cell nucleus which determines a person's appearance.

chrysalis the pupa of a butterfly, the stage that occurs between caterpillar and adult.

compound eye type of eye found in many insects, made up of many units or facets.

corrode to rot, break down, oxidize or lose its structure.

crystal a regularly shaped structure created by the precise way in which some atoms combine together in chemical elements and compounds. Diamond is a crystal formed by the regular bonds between atoms of carbon. Various chemical compounds have characteristic crystal shapes.

crust the outer layer around the earth on which we live. The crust is made up from three types of rock – igneous, sedimentary and metamorphic.

dermis the lower layer of skin on a human body.

digestive system the body's food processing system, which includes the mouth, pharynx, esophagus, stomach and the small and large intestines.

disease an illness with a specific cause and recognizable signs and symptoms. Some diseases are caused by microbes.

DNA short for deoxyribonucleic acid. DNA is a chemical blueprint for living things. It carries coded information that determines the features of a creature and ensures that these are copied and passed on to any offspring.

duct a tube down which liquids flow in an animal's body.

egg the female reproductive cell.

element a substance composed of just one type of atom, such as gold, silver, oxygen gas.

enzyme a type of protein produced by the body which speeds up chemical reactions.

epidermis the upper layer of skin on a human body.

fingerprint the mark left by the tiny ridges of a person's fingers and thumbs on an object they touch or pick up.

forensic term relating to the use of clues and evidence in a court of law. Forensic medicine is the use of medical knowledge in legal problems.

fossils the preserved remains of animals and plants.

gills in fungi such as mushrooms, one of the vertical sheets of tissue under the cap that bear the spores.

haustoria an outgrowth from a parasite that penetrates the body of its host and extracts food.

heart the muscular organ which acts like a double pump to push blood into the lungs and around the body. It is situated between the lungs, slightly left of center in the chest.

hormones the body's chemical messengers. They flow around the blood system and control tissue growth and development.

hyphae the branching filaments that make up the body of many fungi. They may be visible or underground.

igneous rocks form part of the earth's crust and were once molten material, such as lava from a volcanic eruption.

infection the invasion of the body by a harmful microbe.

Iron Age the name given to the period in Europe when people used iron for their tools and weapons. In Britain the Iron Age lasted from about 700 B.C. to A.D. 43.

larva young insect which has hatched from its egg and must become a pupa.

laser a source of intense pure light of a single color. Laser stands for light amplification by stimulated emission of radiation.

maggot a larva such as that of many flies, which has no legs and moves by wriggling. The head is usually poorly developed and usually at the narrow end of the maggot.

magma the molten rock below the earth's crust.

magnification the number of times the diameter, or distance across, something appears to be enlarged or made bigger.

manmade fiber a fiber made of polyester, nylon or other artificial substance.

metamorphic rocks sedimentary or igneous rocks which have been changed by pressure, heat or chemical action.

metamorphosis an obvious change of body shape and structure that takes place during the life of an animal.

microbe any organism too small to be seen by the naked eye. Also known as microorganisms, microbes include protozoa, bacteria, viruses, and some fungi and algae, many of which can cause diseases.

microtome an instrument for cutting sections for light microscopy.

mineral-preservation occurs in organic material when it comes into contact with metal corrosion.

molecule a combination of two or more atoms. A molecule of water, for example, consists of one atom of oxygen combined with two atoms of hydrogen.

molds fungi that produce a network of hyphae visible on the surface of their food, such as those that attack bread an fruit.

molting the way that young insects with incomplete metamorphosis shed their skins in order to grow bigger.

mummies the dried and preserved remains of bodies of people and animals.

natural fiber a fiber such as wool, cotton or silk, produced by animals or plants.

nerve a bundle of fibers that carry information between the brain and parts of the body.

neuron a nerve cell. It consists of a long thin fiber and many short treelike projections called the dendrites.

nodule a small lump, such as that housing bacteria in the roots of peas.

nymph young insects which have hatched from eggs and must undergo incomplete metamorphosis.

organ a major part of the body such as the heart, lungs, eyes, ears or kidneys. Organs are made of one or more types of tissue and each has a particular job to do.

organelle a distinct structure with a living cell, such as the nucleus.

organic materials anything which was once living, such as wood or bone.

ovule the "egg" of a seed plant that after fertilization develops into the seed.

oxygen the gas needed by our body's cells to convert food into energy.

pathologist a doctor specializing in determining the cause of death, illness or disease.

parasite an organism that lives on or in another one, taking nourishment from it.

peldipalps a spider's feelers.

petrification the changing to stone of organic material. Fossils are often petrified animals, trees or plants.

photo-electric a device that produces a small current of electricity when light is shone on it, switching off when the light is interrupted.

pigment a substance that is colored. The green of plants is caused by the pigment chlorophyll.

pollen powdery substance found in flowering plants and trees. Its transfer between different parts of plants is what makes new flowers grow.

proboscis any long extension of the head which looks like a "nose", although its functions may not be noselike. The proboscis of a moth is made up of its mouthparts and forms a drinking straw.

pro-leg a fleshy cone-shaped bump which sticks out under the abdomen of a caterpillar and helps it move.

protozoan a single-celled organism such as the pond creature Amoeba.

pupa the apparently quiet stage in the complete metamorphosis of an insect.

sedimentary rocks are the remains of sediments like mud and sand from long-vanished oceans and seas.

setae tiny hairs on an insect's body which can act as sense organs.

sperm the male's reproductive cells which must fertilize the female's egg before offspring can be produced.

spore a resting or dispersal stage of a plant, usually single-celled, produced without sexual reproduction.

stamens the male parts of a flower. Pollen is produced in the anthers at the top of the stamens.

stigma the sticky tip on top of the female part of a flower (the carpel) which receives pollen.

striations fine lines along the surface of an object. However smooth a surface may appear to the naked eye, under a microscope many bumps, grooves and striations can usually be seen.

thallus the body of a simple plant such as a liverwort. Usually small, and not divided into stem, leaves and roots.

tissue a collection of cells of the same type.

virus a tiny organism, too small to be seen with even a home microscope, which can only multiply inside a cell. Viruses cause unwelcome changes – diseases – in the "host" cells and organisms they infect.

x-ray photographs enable scientists to study the details of objects invisible to the naked eye.

INDEX

Photographic credits
Alexander Keiller Museum, Biophoto Associates, British Museum/ Natural History/ Oxford Scientific Films, Bruce Coleman Ltd, Forensic Science Laboratories (Metropolitan Police), Geoscience Photo Library, Dept of Histopathology, Science Photo Library, Ronald Sheridan, Silkeborg Museum, Topham Picture Library, Roger Vlitos

Illustrations by Ron Hayward, Aziz Khan, Neil Bulpitt and Alex Pang